Dictionaries

Dictionaries

The Art and Craft of Lexicography

SIDNEY I. LANDAU

THE SCRIBNER PRESS

CHARLES SCRIBNER'S SONS

NEW YORK

Copyright © 1984 Sidney I. Landau

Library of Congress Cataloging in Publication Data
Landau, Sidney I.
  Dictionaries : the art and craft of lexicography.

  Includes bibliographies and index.
  1. Lexicography. I. Title.
P327.L3 1984   413'.028   83-27112
ISBN 0-684-18096-0

1 3 5 7 9 11 13 15 17 19   F/C   20 18 16 14 12 10 8 6 4 2

Printed in the United States of America.

To Sarah, Paul, and Amy

Contents

CONTENTS

i x

Abbreviations

ACD	American College Dictionary
AHD	American Heritage Dictionary
AHD2	American Heritage Dictionary, Second College Edition
CED	Collins English Dictionary
COD	Concise Oxford Dictionary
DAE	Dictionary of American English
DARE	Dictionary of American Regional English
DSNA	Dictionary Society of North America
EB	The New Encyclopaedia Britannica (1977)
Harcourt	Harcourt Brace School Dictionary
Hornby	Oxford Advanced Learner's Dictionary of Current English (Hornby)
Lexicography	Lexicography in English (McDavid and Duckert)
Longman	Longman Dictionary of Contemporary English
Manual	Manual of Lexicography (Zgusta)
MW7	Webster's Seventh New Collegiate Dictionary
MW8	Webster's New Collegiate Dictionary, Eighth Edition
MW9	Webster's Ninth New Collegiate Dictionary
NID2	Webster's New International Dictionary, Second Edition
NID3	Webster's Third New International Dictionary
OED	Oxford English Dictionary
Problems	Problems in Lexicography (Householder and Saporta)
RHCD	Random House College Dictionary
World	Webster's New World Dictionary

Preface and Acknowledgments

Although a few institutions offer advanced or graduate courses in lexicography, in the main lexicography is learned, as it has always been, by the apprenticeship method. I have had no formal instruction in lexicography but have learned the craft by practicing it for the past twenty-three years. Many people have helped and encouraged me during my apprenticeship in dictionary work, but three stand out in my mind. None has contributed to this book directly, but without any one of them I doubt the book would have been written.

First, I wish to thank Samuel Davis, who in 1961 taught me how to define in a capacious former stable that housed the Funk & Wagnalls dictionary staff on East Twenty-fourth Street in New York City. Shaded incandescent bulbs hung on long chains from the high ceiling. We worked in a large open space at desks without partitions, a row of dictionaries propped before each of us. No one ever had a gentler, kinder, or more consistently good-humored tutor than I had in Sam Davis. He was a marvelous definer and a born teacher, with that rare ability to know when to stop tampering with a definition. From him I learned that dictionary work is writing for a living and is not to be confused with *belles lettres*.

Second, I recall with gratitude the memory of the late Albert H. Marckwardt, whose many administrative and scholarly achievements need no recital here. Marckwardt was the principal dictionary adviser for Funk & Wagnalls in 1963 when I was placed in charge of the dictionary department. He was much older than I and at the height of a very distinguished career. Yet he was consistently helpful without being officious, and charitable without being condescending. He was incapable of dismissing any idea without rational consideration. If it was worthless, he would get to the heart of its worthlessness swiftly, but with such clear vision that one was compelled to see its emptiness too. His criticism was deft but never hurt, because he so patently meant no hurt. His capacity for quick analysis was amazing. I believe I learned more from Marckwardt's offhand comments over a period of many years than I might have learned from several courses in linguistics. He opened my eyes to the broader fields of language and linguistics in which dictionaries have their roots and stimulated me to read more widely in these areas.

Third, I thank the eminent grammarian Randolph Quirk, whom I first encountered after I had already been in dictionary work for many years. Yet I still had no real sense of the profession of lexicography and felt little kinship with others engaged in the same work. Randolph Quirk has the marvelous habit—whether out of kindness or pedagogical instinct I do not know—of presuming that everyone he meets is as deeply driven and committed as he is to finding out how language works. He also knows everybody in the world of lexicography and has, so far as I can tell, no enemies. He has introduced me or led me to introduce myself to many fine lexicographers and linguists, especially in Great Britain, and whatever attention I have been able to give to contemporary British lexicography in this work is largely owing to his good offices. He has selflessly promoted the careers of a whole generation of linguists and lexicographers, and I gratefully acknowledge his encouragement of mine.

I would also like to thank a number of people who very kindly read selected parts of my manuscript and gave me the benefit of their expert criticism, or who assisted me in other ways. Frederic G. Cassidy and Joan Hall read parts of Chapter 5 relating to regional dialects, particularly to the *Dictionary of American Regional English.* Jeffrey Hirshberg brought to my attention a number of regional maps used by *DARE,* a few of which are reproduced in this book. Walter Glanze read part of Chapter 2, concerning bilingual lexicography. Arthur Bronstein read part of Chapter 3, on pronunciation. Richard L. Venezky and Angus Cameron (whose untimely death in May 1983 is mourned by all lexicographers) read parts of Chapter 7 in draft form. To all of these very busy people who took time out from their demanding day-to-day preoccupations to help me, I offer my sincere thanks. Their comments were always informed by a deep and practical working knowledge of the area in which they were asked to read, and this book has profited greatly from their help. However, they should in no way be held responsible for any errors or omissions that occur in the sections they read or in any other part of the book. Although they saved me from many a blunder, I alone am responsible for those that remain, as well as for the opinions expressed in these sections, as elsewhere.

I am deeply in the debt of my friend and colleague Herbert Gilbert, who read the entire manuscript and made a number of telling criticisms and comments based on his long experience in the reference book field, both as an encyclopedist and as a lexicographer.

Finally, I want to thank my wife, Sarah Bradford Landau, who did *not* type my manuscript but who urged me to write this book, and set an example for me to follow by her own industry and scholarly diligence. Her encouragement was a constant source of strength that I am afraid I took for granted but that I am now pleased to record, with gratitude and love.

Introduction

This book is intended for all those interested in or professionally associated with dictionaries and other reference books. It is specifically meant for students as a text or supplementary reference; for librarians; and for compilers of dictionaries, lexicons, glossaries, indexes, and other language reference books. It is also for those who would never dream of making a dictionary but would just like to know more about such works and how they are made. The focus of attention is English dictionaries of various kinds: for adults and for children, for native speakers and for the foreign born, for general audiences and for special or technical audiences. Some attention is also given to bilingual dictionaries, but chiefly as a means of contrasting the problems of bilingual lexicography with those of monolingual.

Apart from generally brief field guides for the collection of linguistic data, there are at this writing very few works dealing with dictionary making in any depth. Ladislav Zgusta's *Manual of Lexicography* (The Hague: Mouton, 1971), combining the contributions of a number of Czech scholars, is intended primarily for lexicographers working with languages "that do not enjoy a long philological or even lexicographical tradition, as is frequently the case of the languages of Africa and Asia" (page 10). R. R. K. Hartmann's *Lexicography: Principles and Practice* (London: Academic Press, 1983), a less substantial work than Zgusta's, is an international survey of various aspects of lexicography by eighteen contributors, mainly British and European linguistic scholars, with emphasis on how linguistic theory underlies lexicographic practice. My work, on the other hand, is devoted to

American and English lexicography, and with greater attention to the practice of lexicography than to its semantic or lexicologic underpinnings. There is no up-to-date work that answers the need for a general, practical, and readable guide to English-language lexicography. This book is intended to meet that need.

In order to understand how to construct a dictionary, one must first appreciate both what a dictionary is and what it is not, what kinds of information it is designed to convey and what it cannot. I begin, therefore, by drawing distinctions between dictionaries and encyclopedias and by defining the various types of dictionaries and related language reference works. Clearly some knowledge of the history of lexicography is essential as background for current practices. Accordingly, Chapter 2 consists of a brief history of English and American lexicography. The next three chapters are devoted to the various kinds of information given in a dictionary, with definition and usage each allotted an entire chapter.

Definition is so complex a subject that it cannot be dealt with adequately merely as one aspect of a dictionary entry. My emphasis is on the practice of defining, not on its theoretical or philosophical aspects. It is essential, however, to consider not only lexicographic conventions but also some aspects of the nature of meaning, at least those with relevance to lexicography. Some treatment of the underlying principles of lexicography (i.e., lexicology) is also necessary, though not my main purpose. However, semantics (the study of meaning, also called semasiology) is treated only tangentially, and semiotics (the study of linguistic or nonlinguistic signs) is clearly beyond the scope of this book.

Meaning relates to virtually every branch of philosophy. It also has a profound bearing on psychology and sociology as an aspect of human behavior (see, for example, Ogden and Richard's *The Meaning of Meaning;* Skinner's *Verbal Behavior*), on anthropology (the pioneering American linguists, such as Edward Sapir and Benjamin Whorf, were anthropologists studying the languages of American Indian civilizations), on history, archeology, religion, and other disciplines. It was clearly necessary to limit the analysis of definition and its relation to meaning within fairly narrow confines, else the discussion would have been diffuse and disorganized and lost conviction.

Usage is a subject of particular interest to me and, I believe, to the general public, witness the display racks with scores of guides to usage, books about usage, study guides to usage, and the like. Though a complex subject, usage is fortunately less philosophical and more easily confined to the subject of lexicography than is definition. Chapter 5 is a critical discussion of the kinds of usage information given in dictionaries and of past and present attitudes toward usage.

Chapter 6 describes how dictionaries—especially commercial monolingual dictionaries—are made. The various stages of dictionary preparation are considered in detail. The emphasis throughout is practical, with most of the recommended procedures deriving from my own experience in lexicography.

Chapter 7 assesses the future of dictionary making. Not surprisingly, the role of the computer is central to this discussion. I do not pretend to be a computer expert, but anyone who has lived through the development of a computerized database for a major dictionary has learned something of the blessings and pitfalls of computer use, and I would like to share my experiences, both good and bad, with the reader. Finally, Chapter 8 is a miscellany covering everything I had wanted to say earlier but couldn't find a convenient place for.

It must be emphasized that this book is critical as well as descriptive. I realize fully the enormous work that goes into the making of any dictionary, and my criticisms will be tempered by the natural sympathy that exists between people who have suffered from the same indescribable need for patience bordering on faith in traveling a long, tortuous, and uncharted course leading from the beginning to the end of a major project. Nonetheless, that I have traveled it too gives me claim to the right to criticize and, I hope, the knowledge to do it well.

A word about the use in this book of "he" as a neuter pronoun. Some linguists and feminist writers have alleged that, in many cases of actual usage, *he* or *him,* used with ostensible neutrality, in fact refers to men only. They are right. Although I do not agree that the motive is deliberately to exclude women from notice, it certainly does perform this function. The real causes are tradition, as well as ignorance or indifference on the part of most writers, whether male or female. For example, here is an instance in which the masculine pronoun is presumptively neutral but clearly implies gender: "This interesting and growing phenomenon permits the teacher to construct his course materials entirely to his liking without having to depend on the approach of another man's textbook."[1]

The cumulative effect of the iteration of masculine pronouns obliterates the female from one's consciousness. The problem is what to do about it. Proposals to correct the situation strike me as impractical or ludicrous.[2] My own solution is to recommend that men use masculine pronouns for neutral use, because they naturally identify with the masculine gender, and that women use feminine pronouns for the analogous reason. Accordingly, since I am a man and feel comfortable with the masculine pronoun, I will use it in this book. I trust, however, that the context will make clear whether I mean the pronoun to convey physical or grammatical (neutral) gender.

Finally, I would like to say something about the supposed dryness of dictionary editing. Lexicography involves, uniquely in my experience, an immense amount of work that would be routine if it didn't require so much prior knowledge about the scope and priorities of the enterprise. Sometimes one can deceive oneself into thinking that because the work is often repetitious anyone could do it, which is not true. The work is repetitious because it is vast, but buried within the repetitions are thousands—many thousands—of exceptional cases that require an informed and usually very quick judgment. The naïve idea that because dictionaries take years to produce the editors have a great deal of time at their disposal is completely misconceived. The vastness of the amount of work to be done demands a very rapid rate of work, especially in the case of commercial dictionaries. Only those who have labored to produce a new dictionary can comprehend the sheer volume of work to be done. I hope that Chapter 6 in particular will make the actual case clear.

In spite of the work to be done, or perhaps because of it, lexicography provides at its best a joyful sense of busyness with language. One is immersed in the details of language as in no other field. Sometimes the details are so overwhelming and endless they sap the spirit and depress the mind. Often at the end of a hard day's work one realizes with dismay that the meager stack of finished work one has accomplished has an immeasurably slight impact on the work as a whole. But the simple fact, not widely appreciated, is that dictionaries are made by writers. As I hope the readers of this work will come to understand, dictionaries do not spring into being. People must plan them, collect information, and write them. Writing takes time, and it is often frustrating and even infuriating. No other form of writing is at once so quixotic and so intensely practical.

Dictionary making does not require brilliance or originality of mind. It does require high intelligence, mastery of the craft, and dedication to hard work. If one has produced a dictionary, one has the satisfaction of having produced a work of enduring value. Dictionaries ordinarily outlive their creators by many years. Samuel Johnson was a poet, a playwright, a biographer, a political polemicist, a brilliant talker and debater, and a man whose breadth of reading and command of classical literature and language astonished his contemporaries, yet it is as a lexicographer that he left his most enduring legacy to mankind.

CHAPTER ONE

What Is a Dictionary?

Dictionaries and Encyclopedias

Dictionary is a powerful word. Authors and publishers have found that if they call a reference book a dictionary it tends to sell better than it would if called by another name because the word suggests authority, scholarship, and precision. It should come as no surprise, then, that all kinds of books are described as dictionaries. There are dictionaries of pottery, flowering plants, textiles, metal-cutting machine tools, highway traffic, careers, chemical equations, and secret societies. There is a dictionary of heresies, a dictionary of love, and a dictionary of insult. Had Ambrose Bierce called his work *Bierce's Aphorisms* instead of *The Devil's Dictionary* the book would have suffered the neglect it deserved, but I suppose one must give the devil his due.

To most people, dictionaries and encyclopedias are closely linked and are sometimes considered interchangeable, but they are essentially different kinds of reference works with different purposes. A dictionary is a book that lists words in alphabetical order and describes their meanings. Modern dictionaries often include information about spelling, syllabication, pronunciation, etymology (word derivation), usage, synonyms, and grammar, and sometimes illustrations as well. An encyclopedia is a collection of articles about every branch of knowledge. Although the articles are usually arranged alphabetically, and though they often include definitions, their descriptions go far beyond the information given in a dictionary.

Dictionary definitions are usually confined to information that the reader must have to understand an unfamiliar word. The emphasis is on the word, and all the information given bears directly on the meaning, pronunciation, use, or history of the word. Encyclopedic articles are essentially topical, dealing with the entire subject represented by the article's title. An encyclopedia article on religion does not merely say what the word *religion* means or has meant in the past or how it is pronounced or used; it systematically describes the religions of the world: their histories, doctrines, and practices. The difference is sometimes stated, perhaps a bit too simply, by the apothegm, "Dictionaries are about words, encyclopedias are about things." This is true enough if we look at dictionaries and encyclopedias as a whole, but it admits of many exceptions if we try to apply it to every entry in each type of work.

It is difficult to make grand generalizations about dictionaries. They are not encyclopedias, but what are they? They are protean in form, so that any generalization that may apply to one or several types of dictionaries may not apply at all to others. It will therefore be necessary, before we proceed much further, to analyze the various types of dictionaries and related language reference books. Though this survey will take in many types, the reader must forgive me if I omit discussion of dictionaries of love and insult and other such oddities and confine myself to the more common, if less intriguing, varieties.

A Survey of Types of Dictionaries and Other Language References

Dictionaries can be classified by many criteria, some of them obvious to everyone, such as size, but there is no standard, agreed-upon taxonomy for dictionaries. A few intrepid souls have, however, made an attempt to construct an organized scheme of classification, or typology; before we start our own survey, it will be worth taking a look at the most thoughtful and discriminating typology yet devised, by the linguistic scholar Yakov Malkiel.[1]

Malkiel says dictionaries can be distinguished by three categories: range, perspective, and presentation. Range refers to the size and scope of the dictionary: how well does it cover the entire lexicon? He calls this quality density. When dealing with an entire language, range is almost impossible to establish; who knows the total extent of the lexicon? But when the designated lexicon, or corpus, is limited to a specific work, the range can be comprehensive. Another aspect of range is the number of languages covered, whether it is monolingual, bilingual, or multilingual (more than two languages, sometimes called plurilingual). The third aspect of range is the extent of concentration on lexical data; in other words, how encyclopedic is the work?

Perspective is based on how the compiler views the work and what approach he takes. First, is the work diachronic (covering an extended time) or synchronic (confined to one period)? Second, how is it organized—alphabetically, by sound (as in rhyming dictionaries), by concept (as in some thesauruses), or by some other means? Third, is the level of tone detached, preceptive (didactic), or facetious?

Presentation signifies how material of a given perspective is presented; specifically, how full are the definitions? Monolingual dictionaries tend to have fuller definitions than bilingual works. What form of verbal documentation is employed? For example, one work may cite illustrative quotations, another invented phrases, a third bibliographic references. Are graphic illustrations included? Finally, what special features, such as pronunciations and usage information, are included?

Malkiel's classification is valuable because it suggests relationships between types. For example, diachronic dictionaries tend to have few or no pictorial illustrations; bilingual dictionaries are seldom diachronic and usually alphabetic in arrangement. Virtually every type of dictionary can be analyzed with reference to the three categories of range, perspective, and presentation.[2] Malkiel's system, while elegant, is not very serviceable as a teaching tool. Accordingly, I offer my own less elegant survey, which is not intended to be a formal typology but merely a convenient way to highlight significant differences among dictionaries. The categories are not exclusive. This arrangement will give the opportunity to explain in what ways types of dictionaries differ and are alike.

The Number of Languages

Dictionaries differ in the number of languages they contain. The difference between a monolingual dictionary and a bilingual one consists not only in the number of languages in which they are written but in their essential purpose. A bilingual dictionary consists of an alphabetical list of words or expressions in one language (the "source language") for which, ideally, exact equivalents are given in another language (the "target language"). The purpose is to provide help to someone who understands one language but not the other. More, the presumption is that one of the languages is the user's native language.

A monolingual dictionary, written entirely in one language, is intended chiefly for the native speakers of that language, though sometimes for those learning it as a second language. It provides many kinds of information about its entry words but most importantly gives definitions; that is, each of the entry words or expressions is rephrased in words of the same language as the entry word. (The principles of defining are discussed in Chapter 4.) The chief purpose of a monolingual dictionary is to explain, in words likely to be understood by native speakers, what other words mean. Thus, whereas bilingual dictionaries provide equivalents in another language of their entry words, monolingual dictionaries provide periphrastic definitions in the same language.

Bilingual dictionaries may be unidirectional (monodirectional) or bidirectional; that is, they may go in one direction only, from English, let us say, to French, or be combined with another dictionary that goes from French to English. In this case there are really two dictionaries. There are also dictionaries in which the entry words are translated into two other languages (trilingual dictionaries) or more than two other languages (multilingual).

There are two main purposes for using a bilingual dictionary: for comprehension, as in reading, of the source language; or as an aid in expressing oneself, as in writing, in the target language. A speaker of English, for example, will consult a French–English dictionary to help him understand unfamiliar French words he encounters in his reading. On the other hand, a French speaker who must write an essay in English may consult a French–English dictionary to help him find the right words to express himself. Many bilingual lexicographers have observed that it is impossible to construct a unidirectional bilingual dictionary for speakers of both languages. The compiler has, or ought to have, one group in mind, else the dictionary is likely to be satisfactory for neither. As one linguist comments, "Book-publishers can scarcely be expected to take kindly to the thought, but it is nevertheless true that bilingual dictionaries should be titled in such a way that the language of the intended user is made clear, e.g., *French-English Dictionary for Americans* as against *French-English Dictionary for Frenchmen.*"[3]

Why is this so? First of all, there is often no equivalent in the target language for entry words in the source language, not only in the obvious instances of indigenous flora and fauna but for many common words as well. Ladislav Zgusta cites the English word *girlhood* as an example that poses problems in providing an exact French equivalent. *État de fille* is an explanatory equivalent, but it will be of no use to the French speaker who wants to translate *girlhood* into French in a sentence such as: "In her girlhood, she used to read Tennyson."[4]

Many words, too, are culture specific (or culture bound, as some linguists prefer). For example, American and Canadian football terms like *tackle* have no equivalents in countries where this sport is unknown.[5] Many social terms (such as those referring to family relationships), culinary words, political terms, and religious words have no equivalent in the target language and require explanations instead of or in addition to some approximate translation.[6] The lack of equivalence is particularly acute, of course, when the two languages are used in cultures that differ greatly in cultural background, but it occurs with surprising frequency even in cultures with a similar heritage.

It is crucial for the lexicographer to decide in advance, therefore, whether the dictionary—as for example an English–French dictionary—is intended to help French speakers comprehend English or to help English speakers express themselves in French. His decision will affect not only the kind of translational equivalents he provides and the fullness of the equivalents, but the choice of entries themselves. If the English–French dictionary is intended for French speakers, the inclusion of culture-specific words like *tackle* in its football use would make sense; the French speaker would be puzzled by this unfamiliar word. But if the dictionary is intended to help an English speaker express himself in French, *tackle* has no place in the dictionary. Moreover, for the English speaker, many uncommon or difficult words, such as *circumnavigate,* would be unnecessary, for if the English speaker wanted a French equivalent he could seek the same sense under simpler entry words, such as *sail around.*[7] Yet for the French speaker, uncommon and difficult English words are of considerable importance. If the equivalent of a common word in the source language (English) is an uncommon or difficult word in the target language (French), the disparity is of less consequence to the French speaker than to the English speaker, who may use the uncommon French word in an altogether unsuitable context unless the dictionary specifies its limited usage. Few dictionaries have space for such information.

There is a close parallel between bilingual dictionaries made to help target language speakers express themselves in the source language and synonym dictionaries or thesauruses. Although the latter are monolingual, they function much as do bilingual dictionaries. Thus, it hardly helps a thesaurus user to be presented with a list of rare and difficult entry or index words that would never occur to him to look up, as in the case, for example, in *Webster's Collegiate Thesaurus* (1976). (See Chapter 7, page 273.)

Mary R. Haas lists a number of desiderata for a bilingual dictionary, including the following:

1. It provides a translation for each word in the source language
2. Its coverage of the source language lexicon is complete
3. Grammatical, syntactic, and semantic information is provided

4. Usage guidance is given
5. Names are included
6. It includes special vocabulary items, such as scientific terms
7. Spelling aids and alternative spellings are indicated
8. Pronunciation is included
9. It is compact in size—which obviously limits its coverage of items 1–8[8]

Zgusta's *Manual of Lexicography* is particularly good in its treatment of bilingual dictionaries and the problems of selecting entries and providing equivalents. The author gives copious illustrations of the complexities of translation; for example, an encyclopedic term in one language—he cites *Red Guards* in English—may not be encyclopedic in the target language, i.e., in Chinese.[9] Even so basic a category as proper versus common nouns can be confuted in translation.

Given the complexities of accurate translation, which I have barely touched upon but which give some idea of the difficulties, one can see that the compilers of multilingual dictionaries face formidable problems. Translating into two or more other languages makes any sophisticated equivalence to the source language impossible. Linguists use the word *anisomorphic* (from *an* = not + *iso* = same + *morph* = form) to describe languages composed of lexical forms that are not parallel. Trilingual dictionaries are comparatively rare, but those that do exist generally consist of two widely understood languages, such as English and French—or, in the past, Latin and English or a Romance language—plus one language having much more local use, such as a little known African language. Such dictionaries were often created by missionaries to help them communicate with prospective converts in an unknown language having no relation to their own. Thus these dictionaries had in effect two source languages and one target language, a language largely anisomorphic to their own language. Needless to say, such dictionaries are necessarily elementary and practical, more closely resembling travelers' word guides than bilingual dictionaries. The more languages included, the more difficult the problems become. Zgusta remarks that multilingual dictionaries are justified only for technical terminology, when other meanings can be ignored.[10]

The Manner of Financing

Dictionaries differ in how they are financed and in the expectation of profit. Scholarly dictionaries, such as the *Middle English Dictionary* in preparation at the University of Michigan, or the *Dictionary of American Regional English* at the University of Wisconsin, are often financed by government or foundation grants in addition to university support, and are not designed principally to make money for investors. Commercial dictionaries, such as the Random House or the Merriam-Webster line of dictionaries, are supported by private investors who expect to make money by their sale.

Though I choose to focus on the manner of financing as the key difference, there are other profound distinctions between scholarly and commercial dictionaries. The scholarly dictionary appeals to a much narrower segment of the population, but within that segment it is likely to be very well known. In the jargon of publishers, its market is vertical. General commercial dictionaries, on the other hand, appeal to a broad spectrum of the population, but this spectrum's attachment to the particular work is relatively weak—their market is horizontal. Commercial dictionaries, of course, have competitors of the same type, whereas there is no other Middle English dictionary competing for the attention of Middle English scholars.

In market appeal, scholarly dictionaries resemble specialized commercial dictionaries, such as a dictionary of biochemistry or of machine tools. In both cases the market is sharply defined and vertical, but the manner of financing and purposes differ. The primary purpose of the scholarly dictionary is to describe data and communicate knowledge; a secondary purpose may be to promote the name of the supporting institution or to acquire prestige for it by publishing a major work. The primary purpose of a commercial dictionary is to make money, although to the people writing it the day-to-day purpose is usually indistinguishable from that of a scholarly dictionary. The real difference is that the commercial lexicographer is in the business of communicating knowledge, whereas the scholarly lexicographer is not engaged in business, though he is often enough engaged in raising funds.

Whereas scholarly dictionaries may take many years to complete—the *Middle English Dictionary* began publishing parts in 1952 and had reached the halfway point by the early 1980s—commercial dictionaries are done at a much accelerated rate, though often not fast enough to satisfy their publishers. However, the pressure to produce quickly is not confined to commercial lexicographers.

> When one thinks of tying up $2 million for five or six years and imagines what one could do with that money by investing it, one can see why scheduling is so important, and what an unusual act of faith it is to put so much money into the making of a dictionary. During all those years of preparation, no money is coming in. Voices have been known to be raised at board of directors' meetings about whether this is the best use of such a large amount of money. The pressure gets transmitted, ultimately, to the editor in chief. Anyone who has read *Caught in the Web of Words,* the biography of James A. H. Murray, the chief editor of the *Oxford English*

11

Dictionary, knows what severe pressure even so distinguished a lexicographer as Murray was placed under, and what ignominious explanations he was forced to make to defend himself. And the *OED* is hardly a commercial dictionary. His situation was all too typical. Every working lexicographer has had similar experiences.[11]

I do not mean to make them heroic, but commercial lexicographers often do resist intense pressures, sometimes even at the threat of losing their jobs, to maintain the standards they feel they must. The argument is seldom represented as an ethical imperative, which would compel any corporate financial officer to regard one as a lunatic, but on the safe, hard-headed, practical grounds of keeping the quality on a level with the competition in order to preserve sales. Nonetheless, in the privacy of the lexicographer's own home—as the Soviet citizen clandestinely curses the Party leaders—one is free to indulge in good intentions. In any event, the wonder is that the level of commercial dictionary making in the United States is so high, not—as some critics complain—that it fails to match the breadth of scholarly dictionaries.

James Sledd, an authority on the history of lexicography and a writer noted for the acerbic temper of his style and the keenness of his wit, has lost patience with commercial lexicography and appears to call for government to step in and organize the preparation of a scholarly, descriptive dictionary to undo the mischief of Merriam, Random House, and others. "Really useful things in lexicography," he says, "can now be done only by large, permanent staffs, operating under the direction of scholarly editors with plenty of money at their disposal and under no pressure to recover what they spend. But profit is what commercial publishing is all about."[12] Sledd overstates the case, yet he is not far off the mark. Of course, we should all like to have plenty of money at our disposal and be under no pressure, and I confess to being stung by the alleged necessity that such works be directed by "scholarly editors." It may surprise Professor Sledd to learn that plain old profit-making dictionary editors would do splendidly with plenty of money and no pressure, and that all of the defects he justly criticizes in commercial dictionaries would be swiftly corrected.

Sledd sees no value in the public response to dictionaries as a means of maintaining quality: "The average man and the average reviewer cannot demand the best in a big dictionary, because they have no idea what the best might be: and even if they did demand the best, the businessmen who run commercial publishing houses would not give it to them unless they saw a direct relation between quality and profits."[13]

Sledd is right about the inability of the public or the reviewer to recognize merit in a dictionary, big or little, at least in North America. British reviewers are usually better informed, though sometimes biased against American dictionaries. (The state of dictionary criticism will be discussed in Chapter 8.) But the indignant tone with which Sledd accuses businessmen of denying quality to dictionaries is misplaced, for once again the case is overstated. Businessmen do not tell the lexicographer what should go in his dictionary. To quote myself,

> Few investors are willing to turn over several million dollars to a group of scholars and say, in effect, "Do what you like with it." It is nonetheless surprising how much freedom the dictionary editor has, not because the investors—or their representatives, the publishers—are so trusting, but because they know so very little about dictionaries. The canny lexicographer can pretend to be a scholar among businessmen and a businessman among scholars. By making judicious indiscretions within both groups—he goes on and on to the board of directors about phonemes and complains loudly to the scholars about the cost of authors' alterations—he can do pretty much as he wants. In spite of these stratagems, however, there are limits to his freedom....[14]

Yes there are limits to his freedom, painful ones that Sledd rightly deplores; but the problem is not simply that profits may decline slightly if a particular item that enhances quality is incorporated. The problem is that many innovations urged by scholars might cost a company many millions of dollars in sales. Scholars will applaud, but the company will discharge its dictionary staff and numerous other guiltless employees. We are not now talking about stingy bosses fussing over niggling amounts. If the dictionary is a disaster, their heads will roll, too. I do not disagree with Sledd's point, but his indignation is out of place. Businessmen-lexicographers don't have tenure.

The Age of Users

Dictionaries differ in the age of the intended user: some are aimed at children, others at adults. Many of the Latin–English dictionaries of the sixteenth century and earlier were designed to help students. Indeed, as Chapter 2 will make clear, monolingual English lexicography developed from such dictionaries, and some of the earliest monolingual dictionaries were compiled by schoolmasters for the edification of young scholars and other untutored people. In this sense school dictionaries are as old as lexicography; the pedagogical purpose was original, and broader purposes developed from it. But school dictionaries as we know them, with simplified and graded vocabularies, large type, and attractive graphics, are strictly a twentieth-century development. In the early twentieth century and before, any small-sized dictionary was considered suitable for schoolchildren; no concession to simplicity was made in the treatment of vocabulary.

The pioneer in children's dictionaries was Edward L. Thorndike, who "applied the principles of the psychology of learning to dictionary making" in the 1930s.[15] Thorndike edited a series of Thorndike-Century dictionaries in the 1930s and the '40s for three levels of school-age children. An educational psychologist before he was a lexicographer, Thorndike had compiled the *Teacher's Word Book* in 1921 and enlarged it in 1931 to twenty thousand words. The words were listed according to their frequency of occurrence in a large corpus of material examined for this purpose. Subsequently combined with word counts of Irving Lorge and expanded to thirty thousand words, the list was published in 1944 as *The Teacher's Word Book of 30,000 Words* and, in spite of its imperfections (such as the failure to discriminate between different meanings of the same word in making a count of its occurrences), the work remained for many years an extremely valuable tool for teachers, psychologists, and lexicographers. The editor of the *American College Dictionary* (1947), Clarence L. Barnhart, has said that "without the basic research that had been done on the *Thorndike-Century Senior Dictionary . . .* it would have been impossible to produce the *ACD* in the two years of its actual production."[16]

A whole series of dictionaries have now been produced, in a highly competitive market, for children of ages ranging from eight or nine years—third- or fourth-grade level—through senior high school. The dictionaries are usually divided into three tiers: elementary school (grades three–eight), middle school (grades six–ten), which are the most popular, and secondary school (grades nine–twelve). (One must take these grade levels with a grain of salt: few tenth graders would or should use a middle school dictionary, and few third graders are capable of using an elementary school dictionary.) There are also picture books, often called dictionaries, for beginning readers, but until the user has acquired the skills necessary to look up a word and read its definition, he is not using a dictionary, whatever it may be called.

The skills required to use a dictionary are often taken for granted by adults; teachers, however, know very well that they must be taught and are not easily mastered by everyone. One's grasp of the alphabet must be secure, and more, one must grasp conceptually the sequential way in which alphabetizing is done. Even if the child can perform the operation of finding the word he seeks, if it is a great chore filled with false starts he is likely to give up the battle. This is a pity, because the habit of using a dictionary is formed early in life, and if the skills to use it are neglected, the student may never be comfortable using dictionaries. Dictionary publishers have accordingly made their school dictionaries as inviting as possible. The type is large, the

14

format attractive, and illustrations, sometimes in color, abound. In fact, it has been suggested that children's dictionaries have been made so attractive and simplified that they do not prepare children adequately for using adult dictionaries. Some critics have claimed that the use of school dictionaries actually discourages children from using adult dictionaries, which by comparison are formidable books filled with small type and small, spare illustrations.

The theory underlying school dictionaries, begun by Thorndike's analysis of the frequency of word use, is that dictionaries for children should be written in words that children can understand. This may appear to be a truism, but it is not. One learns new words by encountering them, either in speech or writing, and by making a shrewd guess, based on the context in which they occur and one's knowledge of similar words in similar contexts, as to what they mean. It is therefore not self-evident that a dictionary or any other book for children should avoid using words that challenge the reader to add a new word to his vocabulary. On the other hand, the user of a dictionary is presumably already on the track of a new word and would be ill served by spicing the special context of definition with another word he doesn't know.

If one accepts the latter view, it follows that the children's dictionary should have a controlled vocabulary. Now in one sense every dictionary's vocabulary is controlled; every word used in a definition is, or ought to be, itself defined as an entry. But some children's dictionaries go further, confining the defining vocabulary to a more limited range than that embraced by the entry words. (A controlled defining vocabulary is also used by some dictionaries for the foreign born, which share some characteristics with children's dictionaries.) Moreover, some children's dictionaries have graded vocabularies; that is, they assign a grade level to each vocabulary entry, and attempt to define that entry in words presumably understood by most children at that grade level. I say "attempt" advisedly, because the state of knowledge of the vocabulary skills of most children at any grade level is still primitive, and as a practical matter it would be impossible to define every term by other words of that grade level, even if we knew what they were.

The best available study of graded vocabularies is the *American Heritage Word Frequency Book*.[17] This is a computerized study of some 5 million words collected from more than 1,000 different sources, mainly textbooks for grades three through nine, but with some selections from ungraded magazines. The results, which were used in the preparation of the *American Heritage School Dictionary,* are an impressive list of 86,741 different words printed alphabetically and in rank order, with their overall frequencies and frequencies in grades three through nine. Much—in fact, too much—other information is also included, but the work is useful and was obviously assembled diligently and thoughtfully.

My only serious criticism of the *Word Frequency Book* is that it is largely based on textbooks supposedly written in controlled vocabularies for students of particular grade levels. In the absence of any systematic vocabulary studies, how did the authors of those textbooks know what a third- or fourth- or fifth-grade-level vocabulary was? The schoolbooks I have read in the course of compiling a school dictionary (the *Harcourt Brace School Dictionary*) showed no uniform sense of the vocabulary of a particular grade level; their vocabularies varied greatly. Moreover, are these the books children actually read? It strikes me as rather wonderful that the textbook authors whose works the *Word Frequency Book* was based on will henceforth use the *Word Frequency Book*'s findings as justification for composing new texts with the same grade-level vocabularies! It must be asked whether controlled vocabulary textbooks give a more accurate picture of the vocabulary acquirements of children than Kipling or *Winnie the Pooh* or *Tom Sawyer,* which certainly do not have controlled vocabularies.

If one criticism of school dictionaries is that they may make some children reluctant to switch to adult dictionaries, another is that there are just too many school dictionaries for various grade levels. The second criticism has more merit than the first. Although a dictionary for grades four–eight may make sense, by the time the student is in high school—certainly by the tenth grade—he should be using an adult dictionary. The old "junior" or school dictionaries for grades four–eight, generally contained forty thousand to sixty thousand entries. "Intermediate" dictionaries span a somewhat more advanced range, usually grades six–ten, and have the same or a slightly higher number of entries. High school dictionaries contain seventy-five thousand to one hundred thousand entries. In fact if not in name, most high school dictionaries closely resemble adult desk dictionaries but are set in somewhat larger type, with more illustrations, and have sturdier bindings. There is some deception in the idea that the public is getting a unique work for the high school student. Students with special problems may well need simpler dictionaries at the high school level, but high school dictionaries will not help them. They will need a lower-level dictionary.

Although there may be some justice to the charge that school dictionaries retard the rate at which some children acquire adult dictionary skills, surely this is overbalanced by the benefit to the far greater number of children who would otherwise find dictionary use a daunting experience. Too, a good teacher will encourage bright students to use adult dictionaries—not just college dictionaries but an unabridged dictionary—whenever their skills are equal to the task. Also, since good elementary dictionaries contain entry words of various levels of difficulty, the bright fourth or fifth grader can be challenged by the more advanced words in a school dictionary. These dictionaries include words like *disreputable, dissertation, nuclear fission,* and *portraiture.* School dictionary definitions are somewhat simpler than those of most adult dictionaries, but their vocabulary is various enough for the student to find his own level and progress far along the way to achieving a mature vocabulary.

The Size of Dictionaries

Dictionaries differ in how fully they cover the lexicon. Since the size of the lexicon varies from language to language, the number of entries in a dictionary is a measure only of its relative size compared with other dictionaries of the same language. As Zgusta has observed, only dead languages can be exhaustively described in a dictionary, because "no new sentences are produced in a dead language."[18] Whenever the possibility exists of new utterances being generated, there is the likelihood that new senses and new words will also be generated.

How large is the English lexicon? Allen Walker Read estimates its extent at about 4 million.[19] He adduces this figure by citing 700,000 words in the Merriam-Webster files and at least 1 million words in the scientific vocabulary. There are in addition nonce words (words coined for a particular occasion), dialectal words, slang, neologisms (new words), exotic words (words introduced from other languages but not yet naturalized), trade names, and words derived from place names, such as *New Yorker* or *Michigander.* Read's is as good a guess as any, but even so it is not very meaningful. Does one include all obsolete words, and all forms (or spellings) of each of them? If one admits lexical units larger than words, where does one draw the line? How shall we define *word?* Scholars have long disputed the answer to this question, and there is no indication of an approaching consensus. Are proper nouns to be considered words? Are compounds like *pull toy?* In asking these questions, I am deliberately skirting semantic theory, a subject beyond the scope of this book. I raise the question simply to illustrate the problem.

The estimate of the extent of scientific vocabulary is open to serious question. Over 6 million chemical compounds are registered with *Chemical Abstracts,* and more are being discovered every day. Are these lexical units? Many are of great importance in industry and medicine, and some, like *sodium bicarbonate* or *potassium nitrate,* are included in general dictionaries. Medical terms—excluding chemical compounds used in medicine—

17

are probably close to 200,000 in number. These include many Latin anatomical words and expressions; are these to be considered English? They are when used in medicine and they're not when used otherwise.

The question, How many words are there in English? cannot be answered in any satisfactory way. It depends on what one means by "words" and by "English," and even if one could decide the limits to each, the answer would be little more than a guess.

It is widely believed that an unabridged dictionary includes all the words in the language. The only truly unabridged work in the English language is *Webster's Third New International Dictionary (NID3)*.[20] It contains 450,000 words, and as its editor, Philip Babcock Gove, explains in his Preface, omits all those terms that had become obsolete by 1755 "unless found in well-known major works of a few major writers," a comment that echoes Samuel Johnson's criterion for including obsolete words in his *Dictionary* of 1755. Gove also remarks that "the number of words available is always far in excess of . . . the number that can possibly be included."

What then is an unabridged dictionary? It is a dictionary that gives full coverage to the lexicon in general use at a particular time in the history of a language and substantial coverage to specialized lexicons, with quotations given to support its definitions, illustrate context, and suggest typical varieties of usage. By "general use" I mean in common use in the public press and in ordinary speech in both informal and reserved styles (such as those used in business), as distinguished from specialized lexicons such as those of law, medicine, or the physical sciences. In practice, *unabridged* usually refers to a dictionary of 400,000 to 600,000 words. In the sense of "not abridged," *unabridged* is a misnomer, since many smaller dictionaries are also unabridged from a larger work. They may be based, for example, on a collection of glossaries, or be derived from several other dictionaries. By the same token, some abridged dictionaries are bigger (and better) than some unabridged dictionaries.

The next recognized category is that of college dictionaries, defined by Clarence Barnhart as "desk dictionaries usually containing from 130,000 to 160,000 entries, which are sold widely in bookstores and used in colleges and schools in the United States."[21] These are by far the most popular dictionaries in the United States, and recently two works of comparable size and scope, *Collins Dictionary of the English Language* and *Longman New Universal Dictionary,* have appeared in Britain.[22] I would adjust Barnhart's figures upward to the range of 150,000 to 170,000. Since the most obvious way to best one's competitor is to have or claim to have more entries, college dictionaries have inexorably slipped upward in entry count like gliders wafting on hot air.

Those dictionaries intermediate in size between college and unabridged, like the *Random House Dictionary* with 260,000 entries (including many proper nouns), have been called "semi-unabridged". They might with equal logic be called "semi-abridged" and mean the same thing, or "super-college" ("university"?) dictionaries, because they are really best described as bigger-than-college dictionaries.

One step below the college dictionaries are the desk dictionaries. (The alert reader will have noted that Barnhart defined college dictionaries as desk dictionaries. "Desk dictionary" can mean any dictionary that one can pick up easily and use at a desk, but I discuss it here in its more restricted sense.) Desk dictionaries, like the *Thorndike-Barnhart Comprehensive Desk Dictionary* or *The Doubleday Dictionary,* contain from 60,000 to 100,000 words.[23] They not only have fewer entries than college dictionaries, but their definitions are briefer and fewer senses are given for each word. Etymologies, if given at all, are in telescoped form. Pronunciations are usually included. As noted earlier, the relationship between desk dictionaries and school dictionaries for high-school-age children is fairly close.

The next step takes us to the paperback or "pocket" dictionaries, cheap dictionaries of small size (usually $4'' \times 6''$) with paper covers. These may have 40,000 to 60,000 entries or more. If one's primary need is for a spelling book they are a good buy, but their definitions are often little more than strings of synonyms. They may include pronunciations but seldom etymologies; given their size, this is a sensible omission. They often include useful encyclopedic information such as small maps, population statistics, and the like. Because of the cheap paper used and the massive print runs employed in their manufacture, the quality of printing tends to vary greatly.

The paperback size is the smallest dictionary of any use. There are much smaller, "vest pocket" dictionaries, often quite handsome in appearance, resembling slim address books with plasticized covers and neat, legible type. But these are so slight in coverage as to be practically fraudulent for bearing the word *dictionary*. Though apparently modeled on brief, bilingual travelers' guides, which if not elegant are at least useful, vest pocket monolingual glossaries are often elegant but seldom useful.

The Scope of Coverage by Subject

Dictionaries differ in scope in respect to the subjects they cover. I make a distinction between dictionaries confined to a special subject, such as law or medicine, and dictionaries limited to an aspect of language, such as a pronouncing dictionary or a slang dictionary. The latter will be addressed in the next section.

19

"Special-field" dictionaries, to use Barnhart's term, have been with us a long time. Medical and legal dictionaries in Latin, and dictionaries of military and nautical science, in particular, existed long before the development of English monolingual dictionaries. Today's interest in specialized vocabularies is by no means unique to the twentieth century but rather carries on the tradition of earlier English dictionaries such as *Cocker's English Dictionary* of 1704, which boasted of the inclusion of many military and commercial terms. John Harris's *Lexicon Technicum,* also of 1704, was an early subject-field dictionary, in Latin, devoted to terms in the sciences and the arts and was of considerable importance in the history of English lexicography.

Subject-field dictionaries, like scholarly dictionaries, are directed to a vertical and restricted market. Unlike scholarly dictionaries, however, which are as a rule entirely descriptive and lexical, subject-field dictionaries often have a normative purpose as well as an informative one, and they tend to be more encyclopedic in content. It is instructive to draw a distinction between the way general words and scientific words are defined:

> General words are defined on the basis of citations illustrating actual usage: the meanings are EXTRACTED from a body of evidence.... The meanings of scientific entries, on the other hand, are IMPOSED on the basis of expert advice. The experts may have sources apart from their own knowledge and experience, but their sources are informative or encyclopedic rather than lexical, that is, they are likely to consist of authoritative definitions composed by other experts whose concern is maintaining the internal coherence of their discipline rather than faithfully recording how terms are used. Their goal is ease and accuracy of communication between those versed in the language of science.[24]

On the other hand, it is not true to say that usage plays no part in the dictionary treatment of a scientific vocabulary. When a dozen or so terms are used to describe exactly the same concept—a common circumstance in medicine, for example—usage is the most important criterion for determining what the preferred term should be. The problem is that it is very difficult, if not impossible, to determine which of the variants is most widely used. Citation files for technical terms do not exist; no frequency count is possible. The specialist is forced to rely on his own experience, which is necessarily limited both in time and place, and in cases of disputed usage is apt to be parochial. Therefore, other criteria are often essential. Furthermore, even if usage can determine the preferred term, it has a limited role in determining its meaning. That is usually imposed, as I have said, by the demands of the discipline rather than extracted from citations of actual usage. For example, the standard dictionary of electrical and electronics terms identifies every definition with one or more numbers that correspond to various official terminologies. A typical definition plainly reveals the imposed nature of material:

design C motor   an integral horse-power polyphase squirrel-cage induction motor, designed for full-voltage starting, with normal locked-rotor and breakdown torque and with locked-rotor current not exceeding specified values.[25]

What has changed in the last fifty years is the proportion of the entries in general dictionaries devoted to the scientific and technical vocabulary. It is a commonplace that the specialized vocabularies of science have increased enormously in this period, but what is not so often realized is the increased weight given them in relative importance in our dictionaries, compared to the general vocabulary. I have estimated conservatively that more than 40 percent of the entries in *NID3* are scientific or technical, as are 25–35 percent of those in college and desk dictionaries.[26] Clarence Barnhart has estimated that almost 40 percent of the contents in college dictionaries are scientific or technical.[27] The proportion is likely to become even higher in the future. In fact, the larger general dictionaries are becoming a collection of subject-field dictionaries merged with a general dictionary, which is being compressed into an ever smaller proportion of the total work.

Why is this so? The answer is twofold. First, the growth in the vocabulary of our language has been disproportionately in the scientific and technical vocabulary. Second, and more profoundly, the greater space provided technical terms in our dictionaries mirrors the prevailing cultural view of our society that science and technology are of the highest importance.

General dictionaries have always relied chiefly on subject-field dictionaries for technical definitions. Therefore, although the chief market of specialized dictionaries is relatively restricted, their influence is in reality much broader. The inclusion of specialized scientific terms in such large numbers in our dictionaries diminishes the force of the claim that definitions are based on actual usage as revealed by a collection of quotations exemplifying particular words and meanings. It also introduces, even in the most determinedly descriptive work, a normative element, since such definitions often have a prescriptive purpose. The overall descriptive nature of the dictionary is thus very substantially blurred.

There are subject-field dictionaries in almost every subject one can think of. Among the most widely used are those of law, medicine and other branches of biology, electronics, and architecture. Some specialized works, however, though called dictionaries, are entirely encyclopedic in content, depending on concepts rather than terms for classifying their information. Many of the smaller dictionaries are amateurish, compiled by people who may be expert in their subjects but who are often ignorant of the basic principles for writing definitions. These works, sometimes little more than glossaries, may be entertaining but are seldom useful for the serious student. Among the few notable exceptions are Robert S. Gold's *Jazz Talk* (1975), a sound historical dictionary with copious citations, and *Webster's Sports Dictionary* (1976), compiled by Robert Copeland, a first-rate dictionary of all the major sports and a good many minor ones, with well-chosen, informative illustrations.

Some special-field dictionaries are sponsored by professional organizations that appoint committees to study the nomenclature of the field, resolve cases of conflicting and disputed usage, settle on preferred terms, and write official definitions for them. The differences in international usage of the same concept, even in English, but much more so when different languages are involved, are very difficult to resolve and have confounded the experts in many disciplines, especially in medicine, for at least a century. Indeed, there is even considerable confusion over what to call reference works that attempt to classify or define technical terms. As one medical lexicographer says in despair, "Some of the names given to terminological reference works—particularly 'glossary,' 'vocabulary,' and 'dictionary'—have been so misused that there is complete confusion, and the title on the cover of a book is no safe guide to its content."[28] Figure 1 shows one of the clearest and most comprehensible attempts to define these terms. I would only note that the word *lexicon* is often used interchangeably with *vocabulary* in all three senses defined below, and is so used in this book.

Limitations in the Aspects of Language Covered

Dictionaries differ in scope in respect to the aspect of language covered. Dictionaries limited to one aspect of language are called special-purpose dictionaries by Barnhart and restricted (or special) dictionaries by Zgusta. Neither name is entirely satisfactory, but Barnhart's term is preferable because less ambiguous.

Special-purpose dictionaries range from scholarly works, such as Joseph Wright's monumental *English Dialect Dictionary* in six volumes (1898–1905), to "pop-up" picture dictionaries for preschoolers; from Charles Talbut Onions's *Oxford Dictionary of English Etymology* (1966) to popular, commercial books designed to help people increase their vocabularies or improve their style of writing or harness their usage to prescribed models of correctness—or lure them into buying such books in the hope that they will. Such books—for here we must enlarge our survey to include reference works other than dictionaries—may deal with etymology, pronunciation, spelling, vocabulary, usage, synonymy, offensive and taboo words, slang,

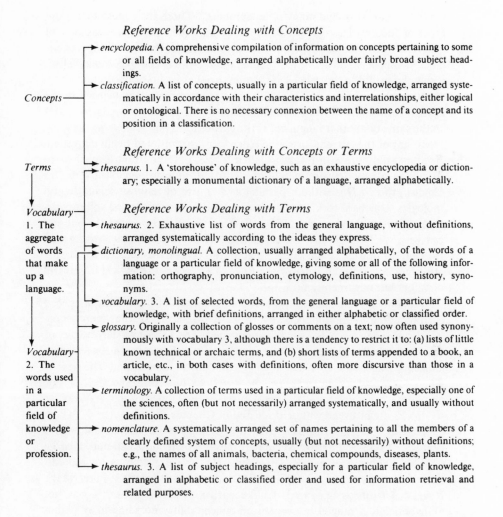

Reference Works Dealing with Concepts

Concepts —

encyclopedia. A comprehensive compilation of information on concepts pertaining to some or all fields of knowledge, arranged alphabetically under fairly broad subject headings.

classification. A list of concepts, usually in a particular field of knowledge, arranged systematically in accordance with their characteristics and interrelationships, either logical or ontological. There is no necessary connexion between the name of a concept and its position in a classification.

Reference Works Dealing with Concepts or Terms

Terms

thesaurus. 1. A 'storehouse' of knowledge, such as an exhaustive encyclopedia or dictionary; especially a monumental dictionary of a language, arranged alphabetically.

Reference Works Dealing with Terms

Vocabulary
1. The aggregate of words that make up a language.

thesaurus. 2. Exhaustive list of words from the general language, without definitions, arranged systematically according to the ideas they express.

dictionary, monolingual. A collection, usually arranged alphabetically, of the words of a language or a particular field of knowledge, giving some or all of the following information: orthography, pronunciation, etymology, definitions, use, history, synonyms.

vocabulary. 3. A list of selected words, from the general language or a particular field of knowledge, with brief definitions, arranged in either alphabetic or classified order.

glossary. Originally a collection of glosses or comments on a text; now often used synonymously with vocabulary 3, although there is a tendency to restrict it to: (a) lists of little known technical or archaic terms, and (b) short lists of terms appended to a book, an article, etc., in both cases with definitions, often more discursive than those in a vocabulary.

Vocabulary
2. The words used in a particular field of knowledge or profession.

terminology. A collection of terms used in a particular field of knowledge, especially one of the sciences, often (but not necessarily) arranged systematically, and usually without definitions.

nomenclature. A systematically arranged set of names pertaining to all the members of a clearly defined system of concepts, usually (but not necessarily) without definitions; e.g., the names of all animals, bacteria, chemical compounds, diseases, plants.

thesaurus. 3. A list of subject headings, especially for a particular field of knowledge, arranged in alphabetic or classified order and used for information retrieval and related purposes.

FIGURE 1.   Reference works dealing with concepts, terms, or both. From A. Manuila, ed., *Progress in Medical Terminology* (Basel, Switzerland: S. Karger, 1981). p. 58. Reprinted by permission.

dialect, neologisms, and many other subjects.[29] There are scores of different types of such works, represented by many hundreds, perhaps thousands, of different titles. Although I will discuss a number of these works in various parts of this book, no systematic survey of all types is possible. Nonetheless, it may be useful to describe some major varieties.

Etymological dictionaries are alphabetic lists of words showing how the current forms were derived from older ones (called *etyma,* singular *etymon*) in the same or another language. If the earlier form had a meaning different from that of the current form, the older form is translated by an equivalent word or brief phrase in English (called a *gloss*). The current English word usually is briefly defined, merely to identify it, in each important sense. In English, the *OED* is without parallel as a source of reliable, scholarly etymologies. Onions's work, previously cited, is the best of the one-volume dictionaries; it is based on the *OED* (of which Onions was one of the editors) but with many additions and corrections. It is an exemplary work, giving the century in which each sense of each word originated. Walter W. Skeat's *An Etymological Dictionary of the English Language* (1879–82) is also still of value, but now mainly of historic interest.

Pronouncing dictionaries provide transcriptions of the sounds of speech corresponding to an alphabetic list of words so that the reader may understand how each word is usually pronounced. The classic modern works of this kind, one British and one American, are Daniel Jones's *An English Pronouncing Dictionary* (first ed. 1917) and John S. Kenyon and Thomas A. Knott's *A Pronouncing Dictionary of American English,* respectively.[30] For up-to-date pronunciations, the best source in the United States is *NID3.*

Books about usage will be discussed in Chapter 5.

Synonym dictionaries have existed in English since the early nineteenth century. Taylor's *English Synonyms Discriminated* (1813) and George Crabb's *English Synonymes* (1816) are two early examples; a revised edition of Crabb's work was reprinted as late as 1917. In 1852, Peter Mark Roget's *Thesaurus* appeared. Unlike earlier synonym books, it was not alphabetically arranged but organized conceptually according to an elaborate philosophical scheme. So successful was the idea that it spawned a number of similarly organized works, and the word *thesaurus,* which had until then meant an exhaustive dictionary or survey of the entire lexicon of a language (literally "storehouse"), now usually refers to a synonym dictionary, whether conceptually organized or alphabetic. Incidentally, the term *Roget's,* like *Webster's,* is in the public domain and can be used with impunity by any publisher. (See page 104 for further discussion of synonym dictionaries.)

What is slang? Slang is usually defined as words or expressions that originated in cant (the familiar, nontechnical vocabulary restricted to a particular occupation, age group, or any group sharing a special interest), jargon (a technical vocabulary restricted to a particular occupation or special-interest group), or argot (the vocabulary peculiar to thieves and other criminals) but that have become more widely known and are used by some segments of the general population. Most slang is colorful, irreverent, or facetious, but it is not to be confused with taboo words. Although slang is often meant to shock the staid or discomfort the pretentious, it is not intended essentially to violate the proprieties of common decency, although it may, depending upon what one's proprieties are. Many taboo words are not slang, and most slang expressions do not deal with sexually or scatologically offensive concepts. As Stuart Berg Flexner has pointed out, "Many so-called bedroom words are not technically slang at all, but are sometimes associated with slang only because standard speech has rejected them as taboo. However, many of these taboo words do have further metaphorical meanings in slang: *fucked, jerk, screw you,* etc."[31]

The two best current slang dictionaries are Eric Partridge's *A Dictionary of Slang and Unconventional English* (fifth supplemented ed. 1961; first ed. 1937), which describes British slang from a historical point of view, and Wentworth and Flexner's *Dictionary of American Slang.* The latter work was based on material originally compiled by Harold Wentworth, whose *American Dialect Dictionary* (1944) was derived from these collections. Flexner added much new material and brought the work to completion. Both slang dictionaries have been criticized for dubious and speculative etymologies, but etymologies for slang must always be speculative, and both works are impressive collections that fill a void in the coverage of the language. (See page 189 for additional discussion of slang.)

In dialect studies, Joseph Wright's *English Dialect Dictionary* is the outstanding work. There are a number of linguistic atlases in both Britain and the United States that map the geographic distribution of uses of particular vocabulary items or features of pronunciation. These are for the specialist and scholar rather than for the general public. A major new work, the *Dictionary of American Regional English* (*DARE* for short), was begun in 1965 based on the files of the American Dialect Society. Under the editorship of Frederic G. Cassidy, it has completed a survey of native speakers in all parts of the United States based on over one thousand lengthy questionnaires personally collected by field workers, mostly graduate students. The resulting work is certain to be an invaluable aid to linguistic scholarship and lexicography, since no work based on original research of this scope has ever before been attempted.[32] (See page 221 for further information about DARE.)

Collections of new words (neologisms) vary from flippant newspaper glossaries to extensive dictionaries with illustrative quotations documenting each new term. Currently, the best such dictionaries are those edited by

Clarence L. Barnhart, Sol Steinmetz, and Robert K. Barnhart, the first in 1973 and the second in 1980: *The Barnhart Dictionary of New English Since 1963* and *The Second Barnhart Dictionary of New English,* respectively. Each is distinguished by handsome format, extensive quotations, and notes dealing with etymology or usage, and (in the second book) with notes on linguistic terminology such as *euphemism.* Merriam-Webster has also issued a supplement to *NID3* called *6,000 Words* (1976), which includes some brief illustrative quotations along with definitions. All three books include a large percentage of technical and scientific words, a tradition at least three centuries old. (Cf. Edward Phillips's *The New World of English Words* [1658] cited in Chapter 2.) Many of the scientific words listed are by no means new but have supposedly only recently entered the common vocabulary. So much is acknowledged in the Explanatory Notes of the first Barnhart dictionary, but the result is still somewhat misleading, because it is often difficult to say when a term has become general. Its use in a quasi-popular scientific magazine that provides synopses of scientific papers or in the "new scientific words" section of an encyclopedia does not persuade me that a word, such as *methicillin* or *methotrexate* or *Marburg virus,* is passing into common usage. In this respect, the criterion for selection in *6,000 Words,* which is not limited to new words and senses but also includes those "for various reasons" omitted from *NID3,* is even more inscrutable. Illustrative quotations are seldom given in *6,000 Words* for scientific and technical entries, yet terms like *indocyanine green* (a dye) and *maneb* (a fungicide) are included. We are left guessing as to why these, and not hundreds more like them, were chosen.

The Lexical Unit

Dictionaries and other language reference books differ in the size of the unit cataloged. Some confine themselves to words or lexical units; others to phrases, set expressions, or longer quotations. General monolingual dictionaries are limited mainly to words or expressions that convey a distinctive lexical meaning. Dictionaries of idioms are limited to expressions that in set combinations convey distinctive meanings. Dictionaries of proverbs and quotations consist of items that contain one or more sentences and are based on other criteria: traditional use in the first instance; especial aptness or wit, or the fame of the person quoted, in the second.

There are many types of indexes, but essentially an index is a reordering of the important words in a text in alphabetical order so as to provide access to particular parts of the text where each word is used. If the repeated words constitute a fairly exhaustive list of all the words in the text, the index is

26

called a concordance. In a concordance, the immediate passage in which the word occurs is often printed next to the index entry. A concordance may be of a particular work or of all the works of a particular author.

If the repeated words are selective rather than exhaustive, and the purpose is to find not only where particular words or names occur in the text but where broader concepts are discussed, the list is commonly called an index. Indexes may be simple or complex. Complex indexes may be hierarchically constructed, so that under the name of someone discussed one may find a subentry reading, "early years in Monticello," "first marriage to Mme Swann," and so forth. Such indexes are far more than a listing of words used in a text; they constitute a narrative or conceptual outline of the work.

An exegesis, or exegetic dictionary, explains a text, such as the Bible, by means of an index to particular words used in key passages. Under each entry word the passage is explicated in a broad, conceptual analysis.[33]

There are also dictionaries of foreign words and expressions, dictionaries of acronyms, and dictionaries of abbreviations. The chief difficulty with such works is that the criteria for selecting entries are often uncertain. Presumably a dictionary of foreign words should include only those terms that are in the process of becoming assimilated but are not yet accepted as English. Admittedly, the decision is often difficult, but in practice such dictionaries routinely include patently foreign terms.

An abbreviation is a shortened form for a word or phrase, consisting of part of the word or the first letter of each of the words in the phrase, or sometimes the first two letters. An acronym is a form of abbreviation composed of the first or the first two letters, or a syllable from each of the words in a compound term or phrase, so ordered that the resulting series of letters is usually pronounced as a word. The distinction between abbreviations and acronyms is often arbitrary because the same designation may be pronounced by some as a word and by others by reciting the names of the letters, as *AWOL* (away without leave). Some dictionaries of abbreviations and acronyms are limited to a particular subject field, such as medicine or law, and these may be particularly useful, since their narrower focus would theoretically suggest more complete coverage. In practice, however, many of these works are haphazardly put together; one finds common abbreviations in the discipline missing and numerous abbreviations that one has reason to doubt have ever existed. My guess is that the compilers of abbreviation and acronym dictionaries tend to copy from one another, sometimes uncritically, and that "ghost" abbreviations are thus created.

A ghost word is a word that has never existed in actual usage but that appears in dictionaries through the lexicographer's error. Ghost words are

27

introduced in dictionaries iatrogenically, so to speak, as diseases are sometimes introduced in well patients by the physician's treatment. Once a term
is in a dictionary it acquires the quiet authority of print and may spread to
other innocent dictionaries, thus acquiring more authority, until it appears,
by virtue of its ubiquitous representation, to be firmly established in the
language. The medical literature abounds with mistranslations of diseases
into expressions that had never been used in the target language but for
which meanings were invented based on the mistranslations. These ghost
terms were subsequently adopted as genuine by other works in the target
language until they gained widespread currency, much to the confusion of
all concerned.[34]

Among dictionaries of idioms, the most historical and scholarly is *The
Kenkyusha Dictionary of Current English Idioms* (1964), edited by Sanki
Ichikawa and four other Japanese scholars. It is an impressive work, organized by key words, with clear, accurate definitions and with extensive citations illustrating each idiom. The citations are precisely identified biblio-
graphically. There is also an index so that if the reader missed *hate like
poison,* for example, by seeking it under *hate* instead of *poison,* he will find
it in both places in the index. It is an elegant work, put together with taste
and care. However, its coverage is somewhat dated and it is far from
complete.

The United States is lamentably backward in its attention to foreign-
born speakers of English, a field known among professional teachers and
linguists as "English as a second language" (ESL) or "English for the foreign learner" (EFL). Not so Great Britain. The reference department of
any large bookshop in England is likely to have an entire section devoted to
ESL, including a good many dictionaries. It is no surprise, then, to find that
the two best up-to-date idiom dictionaries—both intended for the ESL market—are British.[35]

The first is the *Oxford Dictionary of Current Idiomatic English,* in two
volumes (Vol. 1 by A. P. Cowie and R. Mackin, 1975; Vol. 2 by Cowie,
Mackin, and I. R. McCaig, 1983). Volume one deals entirely with idioms
consisting of verbs with prepositions and particles; volume two with phrase,
clause, and sentence idioms. The dictionary contains a massive amount of
information compressed into two small volumes. In many ways it is an innovative and challenging work. The editors attempt to provide clues to the
customary context (or collocation), and indicate common subjects and
objects, called *collocates.* Illustrative quotations with cited sources as well
as invented phrases are included to exemplify context. A vast amount of
grammatical and contextual information is provided about each expression.
Abbreviations and symbols abound in order to save space, and the explanatory introduction runs to eighty-one pages. It is a thoroughly scholarly

work, but in an effort to give their readers as much guidance as possible in the available space, the editors may have made access to some of their data too difficult for many. If that is a fault, it is surely better than the opposite and more common circumstance in which essential information is omitted lest the reader be challenged. Incidentally, dictionaries are notoriously difficult to typeset, and I have never seen a dictionary with a more complex mix of typefaces and symbols than this work. Technically the *Oxford Dictionary* is a work of consummate typographical virtuosity, and editorially it is ingenious.

The second work, published in 1979, is the *Longman Dictionary of English Idioms,* edited by Thomas Hill Long. It is a smaller work and has a much less dense look to it than the *Oxford Dictionary.* It also seems much easier to use with the pages of its explanatory section totaling a mere baker's dozen. Its definitions are written in a controlled vocabulary listed at the end of the book.

Baker's dozen is included in the *Longman Dictionary* with a citation from Dickens and an explanation of the origin of the term: to avoid being punished for selling bread under weight, bakers added a thirteenth loaf to each dozen without extra charge. The reader is told that the expression is not formal and that it is a noun phrase usually used as the object of a verb or preposition or as the complement of a verb.

The striking fact about both these dictionaries is that they are not content with the goal of aiding comprehension of unfamiliar idiomatic expressions. They try to provide enough information so that the foreign-born speaker can use the expression. The *Oxford Dictionary* would be of more help than the *Longman Dictionary* in expression, but both are excellent dictionaries.

The Primary Language of the Market

Monolingual dictionaries differ in the primary language of their intended users, i.e., some are designed for those who are learning English as a second language (ESL), as distinguished from native speakers of English. ESL dictionaries combine many of the features of foreign-language instruction, such as providing detailed information on pronunciation, verb patterns, and collocations, with some characteristics of children's dictionaries: definitions are expressed in simplified language and sometimes in a controlled vocabulary. Unlike monolingual dictionaries, most ESL dictionaries are designed to enable the foreign learner to produce utterances in English, not just to comprehend them. Like children's dictionaries, ESL dictionaries have an essentially pedagogical purpose, and there are ESL dictionaries—as there are

29

school ones—for beginning, intermediate, and advanced students. However, since these works are for adults, the tone of the definitions and to some extent the selection of entries differ from those of school dictionaries. In common with bilingual dictionaries, the vocabulary of ESL dictionaries contains many idiomatic expressions and culture-specific terms.

A number of linguistic scholars, such as the late Albert H. Marckwardt, observed in the 1960s and 70s that dictionaries had not been much influenced by recent advances in the study of linguistics. Although still true of general dictionaries, it is much less true of ESL dictionaries, in no small measure through Marckwardt's own efforts. ESL dictionaries are more sophisticated and more demanding of the user than other dictionaries because they are based on the assumption that the foreign-born user is more highly motivated than the native speaker and is willing to take the trouble to learn how to use a book that requires some time to master. It is also assumed that the ESL user will not be nonplussed by verb paradigms or by the International Phonetic Alphabet; in short, that he will have some familiarity with the pedagogical tools of foreign-language instruction. It may well be that this assumption cannot yet be safely made in the United States.

I have already discussed dictionaries of idioms for the foreign born. There are also a splendid and growing series of general dictionaries for the foreign born, some of which are in the vanguard in applying linguistic research to the practical aim of helping people learn English. For example, the *Longman Dictionary of Contemporary English* (1978), edited by Paul Procter, has used material from the Survey of English Usage directed by Professor Randolph Quirk at University College London.[36] This material provides a firm basis for indicating collocations for particular words and expressions and is of immense practical help, since it relies on actual usage rather than informed guesses. This dictionary, like others of its kind, provides a plethora of information that ordinary monolingual dictionaries do not. It tells the reader which nouns are countable (called count nouns, which can be made plural, like *substance*) and which are not (called mass nouns, like *inventiveness*). It tells the reader not only whether verbs are transitive or intransitive but what sort of objects they take if they are transitive. It tells him how to inflect verbs and how to compare adjectives and adverbs. It tells him whether adjectives are apt to occur before a noun or following a verb. It tells him how words are pronounced in British English and in American English, and how compounds (like *high hat*) are stressed. Its pronunciation system is less ambiguous and shows more variant pronunciations than that of other kinds of dictionaries of similar size.

The pioneer in ESL lexicography is A. S. Hornby, who with A. P. Cowie edited the *Oxford Advanced Learner's Dictionary of Current English* (1980;

first ed. 1948; hereafter called *Hornby*). Beginning in 1936 with his work on the *Idiomatic and Syntactic English Dictionary* for Japanese speakers of English, Hornby produced a series of ESL dictionaries and other language reference books at all levels that drew upon the best available scholarship of the time and that have been enormously influential in accelerating the spread of English as an international language. Hornby's dictionaries are the standard by which all other dictionaries for the ESL market must be measured.

The Period of Time Covered

Dictionaries differ in the period of time covered by their lexicons. Diachronic, or historical, dictionaries deal with an extended period of time, often centuries, with the chief purpose of tracing the development of forms and meanings of each headword over the period covered. Etymology is thus an integral part of such a work, since it illustrates how form and meaning have changed. Indeed, etymological dictionaries are specialized diachronic dictionaries. Synchronic dictionaries, by contrast, deal with a narrow band of time and attempt to represent the lexicon as it exists or existed at a particular point in time—not necessarily the present. *Webster's Third New International Dictionary (NID3)* and the college dictionaries are synchronic works dealing with the present time. Of course, no dictionary can be purely synchronic, since it takes years to produce any dictionary and even synchronic works include some archaic forms.[37] The larger synchronic dictionaries, such as *NID3*, take in a broader band of time than smaller works. As a rule, archaic and obsolete words are the first to go when a dictionary is abridged. Thus in synchronic dictionaries etymology is less important, and the representation of current slang and technological terms is more important than in diachronic works.

Major diachronic dictionaries are scholarly and take a very long time to do. The *Oxford English Dictionary* was originally planned for ten years but actually took nearly fifty (1879–1928); nor does this include the twenty years before, during which the millions of citations forming the basis of the work were collected. Zgusta cites two other diachronic dictionaries, one Dutch and the other Swedish, that took sixty-five years each to produce, and a Danish work that took forty-nine years. In each case they were planned to take one-fourth or less of the actual time required.[38] The *Deutsches Wörterbuch* begun by Jacob and Wilhelm Grimm—known popularly for their fairy tales but to students of language for their discoveries of systematic sound change in philology—was not completed until 1960, over a century after it was begun.

31

Most synchronic dictionaries are commercial, and as we have seen, not everyone is happy about that (see page 12).

The Linguistic Approach Chosen

Dictionaries differ, but less than one might think, in their attitude toward usage. The question is usually phrased in terms of prescriptiveness versus descriptiveness. So far as general monolingual dictionaries are concerned, the question has little meaning.

All dictionaries based on usage—and all competently done dictionaries must be based on usage—are descriptive. Prescription is impossible to distinguish from bias. Any preferred usage or condemnation of existing usage necessarily reflects the educational or cultural background of the editor making such a judgment. Such judgments are obviously welcome if the user consciously or unconsciously admires the educational class or cultural background of the editor; he may even buy the book specifically to get this advice, as is the case with many guides to usage. But they have no place in coloring definitions in a general dictionary any more than editorial opinions belong in straight news articles in the morning newspaper. Usage notes, clearly labeled as such, may provide help to users who want to avoid embarrassment by appearing uneducated or ignorant, but the lexicographer should, so far as possible, abstain from expressing his own opinion about any usage, though reporting to the best of his knowledge what the attitudes of most people (and in particular educated people) are to usages regarded as questionable or obnoxious.

Even if a dictionary is supposed to be prescriptive, as we were told the *American Heritage Dictionary (AHD)* was to be, it cannot be prescriptive and be an honest work.[39] As we will see when we discuss definition in Chapter 4, defining is not a process of value judgment. If one started to make value judgments, one would find oneself contradicting or ignoring the evidence at hand a hundred times a day, and one might as well discard all citations of actual usage and fabricate a metaphysical universe of correct speech forms that would be of interest only to oneself. The definitions in *AHD* are no more prescriptive than those of any of the other college dictionaries. They are based, as they must be—since there is no other basis— on the record of actual usage. *AHD* does take a prescriptive point of view in its usage notes, but that is another matter.

Usage guides, such as Henry Fowler's *Modern English Usage* (first ed. 1926), may legitimately take any view the author wishes, since they are designed precisely to provide guidance to people who feel in need of it. Usage books will be discussed at length in Chapter 5.

The Means of Access

Dictionaries and other language reference books differ in the manner in which access to their information is provided, specifically as to whether their word lists are arranged alphabetically or in some other way.

We think now of dictionaries as being necessarily alphabetical, but as we shall see in Chapter 2, some early dictionaries were arranged by subject rather than alphabetically. Moreover, many technical dictionaries, such as medical ones, are arranged by entry and subentry and are therefore not in strict alphabetical order but alphabetized by the governing noun. (Thus, *infectious hepatitis* appears as a subentry of *hepatitis,* not under *infectious.*) If one broadens the scope of dictionaries to include other word reference books, there are quite a variety of works arranged nonalphabetically.

According to one scholar, the four basic systems of classification are by the alphabet, by the form of the entry words (morphemic), by meaning (semantic), or by no system at all (haphazard).[40] The great advantage of the alphabet is that everybody knows it. A morphemic arrangement, which links words sharing a common form, such as *mishap* and *happen* or all the forms ending in *-ology,* would be of interest mainly to linguists. Semantic arrangements are employed in some thesauruses that, however, also have extensive alphabetic indexes to refer the reader to the various conceptual categories associated with each term.

The *English Duden*—named after the German philologist Konrad Duden (1829–1911)—is a bilingual book semantically arranged and consisting of full-page illustrations in which many kinds of things—types of screws or houses or the parts of a bicycle or motorcar—are individually depicted in careful line drawings and identified in the target language. Based on the German *Duden Bilderwörterbuch* (pictorial dictionary), the *English Duden* includes two alphabetic indexes, one in the source language (German) and the other in the target language (English), linked to numeric references identifying the page and the individual drawing corresponding to each term.[41] Often the reader is uncertain what a term means precisely even in his own (source) language, or what the name is for a thing he recognizes by sight. Thus, as a monolingual dictionary the *English Duden* works in two ways: by providing a means for calling to mind a name for an object one has seen (such as a Phillips head screw) and, more commonly, for identifying by illustration what one has only known by name (such as a monkey wrench). As a bilingual work, the Duden is one-way, from the German term to the picture identified by an English caption. The *English Duden* is most useful for identifying technical or mechanical things and is limited to words denoting things that can be illustrated. It is not designed to cope with words like *justice, mercy, taxation,* or *sorrow.*

33

Some crossword puzzle dictionaries are arranged by the number of letters in each word. All three-letter words are listed together alphabetically, followed by four-letter words (used as a phrase, not as a lexical unit!), five-letter words, and so on. Thus the harried crossword-puzzler can more easily find the answer to his quest.

Word frequency books are often arranged by frequency of occurrence (i.e., by rank), though they may also be arranged alphabetically. Rhyming dictionaries, which are very old, are arranged according to the sound of the ultimate syllables of each word. John Walker produced a rhyming dictionary in 1775 that went through numberless editions and was still in print in the early twentieth century. In recent times, computer-generated reverse dictionaries have been made available on magnetic tape and in book form. These consist of lists of words with each word printed in normal sequence but alphabetized in reverse order of its letters, so that all words ending in *-ology,* for example, appear consecutively. Reverse dictionaries can thus highlight morphemic properties and be of use to scholars by indicating which suffixes are most common.

A fascinating work entitled *A Chronological English Dictionary* (1970) has organized all the words in the *Shorter Oxford English Dictionary* by the date of first occurrence. It therefore essays to list each word in the order in which it first appeared in the English language. Within each year or span of years, words are presented alphabetically.

Note that each of the nonalphabetic methods of organization uses the alphabet in some way. Because it taps a universal skill among the literate, alphabetization is the only way of arranging words for quick access, although alphabetization itself is not always as routine as it may appear. There are many ways to alphabetize, and in scientific and technical vocabularies in particular the decisions that must be made in alphabetizing are by no means simple, as we shall see later in Chapter 3.

CHAPTER TWO

A Brief History of English Lexicography

The history of English lexicography usually consists of a recital of successive and often successful acts of piracy. Representing what may be the least inspiring of all seminal works, Robert Cawdrey's *A Table Alphabeticall . . .* of 1604 is generally accounted to be the first English dictionary.[1] It incorporated almost 90 percent of the words of Edmund Coote's *English Schoole-Master,* a grammar, prayer book, and lexicon with brief definitions published in 1596. Moreover, about half of Cawdrey's three thousand entries were taken from a Latin–English dictionary of 1588, Thomas Thomas's *Dictionarium Linguae Latinae et Anglicanae.* The early history of English lexicography is little more than a record of judicious or flagrant copying from one's predecessors, sometimes with grudging acknowledgment, more often (at least in the seventeenth century) without.

Some of the eighteenth- and nineteenth-century lexicographers publicly acknowledged their indebtedness to specific predecessors. Sad to say, very few twentieth-century lexicographers have done so. The pressures of the marketplace dictate that every dictionary be "new." A really new dictionary would be a dreadful piece of work, missing innumerable basic words and senses, replete with absurdities and unspeakable errors, studded with biases and interlarded with irrelevant provincialisms. Noah Webster's *American Dictionary of the English Language* of 1828, though far from being entirely new, was new enough to subscribe to many of these defects. Webster's dictionary surmounted the infelicities of its originality by the brilliant defining skills of its author and by the business acumen of his publishers.

Fortunately, very few dictionaries are really new, and none of the general, staff-written, commercial dictionaries published by major dictionary houses are. One would think any historian mad who claimed that his new general history was entirely new, spun freshly from his brain without being firmly based on the accumulated store of histories preceding his. Yet the public expects general dictionaries—which are, even if synchronic, histories of the usage of language—to be new in this sense. They are not. They never were and they never will be.

No matter how large a citation file they have at their disposal, modern lexicographers look very carefully at each other's work. Citations, even millions of them, do not cover every aspect of usage in sufficient detail. Even if they did, the working lexicographer simply would not have time to redo the work of hundreds of years of lexicography and analyze the meanings of *set,* for example, which take up more than eighteen pages in the *Oxford English Dictionary (OED).* It could take a highly skilled lexicographer two months or more of uninterrupted work to distinguish the senses and define this word. Listen to James A. H. Murray, the chief editor of the *OED,* on this subject:

> Only those who have made the experiment know the bewilderment with which an editor or sub-editor, after he has apportioned the quotations for such a word as *above* . . . among 20, 30 or 40 groups, and furnished each of these with a provisional definition, spreads them out on a table or on the floor where he can obtain a general survey of the whole, and spends hour after hour in shifting them about like the pieces on a chess-board, striving to find in the fragmentary evidence of an incomplete historical record, such a sequence of meanings as may form a logical chain of development. Sometimes the quest seems hopeless; recently, for example, the word *art* utterly baffled me for several days: something *had* to be done with it: something was done and put in type; but the renewed consideration of it in print, with the greater facility of reading and comparison which this afforded, led to the entire pulling to pieces and reconstruction of the edifice, extending to several columns of type . . . those who think that such work can be hurried, or that anything can accelerate it, except more brain power brought to bear on it, had better try.[2]

And this was said by the man who was quite probably the finest lexicographer in the entire history of English dictionary making. Few modern commercial publishers have an instinct for scholarship so pure that they will spend millions of dollars to redo what other, better scholars have done before them.

So before we begin to fulminate at the supposed chicanery of the early English lexicographers, we had best reflect that modern lexicographers, though more discreet, depend heavily on their predecessors as well, and often the line between using another dictionary as a source or reference and copying its definition with trivial changes is a fine one.

Latin and French Glossaries

The earliest word reference books for English-speaking people were bilingual glossaries that provided English equivalents for Latin or French words. In the Middle Ages, as early as the eighth century, difficult words in manuscripts were sometimes glossed, just as current editions of Shakespeare annotate obsolete words for the modern student, with easier Latin words or with the Old English (Anglo-Saxon) equivalent. The practice continued through the sixteenth century. Schoolmasters sometimes collected the glosses and listed them together; the resulting collection, called a *glossarium,* is today called a *glossary.* Although the word *dictionarius* was used as early as 1225 for a list of Latin words, the word was not applied to anything we would recognize as a dictionary until the sixteenth century. Sir Thomas Elyot's Latin–English work of 1538 was originally called *Dictionary,* then *Bibliotheca Eliotae,* and John Withals published a little English–Latin teaching manual in 1553 called *A Shorte Dictionarie for Yong Begynners.*

English–Latin dictionaries also appeared very early as teaching aids. The *Promptorium Parvulorum, sive Clericorum* ("Storehouse [of words] for Children or Clerics"), the earliest known English–Latin dictionary, may have been written as early as 1440.[3] Caxton introduced printing in England in 1476, and in 1480 he printed a French–English glossary without a title. The *Promptorium* appeared in print in 1499 and is one of the earliest printed books in England.

The entire stock of English words in the fifteenth century was less than a fifth of what it is today.[4] It was therefore necessary to turn to other languages to provide descriptions of things for which no English word existed. The interest in Renaissance learning naturally made the classical languages, particularly Latin, a favorite source, and dictionaries were needed to translate a multitude of "hard words" based on Latin. Later called contemptuously *inkhorn* terms, not without justification, since the coinages went far beyond what was necessary for utility or clarity, they often represented little more than the writer's desire to appear elegant and sophisticated at the expense of the reader's understanding.

In 1500, the *Hortus Vocabularum* ("garden of words"), a Latin–English dictionary, appeared (the title page bore the term "Ortus Vocabularum," by which it is sometimes called). This work was a collection of glossaries arranged by subject rather than in one alphabetic listing. Thus, all the terms of parts of the body might appear together, similar in arrangement to that of the *English Duden* and others in the Duden series. Sir Thomas Elyot's *Dictionary* of 1538, also a Latin–English dictionary, was absorbed in 1565 by a much larger and more important work by Thomas Cooper, *Thesaurus Linguae Romanae et Britannicae* ("Thesaurus of the Roman Tongue and the British"), which influenced seventeenth-century monolingual dictionaries. Allen Walker Read recounts the story of Cooper's misfortune, as told by John Aubrey in *Brief Lives*.

> His wife ... was irreconcileably angrie with him for sitting-up late at night so, compileing his Dictionary. ... When he had halfe-donne it, she had the opportunity to gett into his studie, tooke all his paines out in her lap, and threw it into the fire, and burnt it. Well, for all that, that good man had so great a zeale for the advancement of learning, that he began it again, and went through with it to that perfection that he hath left it to us, a most usefull worke.[5]

Early English Dictionaries:
The Seventeenth Century

Although Cawdrey's dictionary is most often accepted as the first dictionary, Richard Huloet's work of 1552, *Abecedarium Anglo-Latinum,* basically an English–Latin dictionary with French equivalents given as well, did include brief English definitions for the English words. For this reason Frank Vizetelly declared that "Richard Huloet was the first to produce an English dictionary."[6] It is distinctly a minority view.

In truth, the right of primacy in English lexicography is a dubious and feeble privilege. The history of lexicography does not include brilliant innovations or bursts of creativity that leave us in awe, as do some discoveries in science and some masterpieces of art. It is rather a succession of slow and uneven advances in vocabulary and methodology, tempered always in its early stages by outrageous promotional blather consisting in equal parts of self-deification and attacks on the very predecessors whose works one has systematically rifled and without which one's own dictionary would have been impossible. I say this not to condemn the early lexicographers—the marketplace is still very much a reality, and we are not so different from them—but simply because the first English dictionary occurred almost inevitably as a modification of bilingual dictionaries, some of them of far greater importance. The only importance of being first in this case is that of providing an answer to the question, What was the first English dictionary?

Most of the early lexicographers were schoolmasters who compiled glossaries or dictionaries as teaching aids for their students, since there was little else available. In this tradition, Richard Mulcaster's *Elementarie* (1582), a list of some eight thousand English words without definitions, was published. He considered the list worthy of inclusion in a dictionary, defended the power and serviceability of English at a time when such sentiments were not commonplace, and expressed the need for a dictionary of the English language.[7]

Thomas Thomas's *Dictionarium Linguae Latinae et Anglicanae* of 1588, an abridgment of Cooper's *Thesaurus Linguae* of 1565, was as noted a primary source for Cawdrey and others and probably spread the idea of including certain kinds of encyclopedic material in dictionaries. Early seventeenth-century dictionaries included many of Thomas's Latin terms with slight changes to make them appear Anglicized, a convenient way to increase the number of vocabulary entries and give their own work a competitive edge over their rivals. The practice continues today, but scientific terminology is now preferred over Latin.

Although Latin was the most commonly preferred second language in bilingual dictionaries, the Renaissance inspired interest in other languages as well, and Spanish, French, and Italian were not ignored. In 1598, John Florio's massive *A Worlde of Wordes* appeared. This Italian–English dictionary was far ahead of its day in many respects, and by comparison the early English dictionaries are mean affairs. Florio included citations for contemporary Italian authors in illustration of his definitions, a practice that was not adopted in any systematic way in English lexicography until the time of Johnson one hundred and fifty years later. Florio also included slang and even what we would now call taboo words, such as *pesca* (peach) in the sense of a "yoong man's bum" and *fava* (bean) as a vulgar word for penis. In his definition of *fottere,* Florio's work includes one of the earliest printed records of *fuck:* "To iape, to sard, to fucke, to swiue, to occupy."[8]

Specialized dictionaries of law, religion, military science, and other subjects appeared in the sixteenth and seventeenth centuries as well, some of them remaining in print for many years.

Robert Cawdrey's dictionary of 1604 is a small octavo volume of some twenty-five hundred vocabulary entries. Its title is usually abbreviated to *A*

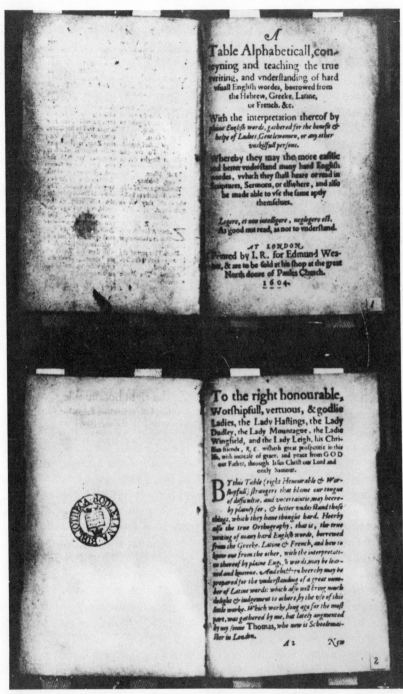

FIGURE 2. Title page of a facsimile edition of Robert Cawdrey's 1604 dictionary, *A Table Alphabeticall*. From the Collection of The Public Library of Cincinnati and Hamilton County.

Table Alphabeticall because the full title, like that of many works of its day, filled the title page. It does specify that it deals with "hard usuall English wordes, borrowed from the Hebrew, Greeke, Latine, or French, &c ... gathered for the benefit & helpe of Ladies, Gentlewomen, or any other unskilfull persons." Because women ordinarily received much less schooling than men, they were more likely to need help in deciphering "hard" words derived from Latin, or so Cawdrey and other lexicographers thought, for it was not uncommon to specify women as their chief audience. Cawdrey gives some rudimentary etymological information by marking the words derived from French and Greek by distinctive symbols, and by leaving words derived from Latin unmarked. His word list, as noted, is based almost entirely on two previous works.[9] Moreover, a close comparison between Cawdrey, Coote, and Thomas shows that Cawdrey used many of their definitions with little or no change. His work was wholly unoriginal. He may have derived the idea for a dictionary from Mulcaster and, capitalizing on the tradition of bilingual dictionaries in explaining "hard words," quietly adopted their substance as well as their method. All that we can say about him is that he had the industry and business sense to do it.

The next English dictionary, *An English Expositor* (1616), was that of John Bullokar and was more of a "hard word" dictionary than Cawdrey's, containing about twice as many words. As was the custom, he lifted many terms from Cawdrey as well as from Thomas Thomas's *Dictionarium Linguae Latinae et Anglicanae,* which apparently Cawdrey had not fully exploited. Bullokar thus included more foreign terms (from Thomas) and more obsolete ones. It is a real question whether these early dictionaries, consisting mainly of Latin words somewhat Anglicized in form, were truly English dictionaries or whether they were a subspecies of the Latin–English dictionaries they so closely resembled. In this respect Cawdrey's work was more English than Bullokar's. Bullokar was a doctor of physic (medicine) and included terms not only from medicine but from logic, philosophy, law, astronomy, and heraldry. He sometimes identified such terms as specialized by saying "A term in Herauldrie," etc. Cawdrey's dictionary is exceedingly rare, with only two reprintings, but Bullokar's was reprinted many times, the last in 1731, more than a century after the first printing.

In 1623, Henry Cockeram's *The English Dictionarie: or, An Interpreter of Hard English Words* appeared. Cockeram was not noted for his modesty. In his Introduction he stated: "what any before me in this kinde have begun, I have not onely fully finished, but thoroughly perfected."[10] Cockeram's was the "hard word" dictionary par excellence, containing words like *abequitate, bulbulcitate,* and *sullevation.* Cockeram mercilessly raided Bullokar for word lists and definitions, and anything that Bullokar had neglected in Cawdrey was seized by Cockeram. His dictionary is arranged in three parts. The first lists "hard words" with simple equivalents, as in a Latin–English dictionary. The second gives simple words with their fancy equivalents, i.e., English–Latin. The third is an encyclopedic section listing gods and goddesses, mythological creatures, birds and beasts, rivers, trees, and so on, a section drawn largely from earlier Latin dictionaries, especially that of Thomas. Cockeram was much criticized for including many terms that had probably never been used in English. For example, what might be listed as *Necessitudo* in Thomas's Latin dictionary would be listed as *Necessitude* in Cockeram. His definitions were brief and sometimes unintentionally funny. *Commotrix* is defined as "A Maid that makes ready and unready her Mistris." *Parentate* is "To celebrate ones parents funerals." *Phylologie* is "Love of much babling."[11]

On the principle that turnabout is fair play, Bullokar's edition of 1663 included encyclopedic entries copied from Cockeram, who in *his* subsequent editions lifted even more material from Bullokar. Copyright laws were, of course, nonexistent. However, it is not entirely fair to judge seventeenth-century authors by twentieth-century publishing standards. Anything published was fair game, and copying was widespread. Exclusive ownership of published material, though doubtless cherished, was not a reasonable expectation if its commercial value was likely to be great. The indignation sometimes expressed by early lexicographers did not make them stint from copying from others. The practice cannot simply be written off as hypocrisy, though there was much of that, to be sure, as there is today. But, so far as one can judge from a distance of three centuries, what we should call plagiarism was then a far less serious offense. One must think of it more as a breach of courtesy or common decency than as theft of property.

The next English dictionary to be published (1656) was Thomas Blount's *Glossographia: or, A Dictionary Interpreting all such Hard Words ... as are now used in our refined English Tongue.* This was a more ambitious and somewhat more original work than any of its predecessors, although Blount took more than half of his terms from Thomas and from Francis Holyoke's *Dictionarium Etymologicum,* a Latin–English dictionary.[12] Blount's use of Thomas and Holyoke represented many new Anglicized Latin words as English; although some of them would never become English, many Latin words were by such means assimilated in English. Though his judgment of what constituted a suitable entry was sometimes suspect, Blount did collect words from his own reading and often cited the source; he also included a considerable number of technical and scientific terms and was the first to attempt etymologies.[13] More important, Blount recognized the changing nature of language and defended the introduction of new words from Latin and other languages as a source of enrichment. He broke new ground among English dictionaries by including two woodcuts in illustration of heraldic terms. Blount, like his predecessors, relied heavily on other works for the great majority of his terms, yet he showed a measure of discrimination in rejecting some of their terms and in altering, often expanding, many of their definitions.

Two years after Blount's *Glossographia,* in 1658, Edward Phillips's *The New World of English Words* appeared in the first folio edition of any English dictionary. Although Phillips, who was Milton's nephew, gave no credit to Blount and even publicly disparaged him, his dictionary is a close copy of Blount's, with a number of encyclopedic entries added. His dictionary contained some eleven thousand words, including proper names and historic and mythological terms taken from earlier sources. Blount, enraged, published *A World of Errors Discovered in the New World of Words* (1673), in which he attacked Phillips and cataloged numerous mistakes in his dictionary. He listed Phillips's incomplete or ambiguous definitions, obviously carelessly abridged from Blount, sometimes uncritically repeating Blount's own mistakes, at other times introducing his own, to which Blount frequently appended sarcastic comments. However, in spite of the unscrupulous character of the work, *The New World of English Words* did initiate several ideas. Phillips included a long list of prominent specialists and gave the impression that they had contributed to or approved certain definitions, a claim that Blount disputed. There is no evidence to confirm Phillips's claim and it is doubtful that the specialists actually contributed to his dictionary.[14] Nonetheless, the idea of enlisting the support of specialists was a new one in English lexicography. Phillips indicated the subject field of each term and also gave, as others had before him, the language of origin.

In 1671, the *Etymologicon Linguae Anglicanae* was published. Its compiler was Stephen Skinner who, taking a leaf out of Phillips's own book, attacked Phillips while borrowing much of his dictionary. Skinner devoted most of his attention to etymology, as his title suggests, and for this reason his work influenced a number of successors, including Johnson.

Another work based on Phillips's but much expanded was Elisha Coles's *An English Dictionary,* of 1676. Still in the "hard words" tradition, Coles, a schoolmaster, included thousands of "old words," obsolete ones from Chaucer's day. His dictionary contained twenty-five thousand words, eight thousand more than the last, augmented revision of Phillips. He shortened Phillips's already brief definitions in order to include more words and more etymological information. Coles did break new ground in including cant (thieves' argot) and dialectal terms. These, taken from other specialized dictionaries, had never before been included in a general English dictionary.

The Beginning of Modern Dictionary Practice:
The Eighteenth Century

In the early eighteenth century the "hard words" tradition finally began to give way before the more useful philosophy of serving the reader's more general need to know the meanings of all sorts of words. John Kersey, regarded by Allen Walker Read as the first professional lexicographer, was reputedly the editor of *A New English Dictionary* (1702). It was the first English dictionary to attempt systematic coverage of common words as well as difficult ones.[15] Though small in size, the dictionary contained about twenty-eight thousand words, many of them included for the first time in any English dictionary. The work marked a new direction in English lexicography, for Kersey deliberately set about to make the book a dictionary of English words, rejecting doctored Latin terms, obsolete terms, and the too specialized vocabularies of the arts and sciences. The work thus parts company with the bilingual Latin–English dictionaries which, up to this time, English dictionaries had taken as their model. His work is more closely allied to spelling books, which had included common words but without definitions.[16] Although Kersey's definitions were brief and often inadequate, his work in this and in his subsequent compilations was a turning point in English lexicography. *A New English Dictionary* was very popular and remained in print for seventy years.

Kersey next thoroughly revised Phillips's *New World of English Words*. In 1706 the new volume appeared, almost twice the size of Phillips's original dictionary. Kersey added some twenty thousand words to bring the word list to thirty-eight thousand. Many of the new words were scientific terms, which he obtained chiefly from an influential work of 1704 by John Harris, *Lexicon Technicum: Or, An Universal English Dictionary of Arts and Sciences* ... Harris had produced an excellent illustrated compilation of technical and scientific terms. Kersey was only the first of a long line of lexicographers to use Harris's work as a source of technical terms, together with rephrasings of Harris's definitions. Kersey also improved and expanded Phillips's definitions. He was one of the first English lexicographers to recognize and list multiple meanings (polysemy) of the same word. His etymologies represented no advance, however, over those of his predecessors.

An Universal Etymological English Dictionary (1721), by Nathan Bailey, represents another major advance in English lexicography. Bailey, like so many of his predecessors, was a schoolmaster, but he seems to have become a professional lexicographer, for his achievements were prodigious. The *Universal* contained about forty thousand words, even more than the Kersey-Phillips, and unlike that work gave great attention to etymology.

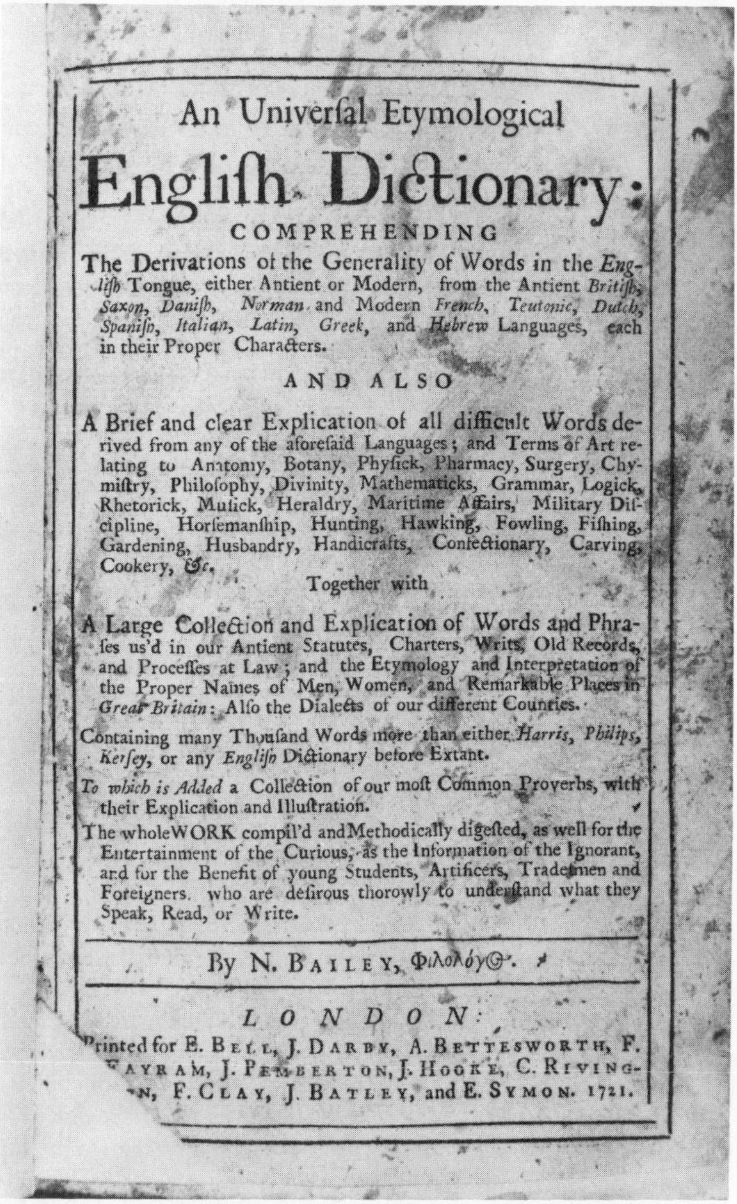

An Univerſal Etymological

Engliſh Dictionary:

COMPREHENDING

The Derivations of the Generality of Words in the *Engliſh* Tongue, either Antient or Modern, from the Antient *Britiſh, Saxon, Daniſh, Norman* and Modern *French, Teutonic, Dutch, Spaniſh, Italian, Latin, Greek,* and *Hebrew* Languages, each in their Proper Characters.

AND ALSO

A Brief and clear Explication of all difficult Words derived from any of the aforeſaid Languages; and Terms of Art relating to Anatomy, Botany, Phyſick, Pharmacy, Surgery, Chymiſtry, Philoſophy, Divinity, Mathematicks, Grammar, Logick, Rhetorick, Muſick, Heraldry, Maritime Affairs, Military Diſcipline, Horſemanſhip, Hunting, Hawking, Fowling, Fiſhing, Gardening, Husbandry, Handicrafts, Confectionary, Carving, Cookery, &c.

Together with

A Large Collection and Explication of Words and Phraſes us'd in our Antient Statutes, Charters, Writs, Old Records, and Proceſſes at Law; and the Etymology and Interpretation of the Proper Names of Men, Women, and Remarkable Places in *Great Britain*: Alſo the Dialects of our different Counties.

Containing many Thouſand Words more than either *Harris, Philips, Kerſey,* or any *Engliſh* Dictionary before Extant.

To which is Added a Collection of our moſt Common Proverbs, with their Explication and Illuſtration.

The whole WORK compil'd and Methodically digeſted, as well for the Entertainment of the Curious, as the Information of the Ignorant, and for the Benefit of young Students, Artificers, Tradeſmen and Foreigners, who are deſirous thorowly to underſtand what they Speak, Read, or Write.

By N. BAILEY, Φιλολόγ℗.

LONDON:

Printed for E. BELL, J. DARBY, A. BETTESWORTH, F. FAYRAM, J. PEMBERTON, J. HOOKE, C. RIVINGTON, F. CLAY, J. BATLEY, and E. SYMON. 1721.

FIGURE 3. Title page of Nathan Bailey's *An Universal Etymological English Dictionary* (1721). From the Collection of The Public Library of Cincinnati and Hamilton County.

Bailey listed not only the immediate source of the English word (etymon), but often earlier forms in other languages, a practice now commonplace in our dictionaries but then a novelty. As is to be expected, many of his etymologies appear wildly speculative from our vantage point, but Bailey was working a century before the great advances in Germanic philology.

The word list of the *Universal* was borrowed from a number of sources, including Kersey's *Dictionarium Anglo-Britannicum* of 1708.[17] Bailey often acknowledged the sources of his etymologies. He included cant, dialect terms, and obsolete terms used in literature, and cited expressions used by Spenser, for example. Bailey certainly had no clear idea of the distinction between dictionary and encyclopedia or, if he did, suppressed it in the interests of satisfying his customers, for his dictionaries contain many entries that have no lexical relevance. For example, he included discussions of proverbs. The following disquisition appears under "A Rolling Stone gathers no Moss":

> There are a Set of People in the World of so unsettled and restless a Temper, and such Admirers of Novelty, that they can never be long pleased with one Way of living, no more than to continue long in one Habitation; but before they are long entered upon one Business dip into another; so that they are always busily beginning to live, but by reason of Fickleness and Impatience, never arrive at a Way of Living: Such Persons fall under the Doom of this Proverb, which is designed to fix the Volatility of their Tempers, by laying before them the ill Consequences of such Fickleness and Inconstancy.[18]

Then follow Latin, Greek, French, and Italian versions of the proverb. Such a profligate use of space strikes us today as very odd in a dictionary, where space is always at a premium.

Bailey's dictionary proved to be immensely popular and remained in widespread use throughout the eighteenth century. Its thirty editions spanned a period of over eighty years, from 1721 to 1802. Bailey's dictionaries were the chief competitors of Johnson's great work and were probably more popular.

Subsequent editions of Bailey's work included indications of word stress. The verb *descend* was represented as DESCEND', *describe* as DESCRI' BE, *fraction* as FRAC'TION. Unfortunately, Bailey used full capitals for all of his entry words. The placement of the stress mark (beginning with 1740 edition) was supposed to do double duty by indicating vowel quality. A mark that followed immediately after a vowel, as in *describe,* indicated a long or "open" vowel, whereas one that followed a consonant, as in *fraction,* indicated that the preceding vowel was short or "closed." No attempt was made to indicate vowel quality beyond this rough guide, and no other pronunciation aid was provided.[19]

In 1727, Bailey issued a supplementary volume, sometimes called Volume II, to the original edition. The supplementary volume was divided into two parts: one part contained words ostensibly omitted from Volume I (though in fact some were included in some editions), and the other part contained a miscellany of encyclopedic information: names, places, theological and mythological terms, and so on. It also gave some usage guidance by marking some words with symbols that signified either that the term should be used with care or that it was certifiably good usage. The second volume was much modified in later editions to prune it of some of its encyclopedic excesses, though it remained a curious mixture of thieves' argot, specialized terms, and names of people and places. The 1731 edition was much expanded and improved and was the basis for numerous future editions.

Bailey made a genuine attempt to represent the language as it was used and to represent as much of it as he could. Kersey deserves much credit for making a start in that direction, but Bailey's treatment of definition reflects a much greater degree of sophistication. Although Bailey continued the tradition of including many obsolete and rare terms, he also took pains to include the common words of the language, including vulgar and taboo words. For example, *shite* is defined as "to ease Nature, to discharge the Belly." *Fuck* is also entered with a full etymology, but defined only in Latin: "Foeminam subagitare." Other common taboo words that have only recently made their reappearance in English dictionaries—to much fanfare—also appear in Bailey.

In 1730, Bailey's great folio dictionary, *Dictionarium Britannicum,* was published. It is this dictionary that Johnson used as a working base for his own dictionary.[20] A massive work by the standards of its time, it contained forty-eight thousand terms, ten thousand more than Kersey-Phillips, and represented an amalgam of the two volumes of *An Universal Etymological English Dictionary* with additional material. It was illustrated with many woodcuts but omitted some of the more extravagantly encyclopedic material, such as proverbs and legendary names, though it included some encyclopedic articles based on Ephraim Chambers's *Cyclopaedia: Or, An Universal Dictionary of Arts and Sciences* (1728). Chambers, like Harris before him, was to provide a veritable army of lexicographers with scientific and technical terms to increase their vocabulary coverage. Bailey's dictionary included encyclopedic articles, such as one on "Gothick Building," which discussed the history of this architectural style, denouncing it, of course, as "incorrect."[21] Nonetheless, *Dictionarium Britannicum* of 1730 was, after the Kersey-Phillips work of 1706, the standard bearer in English lexicography until 1755 when Samuel Johnson's dictionary appeared.

Samuel Johnson's Plan

"The triumphant completion of the *Dictionnaire de l'Académie française* in 1694," say Starnes and Noyes, "made the English uncomfortably aware of their backwardness in the study of their own tongue, and from then on the air was full of schemes for improving the English language and giving it greater prestige."[22] Daniel Defoe and Jonathan Swift made proposals for establishing authoritative standards that would halt language change and fix it in its present "pure" form forever. Addison proposed a dictionary with quotations from literature, a proposal Johnson knew of. Pope was also much interested in the proposed dictionary. The time was ripe for a great literary figure to undertake the task of establishing the standard by making a dictionary that attempted to survey and record the language, especially the literary language, as it had never been recorded. It was Samuel Johnson who undertook the task, and his *Plan of a Dictionary of the English Language,* published in August 1747 and addressed to the Earl of Chesterfield, is a masterful analysis of what would be required to do it. Although a number of his specific proposals as outlined in the *Plan* would be changed or abandoned as unworkable in the face of the punishing realities of putting together a massive dictionary virtually single-handedly, the *Plan* remains a remarkable document. For someone who had never before compiled a dictionary, Johnson's grasp of the lexicographic problems he would be confronted with is extraordinary. What the rest of us are forced to learn through years of experience, Johnson realized at once through the brilliance and originality of his mind. With characteristic humility, though in this instance somewhat artfully contrived to enlist the sympathetic attention of Lord Chesterfield, his would-be patron, Johnson described the lowly status of the lexicographer:

> I knew, that the work in which I engaged is generally considered as drudgery for the blind, as the proper toil of artless industry, a task that requires neither the light of learning, nor the activity of genius, but may be successfully performed without any higher quality than that of bearing burthens with dull patience, and beating the track of the alphabet with sluggish resolution.

He continues in the same vein, suggesting that the occupation of lexicography, "tho' not splendid, would be useful . . ." He goes on to examine the

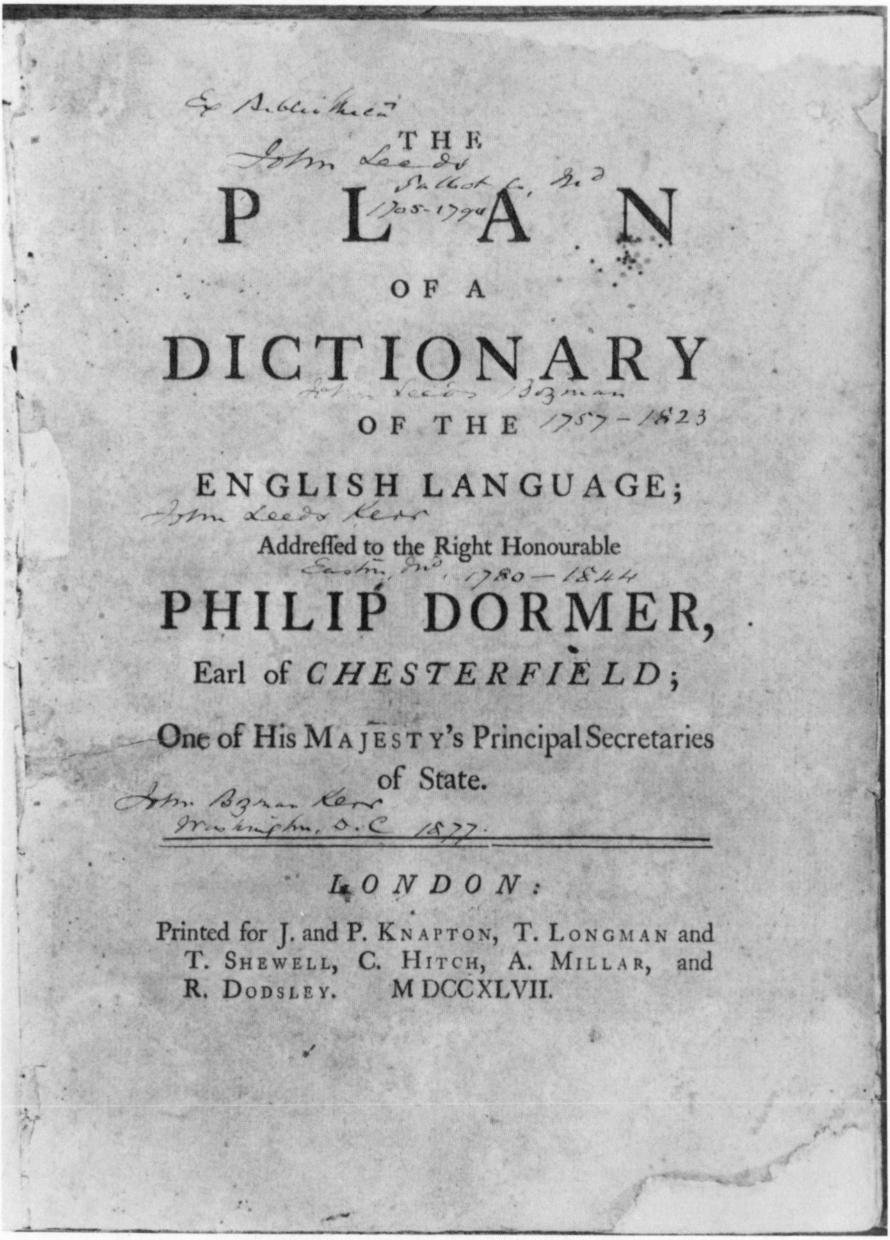

THE

PLAN

OF A

DICTIONARY

OF THE

ENGLISH LANGUAGE;

Addreſſed to the Right Honourable

PHILIP DORMER,

Earl of *CHESTERFIELD*;

One of His MAJESTY's Principal Secretaries of State.

LONDON:

Printed for J. and P. KNAPTON, T. LONGMAN and
T. SHEWELL, C. HITCH, A. MILLAR, and
R. DODSLEY.   MDCCXLVII.

FIGURE 4.   Title page of Samuel Johnson's *Plan of a Dictionary of the English Language* (1747). From the Collection of The Public Library of Cincinnati and Hamilton County.

difficulty of selecting terms; in a memorable passage he argues that usefulness is the prime consideration:

> The value of a work must be estimated by its use: It is not enough that a
> dictionary delights the critic, unless at the same time it instructs the
> learner; as it is to little purpose, that an engine amuses the philosopher
> by the subtilty of its mechanism, if it requires so much knowledge in its
> application, to as be of no advantage to the common workman.

On this basis, it is unwise to exclude terms of science and art. Johnson draws
a distinction between naturalized terms and foreign ones, which he will
exclude as a rule, although even some foreign terms must be included as a
practical matter. The use of technical terms in nontechnical contexts, he
says, justifies their inclusion in a general dictionary. He discusses the criteria
for inclusion of specialized terms of war and navigation, law and industry;
the necessity for including common words like *dog* and *cat* and the difficulty
of defining them. He discusses by turns orthography (he will follow traditional spelling and shun innovation), pronunciation (where his ambitious
and impractical plan to list words rhyming with the entry words was never
fully implemented), etymology, grammar (the treatment of verbs and adjectives and their inflections and comparative forms), what he calls "syntax"
but what we should now call collocation or context, and idiomatic expressions. He also intended to enlist the aid of experts to include encyclopedic
material under some terms. His *Dictionary* did indeed include encyclopedic
material, but for the most part he relied on Chambers's *Cyclopaedia* and
Harris's *Lexicon Technicum* rather than on contributors.

Johnson's views on the question of whether language can or should be
"fixed" in a presumably pure state have been variously interpreted, partly
because his position changed markedly from the time of the *Plan* (1747) to
the publication of his *Dictionary* (1755), but partly because his own position
was inconsistent. About whether it is desirable for language to be stabilized,
there is no doubt: Johnson thought it desirable and wished that change could
be retarded or stopped. But by the time the *Dictionary* was published, he
seems to have realized that achieving such a goal was impossible. The *Plan,*
on the other hand, is rife with expressions of determination to fix the language much as the French Academy was setting about to fix the standard
in French. We must remember that the strength of Johnson's views of the
role of authority may well have been influenced by his awareness that Chesterfield clearly favored such an approach.[23] Nonetheless, his position must
be taken as his own. "The chief intent of . . . [the *Dictionary*] is to preserve
the purity and ascertain the meaning of our English idiom. . . ," he says.
And again, in connection with pronunciation; " . . . one great end of this

undertaking is to fix the English language . . ." And again, in connection with etymology: "By . . . not admitting, but with great caution, any [word] of which no original can be found, we shall secure our language from being over-run with *cant,* from being crouded with low terms . . ." Wistfully, he asks, "who . . . can forbear to wish, that these fundamental atoms of our speech might obtain the firmness and immutability of the primogenial and constituent particles of matter . . ." And again: "With regard to questions of purity, or propriety, I was once in doubt whether I should not attribute too much to myself in attempting to decide them. . . ; but I have been since determined by your Lordship's opinion, to interpose my own judgment . . ." In summary he says this is his idea of an English dictionary, "a dictionary by which the pronunciation of our language may be fixed; . . . by which its purity may be preserved . . ." As part of the same goal of moral uplift, Johnson proposes to prefer quotations from writers of the "first reputation to those of an inferior rank," and hopes to convey "some elegance of language, or some precept of prudence, or piety," in his illustrative quotations.

Yet even in 1747 he hinted at the futility of attempting to fix an arbitrary standard. "And though, perhaps, to correct the language of nations by books of grammar, and amend their manners by discourses of morality, may be tasks equally difficult . . ." suggests as much.

Though ingenious, the *Plan* was far too ambitious. The stated goal was nothing less than to survey the whole of the English language and to show the history of every word. "[T]he reader will be informed of the gradual changes of the language, and have before his eyes the rise of some words, and the fall of others," a description that sounds more like that of the *OED* than of Johnson's *Dictionary,* though Johnson sensibly adds that such observations are "to be desired rather than expected." Indeed, as critics of the *Dictionary* were quick to observe, he did not meet such expectations, but it was unreasonable to expect any one man to do more.

Johnson's Dictionary *and Its Competitors*

Two years after Johnson's *Plan,* Benjamin Martin's *Lingua Britannica Reformata* appeared. Martin's work, unlike most of his predecessors', dealt at length in his Preface with definition and proffered a theory by which the senses of words ought to be arranged. In some ways Martin's treatment resembles that in Johnson's *Plan,* and may have influenced Johnson. Be that as it may, Martin's plan was well thought out, and he tried to put his theories into practice before Johnson. Basing his sense division on a French and

Latin dictionary, he divided senses into numbered definitions and put more effort into such distinctions of meaning than anyone had before him. In practice, however, Martin's definitions are sometimes too brief to make clear the distinctions in meaning he attempts to make.[24] Martin's use of the bilingual dictionary treatment of polysemy is an interesting step backward since, as we have seen, Kersey and Bailey had moved away from that tradition. Yet it was a sensible and fruitful one, for in this respect bilingual lexicography was far advanced over monolingual English dictionaries.

The booksellers of Bailey's dictionary—in those days the booksellers were also publishers—knew from 1747 that Samuel Johnson's *Dictionary* would be formidable competition and set about improving the *Dictionarium Britannicum*. Called the Scott-Bailey after Joseph Nicol Scott, a well-known scholar in the worlds of religion and science (he was a practicing medical doctor and an accomplished author of sermons), the revised dictionary was really a pastiche of the *Dictionarium Britannicum* and Johnson's *Dictionary*, which was freely pirated for definitions and quotations (often in shortened form), and combined with additional material obtained elsewhere. Entitled *A New Universal English Dictionary* (1755), it was a multiauthored work, of which Scott was only one of the contributors, but the best known. It attempted to provide a cheaper alternative to the expensive two-volume Johnson *Dictionary*. Accordingly, Scott-Bailey was printed in small type in one large folio and contained many more terms than Johnson, perhaps sixty-five thousand as compared to Johnson's forty thousand.[25] Johnson had deliberately excluded many obsolete and foreign terms as well as most scientific terms, and did not include names. The Scott-Bailey was designed to appeal to common people who wanted a basic tool without frills, as distinguished from the literary appeal of Johnson's work, with its extended quotations from great writers of past and present.

Johnson's *Dictionary* was published nine years after he had signed a contract (on June 18, 1746) to produce it. It was a prodigious achievement. Remarking on the impossibility of resolving many questions without unduly delaying the project, Johnson wrote eloquently in his Preface of the necessity for setting limits to scholarly inquiry.

> To deliberate whenever I doubted, to enquire whenever I was ignorant, would have protracted the undertaking without end, and, perhaps, without much improvement; for I did not find by my first experiments, that what I had not of my own was easily to be obtained: I saw that one enquiry only gave occasion to another, that book referred to book, that to search was not always to find, and to find was not always to be informed; and that thus to persue perfection, was, like the first inhabitants of Arcadia, to chace the sun, which, when they had reached the hill where he seemed to rest, was still beheld at the same distance from them.

All dictionary makers are sometimes faced with the necessity to make decisions without full information, which is sometimes impossible to obtain. Of course, Johnson's problem was particularly acute compared to that of a large staff which can call upon specialists to provide information and guidance. But so vast is the scope of the subjects covered by any large dictionary that experts cannot be found in every branch of every field without an effort out of all proportion to the likely benefit. Truly, one would need an army of specialists to cover every definition expertly. Such is not practicable, and it is not done, even today. Many decisions in contemporary dictionaries are still made as Johnson made them in his. In Johnson's words, "he, whose design includes whatever language can express, must often speak of what he does not understand." Unlike most of his predecessors, Johnson acknowledged his debt to other dictionaries, citing in particular Bailey, Phillips, and Ainsworth.[26]

Johnson discusses in his Preface the principles of defining and the purposes of illustrative quotations. He acknowledges the difficulty of defining common words without using more difficult words in their definitions. Definitions are to be given in historical sequence to show the development of meaning. (In practice he was not consistent in applying this principle, and some critics rightly took him to task.) The illustrative quotations are designed to elucidate shades of meaning, show examples of "pure" English, and illustrate its range of usage and ordinary context.

On usage Johnson remains ambivalent. He still believes it is the task of the lexicographer "to correct or proscribe . . . improprieties and absurdities," and feels it his obligation to rescue English from corruption by Gallicisms. On the other hand, he says plainly that it is not his task to "form, but register the language. . . ; not [to] teach men how they should think, but relate how they have hitherto expressed their thoughts." His most celebrated statement on "fixing" the language clearly shows a considerable evolution in thought from the views expressed in the *Plan:*

> Those who have been persuaded to think well of my design, require that it should fix our language, and put a stop to those alterations which time and chance have hitherto been suffered to make in it without opposition. With this consequence I will confess that I flattered myself for a while; but now begin to fear that I have indulged expectation which neither reason nor experience can justify. When we see men grow old and die at a certain time one after another, from century to century, we laugh at the elixir that promises to prolong life to a thousand years, and with equal justice may the lexicographer be derided, who being able to produce no example of a nation that has preserved their words and phrases from mutability, shall imagine that his dictionary can embalm his language, and secure it from corruption and decay, that it is in his power to change

53

sublunary nature, or clear the world at once from folly, vanity, and affectation.

In the next breath he speaks of commerce corrupting the language. He urges struggle against linguistic change even while acknowledging the futility of such a struggle. He opposes the formation of an English Academy modeled after the French Academy as contrary to "the spirit of English liberty." His final advice is that though language change cannot be stopped, "we retard what we cannot repel, . . . we palliate what we cannot cure."

Johnson's profound commitment to tradition would not permit him to accept linguistic change philosophically; it ran counter to everything he believed in. But he was never one to turn his back on the real world. He was neither naïve nor so ideological as to be unable to face unpleasant facts. He accepted the role of the lexicographer as the recorder of actual usage, but nonetheless felt it his duty to expose "barbarous" expressions and infelicities of usage, for even though such an effort might have no influence on the course of actual usage, it was the only honorable course of action to take. Johnson always viewed the *Dictionary* not only as an educational enterprise but in part a moral one, and just as he reprimanded himself for idleness he felt it was his responsibility to act morally, for the good of his own soul, in instructing others in correct usage. Though the explanation sounds quixotic, and Johnson was preeminently practical minded, it was, I think, characteristic of Johnson to act on the basis of personal moral conviction even when it came into conflict with practical effect.

The Preface is a remarkable piece of writing: humble without being false to Johnson's own estimate of the magnitude of his achievement, honest in recognizing the limited influence of lexicography on language, moving in its dignified allusion to the personal hardships and suffering he endured while carrying on his work. He acknowledges ruefully that "I have not always executed my own scheme, or satisfied my own expectations." Nonetheless, "when it shall be found that much is omitted, let it not be forgotten that much likewise is performed . . ." Although the world is little interested in what caused the faults its critics condemn, "the *English Dictionary* was written with little assistance from the learned, and without any patronage of the great; not in the soft obscurities of retirement, or under the shelter of academick bowers, but amidst inconvenience and distraction, in sickness and in sorrow . . ." He alludes also to the failure of the Earl of Chesterfield to contribute to his support, and the hardship this caused him; to his life-long battle with debilitating, chronic illnesses (scrofula, nervous disorders, bronchitis); and to the death in 1752 of his beloved wife, Tetty.

54

Johnson's *Dictionary* is often cited as the first to include illustrative quotations, a claim that is not justified. As already noted, John Florio's Italian–English dictionary of 1598 included such quotations, as had Greek and Latin dictionaries of the sixteenth century. In fact, some of these dictionaries—with which Johnson was certainly familiar—were more copious and various in their selections and more precise in their quotations than was Johnson's but, of course, they were the works of academies such as the Accademia della Crusca, not of one man.[27] Johnson is also often credited with being the first to divide and number different senses of a word, but Benjamin Martin had already elaborated such a system in 1749, and Latin–English and French–English dictionaries had already used such discriminations. In fact, Johnson's *Dictionary* is not distinguished by its innovation in either the use of illustrative quotations or divided and numbered senses, but by the skillful and original execution of these methods. What he did he did supremely well. It is no criticism of Johnson to say that he was thoroughly conversant with the practices of contemporary and earlier bilingual dictionaries, and wise enough to draw upon their established methods to make his own *Dictionary* more useful and up to date than any prior English dictionary.

In his treatment of pronunciation, Johnson made some advances over the past. Although he showed only stress as a rule, without indicating vowel quality, he did sometimes indicate pronunciation by citing a word with the same vowel quality (as he said he would in the *Plan*) and, less often, when the sound was "irregular," by respelling. There is some disagreement among scholars on how innovative these steps were and how important Johnson was in the development of pronunciation systems used in dictionaries.[28]

Critically, the reception of Johnson's *Dictionary* was mixed. It was said to have too many quotations, sometimes from writers "of no authority." (Such criticism eerily evokes the reception of *NID3* in 1961, which was denounced because it quoted Art Linkletter and Ethel Merman.) The etymologies were attacked and even ridiculed, but much of the criticism was undeserved. As one twentieth century lexicographer puts it, "Everyone remembers Macaulay's snap verdict: 'Johnson was a wretched etymologist.' He does not tell us who knew any better. Who *should* etymologize, beyond the limits of the obvious, in that pre-Copernican age before philology was born?"[29]

Johnson was criticized for not including more specialized terms of the arts and commerce and for including too many artificial or purely literary words. However, on the whole his *Dictionary* was praised, his choice of spellings recognized as authoritative, and his definitions much admired.[30] Later, in America, the two great nineteenth-century lexicographers, Noah Webster and Joseph E. Worcester, would take diametrically opposed views, with Webster attacking virtually every aspect of Johnson's work (at the same time that he relied heavily on it in his own dictionaries) and Worcester praising Johnson with equal vigor. Worcester's judgment was much the soberer, less biased, and historically more accurate. In 1847, in the Introduction of his own dictionary, Worcester pointed out that Johnson's *Dictionary,* "from the time of its first publication, has been, far more than any other, regarded as a standard for the language. It has formed substantially the basis of many smaller works, and, as Walker remarks, it 'has been deemed lawful plunder by every subsequent lexicographer.'"[31]

Although Johnson's choice of illustrative quotations and his finely crafted definitions are justly regarded as major advances in the practice of lexicography, his real achievement lay in his success in fulfilling—grandly—the expectations of the literary English establishment, and through its influence of a much wider segment of the public, that the English language was every bit as worthy of study as the French or German. Johnson's *Dictionary* was mighty and tangible evidence that English was sufficiently developed to be analyzed and studied with sophistication and informed historical judgment. In this sense it paved the way for the *Oxford English Dictionary.* Without Johnson's *Dictionary,* it is doubtful that Dean Trench, a century later, would ever have set his goals so high for the historical survey of the development of English, or seen the deficiencies in earlier English dictionaries so clearly.[32]

By the force of his reason, his wide reading and the excellent memory with which he put it to use, and his masterly command of the art of lucid expression, Johnson fashioned a work that engendered such respect that for well over a century it was without peer as the most authoritative dictionary in English. Revised by Henry John Todd in 1818 and again in 1827, Todd-Johnson, as it came to be known, was esteemed the best of dictionaries in both England and America until well into the nineteenth century. Indeed, it was Webster's ambition, to which he devoted the better part of his life, to supplant Todd-Johnson's place in America as the standard work.

Pronouncing Dictionaries of the Eighteenth and Nineteenth Centuries

The latter part of the eighteenth century saw the publication of a number of dictionaries devoted principally to pronunciation. There was throughout this century and much of the next a lively interest in "correct" pronunciation promoted by "elocutionists"—presumed authorities on pronunciation. But it was not until the publication of Thomas Sheridan's *A General Dictionary of the English Language* in 1780 that a major advance was made in the dictionary treatment of pronunciation.[33]

Although Bailey had already, in 1740, used the stress mark to indicate whether the preceding vowel were "long" or "short," James Buchanan, in his *Linguae Britannicae* (1757), was the first to attempt actual pronunciations rather than simply indicating stress. William Johnston's *Pronouncing and Spelling Dictionary* (1764), a guide to pronunciation without definitions, included an elaborate diacritic system to indicate every sound, but the system was so elaborate that it was difficult to follow. The most popular way to indicate pronunciation proved to be that of William Kenrick in *A New Dictionary of the English Language* (1773); he used tiny numbers placed over individual letters, or sometimes following them, to indicate phonetic quality. So did Sheridan and his successors. Examining a dictionary with diacritic numbers, one can only conclude that eighteenth-century dictionary users had marvelously acute vision. The numerals can easily be mistaken for insect droppings, shredded dots dumped across the page, or the hallucinatory effect of too many brandies. Kenrick's system had diacritic numbers from 0 to 16.

Thomas Sheridan is the first lexicographer who consistently respelled the entry words to indicate pronunciation. His diacritic numbers were used with the respellings rather than with the entry words themselves. Though the idea of respelling was not new—Johnson and earlier lexicographers had sometimes done it—it had been used only exceptionally and in systems that were relatively crude. Sheridan pronounced every word, even simple ones, indicated stress as well as sound in his respellings, and gave greater attention to the hitherto neglected consonants than ever before.

John Walker's *Critical Pronouncing Dictionary and Expositor of the English Language* (1791) was one of the most popular and influential dictionaries ever published. It went through countless editions and remained in widespread use well into the nineteenth century. The work had an incalculably great effect on the treatment of pronunciation in other dictionaries as well as on schoolbooks, and many pronunciations still taught as correct in our schools can be traced to Walker's dictionary. Walker's prescription for popularity was simple. He used, with due acknowledgment—"I have scrupulously followed Dr. Johnson," he says in his Introduction—Johnson's definitions. He omitted all illustrative quotations and etymologies, added some words that had been inadvertently neglected, and employed his detailed pronunciation system. A key to the system, which is fully explained in the front matter, appears at the head of every page. It is a fairly simple but adequate system, and it is easy to use.

Walker's system, a refinement of Sheridan's, is not much different from those used even today in abridged dictionaries, except for the modern replacement of Walker's numerals with diacritic marks. Walker respelled, showed primary (but not secondary) stress, syllabication, and vowel quality, and used special symbols to distinguish pairs of voiced and voiceless consonants, as the *th* of *that* and *throw*. Whereas Sheridan generally tried to follow actual usage in rendering his pronunciations, Walker wanted to "correct" certain pronunciations and often included monitory notes to the reader. For example, under *decrepit,* he says: "This word is frequently mispronounced, as if spelled *decrepid.*" (Interestingly, *NID3* of 1961 still gives the voiceless /-ət/ ending as preferred, but adds, | usu. əd · + V |, which means, usually /-əd/ if followed by a vowel without pause, as in "a decrepit old house." This is a very conservative treatment which still shows Walker's influence. I wonder how many people use /-ət/ in a "decrepit person." To my ear the /-əd/ is no less likely in this frame than if followed by a vowel.) Sheldon cites Walker's insistence that unstressed syllables be pronounced precisely and that every syllable be given its due weight. For example, he deplored the pronunciation of /med'sin/ for *medicine,* which Sheridan had accurately given. Walker preferred /med'de-sin/, which remains the usual pronunciation in the United States, whereas /med'sin/ remains the usual one in England. For Walker, a word's spelling and etymology were more important criteria than its actual usage, even among educated speakers. It was Walker who preferred the /syoo/ pronunciation in words like *suicide* and *super,* which in the eighteenth century were commonly pronounced /shoo/ as in *sugar* and *sure* today. If usage clearly favored a form of which Walker disapproved, he would indicate the actual usage but include a note warning the reader not to use it. For the millions of linguistically insecure immigrants pouring into the United States in the early nineteenth century and for the legions of upwardly mobile middle-class people, Walker's advice was a much appreciated help. Walker urged them to say inter*e*sting, not *intristing;* laboratory, not *labratory;* bound*a*ry, not *boundry.*[34]

I should be surprised if Walker's strictures are not still being applied in oral instruction in many schools. Every time I have served on jury duty in New York County (Manhattan), I have been struck by the unusual and emphatic pronunciation of the second syllable of *juror* when uttered by lawyers or judges. It received equal stress with the first, as though equal stress on every syllable were somehow suitable for dignified and solemn occasions as befit a court of law.[35] The same measured kind of Gilbert and Sullivan pronunciation was heard for the last syllable of *defendant,* which left no doubt as to the *-ant* spelling. Perhaps these pronunciations have long traditions in the legal profession, but I wonder whether they are not uttered, by way of many intermediaries, in obedience to Walker's admonitions in

1791 against the "slurring" of unaccented syllables. The reluctance to pronounce part of an important word as unstressed is analogous to the reluctance to use lower-case initial letters in writing nouns like *Hope, Charity, Love,* or *Nation,* which were traditionally capitalized and still are in formal documents.

Webster and the Nineteenth Century

Noah Webster's name became famous because of his "blue-backed speller," *The American Spelling Book,* first published in 1783 as part of *A Grammatical Institute of the English Language.* It went through many editions and at least two hundred sixty impressions from 1783 to Webster's death in 1843, becoming one of the most widely used books in America after the Bible and the most popular schoolbook ever published.[36] By 1850, when the U.S. population was scarcely more than 23 million, Webster's *Spelling Book* sold the phenomenal total of about 1 million copies annually.[37] It has been estimated that by the end of the nineteenth century 100 million copies had been sold.

In 1806, Webster's first dictionary appeared, a modest effort entitled *A Compendious Dictionary of the English Language.* It was based, by Webster's own acknowledgment, on John Entick's *Spelling Dictionary,* published in London in 1764, though reprinted many times and widely used in America. Even at this time, Webster had ambitious plans to produce a much larger dictionary, one that would excel Johnson's and establish himself as the first among lexicographers.[38] Webster improved Entick's definitions and added about five thousand terms, many of them scientific and technical or Americanisms. Unlike Johnson, Webster had no desire to "fix" the language but welcomed change as invigorating force. Although the *Compendious* has no etymologies, it included certain features that have since become more or less standard in American dictionaries, such as the inclusion of the past tense and past participle of strong verbs and the inclusion of appendixes of weights and measures and of U.S. population figures.

Webster attacked Johnson for including rare and difficult terms and for including vulgar words that Johnson had included because of their use in literary works. Webster omitted *fart* and *turd,* for instance, and any term having sexual or excretory meaning. He maintained an abhorrence of indelicate words throughout his life and never entered them in his dictionaries. (Such was the difference between the eighteenth and nineteenth centuries!)

Originally, Webster opposed any spelling change, and with characteristic exuberance ridiculed the omission of *u* from *favour* and *e* from *judge-*

ment. By 1789 he had changed his mind and had gone to the other extreme, endorsing *bred* for *bread* and *tuf* for *tough,* spellings advocated by Benjamin Franklin. But by 1806 his position had moderated and he endorsed certain changes in conformity with the principle of analogy and, if illustrative, of etymology. Although not entirely consistent, he dropped the final *k* from *musick, logick,* etc., used the *-er* ending in words like *theater* and *meter,* dropped the *u* in *honor, favor,* etc., used *check* and *mask* for *cheque* and *masque* and *defense* for *defence.* He also dropped the final *e* from words like *determine, examine,* etc., the only change that did not last.[39]

The *Compendious* did not take the world by storm. Some Americans were offended by Webster's brash assertions of the inadequacies of Johnson and of his own superiority, and British conventions in language were still considered proper and safe. "Johnson, Walker, and Company still had, if not a monopoly, something comfortably close to one, on both sides of the Atlantic."[40]

In 1818, Henry Todd's edition of Johnson appeared. Todd revised Johnson's etymologies, added to the vocabulary, and corrected errors, but did not alter the definitions much. In 1820, Albert Chalmers issued an abridged edition of Todd-Johnson with Walker's pronunciations, and in 1828, Joseph E. Worcester edited Chalmers's work.

Noah Webster was seventy years old when his great two-volume quarto work, *An American Dictionary of the English Language,* was published in 1828. It contained about seventy thousand words, as compared to about fifty-eight thousand in Todd-Johnson. Webster's work was superior to Todd-Johnson in its coverage of scientific and technical terms, thousands of which were added. Webster also included many eponymous words like *Newtonian* and gave encyclopedic information on the bearer of the name. Webster was a brilliant definer, although sometimes he lapsed into provinciality or wordiness or became too encyclopedic. Like everyone else, he owed the substance of many of his definitions and citations of authority to Johnson, whom he attacked for including so many illustrative quotations.[41] Webster included very few and was himself severely rebuked by Dean Trench on this account. Webster believed that illustrative quotations were unnecessary in most instances, and he invented an illustrative phrase in those contexts where a quotation was deemed useful. His definitions were, however, fuller than Johnson's and well divided into senses.

Always the patriot, Webster included many new terms and senses that had originated or been changed by usage in America. In spite of his excessive claims for American English and his exaggeration of the differences between British and American English, many of his observations on the need for recognizing a distinctively American English were sensible, informed, and foresighted. American culture, customs, and political institutions differed from the British, and different words were used to describe them in each country. Moreover, the same word, such as *congress* or *plantation,* often took on quite different meanings in America from those in Britain. Thus, he argued, America needed an American dictionary. The same argument, and with equal justification, has been made by others about Canada, Australia, and other English-speaking countries.

Webster's spellings were only slightly adjusted from his 1806 dictionary. The final *e* was restored to words like *doctrine;* the final consonant in words like *worship* was not doubled in the past tense and present participle, a practice never adopted by the British and in recent years often eschewed in America; *-ize* was used in preference to *-ise* in most words having such an ending. "There is a retreat to conventional spelling in a number of instances . . ."[42]

Webster's provinciality showed through markedly in his pronunciations, which were those of New England. The rest of the country was ignored or was considered to speak incorrectly. His pronunciation system was not even as sophisticated as Walker's of 1791, and the pronunciations were not based on actual usage but on what one would suppose a pronunciation ought to be because of its correspondence to another word of similar form.

Webster's etymologies, for which he had taken ten years to study the world's languages, were sadly deficient, even for his own time. It was Webster's ill fortune to publish his dictionary in a time of great ferment and rapid progress in the understanding of linguistic change. The major discoveries of the German philologists, especially Jacob Grimm, were just becoming widely known, but Webster's natural arrogance, contentiousness, and contempt for any theory that controverted his own blinded him to the significance of even those discoveries with which he was familiar. Many of his etymologies were fantastic speculations, devoid of any value save that of historical curiosity.

Webster's *Dictionary* was not a great commercial success. It suffered from the same disadvantage—high price—that Johnson's had. Although the *Dictionary* was important in its day, apart from its influence on American spelling and a few other minor conventions of lexicography it would have had no lasting effect had it not been vigorously promoted and extensively revised by Webster's publishers. George Philip Krapp commented, "If it were not for elaborate publishers' revisions of Webster's work, revisions with which he had nothing to do but which nevertheless did retain what was genuinely good in the dictionary of 1828, Webster's name would probably now be unknown in the land."[43]

In 1830, Joseph Worcester's *Comprehensive Pronouncing and Explanatory Dictionary of the English Language* was published, and several years later Webster accused Worcester of having plagiarized his *American Dic-*

tionary of 1828. Worcester had formerly worked for Webster and had revised the *American Dictionary,* abridging definitions but adding vocabulary entries and deleting most of the etymologies for an octavo edition. Webster, then in his seventies, did not approve of many of the changes, but apparently Webster's son-in-law, Chauncey Goodrich, did, and Goodrich was directing the work. One can understand Webster's feeling, then, if one year after the publication of the octavo edition of the *American Dictionary* another dictionary by Worcester appeared under his own name. The charge, however, was unfounded, since Worcester had been working on his own dictionary before he began abridging Webster's, and he was able to point to many differences between his work and Webster's. Of course, a relationship between the two works is undeniable, but anyone who has read this brief history of lexicography is by now aware of how much each lexicographer owes to his predecessors. This is as true of Webster as of Worcester. Both borrowed from other sources, but neither did so systematically and egregiously, as had commonly occurred in the early days of English lexicography in the seventeenth century.

Worcester's dictionary contained about forty-three thousand entries in four hundred pages, included no etymologies, but had a better pronunciation system than Webster's, showing more variants. His approach was more detached and objective than Webster's in that he sought to establish what the cultivated pronunciation was rather than saying what it ought to be on the basis of analogy or etymology. Worcester included a number of neologisms of his day but, like Webster, omitted vulgar and taboo words.

A new edition of Webster's *Dictionary* was published in 1841, two years before his death. In 1846, Worcester's *Universal and Critical Dictionary of the English Language* appeared and the battle was joined. Joseph Friend comments: "What had begun as a personal quarrel in print between rival lexicographers and their partisans was now clearly a fight for the market between publishing firms as well as a linguistic dispute involving regional, class, and academic antagonisms."[44] Webster was identified with Yale University, Worcester with Harvard. Webster was brash, cocky, contemptuous of tradition, and 100 percent American; Worcester was staid, solid, scholarly, and admired the British tradition in lexicography. As a modern lexicographer observes, "To conservative people of the time, Worcester's books seemed preferable to Webster's because of their closer approximation to British standards, their use of what seemed a more refined type of pronunciation ... and their preference for established usage in spellings."[45] Although some of these differences were reflected in the works themselves, one wonders how much the different outlooks were exaggerated by publishers eager to play upon the prejudices of the marketplace.

Worcester's *Dictionary* of 1846 includes an extensive discussion of pronunciation; the traditional English grammar; a brief history of the English language; archaisms, provincialisms, and Americanisms; and a scholarly and accurate history of English lexicography, including a catalog of dictionaries and encyclopedias. Worcester is disinterested enough to credit Noah Webster's 1828 dictionary as "a work of great learning and research, comprising a much more full vocabulary of the language than Johnson's Dictionary, and combining many and great improvements with respect both to the etymology and definitions of words"—an assessment much too kind in etymology—then adds: "but the taste and judgment of the author are not generally esteemed equal to his industry and erudition."

The scholarly nature of Worcester's work is illustrated by his notes on orthography. For example, under the entry for *judgment,* so spelled in the quotation above and in the text of his dictionary, there is a long note tracing Johnson's usage (without the intermediate *e*) to Todd's (inserting it), up to the present, and ending with the reasonable statement that usage remains divided and is still undergoing change.

The "war of the dictionaries," as it is called, lasted from 1830 to 1864 and was filled with charges and countercharges, endorsements by authorities, invidious publicity releases, and unscrupulous marketing tactics by both publishers, who put pressure on booksellers to stock only their own dictionary. In 1860, Worcester's magnum opus, *A Dictionary of the English Language,* appeared. It was the culmination of his life's work and was seen as an immediate threat by Webster's publishers. Worcester's *Dictionary* was impressive. A large quarto, it included 104,000 entries in 1,800 pages and was illustrated with 1,000 woodcuts (in response to an illustrated edition of Webster's issued the previous year). Its pronunciations, developed from Worcester's 1846 work, were far fuller and more accurate than Webster's. Though its definitions were on the whole briefer, its coverage of the vocabulary was better and its preferred spellings remained traditional. The etymologies, though less speculative and pretentious than Webster's, were unexceptional but adequate. Worcester introduced illustrative quotations in this work to support definitions and, while acknowledging his debt to earlier works comparing synonyms, included thousands of discussions in which groups of synonyms were discriminated, a feature that has become standard in modern dictionaries.

Although Worcester's new dictionary was widely acclaimed as the best and most comprehensive since Johnson's and occasioned another exchange of pamphlets from each side, it was in fact Worcester's last hurrah. Webster's son-in-law, Chauncey Goodrich, had commissioned the German philologist C. A. F. Mahn to redo Webster's etymologies, and in 1864 the new work, edited by Noah Porter but known as the Webster-Mahn, or "the unabridged," was published. Its official title was *A Dictionary of the English Language.* It ended the war of the dictionaries, ironically by abandoning everything characteristic of Webster and adopting Worcester's virtues: in the words of Joseph Friend, "neatness, precision, caution, moderation, and elegance, together with his handling of synonymy and . . . divided usage and idiomatic phrases . . . Worcester deserves a considerable share of the credit so unjustly monopolized by Webster's popular reputation."[46] The line of dictionaries now known as Merriam-Webster dictionaries evolved from the Webster-Mahn of 1864.[47]

Modern Unabridged Dictionaries

In 1909, the first of Merriam's international dictionaries was published, based most directly on its 1890 *International Dictionary* but greatly expanded and including many scientific and technical terms, a policy it has continued to this day. Its etymologies were scholarly, its pronunciations conservative, and encyclopedic appendixes were included. The second edition of *Webster's New International Dictionary (NID2)* appeared in 1934 and takes the prize as the largest lexicon in English, with 600,000 vocabulary entries.[48] Its pronunciations retained Webster's eastern, conservative bias. Its coverage of both current and obsolete and rare terms was immense, and the second edition still figures in the minds of many middle-aged and elderly Americans as the dictionary par excellence.

Webster's Third New International Dictionary (1961), edited by Philip Babcock Gove and based on a huge stock of citations, cut back its vocabulary coverage to 450,000. Of this total about 100,000 entries were new; thus no fewer than a quarter of a million words were dropped from the second edition. One of the compelling reasons for the limitation in size of the third edition was the staggering cost of hand-bound books. No machinery could bind books with a bulk (the extent of a book measured horizontally across the spine) of five inches, such as *NID2,* and the cost of labor had gone up precipitately from the mid-thirties to the 1960s. Accordingly, by trimming the number of entries substantially, *NID3*'s bulk was reduced to less than four inches, and the books could be bound largely by machine, at great savings in cost.

NID3 was neither as innovative as its detractors claimed nor as traditional as some defensive comments from Gove and others have made it appear. Encyclopedic entries were dropped, as were many thousands of rare and obsolete terms (all those before 1755). In spite of some imperfections and some overelaboration, the treatment of pronunciations in particular was greatly improved from *NID2's,* and in my judgment Harold Artin, the pronunciation editor, has yet to receive the recognition he deserves. It is no exaggeration to say that for the first time in any general English dictionary the great advances in phonological research of the twentieth century were systematically utilized.

During the latter half of the nineteenth century a number of influences contributed to making dictionaries extraordinarily popular among great masses of people in America. The growth of linguistic knowledge marked by the studies of Franz Bopp, Rasmus Rask, Jacob and Wilhelm Grimm, and others was rapid and in some ways revolutionary. For example, Grimm's Law (after Jacob Grimm) accounted for correspondences of certain sounds between the Germanic languages and Greek and Latin; at one stroke it rendered earlier theories of sound correspondences, such as those used by Webster, obsolete. The rapid growth of industrialization and technology spawned a new vocabulary and gave it greater importance than ever before. The growth of population and of public education as a means of self-improvement in a free society created an enormous demand for books that would teach recent immigrants and others how to speak and write correctly. Advancement depended on how one behaved rather than on the advantages of birth. Breeding could be acquired through education and hard work. Dictionaries naturally assumed large importance as authorities to be relied on to settle questions of usage and pronunciation. If a word wasn't in the dictionary, it wasn't a word. Whatever was in the dictionary was venerated as the unquestioned truth. To a considerable extent these generalizations still obtain, much more so in the United States than in Britain, where tradition dictated more independence and less linguistic insecurity among all classes than in America.

Thus it is not surprising that Merriam-Webster should have competition even after it disposed of Worcester. Its 1890 *International* was challenged by Funk & Wagnalls' new unabridged *Standard Dictionary of the English Language* (1893). Edited by Isaac Kauffman Funk, the *Standard* and its enlarged revision of 1913, the *New Standard Dictionary,* with 450,000 terms, were worthy competitors of the Webster dictionaries.[49] They also introduced certain changes in lexicographic practice. The etymology was placed at the end of the entry rather than at the beginning; definitions were presented with the most common meaning first rather than in historical order. Etymology was thus recognized as less important than meaning and

65

pronunciation. These innovations have been maintained by other dictionaries, though not by all. Less enduring were the attempts to introduce simplified spellings—a pet project of Theodore Roosevelt—which played a conspicuous part in Funk & Wagnalls dictionaries until the 1940s, and unquestionably contributed to their relative lack of success. Unfortunately, though the company remained active in lexicography through the 1960s, it never revised the *New Standard Dictionary* of 1913, relying instead on periodic updatings that became less and less noticeable as the years passed. When there was no response following Merriam-Webster's *NID2* of 1934, Funk & Wagnalls ceased to be a major competitor.

The Oxford English Dictionary *and Other Historical Dictionaries*

A remarkable and unique work in the history of lexicography appeared serially from 1818 on. First published as part of *Encyclopaedia metropolitana,* it consisted of a great many illustrative quotations drawn from literature, but with relatively few and brief definitions. It was compiled by Charles Richardson, a disciple of John Horne Tooke, who had been one of Johnson's severest critics. Tooke had elaborate and rather fantastic theories on the importance of etymology; Sledd and Kolb, not usually given to wild overstatement, describe him as "one of the most systematically frantic etymologists who ever lived. By pure reasoning a priori he reached certain conclusions about language, which he then attempted to support—naturally with complete success—by the appeal to etymology."[50] Richardson's approach was based on the notion that quotations alone, if sufficient in number, could serve to elucidate "true etymological meaning." He went far beyond Johnson in collecting quotations, beginning at the fourteenth century. In *A New Dictionary of the English Language,* collected and published in book form in 1837, Richardson sought by his vast collection of quotations to justify the preposterous theory of John Horne Tooke that each word had a single immutable meaning. He wrote lengthy essays attacking Johnson for attributing many different meanings to ordinary words. In his own work, each word and its derivatives were given one etymology and one meaning. His etymologies were as preposterous as his theories, but his dictionary was of great interest to lexicographers because it foreshadowed the historical collections of quotations that were later to form the basis of the *Oxford English Dictionary.*

In November 1857, Richard Chenevix Trench, Dean of Westminster, presented two papers before the Philological Society that are widely credited with inspiring the undertaking of the finest dictionary in the English language. The papers, published by the Society under the title *On Some Deficiencies in Our English Dictionaries,* were specific, informed, thoughtful, and notably devoid of pettiness. Before then most criticisms of dictionaries had been made by partisan lexicographers whose arguments were always colored by the fact or suspicion of self-interest. Dean Trench was clearly an observer and his criticisms, though firm and unequivocal, were never harsh or contemptuous—as Webster's, for example, were wont to be—but addressed themselves always to the issues, and always with some expression of respect for what had been accomplished.

Trench lists seven ways in which past dictionaries had been defective, and gives examples for each. The seven areas are:

1. They failed to include obsolete terms by any consistent method
2. Families or groups of words were inconsistently entered in dictionaries
3. Earlier and later examples of illustrative quotations could be found other than those listed in dictionaries
4. Coverage of important early meanings was defective, especially important for understanding the historical development of the word
5. Synonym discriminations were neglected
6. The literature had been inadequately surveyed for apt quotations to illustrate the first use of a word, its etymology, and its meaning
7. A miscellany of irrelevant and redundant information—mythological characters, encyclopedia articles, and so on—was cluttering up dictionaries needlessly

The history of lexicography is not studded with perceptive criticisms on this order, nor are they any more common today. For this reason, and because many of Trench's criticisms apply still to current dictionaries, it will be worth our while to take a closer look at what the dean was saying. His idea of a dictionary is straightforward and simple: a dictionary is "an inventory of the language." "It is no task of the maker of . . . [a dictionary] to select the *good* [his italics] words of a language. . . . He is an historian of . . . [the language] not a critic." The public "conceive of a Dictionary as though it had this function, to be a standard of the language." But that is a misconception, which he blames the French Academy for fostering. Echoing Johnson, Trench demands to know how anyone with a spark of "vigour and vitality" could allow "one self-made dictator, or forty, determine for him what words he should use, and what he should forbear from using." This suggests not just a linguistic objection to prescription but a philosophical and political objection: it is repugnant to the English tradition of individual freedom. He does, however, go on to assert linguistic objections as well, namely, that omitting disapproved forms would diminish the value of the work by falsely representing the language. Instead, he advises the lexicographer to include all words but to state his objections to those deemed affected, pedantic, or otherwise objectionable. "A Dictionary," he says, "is an historical monument, the history of a nation contemplated from one point of view, and the wrong ways into which a language has wandered . . . may be nearly as instructive as the right ones . . ." This is brilliant criticism indeed and is true of all history, not simply the history of a language.

Although some of Trench's specific likes and dislikes can be questioned with hindsight—such as his gullible admiration for Richardson's etymologies and his unduly harsh criticisms of Webster—seen in their entirety, Trench's remarks constitute a profound *raison d'être* for historical lexicography. The role of the lexicographer as a recorder of actual usage—*all* actual usage—is clearly and unequivocally delineated. It is a curiously modern credo, one that would even today evoke cries of derision and outrage among linguistic conservatives if recast in contemporary idiom and printed opposite the editorial page of the *New York Times*.

The massive task of perusing the whole of English literature is far beyond the power of any man, Trench says, and must be "the combined action of many." Although he does not call for a new dictionary, he calls for a concerted effort by the members of the Philological Society to contribute to an inventory of the whole of the English language to supplement existing dictionaries and to aid future dictionaries. Given this purpose, it is easy to see why Trench admired Richardson, who had compiled a prodigious number of quotations. By providing an example of the value of historically ordered quotations, Richardson was indeed important, however misguided his underlying theories were. The example of Jacob and Wilhelm Grimm, who in 1852 had issued the first part of the great historical dictionary of the German language, *Deutsches Wörterbuch,* was also on Trench's mind. The Grimm brothers had a large group of volunteer readers to assist them. Dean Trench provided the descriptive, inclusive rationale for the collection of quotations and their use that had been missing in English lexicography up to this time. Once such an inventory of the language was seen as a desideratum, it was just a matter of time before the proposal would turn into a call for a new dictionary.

The history of the origin of the *Oxford English Dictionary,* fully described in the Introduction to that work, apparently began with a suggestion from F. J. Furnivall to Dean Trench that resulted in his analysis of the deficiencies in English dictionaries. Following Trench's talks, the Philological Society decided that rather than merely supplementing the dictionaries of Johnson or Richardson, a new dictionary was needed—hence the work's original title: *A New English Dictionary on Historical Principles.* The first editor, Herbert Coleridge, was appointed in 1859. Though able and industrious, he lived but a short time, dying in 1861 at the age of thirty-one. Through the efforts of Furnivall and Coleridge, volunteer readers were organized to inventory the entire literature of the English language as Dean Trench had urged. Furnivall, colorful, dynamic, and indomitably cheerful, took over the editorship at the age of thirty-six.[51] He was instrumental in greatly expanding the reading by enlisting the aid of the English Text Society, which compiled invaluable Middle English material for the dictionary.

The real beginning of the dictionary can be placed at 1879, when James A. H. Murray, a Scottish schoolmaster and an active member of the Philological Society, was persuaded to take over the editorship. Murray had the patient and scholarly temperament ideally suited for the position. At that time the dictionary was supposed to take ten years to complete; in fact it would take fifty. The length of the project was not occasioned by any laxness in pursuit of its completion. On the contrary, Murray and his assistants worked rapidly and efficiently; the scope of the project was simply enormous. By the time of its completion the dictionary, published in fascicles from 1882 to 1928, numbered 15,487 pages, each of which contained three columns of type. Based on a file of 5 million citations, it printed more than 1.8 million. It includes more than 240,000 headwords and, counting subordinate words and combinations, contains over 400,000 entries.

Each of the 5 million citations had to be painstakingly collected—a process conducted largely from 1858 to 1881—subsorted (i.e., alphabetized and divided in a preliminary way by sense); analyzed by assistant editors and defined, with representative citations chosen for inclusion; and checked and redefined by Murray or one of the other supervising editors. Even this sketchy summary omits many other necessary steps. Far from being surprised at the time required to complete the project, we should be amazed that it was ever completed at all. That the first fascicle was published in 1882, only three years after Murray assumed the editorship, is impressive testimony to the diligence of Murray and his staff.

In 1888, Henry Bradley was invited to become an editor of the dictionary with his own staff to speed the progress of the work. In 1901, William Alexander Craigie was enlisted in a similar capacity, and in 1914 Charles Talbut Onions was added as a fourth editor. Murray, who died in 1915, had spend thirty-eight years of his life working on the dictionary and was responsible for editing nearly half of the entire work. Bradley and Craigie were each responsible for very large segments, with Onions, who joined the group much later, for substantially less. The *Oxford English Dictionary,* as it came to be called, is a monumental achievement, without parallel in the English language and in few others. Every dictionary thereafter is indebted to it. It

FIGURE 5. James A. H. Murray, the chief editor of the *Oxford English Dictionary*. Courtesy of K. M. Elisabeth Murray.

is as unthinkable that any contemporary lexicographer be without the *OED* as it is that a professional photographer fail to own a tripod to support his camera when needed. It provides the solid base for all he does, and without it his work is apt to be as blurred and undefined as a picture taken in the twilight of underbrush with a hand-held camera.

The *OED* not only provides a historical record of the development of meaning of each word, with illustrative quotations and definitions for each sense. It also shows the changes in spelling, the different forms each word assumed during its history. It gives by far the most complete and authoritative etymologies that existed up until that time, a body of information that is still unchallenged as a whole. The divisions of sense are the most detailed and exacting, the definitions the most precise and clearly substantiated, of any English dictionary.

Even with such great merits, the *OED* is not without its defects. Its pronunciation system is adequate but not as sophisticated as it might be. More serious, its coverage of words native to North America is notably deficient. Words considered vulgar or taboo were not admitted, in clear violation of Trench's philosophy. The scientific and technical vocabulary was largely ignored. In this case the policy accords with Trench's criticism of including such terms, which he considered extraneous. Given the increasingly common usage of many such terms, it is nonetheless unfortunate.

The English tradition in lexicography, as opposed to the American, depended upon the educated generalist, the Oxford- or Cambridge-educated scholar who was in the best sense of the word an amateur. The army of volunteer readers was largely composed of such people. The ideal of the educated gentleman or woman of broad knowledge and exquisite taste was vitiated by narrowly specialized expertise such as that required in the sciences. I believe the absence of scientific terms from the *OED* is due not only to the limitations of space—for in spite of its huge size the *OED* editors were pressed to omit many quotations—or to the theoretical objections of Dean Trench, but also to a distaste for such special subjects, as for commerce and industry, as being profoundly incompatible with the generalist orientation of the upper class. In fact, this tradition in British lexicography was not really breached until the 1970s. In this respect it was far behind American lexicography, which has long recognized the importance of the scientific and technical vocabulary.

Because the volumes of the *OED* were published over a period of forty years, from 1888 to 1928, by the time the last volumes appeared the earliest needed revision, and a supplement was therefore issued in 1933 to record changes in the earlier volumes. But even the supplement was soon outdated, and in 1957 a New Zealand–born Oxonian scholar, Robert W. Burchfield, was asked to edit a multivolume supplement not only to fill in the gaps of

71

the historical record but to correct errors, add the sexual and scatological words that had been omitted, and try to capture at least the basic lexicon of science and technology. For the first time, the *OED* staff drew upon the specialized knowledge of experts. A concerted effort was made also to report uses of English in Australia, New Zealand, and elsewhere as well as in the United States and Canada. Three of the *Supplement*'s four volumes have now been published and they are admirable works, of a quality commensurate with the *OED* itself.[52]

In an effort to fill in the gaps in the *OED*'s coverage of Americanisms, William A. Craigie, one of the four *OED* editors, with James R. Hulbert, edited *A Dictionary of American English* in four volumes.[53] It included words first arising in the United States and also words revealing the cultural life of the American people. In 1951, Mitford M. Mathews's *A Dictionary of Americanisms* appeared.[54] This work was limited to Americanisms, i.e., to words that originated in the United States; but as Allen Walker Read observes, Mathews unfortunately excluded those terms that had survived in the United States while becoming obsolete in Britain, simply on the grounds that they had not originated in the United States.[55]

In 1850, John Ogilvie's *The Imperial Dictionary* ... was published, acknowledged even in its long title to be based on Webster's *Dictionary*. In 1882, Charles Annandale greatly enlarged Ogilvie's dictionary, which came to be the basis for *The Century Dictionary,* an American work modeled after the *OED*. William Dwight Whitney, a well-known Sanskrit scholar and linguist, was the editor. Published in six volumes from 1889 to 1891, it was subsequently issued in ten volumes, along with two volumes of names and an atlas.[56] It includes much encyclopedic material even in its A–Z section, many thousands of illustrative quotations, and numerous fine pictorial illustrations. Beautifully printed and bound, it is surely one of the handsomest dictionaries ever made. In spite of the competition of other large but less expensive dictionaries—the Funk & Wagnalls *Standard,* the 1890 Webster's unabridged—it was highly successful, but was unfortunately never revised. A two-volume abridgment, *The New Century Dictionary,* appeared in 1927. Both *New Century* and *Century* were important sources for the celebrated *American College Dictionary* (1947).

College Dictionaries

Although Merriam-Webster "collegiate" dictionaries were published beginning in 1898, and the Webster collegiate dictionaries were widely used, the

1940s saw the development of college dictionaries—as they came to be called—as ends in themselves rather than as handy abridgments of larger works. The *American College Dictionary (ACD)*, edited by Clarence L. Barnhart, drew upon a distinguished group of linguistic advisers.[57] Kemp Malone was in charge of etymologies, W. Cabell Greet of pronunciations; Leonard Bloomfield, Irving Lorge, and Charles C. Fries rounded out the Editorial Advisory Committee. It is difficult to imagine a more celebrated group of linguistic scholars of the period. What distinguishes the *ACD* most from its predecessors is that it drew upon the best available scholarship and linguistic studies of its time, such as the Irving Lorge and Edward Thorndike *A Semantic Count of English Words* (1938), and applied them in its dictionary. It was the first general, adult dictionary to use the schwa (ə) in pronunciations, now a standard feature of almost all dictionaries.[58] It included a large number of technical terms and used a team of experts to check its definitions in these fields. The *ACD* managed to be successful not only among scholars but with the general public.

A Funk & Wagnalls college dictionary, the *New College Standard*, edited by Charles Earle Funk, was also published in 1947; but though larger in vocabulary—145,000 to the *ACD*'s 132,000—it was no match for the *ACD* in popularity. In 1953, *Webster's New World Dictionary of the American Language* appeared.[59] Edited by David B. Guralnik and Joseph H. Friend, it simplified its technical definitions to make them more understandable to the layman, gave full etymologies, and used no undefined (or "run on") derivatives, a policy changed in later editions. In 1963, *Webster's Seventh New Collegiate Dictionary*, edited by Philip Babcock Gove and based on *NID3*, appeared, and that same year the ill-starred Funk & Wagnalls' new dictionary, the *Standard College Dictionary*, was issued. In 1966, Random House, publisher of the *ACD*, issued a larger work, *The Random House Dictionary of the English Language*, which it called unabridged but which was really an overblown college dictionary stuffed with encyclopedic entries. Two years later the *Random House Dictionary, College Edition*, appeared (later called the *Random House College Dictionary, RHCD*), with 155,000 entries, more than any of the other college dictionaries up to that time.[60] The following year saw the publication of the *American Heritage Dictionary*, which had begun in design as an unabridged dictionary to answer *NID3*'s supposed permissivism but which through miscalculations and mistakes—and the grim realization that with all the money in the world an unabridged dictionary could not be created from scratch in the 1960s—shrank in conception to its collegiate size. In 1970, still another edition of a college dictionary appeared, this time the second edition of *World*, with 157,000 entries. In 1973, the eighth edition of *Webster's New Collegiate*

Dictionary, much expanded in vocabulary from the seventh edition, was published, and ten years later *Webster's Ninth New Collegiate Dictionary,* enlarged still more, with nearly 160,000 entries, appeared.[61]

The *World Book Dictionary,* edited by Clarence L. Barnhart and his son Robert K. Barnhart, originally published in 1963 with about 170,000 terms, was marketed with the *World Book Encyclopedia* and therefore excludes all biographical and geographical entries; its entry count thus consists entirely of lexical items. Based on the Thorndike-Barnhart line of dictionaries and on *The Century Dictionary* files, with the addition of some 3 million citations collected by the Barnharts, this dictionary is one of the finest available, containing copious illustrative quotations and full definitions. It has grown with each edition, by 1981 amassing 264,000 vocabulary entries.[62] The dictionary is written on a somewhat simpler level than that of the college dictionaries since, like the *World Book Encyclopedia,* it is targeted chiefly at a high-school-age audience.

How are we to explain this explosion of new dictionaries in the 1960s and 70s? First, we can assume that the market for college dictionaries is huge and that Merriam-Webster was considered vulnerable because of the severely critical reception accorded *NID3.* Second, in the 1950s and 60s, when these dictionaries were being prepared, it was still possible to engage large dictionary staffs. It is still possible, but the costs have increased enormously. Third, college dictionaries containing 130,000 to 160,000 entries and then selling for ten to twelve dollars were a good buy. They were neither so large and bulky as to be cumbersome nor so expensive as to preclude their purchase as convenient gifts, and they were full enough in content to satisfy almost all the needs of the average dictionary user. In other words, they were popular because the public knew a good thing when it saw it, and as the market expanded publishers jumped in with new dictionaries.

Several of the college dictionaries have made important innovations. The Funk & Wagnalls *Standard College Dictionary* included many usage notes based on Margaret Bryant's scholarly survey *Current American Usage*[63]; the *AHD* reintroduced taboo words like *fuck*—excluded from general dictionaries since Bailey's time in the eighteenth century.[64] This was an important and courageous step in reporting the actual usage of commonly used words, and every other college dictionary with the exception of *World* soon followed suit. *RHCD* gave greater attention to scientific and technical terms than any other and treated them in a more encyclopedic way. It may have gone too far—I happen to think it did—but other dictionaries had not gone far enough, and *RHCD* forced them to pay closer attention to technology. *World* is especially strong in its coverage of Americanisms and endorses a generalist approach to technical definitions. *MW8* is a particularly fine work and has been deservedly popular. Drawing upon Merriam-Webster's huge citation file, it includes illustrative quotations in addition to invented illustrative phrases. Its pronunciations, though briefer than those of *NID3*, were superior to those of the other college dictionaries, and its definitions were rigorously and often elegantly crafted. *MW9* has inherited these virtues and added the etymological datum of including the year in which each entry word presumably first appeared in English. It is still too early, however, to say whether *MW9* will measure up to the quality of *MW8*. Finally, in 1982 a revised edition of *AHD* appeared with a new subtitle, *Second College Edition*.[65] We can without doubt expect new editions from *Random House* and *World* in the next few years, since no.college dictionary can expect to go much more than fifteen years between editions and remain competitive. And it is a most competitive market.

Of course, just as Cockeram copied from Bullokar in the seventeenth century and Blount from Cockeram and Phillips from Blount, so modern lexicographers look at each other's work and strive to improve upon their predecessors.

CHAPTER THREE

Key Elements of Dictionaries and Other Language References

The Entry Term

We turn now to a discussion of the elements that make up a dictionary entry, beginning with the alphabetized headword, or main entry, by which the word or expression being defined (the lexical unit) is identified. The canonical form is the form chosen to repesent a paradigm; most headwords, with the exception of cross-references and names, are canonical forms.[1] (The selection of entries to be included is discussed below in Chapter 6 under "Planning the Dictionary," page 227.) This section will deal with the question of determining the form and placement of the headword for each lexical unit.

In order to have canonical forms, forms that the speakers of a language recognize as representative of grammatical paradigms, there must be a standard language. If there are competing forms with exactly the same meaning, one must arrive at some basis for deciding which of the various usages is to be represented in the dictionary as the canonical form. Thus, before a dictionary can be written for a language, the language must have developed more or less standard spellings or, in a language with various dialects, have a preferred dialect. Variant spellings and dialectal forms can, of course, be given, and for the larger (and especially the historical) dictionaries should be given; but a single form must be chosen as the canonical one.

In English the standard, which emerged during the fifteenth century, was that of the East Midland district that included London. Spelling remained variable throughout the sixteenth century, one of the chief aims of the early English lexicographers, such as William Bullokar and Richard Mulcaster, being to bring about greater uniformity in spelling. Though they directed attention to the problem, they did not succeed in resolving it. In the early eighteenth century individual variations in spelling were widely denounced as intolerable, but it was not until Bailey's dictionaries of the 1730s and more particularly Johnson's of 1755 that the spellings of many words became fixed. In America, Noah Webster was an active and influential spelling reformer, as already noted.[2]

"The first task of the editor of a dictionary," writes James R. Hulbert, "is to decide on the spelling of his word-entry. Usually on a modern dictionary this affords no difficulty, as usage has fixed a single spelling."[3] Spelling, however, is not the only problem. In bilingual dictionaries, for example,

> One of the traditions of Western lexicography is to use the so-called "infinitive" form for both the entry heading and the translation of verbs. . . . In many parts of the world, verbs are usually entered under the plain present (or non-past) form, and it is misleading to translate such headings with English *to* + constructions. Japanese *suru* does not mean "to do"; it means "(someone) does" or "will do." The one advantage of the *to* + translation is that it clearly marks the word as a verb, and in English many verb forms are homonymous with nouns. . . . [4]

Because the user of a bilingual dictionary may not know the canonical forms of the source language, it is particularly important that inflected forms be listed as headwords with cross-references to the canonical forms, especially when the inflections differ markedly from the canonical forms, as *is* and *be*. If space permits, even more closely related inflections, such as *made (make)* and *tried (try)* should also be listed.

In an unabridged monolingual dictionary, virtually all canonical forms are main entries. But in college-level and shorter dictionaries, the canonical forms for many words, chiefly regularly formed adverbs and adjectives but also many nouns, are "run on" at the end of other entries. For example, *conniver* may be run on to *connive,* the presumption being that if one knows the meaning of *connive* and of *-er,* both of which are main entries, one will have no difficulty understanding *conniver*. Sometimes regularly formed nouns in *-tion* or, more commonly, *-ness*, are also run on.

In an effort to cram as many entries as possible into a dictionary—since the run-on derivatives also count as entries—every college dictionary includes thousands of rarely used run-on derivatives, such as *oppressingly, sluggardliness,* and *idioticalness,* which appear in the *Collins English Dictionary (CED)*. Some run-on derivatives may never have been used. Words that could exist but for which no record exists to prove that they have ever been used are called *latent words*.[5]

Though the practice of using rare or latent words to enhance one's entry count is an unfortunate waste of space, it does not contribute to confusion or misunderstanding. But the failure to list semantically important words as main entries is more serious. The *CED* for example, runs on *oppression* to *oppress.* Given the heavy usage in recent years of *oppression* in a variety of senses, this is an abuse of the presumption that derivatives do not require full definition.

The assumption that certain forms are more basic semantically because they happen to be more basic grammatically is not necessarily true. To regard adverbs ending in *-ly* or nouns in *-ness* as less important than the adjectival root indulges the convenience of the definer at the expense of the needs of the user. In many cases, *-ly* words and *-ness* words have acquired senses not adequately covered by the root words. *-ly* is supposed to mean "in a ———— manner." *-ness* is supposed to mean "the state of being ————." Thus, *swiftly* and *swiftness,* run on to *swift,* can be understood to mean "in a swift manner" and "the state of being swift," respectively. Well and good. It is understood in theory, if not always observed in practice, that if a derivative has a meaning not covered by the senses of the form to which it is appended, or not applicable to the formulaic definitions cited, it should be entered separately and defined. As a result, adverbs like *hopefully, incidentally,* and *literally* are defined as main entries in all reputable dictionaries.

But the problem is much broader than that of defining derivatives separately because they include senses peculiar to themselves. To say that *oddly* means "in an odd manner" or that *obviously* means "in an obvious manner" is both misleading and ambiguous. Yet this is routinely done to save space. Even when the adverb is at least as commonly used as the adjective from which it is formed (as, for example, *matter-of-factly* and *matter-of-fact),* it is run on rather than defined. Lexicographic practice does not allow one to run on an adjective to an adverb, so the poor adverb, no matter how widely used, is pushed to the rear of the entry where it is lucky to get a pronunciation, much less a definition. Adverbs are an oppressed part of

KEY ELEMENTS OF DICTIONARIES

speech, and probably bitter about their ill treatment. If they were ever organized, the upper classes of nouns and verbs had better look out.

Even unabridged dictionaries treat adverbs cavalierly. *Webster's Third New International Dictionary (NID3)* defines *oddly* as "in an odd manner or to an odd extent" and cites three illustrative quotations, while the entry for *odd* occupies nearly an entire column of type and is divided into six main senses subdivided into thirty-two subsenses. Are we to understand that *oddly* can mean "in an odd manner or to an odd extent" in each of the thirty-two senses of *odd?* Obviously not. More, in which senses of *odd* is *oddly* most commonly used, and in which is it rarely used? This information is central to an understanding of the use of *oddly,* but it is not given. Many *-ly* words fall into this category: *obviously, openly, modestly, deliberately, centrally, strangely,* and so on. For example, to say that *strangely* in "He was strangely silent" means "in a strange manner" does not explain it. In this context it means "inexplicably" and is not related to *strange* in the sense of "unfamiliar or alien," as in "It was a strange environment for her." Yet *NID3* defines *strangely* as "in a strange manner," without even an illustrative quotation, and college dictionaries either run it on without definition or define it as *NID3* does without amplification. What makes these omissions peculiarly important is that the undefined words are very commonly used. I have suggested elsewhere that modern dictionaries have a bias in favor of scientific and technical terms, and I believe the neglect of common words such as adverbs is the other side of the coin.[6] Dictionaries have increasingly taken on an encyclopedic function that precludes full treatment of common words. Common adverbs are regarded as less important than even those scientific terms rarely used in general contexts.

Why, one might ask, don't dictionaries use word frequency studies to determine which forms should be headwords? First of all, often the most common words do not correspond to the canonical forms. *Is* and *was* are more common than *be.* Even if one ignored frequency in the selection of canonical forms and concentrated on giving equal representation to adverbs and nouns in *-ness,* the frequency lists would be of little help because they are not based on large enough samples (or corpora) of the language to be reliable indicators of frequency, because their choice of corpus material is not representative of the language, and because they are not sophisticated enough in methodology. For example, they do not indicate in which sense each polysemous word is used. Frequency counts are not totaled under the canonical form but are listed separately for each inflection, such as *body, body's,* and *bodies;* capitalized and noncapitalized variants of the same term are listed separately as if they were two different words.

The *American Heritage Word Frequency Book* has already been cited as a valuable but flawed work whose data are questionable because of the selection of its corpus. A widely used frequency study of adult usage, published in 1967 by Brown University and informally known as the Brown Corpus, by Henry Kučera and W. Nelson Francis, is more soundly based. It relies on five hundred samples of two thousand words each, representing a broad variety of subjects and levels of formality.[7] But its entire corpus is only a little more than 1 million words, or tokens, far too slight to give any true indication of the frequency relationships of the entire lexicon. In fact, even the *American Heritage* study is too small. A statistically useful corpus would have to be many times larger than 5 million words.

In a sense, dictionaries do use frequency counts—that of their own citation files. A dictionary citation file is a collection of quotations of actual usage selected to serve as a basis for constructing definitions or for providing other semantic or formal information (such as collocation, degree of formality, spelling, compounding, etymology, or grammatical data). Citation files may also include transcriptions or recordings of spoken forms. The manner of collection and use of citation files for defining will be discussed in the next chapter. Suffice it to say here that as traditionally collected, citation files, however vast—and Merriam-Webster's files reputedly number over 12 million—have been assembled in too haphazard a manner to be used as a reliable guide to frequency. As James A. H. Murray had occasion to remark in connection with the *OED* files, citation readers all too often ignore common usages and give disproportionate attention to uncommon ones, as the seasoned birdwatcher thrills at a glimpse in the distance of a rare bird while the grass about him teems with ordinary domestic varieties that escape his notice.

Scientific and technical dictionaries have terminological difficulties of a different sort. A group of medical experts convened in 1968 to discuss the problems in medical terminology concluded:

> Most diseases are described under several names, some under as many as 20 or 30 different synonyms. The same drug is often designated under numerous different names. ... Equal confusion reigns in such diverse fields as bacteriology, virology, chemistry, to name just a few of the basic sciences, and in nearly all of the medical sciences. A Russian and a French psychiatrist, for example, could never be sure that when using the same term they were designating the same entity, and the same would be true of a German and an American dermatologist.[8]

The problem here is neither of spelling nor of paradigmatic model, but the absence of a standard nomenclature. It is not analogous to the lack of a standard language, as in a country with mutually unintelligible dialects. German and American dermatologists believe they understand perfectly well one another's words, but they attach different meanings to the same medical term. Two people speaking widely different dialects, on the other hand, know very well that they cannot understand each other. The differences in pronunciation, stress, and other features make the same word unintelligible, even though it has the same meaning in both dialects.

How does one go about standardizing nomenclature? In other words, how does one determine preferred terms when there is no agreement among the experts? Recommended criteria, in order of importance, are as follows:[9]

1. Usage, as in textbooks, medical dictionaries, and other reference works
2. Recommendations of authoritative specialist organizations
3. Self-descriptiveness, i.e., giving preference to terms that describe the nature of the concept, as opposed to eponymous terms (terms named after people, such as *Bright's disease*). However, some eponymous terms are so well established by usage that they should be retained.
4. Specificity, i.e., not vague or ambiguous
5. Simplicity, i.e., as short as possible
6. Conceptual relationships, i.e., related concepts should ideally be related in terminology. Two forms of pneumonia should both include the word *pneumonia*. This may seem self-evident to those unfamiliar with medical terminology, but it is very often not the case, sometimes for good historical reasons. For example, often the causes of a newly identified disease are unknown or misattributed. Thus, like many other disorders, *legionnaire's disease* was named after the group of people (*American Legion* members) who, it was mistakenly thought, were the first to contract it. A disease originally thought to be a form of tuberculosis and accordingly named may turn out to be more closely associated with pneumonia, but by that time the original name given to the disorder may be widely known and have been translated into numerous other languages. If the name of the disease were to be changed suddenly it would cause widespread confusion among scientists who had known it only by the original name—and had known very well that it was a form of pneumonia—and even more so among scientists of other countries, because the new translation might be quite dissimilar to the original one. In fact, it is impossible to obliterate forms in widespread usage, and the attempt to do so merely aggravates the problem by multiplying the number of competing usages in currency.
7. Linguistic relationships, i.e., ideally the translations of a term into other major languages should be similar in all languages, so that one can more easily recognize that the two terms are the same.

81

Alphabetization

Dictionaries usually alphabetize letter by letter rather than word by word. They place *power, powerful,* and *power of attorney* in that order, whereas a word-by-word arrangement would place *power of attorney* before *powerful.* Letter-by-letter arrangement has the great virtue that readers need not know whether a compound is spelled as one word, as a hyphenated word, or as two words. Since usage is often divided about compounds—witness *data base* and *database, out of date* and *out-of-date* (as predicate adjective)— and is constantly shifting, the ability to locate such terms is of considerable practical importance.

Verbal idioms are particularly troublesome. No form of alphabetization can successfully deal with all types of idioms without listing each in several places, and no dictionary can afford the luxury of such repetition. Verbal idioms such as *have one's eye on* are usually "run in" at the end of the entry for one of the key words of the phrase, in this instance *have.* The question of which word is most likely to be sought by the user is one that is sometimes impossible to answer. Should the idiom be placed under the first word, or the most important word? Sometimes the first word is variable, as in *shed* or *throw light on.* Sometimes it is not easy to say which word is more important, as in *hang fire.* Most dictionaries prefer to list idioms under the first word, but exceptions are common. Absolute consistency is purchased at the price of the reader's confusion and frustration.

The problems of alphabetization in general monolingual dictionaries are minor compared to those of scientific and technical works, which usually have a much higher percentage of phrasal entries, often 50 percent or more of the total. Rather than try to alphabetize *nuclei nervi vestibularis* letter by letter, for example, medical dictionaries generally employ the main entry/subentry system, alphabetizing under the canonical form of the governing noun and then alphabetizing (usually letter by letter) within the subentry field. The term quoted above is alphabetized under the entry *nucleus.* The fact that its form of *nucleus* is plural has no bearing on its placement amid other subentries that begin with the singular form. Within the field of terms beginning with a form of *nucleus,* its alphabetic place is determined by the letters NERVIVESTIBULARIS. *Dorland's Illustrated Medical Dictionary* lists the following words in this order:

> nucleus nervi vagi
> nuclei nervi vestibularis
> nucleus nervi vestibulocochlearis
> nutrition nucleus
> nucleus of oculomotor nerve
> nucleus olivaris[10]

An exception to letter-by-letter alphabetization is sometimes made by ignoring some prepositions, connectives, or articles; in *accessory sinuses of the nose,* for example, *of* and *the* may be ignored in alphabetization.

The treatment of chemical terms is particularly troublesome, because systematic chemical names (like *methylcellulose*) are formed simply by sticking together the parts necessary to describe the terms chemically, and it is a matter of indifference whether they are written as one word or two. Should *methyl cellulose* be alphabetized under *methyl* or *cellulose? Stedman's Medical Dictionary* partially resolves the problem by making an exception to its usual entry/subentry method of alphabetization.[11] Chemical terms are alphabetized letter by letter but still appear as subentries if listed as two words. Thus, *methyl cellulose* would appear as a subentry under *methyl,* not under *cellulose* but *methylcellulose* would appear in its own alphabetic place as a main entry. Having taken a major step toward resolving the problem of which word in a chemical term governs alphabetization, *Stedman's* then dodges the equally troubling issue of determining whether a chemical term is written as one word or two. That problem could be resolved by making all systematic chemical names main entries: *methylcellulose* and *methyl cellulose* would thus appear consecutively. The drawbacks of this system are illustrated by *methyl blue, methyl green, methyl ether,* etc., which would seem to call for subentry status under *methyl.* No need to belabor the point: in dictionaries, if there is a possibility that certain forms may occur that do not fit into any category, one can be sure that they will occur. The best advice I can give is to set policy only after having had some experience with the kinds of entries to be encountered. Having set it, make minor adjustments or major exceptions when necessary, but once the project is well under way don't make any major systematic changes. Even if the alphabetization is computerized, is the program powerful enough to handle such changes? Reprograming when well into a project can be disastrous. One is better off sticking with a less-than-perfect system than risking a major setback.

Another major problem of alphabetization in technical dictionaries is the ordering of non–English alphabetic characters, of different typefaces of the same letter, of the same letter with superior or inferior figures, letters, or symbols, of entries consisting wholly or partly of numbers, or of nonalphabetic symbols. Practice in these cases varies from one dictionary to the next and, all too often, within the same dictionary. The issue must be addressed in sufficient detail in the dictionary style manual, to be discussed in Chapter 6. The particular order in which the entries are listed is of little importance so long as the problem of determining an order of entries is appreciated early in the project and a start made at elaborating a fixed sequence. Almost surely, new terms will have to be added to the list in the course of compiling the dictionary; but once the order of entries is established, it should not be changed in mid-course. For example, consider the possible ways in which the following entries could be sequenced:

Hg	hg^{-1}
hG	hg_∞
HG	$\sqrt{hg}$
h*G*	HG
1hg	h^g
hg1	

This list is by no means far-fetched. In fact, it is simple compared to many technical glossaries. (See also pages 251–252 on the order of entries.)

Entry Counting

We must now approach the delicate subject of what is meant by saying that a dictionary has 80,000 or 100,000 or 158,000 entries. What is a dictionary entry?[12]

The tradition in British lexicography in the nineteenth and twentieth centuries has been less competitive than the American, hence less dependent on publicizing invidious statistical comparisons, of which the entry count is a favorite. Up until recently, the entry count in British dictionaries was scarcely mentioned in publicity releases, and if it was it usually referred to the number of headwords. That situation is changing, however. The *CED* boasts of 162,000 entries—which it discreetly calls "references"—and obviously employs the American system of entry counting, which includes not just headwords but many other entries as well. Other British dictionaries are sure to follow suit.

The American system of entry counting is based upon two presumptions:

1. Every word or phrase that is explicitly or implicity defined, so long as it is clearly identifiable, usually by appearing in boldface type, is an entry.
2. The more entries one has or can claim, the better.

The American system is designed to maximize the number of entries one can claim, but it is neither illogical nor fraudulent so long as its rules are scrupulously followed. Unfortunately, they are not, and dictionaries have with disturbing frequency made claims that are hard to justify even by the American system. I once had a critic take me to task for the small type of my dictionary and in the next breath praise the legible type of a competitor that claimed almost the same number of entries as my dictionary. Why, he wondered, could we not have produced a work of comparable legibility? The answer was that we forbore to lie about the number of entries, whereas our competitor claimed at least 25 percent more entries than he actually had.

Here is a sample entry article from *The Doubleday Dictionary:*

> **par·a·chute** (par′ə·sho͞ot) *n.* An apparatus of lightweight fabric that when unfurled assumes the shape of a large umbrella and acts to retard the speed of a body moving or descending through air. —*v.* ·**chut·ed**, ·**chut·ing** *v.t.* **1.** to land (troops, materiel, etc.) by means of parachutes. —*v.i.* **2.** to descend by parachute. [< F < PARA— +*chute* fall) — **par′a·chut·ist** *n.*

The following items are entries:

1. The main entry, or headword, i.e., *parachute* as a noun
2. Any other defined part of speech of the headword, i.e., *parachute* as a verb. In an unabridged dictionary each part of speech is generally accorded main-entry status, but in shorter works they are usually combined in a single paragraph.
3. Inflected forms that are actually shown, such as *parachuted* and *parachuting*. Verbs having identical past tense and past participle forms in *-ed* and present participle forms in *-ing,* such as *rush,* usually do not show any inflected forms following the main entry. In that case, no other entries should be counted, even though the reader can surmise by their absence what the inflected forms are. Implication is not enough. A dictionary entry must actually appear in the article.
4. Run-on derivatives, such as *parachutist.*

Thus, the article for *parachute* includes five entries, not one. It is worth pausing to consider what does *not* count as an entry. Transitive and intransitive verb uses, such as definitions 1 and 2 of *parachute,* do not count as two entries. Individual definitions never count as entries. A word like *run* may take up a whole page and count for no more than two entries, one for each part of speech. Pronunciations and etymologies have no bearing on the entry count. Lists of synonyms or synonym discussions do not count as entries, nor do usage notes.

The following items do count as entries, though they do not occur in the entry for *parachute:*

5. Idioms or other defined expressions "run in" an article, such as *take pot luck* and *at sixes and sevens* in the following articles. *At sixes and sevens,* called in lexicographic jargon a *run-in,* is commonplace; *take pot luck,* called a *hidden boldface entry,* is comparatively rare in gen-

eral dictionaries for native speakers, though more common in ESL [English as a second language] works.

pot luck   whatever happens to be available and ready for a meal: usu. in the phrase **take pot luck**.

six   (siks) *n.* **1.** the sum of five plus one; 6; VI. **2.** a set or group of six members. **—at sixes and sevens.** in a state of confusion or indecision. [<OE] **—six** *adj., pron.*

Thus the article *pot luck* counts for two entries. *Six* counts for four, because the run-on derivatives, identified as two parts of speech, count for two.

6. Variants. Variant forms should be counted once only, though they may appear once as a main entry and again under the article of the word of which they are a variant.

di·op·ter   (di·op′tər) *n. optics* the unit for measuring the refractive power of a lens, mirror, etc., determined by the reciprocal of its focal length in meters. Also **di·op′tre**. [<Gk. *dioptra* an optical instrument] **—di·op′tric** or **·tri·cal** *adj.*

The article for *diopter* counts for four entries, including *dioptre;* but if *dioptre* also appears as a headword as a cross-refrence to *diopter,* it should not be counted again.

7. Words in lists following an entry for a common prefix, such as *un-*. Each of these words is a valid entry only if two conditions are met: first, that the prefix is defined in the sense in which it is used in the word; second, that the word sans prefix (in this case, the affirmative sense without *un-*) is defined in the dictionary. If these two conditions are met, the sense of the word can be surmised. Good dictionary practice also requires that if a word has any additional meanings not covered by the basic form that is defined, it should not be entered in a list, although this is not a condition for entry status. For example, the usual meaning of *unexceptional* is "ordinary," although it can also mean "not exceptional." Therefore, it would be misleading to enter *unexceptional* in a list of *un-* words even if *exceptional* were entered and defined.

Lists of this sort may be found in many dictionaries under *in-, non-, re-,* and other prefixes, as well as *un-*. Although sometimes ridiculously inflated to include terms that seldom if ever occur, in principle such lists are legitimate. Some negatives in English are formed with *in-*, others with *un-*. There is no reason to waste the space of an entire dictionary article to convey this information so long as the definition is routine and the meaning clear.

86

Many people believe wrongly and naïvely that if a word does not appear in a dictionary, it does not exist and may not be used. Lists may serve the purpose of comforting such people by including many forms that the compilers would otherwise not have the space to include. The same arguments, by the way, apply to the inclusion of run-on derivatives in *-able* or *-ible*. In run-on derivatives, the stress pattern, which is shown, often differs from that of the headword. For these reasons, both run-on derivatives and lists are useful space-saving devices if used with restraint, and it is perfectly proper to count them as entries.

Encyclopedic entries appearing in the A–Z section of a dictionary count as entries, just as any other headwords. Some dictionaries place biographical and geographical entries in separate sections, and perhaps more dubiously nonetheless count them as dictionary entries. The same applies to lists of abbreviations, common names, and the like. One can be fairly sure that any headword that could possibly be construed as a dictionary entry will be counted as one.

The main entry form in a dictionary serves a number of different purposes:

· It indicates the preferred spelling.

· It indicates the usual printed form of the lexical unit, i.e., whether capitalized or not; whether considered foreign (and italicized) or naturalized.

· In most general dictionaries, it indicates syllabication. This may be shown by a centered period, a light vertical rule, or by some other symbol. A few dictionaries, such as the *CED,* also indicate preferred end-of-line divisions for typists. Some dictionaries, such as the *Concise Oxford Dictionary (COD),*[13] indicate stress pattern and pronunciation in most headwords, thus obviating the need for respelled pronunciations. However, in that case syllabication cannot be shown, because the division of a word that best illustrates its pronunciation is often inconsistent with that of its syllabication.

Almost every criticism made of dictionaries comes down at bottom to the lexicographer's need to save space. The elements of style that so baffle and infuriate some readers are not maintained for playful or malicious reasons or from the factotum's unthinking observance of traditional practice. They save space. Every decision a lexicographer makes affects the proportion of space his dictionary will allot to each component. It is perfectly fair for critics to question his judgment, but they must realize that the length of a dictionary is finite, and as large as it may appear to them, it is never large enough for the lexicographer.

In most American college dictionaries, less than half of the total number of entries are headwords. A ratio of close to 50 percent is high, demonstrating that the dictionary does not have an excessive number of run-on derivatives, lists, or other entries with implied meanings. For many years, *World* maintained a policy of having no run-on derivatives, but the smaller entry count this policy assured eventually compelled the editors to abandon it for competitive reasons. Probably no American college dictionary now has a ratio of headwords to total entries as high as 47–48 percent—they more likely average out at about 44–45 percent. One percentage point represents a substantial shift between headwords and other entries. In a college dictionary, each percentage point represents about 1,500 additional headwords.

It cannot be assumed that smaller dictionaries necessarily have lower ratios, since they also have fewer total entries and there are limits to how many words can be run on as derivatives or entered in word lists. Their ratios are apt to be similar to those of college dictionaries and in some instances higher, depending on the policy on including derivatives. For example, children's dictionaries have far fewer derivatives, hence higher ratios, than adult dictionaries. Children's dictionaries may average 48–49 percent headwords, with most of the other entries coming by way of inflected forms and idiomatic expressions rather than derivatives. Scientific and technical dictionaries generally do not have run-on derivatives or lists of terms; the entry count is based upon headwords (main entries) and subentries. ESL (English as a second language) dictionaries have few run-on derivatives but a multitude of hidden boldface entries that describe idioms, proverbial expressions, or common collocations.

Grammatical Information

Grammatical information is more essential for the person who is trying to speak or understand a foreign language than for the native speaker. It is not surprising, then that ESL dictionaries should provide considerably more grammatical help than monolingual adult or children's dictionaries. The *Oxford Advanced Learner's Dictionary of Current English* (*Hornby*) gives examples of 25 different verb paradigms, with variations, in its front matter. Each verbal entry is identified by an alphanumeric code that refers the reader to the front-matter paradigm illustrating that of the verb. Count nouns are distinguished from mass nouns (see page 30). Thus, *disappointment* in the sense of the state of being disappointed, as in "To her great disappointment, it rained on the day of the picnic," is a mass noun, whereas in the sense of something that disappoints, as in "He had suffered many disappointments in love," it is a count noun.

There is good reason to include such information in ESL dictionaries and in bilingual dictionaries, especially when the translation in the target language is a count noun whereas the source-language term is a mass noun or vice versa. Some scholars have argued that it would be useful to include similar information in monolingual dictionaries. Indeed, it would, but the question of which words are countable for the native speaker is far more complex than for the foreign-born speaker. Like most pedagogical books, ESL dictionaries oversimplify to make a point. For example, the illustrative sentence quoted above as the countable sense of something that disappoints, "He had suffered many disappointments in love," probably more truly conveys the sense "He suffered the state of being disappointed in love many times" or, in other words, many states of being disappointed. *Disappointment* in this sense turns out to be countable after all, contrary to what ESL dictionaries tell us. The native speaker can make almost any noun plural and, given the vastly greater scope and complexity of his possible range of expression compared to that of the learner of a foreign language, he may well have reason to do so. *Hornby* and other ESL dictionaries are certainly right to limit the ESL student to safe idiomatic uses, but we must be wary of presuming that practical guidelines for the foreign-born student of English have any theoretical basis or practical use for the native speaker.

Context and variety of usage determine whether a noun can be made plural. In poetry, anything can happen. In scientific contexts, some words, like *etiology,* are often pluralized, though in ordinary usage they are generally considered noncountable. My experience as a dictionary maker convinces me that it is rash to suppose that any grammatical form cannot occur. Not the least value of lexicography is that one learns to be humble about one's own knowledge of the language.

General dictionaries provide basic grammatical information. Adult dictionaries indicate the part of speech of each entry, and the senses of the verbs are usually distinguished as to whether they are transitive or intransitive. Illustrative phrases serve to show the usual collocations or contexts in which each sense is used, thus providing a variety of grammatical information, such as whether a word takes an indirect object or whether it is usually used in the passive voice. Often other grammatical information is explicitly given. For example, the reader is advised that words like *economics* that are plural in form are construed as singular and that some words like *barrack* are usually used in the plural. Indication of the form of a word, especially capitalization, is also a common feature of dictionaries.

I can hear the reader protesting at this moment, "Doesn't the same argument you made about count versus mass nouns apply equally to any grammatical information given in a dictionary? If a dictionary says, 'usually used in the plural,' isn't it being equally factitious for the native speaker?"

89

My response is that the two cases are dissimilar. When a dictionary says, "usually used in the plural," it may be assumed that the only evidence that the word was ever used in the singular is a single fifty-year-old, smudged and partially illegible citation slip of questionable authenticity. When a dictionary says "usually," one may assume it to mean "almost invariably." The countable/noncountable distinction is hardly so reliable for native speakers. Second, all nouns can be distinguished by countability, whereas other kinds of grammatical information given by dictionaries (except for part of speech) are highly selective. They are not given at all unless the evidence in their support is overwhelming. The obligation to call every noun countable or not countable is far beyond the capacity of dictionary makers to do reliably, since in most cases the evidence is fragmentary and inconclusive.

Beginning children's dictionaries often do not include part-of-speech indications, because such labels would serve only to confuse the child who had not learned the rudiments of grammar. Even dictionaries for grades six through ten deemphasize part-of-speech labels. The Thorndike-Barnhart school dictionaries indicate part of speech at the end of each article. If the article includes more than one part of speech, the labels are all indicated and are keyed to the appropriate definitions.[14] This system has the merit of allowing the editors to arrange the definitions in the order that best clusters meaning rather than separating them by grammatical function. The *Harcourt Brace School Dictionary* places the part-of-speech label after each definition without regard to order.[15] It thus combines the clustering technique of the *Thorndike-Barnhart Intermediate Dictionary* (*TBI*) with a more direct way to identify the part of speech of each definition. The label *adj. use* is employed for noun attributives following immediately upon the noun sense from which they are derived. So, following the definition for the metal *lead,* definition 2 (hereafter def. 2) is "*adj. use:* a *lead* pipe." The technique saves space with no loss of clarity.

Scientific and technical dictionaries provide little grammatical information. Most do not indicate part of speech, although irregular plural forms, as for Latin terms, may be included. But since the study of the grammatical usage of technical terms is spare or nonexistent, there is little basis on which to provide information or guidance. Given the encyclopedic nature of such works, grammatical data are of marginal relevance in any case.

In bilingual dictionaries, the grammatical categories of the source-language vocabulary and its corresponding translations should be consistent. "The reader has a right to expect," one linguist observes, " . . . that if Japanese verbs are usually translated as English verbs, an adjective will not turn up without some compelling reason." If a Japanese adjective is translated as "is dark," for example, it would be misleading to translate a Japanese verb the same way; rather it should be translated as "gets (becomes)" dark, cloudy, etc.[16]

The use of the word *compelling* in the above quotation illustrates one of the most difficult grammatical problems for monolingual lexicographers, namely, how to decide when the present or past participle of a verb should be considered an adjective and entered as a canonical form in its own right. The case for *compelling* is compelling, but the status of many other words is less clear cut: *domed* (stadium), *marbled* (veneer), *tempered* (steel), *hardened* (criminal), *flourishing* (vegetation), *pleasing* (performance). There are thousands of such terms that seem to defy all attempts to place them in lexical categories by which to judge their fitness for entry status. Many, for example, do not have any meanings that are not already well covered by their underlying verbs. Because any verb participle can be used adjectivally in English and many nouns can be used attributively, the mere fact of occurrence with such grammatical functions obviously does not sustain the argument to include them as separate entries. But some participles are used adjectivally much more commonly than others. Some participles seem to have slightly different shades of meaning when used adjectivally in some contexts than one could impute to them simply by knowing their verbal meanings. Yet are the differences substantial enough to warrant entry status? It is very hard to know where to draw the line. Too relaxed a standard would open the floodgates to many thousands of terms that one hadn't the space to include and that would give the appearance of padding one's dictionary with redundant entries. Too strict a standard would demand a close and expert reading of the verb entries on the part of users, which could not be reasonably expected, and would suggest an inadequate survey of the lexicon.

The citation file and other word counts must determine whether participles and nouns are to be included as adjectives or whether they should merely be identified as "noun attrib." or by some other qualified designation. Unfortunately, there are no satisfactory guidelines other than frequency of use to help one in reaching a decision, and sometimes frequency cannot be determined or seems inadequate or even irrelevant. In such ways lexicography remains an art, or at least, to state the matter plainly, something less than a science.

Dictionaries also provide grammatical information about function words, so called because they function primarily as grammatical devices, as to link two words or introduce a phrase, rather than as lexical units. *Of, for, at, and, but,* and *to* are examples of function words. In my view it is misleading to say that function words do not have lexical meaning. Rather, their lexical meanings cannot be conventionally defined, and dictionaries are forced to devise stratagems for coping with them, one of which is to rely on the grammatical label of function word.

Definition will be treated at length in the next chapter, but suffice it to say here that the requirement for substitutability—that the definition for a word be substitutable for the word itself in most contexts—cannot be met with function words. When *Webster's Ninth New Collegiate Dictionary (MW9)* defines *of* as "—used as a function word to indicate a point of reckoning ⟨north ∼ the lake⟩," it is employing a convenient style to get around the impossibility of stating what *of* means in "north of the lake" in a substitutable way. Other dictionaries use different methods. I am not sure what special insight *MW9* hopes to give the reader by repeating "—used as a function word" fifteen times in its article for *of*. The grammatical category is a useful one, but its repetition with each definition, as if to suggest that the very possibility of defining *of* were impure, is typical of the rigid and slightly daft style of the linguistic holier-than-thou.

Pronunciation

The pronunciation system favored by monolingual American dictionaries is one in which the entry word is respelled in alphabetic characters with diacritical marks over certain vowels and with primary and secondary stress marks indicated. Such a system is essentially phonemic rather than phonetic. It is based on *phonemes,* the smallest units of sound that can differentiate between words. Phonemes are theoretical constructs, composites of similar but variously articulated speech sounds. Phonetic sounds, or *phones,* on the other hand, are actual speech sounds classified by the manner and place of articulation, that is, by the way in which air is forced through the mouth and shaped by tongue, teeth, palate, lips, and in some languages by the uvula. The *r* of *run* and of *fur* is articulated differently, thus phonetically different, but belongs to the same phoneme in English and is represented by one symbol in American dictionaries. The same is true of the *p* of *pill* and *spill* and the *l* of *lean* and *feel.* In some languages, the substitution of one of these sounds for the other in the same context would result in two different words; they are phonemically distinct in such languages, though not in English.[17] In the speech of many American southerners, the vowel sound of *pen* and *pin* is in free variation; such speakers are unaware whether they use the high front vowel [ɪ] or the mid front vowel [ɛ] in either context, though in other contexts, such as those of *slept* and *slipped,* a distinction is observed. In contexts like *pen/pin* the difference is not phonemic to southerners, though it is to most other Americans, who interpret the two utterances as different words. If a dictionary were intended for southerners only, [ɪ] and [ɛ] in these contexts would be represented by the same phonemic symbol; but since it is intended for all Americans, dictionaries represent them by two different symbols, usually /i/ and /e/. Parallel situations exist in the dialects in many other regions. For this reason, a phonemic pronunciation system may not serve the needs of all dialectal varieties equally well. It is nonetheless used because it is simpler and more easily understood by most dictionary users.

The chief difficulty in representing pronunciation is that the letters of the alphabet often represent more than one sound, as *a* in *late, can, far,* and *care,* and sometimes two different letters represent the same sound, as *c* and *k* in *cool* and *kin.* Because the letter *a* is pronounced variously, different symbols must be used to represent its different sounds. That the distinction between the sound of *late* and the sound of *can* is phonemic can be demonstrated by comparing *can* and *cane.* A change in the vowel sound changes the meaning of the two words. Thus, the vowel in *late* is represented by /ā/, that of *can* by /a/, that of *far* by /ä/, and that of *care* by /er/ or /â/. These sounds are then linked to "key words," familiar words in which each of these sounds occur. If the reader sees /ä/ in a pronunciation, he looks at the pronunciation key, usually printed on every two page spread, and finds /ä/ identified as the first vowel sound in *father.* The system works so long as everyone pronounces the key word the same way, but in some cases, as we have seen with *pen* and *pin,* not everyone does. In those cases, the system is chiefly of value in providing clues as to how the pronunciations of others differ from one's own.

The alternative to a phonemic system is a phonetic one. The most widely used phonetic system is that of the International Phonetic Alphabet. In the IPA, the sound of *late* is represented by [e], that of *can* by [æ], that of *far* by [a], and that of *set* by [ɛ]. Although a phonemic system can work rather well among native speakers who are all familiar with the basic quality of English sounds, however they may differ in a few particularities, it does not work at all among foreign learners of English, who may not know how to pronounce *late* or *can* and who may bring into play their own foreign-language equivalents of these vowel sounds rather than use the English sounds. The phonemes in their own languages are not likely to be those found in English. For ESL and bilingual dictionaries, then, it is obvious that a phonetic system, usually the IPA or a modification of it, is necessary.

A system based on the manner of articulation can be used to produce the sounds of any language, even a language with which one is entirely unfamiliar. However, the notation to represent such sounds exactly must be much more elaborate than for a phonemic system, for a phonetic system must indicate whether the tongue is high, mid, or low; front, mid, or back; whether a vowel sound is long or short, rounded, diphthongal (consisting of two sounds), or retroflex (made with the tip of the tongue curled up toward the palate). In addition, the movement from one position to another, or glides, must be represented, stress pattern and pauses must be more exactly indicated, and pitch or intonation may also be noted.

In practice, an adequate phonetic system for a general English dictionary need not be much more complicated than a phonemic system. Unfortunately, no American dictionary has successfully employed one. Few have tried. Wyld's *Universal Dictionary of the English Language,* of British origin, is an exception. It includes two pronunciations, one phonetic and one phonemic.[18] The reluctance of Americans to accept a phonetic system seems to stem from the use of nonalphabetic characters, such as [∧] for the vowel sound in *hut* or [ɔ] for that of *law,* or the use of the characters [ð] and [θ] for the *th* sounds of *the* and *thread,* respectively. There are really not very many such characters, and they are not hard to memorize—as any student of an elementary speech or linguistics course can attest—but to the general, lay, dictionary-buying public, they represent a formidable barrier to understanding. It is an unfortunate fact that even the currently used, simplified, phonemic systems of American dictionaries are widely misunderstood by dictionary users. I would guess that at best no more than 25 percent of the users of adult monolingual dictionaries can accurately render the sound of a word by reading its dictionary pronunciation. For ESL dictionary users employing a phonetic system the figure is much higher, because these people are more highly motivated to learn and as a rule have acquired some familiarity with the principles of phonetics in the course of their language study. For ESL dictionary users, pronunciation is of great importance; for native speakers, definition is of central importance and pronunciation usually only of marginal interest.

One of the major problems in pronunciation parallels that of establishing the written canonical form: what pronunciation will be regarded as preferred, if any? In Britain, where dialectal variations are great, one dialect is preferred over others. The Received Pronunciation (RP) of southern England, based on the careful speech of educated speakers, especially those who are products of the best public schools and of Oxford and Cambridge, is still the standard. No general dictionary could possibly do justice to all the varieties in England.

In the United States, on the other hand, there are fewer regional differences, and they are relatively minor. The most widely used pronunciation—whether it is acknowledged to be a standard or not—is the measure of priority. Perhaps the major national difference is that of *r*-pronouncers versus *r*-less speakers (in words like *sore* and *paper*). In American dictionaries, the forms of the *r*-pronouncers are usually given priority, even though the front-matter guide may acknowledge that *r*-less speakers also exist in large numbers and are not speaking incorrectly. "I wonder," says James R. Hulbert, "how many users of our dictionaries realize that when they see *färthar*, they are to understand that in the case of Virginians it means *fätha*?"[19]

There is no question that widespread variations such as the alternative ways of saying *either* with initial /aɪ/ or /i/, must be represented. But what to do about *pen* and *pin,* or *father* with or without the /r/, is another matter. As one pronunciation expert acknowledges, rules for converting one symbol to another based on instructions in the front-matter guide are difficult to follow. "Moreover, the dictionary user requires information to be explicit at the point of entry and rarely consults the good advice given in the introductory sections, which are usually read only by other lexicographers."[20]

The alternative is to show each variation in the pronunciation of each word, the practice generally followed by *NID3*. This takes up much more space and sometimes leads to extraordinarily complicated pronunciations. Here, for example, is *NID3*'s pronunciation for *whir* (or *whirr*):

\R ˈwh|ər *also* ˈw|, + *vowel* ər· :|ə̄, + *suffixal vowel*|ər· *also* |ə̄r, + *vowel in a following word*|ər· or |ə̄ *also*|ə̄r\

Clarence Barnhart quotes approvingly the criticisms of two other lexicographers that the system used by *NID3* is too elaborate and cumbersome.[21] *NID3* is criticized on four grounds: (1) its pronunciation system is too complicated; (2) too many variants are shown; (3) the style used to save space,employing an equals sign to mean "same pronunciation as that of the lexical unit next above," which often looks like this: \↓ = (=) = ↑ = \, is confusing; (4) there is no pronunciation key listed on every two-page spread.

One can sympathize with the critics who find *NID3*'s pronunciations too complex and difficult to follow. On the other hand, it seems to me that the only synchronic, unabridged dictionary in English should record fully the variant pronunciations documented by regional linguistic atlases and by its own phonological records. The pronunciation of *whir* above need not be fully understood for the casual user to grasp the essential pronunciation, namely, \whər\ or \wər\. All the rest is superfluous for most users but of potential value to anyone who wants it. I cannot understand why *NID3* should be criticized for providing extraordinarily full pronunciations and also for dropping the obsolete terms listed "under the line" in *NID2*.[22] Surely the obsolete terms, though a pleasant diversion for rainy days, were more superfluous than are currently used variant pronunciations. The absence of a pronunciation key is unfortunate, but, given the great saving in space by omitting it, one can understand why the decision was made. The pronunciation key in *NID2* filled two full lines of type across all three columns of every page. Since *NID3* has 2,662 pages of three columns each, the pronunciation key would have consumed 15,972 column-lines of type (6 column-lines per page). One can fit a great many entries into 16,000 column-lines!

Yet it must be admitted that the use of an equals sign to represent a part of a pronunciation identical to a corresponding part of a pronunciation of a preceding lexical unit places an intolerable burden on the reader. On this point I agree entirely with Robert L. Chapman, who describes the often futile search to put together the missing pieces of a pronunciation: " . . . [O]ne must go chasing up the column, picking up one element at a time and holding it in mind until all the bits are found, often at some distance from the word itself. The space saved by this ingenuity was too dearly bought."[23] I have often abandoned the attempt to piece together a pronunciation in *NID3,* preferring to turn to another dictionary where I knew I would find at least a basic pronunciation at the point of reference. The equals sign devices were considered necessary because the pronunciations were so full that to repeat all the variants for each similar term would have used an excessive amount of space. The shorthand symbols may well represent all variant pronunciations, but if one need be a certified chess grandmaster to figure them out, would it not have been better to have omitted some variant pronunciations? I may seem to be arguing both sides of this question—for and against full pronunciations—but I do feel that a workable compromise might have been fashioned if the editors had been less rigid in their approach to dictionary style. Surely a less exacting method that gave full pronunciations to many words but that omitted the less common variants in many others—perhaps with a special character indicating such omission—would have served the needs of most readers far better than that used.

One modern critic, Robert H. Secrist, calls rather engagingly for a return to the eighteenth and nineteenth century systems, which generally avoided respelling, instead simply marking certain vowels of the entry word with diacritics to indicate the specific sound.[24] In fact, the *COD* and some technical dictionaries do follow this method to some extent, but for a large general monolingual dictionary to do so would require great courage or poor judgment, depending on one's point of view. In the 1950s Funk & Wagnalls published with great fanfare a new college dictionary, called the Emphatype edition, based exactly on this premise. It was a spectacular failure. The public, evidently, did not regard it as easier to use. Nonetheless, there is much to be said for Secrist's argument that many respellings are unnecessary and could be omitted from abridged dictionaries at great savings in space. Some respellings, he argues, such as /plān/ and /sins/ for *plane* and *since,* are easily mistaken for other words. He even dares to question the almost universally applauded adoption of the schwa in dictionary pronunciation systems, on the ground that it is unnecessary and is used as a catchall for a variety of different sounds. Older systems sometimes italicized the unstressed character now represented by the schwa, as in bitt*e*r or p*o*lice. Italic type, however, is easily overlooked and many readers might feel that the italicized vowel indicated that it should be especially stressed! The schwa removes all ambiguity of that sort. On the other hand, Secrist and other critics are right that the schwa represents a variety of sounds and is in reality neither phonetic nor phonemic, but a convenient catchall for unstressed vowels.[25]

Bilingual dictionaries generally show only one pronunciation. "[T]he foreign learner," one scholar comments, "would be at a loss when offered more than one variant."[26] Furthermore, pronunciation is regarded as of secondary importance in bilingual dictionaries.

Variant pronunciations are also kept to a minimum in children's dictionaries, for much the same reasons. The student, whether native-speaking child or adult foreigner, needs direction. Both works are necessarily normative compared to general adult monolingual dictionaries.

Some scientific and technical dictionaries provide pronunciations and some do not. Because many technical terms are seldom pronounced outside of the lecture hall, it is often difficult to ascertain their pronunciations. Many pronunciations for scientific words are necessarily devised on the basis of analogy with other similar words whose pronunciation is known, since terms like *coccidioidomycosis,* for example, do not turn up frequently in conversation. The scientific vocabulary is preeminently written—numerous terms encountered frequently in print are rarely uttered. Thus, scientific and technical dictionaries necessarily adopt a normative approach to their pronunciations. Where a record of usage does exist, the pronunciations based on usage are given in preference to those based on analogy, but in a large technical dictionary that situation is the exception rather than the rule.

James R. Hulbert remarks that dictionaries are less satisfactory in pronunciation than in spelling, meaning, or etymology.[27] The record of the spoken language is difficult to acquire, difficult to transcribe accurately and unambiguously, difficult to represent understandably in a dictionary transcription, and in most dictionaries of less interest to the user than other kinds of information. For these reasons it is not usually accorded the same degree of attention in general dictionaries as that given spelling, meaning,

97

or etymology. The only comprehensive American pronouncing dictionary, John S. Kenyon and Thomas A. Knott's *A Pronouncing Dictionary of American English,* is out of date. *NID3*'s full coverage of pronunciation can be interpreted as its substitute for a revision of Kenyon and Knott (originally published by G. & C. Merriam), which must have been regarded as commercially unprofitable. For current pronunciations of American English, the reader has no choice but to consult general dictionaries.

Etymology

Whenever the subject at a dinner or cocktail party among fresh acquaintances turns to what each of us does for a living, and I am introduced as a dictionary maker, invariably the first response from my associates is that they find dictionaries fascinating, and in particular the derivation of words. From the number of cocktail party acquaintances who have in all seriousness, but with what sobriety I cannot say, affirmed that they loved to read—"yes, read"—dictionaries, one would suppose the nation to be studded with pockets of people neglecting their work and families to read dictionaries, especially etymologies. Somehow, I doubt it. I have never heard anyone say he loved to read pronunciations. Although meaning is certainly most often sought by dictionary users, it does not have the cachet of etymology, which combines knowledge of other languages, especially the classical languages, with arcane scholarship. It may come as a surprise to some readers, then, to learn that of all the elements included in modern dictionaries etymology has least to do with the essential purpose of a synchronic dictionary. Etymology may be valuable in its own right, but it tells us little about current meaning and is in fact often misleading. Here is what Thomas Pyles, a scholar who has written extensively on English usage, has to say on the subject:

> There is a widespread belief held even by some quite learned people, that the way to find out what a word means is to find out what it previously meant—or, preferably, if it were possible to do so, what it originally meant. . . . [S]uch an appeal to etymology to determine present meaning is as unreliable as would be an appeal to spelling to determine modern pronunciation. Change of meaning—semantic change, as it is called—may, and frequently does, alter the so-called etymological sense . . . which may have become altogether obsolete. . . .
> Certain popular writers, overeager to display their learning, have asserted that words are misused when they depart from their etymologi-

cal meanings. Thus Ambrose Bierce once declared that *dilapidated,* because of its ultimate derivation from Latin *lapis* "stone," could appropriately be used only of a stone structure. [28]

By the same token, Pyles observes, we should have to confine the use of *eradicate* to roots, since it is derived from Latin *rādix* "root"; *calculation,* from Latin *calx* "stone," to counting pebbles; *sinister* to leftists, and *giddy* to those divinely inspired, since *gid* is derived from *god.*

The error of associating current meaning with past etymological meaning is commonplace also in the sciences, particularly medicine, where devotion to tradition and a belief in the sanctity of Latin combine to reinforce the fallacy. As the medical lexicographer A. Manuila points out,

> Many words, whether technical or in ordinary use, have departed so widely from their original meaning that the latter can be of interest only to medical historians or linguists. Thus, etymologically, *thalassaemia* means "sea in the blood," *gonorrhoea* "a flow of semen," *artery* "an air vessel," *asphyxia* "a weak or suppressed pulse," *autopsy* "self-seeing," *embryo* "a young animal," *diploma* "anything folded twice," and *anatomy* "a cutting through."[29]

Yet in spite of all evidence to the contrary, popular writers continue to make the assumption that etymological meaning determines current meaning. For example, in a recent column in the *New York Times Magazine* in which *hazard* was compared to *danger,* William Safire concluded that "The difference is semantically significant: 'Hazard' is from the French *hasard,* a crap game; 'danger' is rooted in the Latin *dominum,* from the absolute power of a lord and master to do harm. With a hazard, at least you have a chance."[30]

Nathan Bailey's *An Universal Etymological English Dictionary* of 1721 was the first English dictionary to treat etymology with consistent purpose and seriousness. Etymology was sometimes included in earlier dictionaries, but in a rudimentary way, often consisting simply of a language designation such as *L* for Latin. Bailey gave the Latin etymon and often more immediate sources, as in Italian or French. Though he too was inconsistent, Bailey's dictionary is credited with having established etymology as "one of the requisites of any reputable dictionary."[31]

How far we have come in our expectations of what general dictionaries should provide by way of etymology is illustrated by criticisms of recent dictionaries. Patrick Drysdale, a British lexicographer formerly active in Canada, lists the following etymological desiderata:

1. Source language or language family
2. First English form and/or immediate source
3. Date or period of entry into English
4. Changes in form and meaning in English
5. Intermediate stages
6. Ultimate known source
7. Semantic development
8. Ultimate underlying or hypothetical form, e.g., an Indo-European root
9. Cognates in related lanquages also derived from the underlying form
10. Other English words derived from the same base.[32]

In the eighteenth century and the early part of the nineteenth, no one could have fulfilled Drysdale's standards for good etymological treatment, because the great advances in philology that were to transform it into a science had not occurred or were yet relatively unknown. What are the principles that the famous philologists of the nineteenth century—Rasmus Rask, Franz Bopp, Jacob Grimm, Karl Verner, Ferdinand de Saussure, Karl Brugmann, and others—elaborated? Essentially, they discovered and proved that sound change was regular rather than hit or miss. Henry Cecil Wyld, in the Introduction to his dictionary, describes the discovery:

> We soon learn to appreciate the truth of the great principle which guides all philological study, that a given sound is always changed, in one and the same dialect, in the same way, under the same conditions. Thus, for instance, in Greek initial *s* becomes the aspirate *h*, and between vowels is lost altogether; in Celtic initial *p* is lost; in Sanscrit, Persian, and the Baltic-Slavic families a sound which appears as *k* in Greek and Latin and as *h* in Germanic, develops into the sound of *sh* or *s*; Germanic has changed old *p*, *t*, *k* into *f*, Þ ("thorn") *h*, respectively, and so on. *These changes take place everywhere, in all words containing these sounds, not in only isolated words here and there.*[33] [Italics added]

The importance of the last sentence above can scarcely be exaggerated, for up until this time etymologists had depended on chance similarities between words in different languages or on wildly speculative theories based on biblical stories to determine the derivation of words. As we have seen, Noah Webster devoted ten years of study to the world's languages with the aim of mastering the science of etymology, but since he was contemptuous of the principle of the regularity of sound change and ignorant of the discoveries based upon it, his etymologies were worthless.

The modern etymologist must explain how every sound in the current canonical form of each word developed from older forms. If he cannot explain certain changes on the basis of systematic sound change according to established principles, he must have some other plausible explanation to account for them. Merely saying that the sounds of /d/ and /t/, for example, are similar will not do. Common sense, however, still plays an important role in good etymologizing. As the famous etymologist Walter Skeat declared, "observe chronology." "The word *surloin* or *sirloin,*" he points out, "is often said to be derived from the fact that the *loin* was knighted as *Sir Loin* by Charles II, or (according to Richardson) by James I. Chronology makes short work of this statement; the word being in use long before James I was born." Borrowings are due to actual contact. When one alleges that a word was borrowed from the language of another culture, there must be evidence that the two peoples actually came in contact. "The history of a nation generally accounts for the constituent parts of its language. When an early English word is compared with Hebrew or Coptic, as used to be done in the *old* editions of Webster's dictionary, history is set at defiance...."[34]

The importance of etymology for historical dictionaries is beyond dispute. The main purpose of a diachronic dictionary such as the *OED* is to trace the development of form and meaning over an extended period of time for each word in the language. This is not exactly the same as etymology, which describes a word's form and meaning when it first appeared in English and describes its intermediate and ultimate forms and meanings in other languages. But it is clearly central to an understanding of the word's development in English.

Synchronic dictionaries, on the other hand, need not deal with etymology at all. Small paperback dictionaries generally omit it. Desk dictionaries include only very brief etymologies. Of the college dictionaries, the *American Heritage Dictionary*'s *(AHD)* first edition gives the fullest etymologies. (*AHD2* has cut back sharply on the etymologies of the first edition, however.) The first edition of *AHD* boasted of an appendix of Indo-European roots, which is an excellent piece of work, but I wonder what percentage of that dictionary's buyers have ever used it. Clarence Barnhart states, with characteristic honesty, "Most dictionary users have little interest in or use for etymologies."[35] How does one square this with my acquaintance with untold numbers of people reading dictionaries and fascinated by the derivations of words? I'm afraid Mr. Barnhart is right. The people who think they love etymology regard etymology as a selection of stories about word histories. Books recounting interesting or odd etymologies have always been popular and successful, such as those of Ernest Weekley in the early part of this century and of William and Mary Morris, Stuart Berg Flexner, William Safire, and others in more recent years. H.L. Mencken's *The American Language* also derived much of its popularity from its etymological information. Such books naturally select just those words and expressions that will provide material for entertaining accounts. Including several hundred words or at most a few thousand, they are usually derivative (Mencken excepted), based on etymological dictionaries or other works of scholarship, or highly speculative. This is not meant in criticism—who would be churlish enough to denounce books that are both educational and fun to read?—but they are not comparable to dictionaries, which must provide an etymology for many thousands of words, the great majority of which do not have charming anecdotes associated with their histories, consisting merely of an uninspiring list of foreign words and a handful of glosses. Nor can dictionaries indulge in clever speculation. *AHD2* has quietly dropped its appendix of Indo-European roots to make room for other material.

Children's dictionaries either omit etymologies entirely or include brief, selective statements, such as: "*Iconoclast* comes from two Greek words meaning *breaker of images*."[36] Subjecting children who are in the process of mastering their own written language to unfamiliar words in other languages does not make a great deal of sense. Etymologies are not included in ESL dictionaries or in bilingual dictionaries. To use space on this subject for a foreign learner, given the many other more profitable uses to which the space could be put, would be foolish, especially when general, monolingual dictionaries cover the ground so much better than any ESL or "translation" dictionary could. Etymologies are almost exclusively for the adult, native speaker.

Etymologies are often included in scientific and technical dictionaries, especially those for the older sciences like medicine, because they are mistakenly believed to be essential to an understanding of meaning. In fact, what is important in medicine is not a knowledge of Latin or Greek but of the modern meanings of combining forms derived from Latin and Greek. It certainly helps, if one has never encountered *nephroureterocystectomy* before, to be able to divide the word into its components, *nephro-*, *uretero-*, *cyst-*, and *-ectomy*, rather than perceiving it as an alphabetic blur. But to know that *nephro-* has to do with the kidney implies no knowledge of the Greek *nephros* underlying it, and a knowledge of the underlying Greek or Latin can, as we have already seen, be misleading by suggesting a relationship that no longer obtains. If one understands the limitations of etymology in conveying modern meaning, it is surely of value to know how the ancients perceived conditions such as *thalassemia* and *gonorrhea* and may even, in rare cases, throw light on some aspect of modern meaning. But etymology's chief value lay in its historic and linguistic interest, not in its relevance to the modern meaning of scientific terms.

Are etymologies useful to anyone? If they do not contribute to an understanding of current meaning, shouldn't they be omitted altogether from non-historical, general dictionaries? It is a question worth pondering. Patrick Drysdale considers the question and cites three reasons for including etymologies.[37] The first is to satisfy the need of the scholar or student of the history of the English language. But surely the scholar will not be satisfied by the treatment in a synchronic dictionary and will seek fuller information in a historical or etymological dictionary. Second, Drysdale says, etymologies increase one's understanding of one's language and stimulate interest in it. But they also increase *mis*understanding of language, given the wrongheaded uses to which etymology is so often put. It is also debatable whether dictionary etymologies stimulate interest in language. Third, according to Drysdale, etymologies provide clues to the history of the culture and its relationships to other words. Here I think he is really on to something.

Without etymologies, the entries in a dictionary appear to have been granted their present shapes by divine right, without relation to any other language and without relation to the past. To divorce a language from its past misses the opportunity to show language in its context, even though particular words may be very well defined without etymology. It is the difference between seeing a lion on the African plains and seeing it behind bars in an old-fashioned zoo. The zoo will afford a better look at the lion—but a much inferior view of lions.

Etymologies demonstrate that language changes in form and meaning. Even the brief etymologies in synchronic dictionaries remind people of this process and sometimes give glimpses of the way other cultures, or our own in times past, viewed particular words. The processes of semantic change, coinages of new words, and linguistic borrowing from other languages (loan words) have been thoroughly explored and discussed in fascinating detail in a number of studies of American English. See, for example, H. L. Mencken's *The American Language* (revised by Raven I. McDavid, Jr.), Thomas Pyles's *Words and Ways of American English*, or Albert H. Marckwardt's *American English*.

It is true that conventional dictionary treatment of etymologies does not usually shed much light on semantic development, but perhaps, as Drysdale suggests, dictionary makers have never really explored the question of how to edit and present etymologies effectively for their chosen audience. It might, for instance, be more helpful for the general user if some words were not etymologized at all so that others might be more fully explored in a style that was understandable to the layman and that placed the word in some meaningful relationship to other words. At all events, of all the elements of the dictionary article, etymology is the least satisfactory in presentation.

Dictionaries are about evenly divided as to whether etymology should appear near the beginning or the end of the dictionary article. Funk & Wagnalls was the first dictionary publisher to place the etymology after the definitions in its dictionaries, beginning with the *Standard* of 1893, and the practice has been adopted by a number of other dictionaries. The reasoning was that since definition is more often sought than etymology, it should appear earlier in the entry. The early placement of etymology in square brackets is seen as a kind of moat that the reader must leap across to reach his quest. I do not think it makes very much difference where the etymology is placed. If it is clearly marked as etymology, one loses no time in sweeping ahead to the definitions. Commercial dictionaries will, of course, go on declaring that they have shattered all precedent and opened communication to millions of frustrated dictionary users by their ingenious innovations, but often it's a matter of Tweedledum and Tweedledee.

Synonyms and Synonym Discussions

One of Dean Trench's criticisms in his paper *On Some Deficiencies in Our English Dictionaries* (1857) was the scant attention given to "distinguishing of synonymous words." He calls for the discrimination of synonyms "likely to be confounded," such as *safe* and *secure*. The first dictionary to include a large number of such discussions was Joseph E. Worcester's great work of 1860, *A Dictionary of the English Language,* perhaps in heed of Trench's criticism. Worcester can be said to have established synonym discriminations as a standard feature of large dictionaries.

Dictionaries of synonym discriminations, variously known in the nineteenth century as *synonymicons* or *synonymies,* have a venerable history. The discussion of synonyms goes back to the ancients, and the earliest synonymies were of Greek and Latin during the Renaissance. French and German dictionaries of synonyms appeared in the eighteenth century. One of the earliest synonym dictionaries in English was John Trusler's *Difference between Words Esteemed Synonymous in the English Language* (1766). Another very early synonym dictionary was that of Hester Lynch Piozzi, more widely known as Hester Lynch Thrale, the celebrated friend of Samuel Johnson. Her *British Synonymy: or an Attempt to regulate the Choice of Words in Familiar Conversation* appeared in 1794. William Taylor's small octavo *English Synonyms Discriminated* was published in 1813, and in 1816 George Crabb's *English Synonymes Explained,* the latter going through many editions. An edition of *Crabb's English Synonymes* was published in 1917, a century after the first edition. Richard Whateley's *Selection of English Synonyms* (1851) was also influential.

The lack of any dictionary of synonyms in English before the end of the eighteenth century is not hard to explain. In the sixteenth and seventeenth centuries the extent of the entire English word stock was much smaller than it is now, and the problem then, as Taylor points out in the Preface to his dictionary, was that the same word had to be used in a variety of contexts with different meanings. As the word stock increased, the lexicon absorbed words that were near synonyms of existing words, or words that evolved in meaning to become near synonyms. It was not until the word stock of English was sufficiently developed to embrace thousands of near synonyms that dictionaries of synonyms could be written with much effect.

As an example of the kind of discriminations given in such early books, here is part of Taylor's essay (page 98) on *mirth* and *cheerfulness,* attributed to Addison:

> Mirth is an effort, cheerfulness a habit of the mind; mirth is transient, and cheerfulness permanent; mirth is like a flash of lightening, that glitters with momentary brilliance, cheerfulness is the day-light of the soul, which steeps it in perpetual serenity.

Sometimes collocation was indicated, as in this essay (page 99) on *brute* and *beast:*

> Both these words are applied to animals, as distinguished from birds, insects, fishes, and man; but the term *brute* is confined to the untamed quadrupeds. [¶] We say, *beasts* of burden, never brutes of burden. The beasts of the field; the brutes of the forest.

At this point we must backtrack a bit and determine just what is meant by synonymy, in the sense of the state of being synonymous. Zgusta specifies three aspects of lexical meaning: the designatum, connotation, and range of application. *Designatum* refers to the essential properties of the thing or concept that define it; *connotation* refers to associated features; and *range of application* refers to the variety of contexts in which the word may be used.[38] Zgusta defines absolute synonymy as occurring when two terms correspond in all three aspects of designatum, connotation, and range. Absolute synonymy is rare among general terms but common among technical ones, especially in medicine. For example, Creutzfeldt-Jakob disease, a progressive degenerative brain disease, has at least ten absolute synonyms (which I prefer to call variants), including *Jakob-Creutzfeldt disease, Jakob's disease, Creutzfeldt-Jakob syndrome, Jones-Nevin syndrome,* and *spongiform encephalopathy.*

If the correspondence is exact in one or two of the three aspects but not in all, the two words are near synonyms. *Beast* and *brute* have the same

105

designatum—an animal other than man—but are dissimilar both in connotation and in range of application. It is precisely the object of synonym discussions to distinguish the ways in which two words differ in one or more aspect, usually that of connotation, and often of range as well. Such discriminations are based on individual point of view and depend for their effect largely on quality of expression rather than cogency of argument. At the end of his discussion of *beast* and *brute,* Taylor adds of another synonymist: "Dr. Trusler gives an opposite account of these words."

Roget's Thesaurus

In speaking of synonym dictionaries, I have been referring to works devoted to brief essays in which synonyms were discriminated. But in 1852, Peter Mark Roget's *Thesaurus of English Words and Phrases* was published. Roget was an English physician who had already made a name for himself with his studies in physiology. The *Thesaurus* was a different sort of book, with words arranged, to use Roget's own description (page xiii),

> ... not in alphabetical order as they are in a Dictionary, but according to the *ideas* which they express. The purpose of an ordinary dictionary is simply to explain the meaning of words. ... The object aimed at in the present undertaking is exactly the converse of this: namely,—The idea being given, to find the word, or words, by which that idea may be most fitly and aptly expressed. For this purpose, the words and phrases of the language are here classed, not according to their sound or their orthography, but strictly according to their *signification.*

Roget elaborated six classes of categories: abstract relations; space; material world; intellect; volition; sentient and moral powers. Within these broad classifications he placed numerous subdivisions, with the subdivisions further divided. He recognized that many words would fall into more than one category and that the placement of a word in one or another category was a difficult decision. Even the first edition included an index to help readers find the signification they were looking for, but the presumption then (page xviii) was that the elaborate classification of thoughts would usually suffice without resort to the index. "By the aid of the table [of classification of subjects into divisions], the reader will, with a little practice, readily discover the place which the particular topic he is in search of occupies in the series. ... [I]f, during the search, any doubt or difficulty should occur, recourse may be had to the copious alphabetical Index of words at the end of the volume. . . ." However ingenious the hierarchy of concepts, it was pure fantasy to suppose that any conceptual arrangement of the vocabulary of English was natural to most native speakers. It cannot be doubted that few readers could have found the meaning sought without recourse to the index, which was been expanded greatly through the work's many editions. The most recent edition (1977) straightforwardly instructs the reader to begin with the index.[39]

Conceptually vs. Alphabetically Arranged Thesauruses

So closely identified is *Roget* with this kind of synonym work that the name, now in the common domain, has been adopted by many other synonym dictionaries, some using a conceptual arrangement and others organized alphabetically with a list of synonyms following every main entry. Alphabetically arranged synonym dictionaries do not have an index, since the presumption is that every word the reader might look up in an index is listed alphabetically as a main entry. Both kinds of works are now called *thesauruses*.[40] The claim by proponents of the conceptual variety that theirs is the only true thesaurus is specious.[41] "Thesaurus" was used long before Roget adopted it for his work in its Greek sense of a storehouse or treasure, with the specific meaning of an exhaustive survey of words, as in Ainsworth's *Thesaurus Linguae Latinae Compendiarius* (1736), and it has retained this sense in English. It was perfectly suitable for Roget to describe his own work by the word *thesaurus,* but there is no historical or logical basis for arguing that his use of the term is the only correct one and that *thesaurus* may not, with equal regard for its history, be used to describe other kinds of synonym dictionaries, and indeed other kinds of dictionaries.

Kenneth Kister, while acknowledging the original sense of the Greek word, claims that Roget "invented" *thesaurus.*[42] I do not know how someone can be said to have invented a word already in use for hundreds of years. Roget's adaptation of the term *thesaurus* to his work was certainly instrumental in its assimilation into English, but his use cannot "fix" the word eternally. If, as Kister seems to imply, *thesaurus* is used by publishers to deceive the public, their motives rather than their diction should be impugned. The word *thesaurus* has no true sense by virtue of priority of use. No word does.

Roget is used in the titles of at least nine different synonym books. The use or nonuse of *thesaurus* and *Roget* is worth millions of dollars to competing publishers. The real conflict is between those who would like to reserve these words for their own exclusive profit and those who fear that their failure to use them would place them at an enormous marketing disadvantage. The unfortunate fact is that most buyers of reference books know very little about the merits of competing works but rely chiefly on a familiarity with their names. The argument that *thesaurus* has a true sense is merely a smokescreen to conceal the battle for commercial profit.

Though the sales pitches for both types of thesauruses expatiate on the unique merits of their own system and inveigh against the cumbersome complexities and inadequate oversimplifications of the other systems, the two methods of arrangement are not really very much different. Both rely on an alphabetic listing of words. But whereas the conceptual organization leads the reader from the index to clusters of words centered upon a congeries of related meanings, the dictionary type of organization strings out the synonyms directly after the index entry. The dictionary arrangement necessitates a great deal of repetition; given the same amount of space, the conceptual arrangement can offer a greater number of different words. Also, by having a whole series of paragraphs of words with similar meanings under each heading, in theory at least the conceptual scheme offers a greater likelihood that the reader will find the word he is seeking. On the other hand, the alphabetical dictionary arrangement is easier to use, since the reader can often find synonyms by looking in one place rather than two or more.

The conceptual arrangement is associated with extreme inclusiveness. Rarely used words, non-English words, names, obsolete and unidiomatic expressions, phrases: all are thrown in together along with common words without any apparent principle of selection. For example, in the fourth edition of *Roget's International Dictionary*—one of the best of the conceptually arranged works—we find included under the subheading *orator:* "Demosthenes, Cicero, Franklin D. Roosevelt, Winston Churchill, William Jennings Bryan." Why not Pericles and Billy Graham? When one starts to include types of things, where does one stop? There is actually a list of insects (paragraph 414.36), which is even more of a random sampling than that of orators. Such works are a potpourri of everything the compiler can think of. The governing principle seems to be that the more there is, the more likely it is something in the collection will prove to be useful. Conceptually arranged works are thus designed for the widest possible market.

The alphabetical arrangement is usually associated with more selectivity. Names, rarely used words, and types of things are generally excluded. In a work based on selectivity, the compilers must have in mind a clear perception of their intended audience. Though the level of difficulty of the synonyms may vary somewhat, the necessity to exclude some words imposes a limited range upon most alphabetical works that is lacking in most perceptually arranged works. Alphabetical thesauruses thus tend to be more homogeneous than conceptually arranged works. The governing principle is that the compilers know best what the user is likely to need.[43]

In this century, books of synonym discriminations have not been nearly as popular as thesauruses, and since they are much harder to prepare, there are fewer of them than of thesauruses. In 1871, Charles John Smith's *Synonyms Discriminated* was published. The second edition (1890) is an impressive work of 870 double-column pages, including etymologies, many quotations from well-known writers illustrating the words discussed, and an index. Smith frequently compares three or more words, and even as many as eight. James C. Fernald's *English Synonyms and Antonyms* was published in 1896 and revised in 1914. Fernald's discussions often involve a dozen words and consist of a sentence about each. He is one of the few synonymists to pay any attention to antonyms, though he merely lists them alphabetically at the end of each essay. The book includes a full index and a question-and-answer section for teachers. An interesting and useful feature is the inclusion of notes "on the correct use of prepositions" with the verbs discriminated. The *Modern Guide to Synonyms and Related Words,* edited by S. I. Hayakawa and the Funk & Wagnalls dictionary staff, appeared in 1968. Finally, *Webster's New Dictionary of Synonyms,* edited by Philip B. Gove, appeared in 1973, a revision of an earlier work.[44]

The much more modest success of books of synonym discriminations, as compared with thesauruses, is not surprising as soon as one realizes that the former are not truly reference works. They may discriminate five to ten thousand words, but even were they to include many more they would hardly be comprehensive enough to assure the user that he will find the word he seeks, as a dictionary or thesaurus does. With few exceptions, the recent history of publishing such books is a record of failure, because dictionaries of discriminations are neither read like a novel nor used as a reference but used to some extent, publishers hope, in both ways. Nowadays, unless such works are attractively packaged and marketed to appeal to some contemporary interest, they are not likely to be successful commercially, however worthy and wise they may be.

Among general dictionaries, the discriminations of *The Century Dictionary* (1889–91) are outstanding for their quality and for the sensitive choice of quotations illustrating each word discriminated. They are neither wordy nor too slight but give fair attention to each word and show typical contexts in addition to the quotations. For newer senses, *NID3* should be consulted, but in many instances the *Century's* treatment has not been surpassed.

Dictionary Treatment of Synonymy

Because general dictionaries are truly reference works, the inclusion of synonym discriminations makes a great deal of sense. When they are not included, they are not missed; when they are included, they are a welcome superfluity. Some usage notes, such as that for *uninterested* and *disinterested,* may masquerade as synonym discriminations, and it is these the user is most likely to seek and find. The words included in true synonym discriminations are unpredictable. Dictionaries sometimes combine discriminations with brief lists of synonyms keyed to specific definitions. Both adult and children's dictionaries include synonymies, but the children's version is apt to be more didactic in keeping with its pedagogical purpose.

ESL and bilingual dictionaries do not include synonym discriminations, since such rarefied distinctions are quite beyond the skills of their users and altogether irrelevant to their purpose. Their aim is not to provide exquisite sensitivity in another language but to provide the means for communicating competently with a native speaker of another language. That goal is tough enough without worrying about the fine distinctions of connotation. Synonym discriminations are strictly for the native speaker.

The larger question of synonymy and bilingual lexicography is a profound one beyond the scope of this book. For example, two words in English may be near synonyms, such as *brute* and *beast,* but their respective translations into another language may be completely unrelated. Contrariwise, two words in English that are semantically unrelated may correspond in translation to two near synonyms in another language. This is an illustration of anisomorphism, discussed by Zgusta at length in his treatment of the bilingual dictionary.[45]

I have mentioned technical dictionaries and said they differ from other kinds of dictionaries in having numerous absolute synonyms. As the reader may have surmised, I am not entirely easy with this statement. Can we really call *Jakob-Creutzfeldt disease* a synonym for *Creutzfeldt-Jakob disease?* It is a mere variant having closer kinship to spelling variants. Even in the case of less similar forms, such as the *Jones-Nevin syndrome* and *spongiform encephalopathy,* the absoluteness of synonymy with *Creutzfeldt-Jakob disease* is of a different order than that of ordinary language. The *Jones-Nevin syndrome* and *spongiform encephalopathy* are based upon a description of a disease that was subsequently found to be identical to one previously described by Creutzfeldt and Jakob. An examination of the usage of these three terms in their immediate linguistic contexts could by no means have established their identity, as would be the case with synonyms of the general language. The three terms are *said* to be the same by inves-

110

tigators on the basis of their examination of the detailed data describing the circumstances of each disease. The terms were not consistently used with the same meaning, but they have been determined to be the same. In fact, subsequent research may even show that what is now supposed to be an absolute synonym is not after all the same and should be reclassified as a slightly different condition. Ordinary language does not behave in this way. For these reasons I feel more comfortable in speaking of technical terms of like meaning as variants rather than synonyms.

Illustrations

Nathan Bailey's dictionaries in the early eighteenth century included a number of woodcut illustrations, but it was not until the publication of John Ogilvie's *Imperial Dictionary* in 1850 that a dictionary gave prominence to pictorial illustration. *The Century Dictionary,* based on Charles Annandale's revision of the Ogilvie dictionary, is justly famous for the quality and number of its illustrations. The *Century* used some of the Ogilvie illustrations, but many others were drawn expressly for it.[46] The illustrations of animals and plants are exceptionally fine and are often initialed by the artists, one of whom was Ernest Thompson Seton. Seton's illustrations of birds are particularly notable. *The Century Magazine,* whose parent company supported the *Dictionary,* was famous for its etchings, and since the manager of the Century Company's art department, W. Lewis Fraser, was put in charge of assembling the *Dictionary*'s illustrations, it is not surprising that the quality is so high. No twentieth-century dictionary comes close to matching the elegance and sophistication of the *Century*'s art.

Nowadays in the United States one takes for granted that every general dictionary will be illustrated, but it has long been debated whether the space used for illustrations contributes much to the basic purpose of a dictionary. To what extent do pictures help the reader understand meaning? To some observers it is obvious that concrete objects such as forms of architecture, animals, plants, and many other things marked by a specific shape, such as geometric figures, are more easily grasped by means of illustration than by verbal description.[47] As a generalization, this is certainly true; but it is misleading and naïve to suppose that an illustration makes the definition superfluous, as Hulbert seems to argue. A picture is at best a representative example of the type of thing defined, yet it does not encompass anything approaching the full range of possibilities defined by the term it is supposed to illustrate. It thus performs graphically what an illustrative phrase or sen-

1 1 1

tence does verbally. To say that a picture obviates the need for definition makes the mistake of substituting an example representing a class of things—in Zgusta's terms the *denotatum*—for the qualities that define the object (the *designatum*). The idea that "simple" words like *dog* and *cat* need no definition will be discussed in Chapter 4; I find it primitive, ill conceived, and vacuous. I should say that simple words need no pictures; they certainly do need definitions.

Zgusta sees the primary purpose of illustrations as that of depicting unusual or unfamiliar things. I agree. No need to illustrate *dog* or *cat,* but *gnu* or *capybara* is another story. "The pictures should not be over-specific," he adds, "but only general lest the user accept a feature only accidental to the picture as criterial to the designatum."[48] In other words, if one's picture of a gnu has a peculiarly long neck, we may wrongly suppose that all gnus have necks that long. This is good advice that is not always easy to observe in practice. If one is depicting a rare animal or plant altogether foreign to one's own culture, one must necessarily base the illustration on a limited number of available photographs or illustrations. One collects what source material is available. Ideally, an expert in zoology should review the drawings to see whether they are accurate; in practice, it is difficult to find experts in every category depicted, or to entrust them if they are found with the ultimate responsibility for warranting that the art is accurate. Some experts, alas, are not conscientious; others, from a misplaced desire to be obliging, are not critical enough to be a reliable help. Frequently the editor must rely on his own judgment, based on the best information available. Nonetheless, Zgusta's advice is important to keep in mind. Although there may be some comparatively short-necked giraffes, we ought not to use them as our model for *giraffe.*

This raises the question of whether drawings or photographs are more useful for dictionary illustration. Photographs are necessarily of unidealized individual things, whether zebras, geese, or medieval churches. Drawings may combine features of many individuals and thus represent a composite distillation of elements regarded as typical. If the drawing is well done, it is usually more informative, with its details more readily apparent, than any photograph (or halftone, as it is called when processed for printing). On the other hand, photographs have an undeniable attachment to reality. There is always, in viewing a photograph, a slight thrill of appreciation that is missing in viewing a drawing; we know that the thing photographed was really there and not designed to illustrate anything. It is authentic.

Halftones are more difficult to use than line drawings, however, and often less satisfactory. For one thing, a photograph must be much larger than a drawing to convey the same sense of distance and space of a skillful drawing. A photograph of a group of people, for example, must be severely reduced in size for dictionary illustration; one feels one is examining a postage stamp. Moreover, in a photograph everything is uniformly reduced, the important foreground as well as the unimportant background. Photographs are often too detailed, too "busy," to highlight the very features that one wants to emphasize. In an artist's drawing, proportions can be doctored to highlight whatever one desires and details can be obscured or omitted. Of course, photographs can be doctored as well, with details brushed out, but the results often *look* doctored and unsatisfactory, and touching up photographs is expensive.

To some extent, dictionary illustration is a matter of fashion. Until the publication of the *American Heritage Dictionary* in 1969, line drawings were *à la mode*. The *AHD,* with thousands more illustrations than any other dictionary, included both line drawings and halftones. Although some of the halftones were of poor quality—always a problem in large printings with relatively inexpensive paper—the overall effect was successful, albeit more from a marketing point of view than a lexicographic one. But it has not so far reversed the trend toward line drawings. From a purely lexicographic point of view, line drawings are more useful; yet certainly halftones lend variety and interest to the appearance of the page, and I would like to see them used more often than they are in certain instances. For example, if one is going to include biographical entries, it is apposite and rather charming to include a photograph of the biographee, as *AHD* often does. Here is a case, after all, where the denotatum *is* the designatum—no ambiguity whatsoever.

Children's dictionaries include many more pictures in comparison to number of entries than do adult dictionaries. Very often an adult seeks a definition merely to confirm what he thinks a word means; this is less often true of a child, who may have no notion of the word's meaning. For example, an adult may know that a dormer is a kind of window in a house, though he may be unsure just what *dormer* means. A definition that reads "a small, roofed structure extending out from a sloping roof and containing an upright window" may therefore evoke in his mind a picture of what he has previously seen but may evoke nothing at all in the mind of a child who has no preexisting visual idea of such a structure.[49] But if a picture is included, the child may then recognize a dormer as something he has seen, or at least be able to identify one in the future. The space limitations of an adult dictionary, with its larger entry count, preclude a copious use of pictures.

The abundant use of illustrations in children's dictionaries also lends a more attractive, varied look to the page. In some dictionaries a second or third (nonblack) color is used to highlight the aspect of the picture relating specifically to the term and to add a decorative element. The strongly competitive market for children's dictionaries demands that each dictionary have comparable features, i.e., a great many pictures. Fair enough. But when the second color is used purely for decorative purposes, it is more of a distraction than a help. For example, one children's dictionary uses a second color as background in every illustration. Printing the key words at the top of the page in the nonblack color is poor graphics as well as poor dictionary practice, since black print is more outstanding than red or any other color; yet a number of dictionaries use the second color for this purpose.

ESL dictionaries can also profit from pictorial illustrations but, unfortunately, pictures must compete for space with other more essential elements, such as grammatical and usage information and collocational aids. Because ESL dictionaries are often used in formal instruction, they must be of portable size. Therefore, although pictures are desirable and some are usually included, there is not much space for them. Within these limitations, *Hornby* is particularly helpful, combining the use of line drawings with quite a few halftones. However, I doubt that its small photo illustrating "American football" would be any more meaningful to a European or Asian than a rugby scrum would be to an American. Such words cannot be effectively illustrated. The key to good illustration is selection, a process discussed in Chapter 6.

Pictorial dictionaries such as *The English Duden* (see page 33) used for bilingual translation make excellent use of illustrations. For the most part, only line drawings are used. It is amazing how much information is packed into each page of the Duden picture dictionaries through the grouping of drawings and the detailed labeling of each illustration. Since a large percentage of Duden illustrations are of mechanical parts or types of things or creatures (from musical instruments to butterflies), Dudens are to a considerable extent bilingual technical dictionaries.

Technical and scientific dictionaries can and often do use pictorial illustrations, as well as charts and tables, to supplement their text. To what extent the pictures are useful is a matter of debate. The difficulty is that technical dictionaries are often intended to serve users on a variety of levels, from student to advanced research scientist. Whereas the student may find illustrations helpful, the more advanced user may regard them as intrusive or oversimple and wish that the space had been used for additional entries. Generally speaking, dictionaries intended for a broad market, such as one-volume medical or biological dictionaries, are helped by illustration. Charts and tables are obviously useful in such works, although as a rule they should not be used to omit entries but rather as a convenient reorganization of included terms. Chemical elements may be included in a table for purposes of comparison, but they should also be included as alphabetic entries. How-ever, in some cases the table can substitute for certain terms. For example, a table of poisonous snakes may make unnecessary the inclusion of each poisonous species so long as the genera are entered with cross-references to the table.

The illustrated Larousse dictionaries combine in one volume an encyclo-pedia and a dictionary, and depend for their appeal largely on colorful and attractive design. They include full-color illustrations, both halftones and drawings, often of large size, so that each page is an interesting layout in itself. The page design resembles that of a magazine rather than a book. In the case of the English Larousse, when so much space is taken up with illus-tration, the text must be reciprocally diminished, and when a small encyclo-pedia is tossed in as well, the dictionary is properly viewed as the space between the illustrations.[50]

Just how important are illustrations in a dictionary? The answer depends on the intended audience. The more elementary or pedagogical the work is, the more useful are illustrations. Scholarly or historical dictionaries have no need of illustrations. Bilingual dictionaries seldom include them, because illustrations of words in the source language are a monolingual function. Illustrations of some words in the target language—which is in effect what the Duden picture dictionaries do—would be helpful, though to my knowledge it is not done, undoubtedly because editors would rather use the space to add entries or expand translational equivalents.

Other graphic elements, such as type size and page layout—at least as important as illustrations—will be discussed in Chapter 6.

Front and Back Matter

Up till now we have been discussing only the A–Z section of dictionaries and ignoring the introductory material and appendixes, called in the book trade *front* and *back matter,* respectively. These sections vary greatly in importance depending on the nature of the dictionary. In adult monolingual dictionaries, a guide to the use of the dictionary is now considered essential, yet it is astonishing how little help was given the reader in early dictionaries. By the time of Johnson, however, it was traditional to include an essay on English grammar and a history of the English language in a dictionary's front matter. History of the language is still a fixture of desk dictionaries, but grammar is less often discussed. More attention is given to pronuncia-tion, usage, and regional varieties of English. Other front-matter articles deal with etymology, the influence of linguistics on lexicography, computer analysis of language, punctuation, Americanisms, Canadian English, and so on. None of these is necessary; convention dictates their inclusion.

Front-matter articles are seldom read by dictionary users but are almost always regarded as important by reviewers. In reviewing a dictionary of sixteen hundred double-column pages, the critic seizes on the most conspicuous elements to read. It takes less time and effort to comment on the front matter and look up one or two favorite neologisms than to make an informed estimate of the value of an entire dictionary. Many a dictionary that has been prepared by dozens of people and that consists of 1 to 3 million words written and revised repeatedly over a period of five to ten years has been judged on the merit of one or two short essays composed in a few days' time by consultants whose contributions to the dictionary did not extend beyond their own essays. One cannot fault critics for reviewing a dictionary's front matter: anything in the book is fair game. Yet compared to the overall effort of producing a dictionary, front-matter articles are of negligible importance. The attention given them by reviewers, however, makes them of considerable commercial importance. Thus, front-matter articles are often written by prominent scholars or educators in an attempt to establish the authority of the work and lend it prestige. In some cases these scholars have been associated intimately with the work, as, for example, Kemp Malone was with the *American College Dictionary;* but as a rule the association is more distant, sometimes little more than window dressing.

Ironically, the guide to the use of the dictionary, which is the only part of the front matter of demonstrable practical importance and the only one that most readers ever use, is almost always ignored by reviewers. In order to detect omissions or ambiguities in the guide, the reviewers would have to have spent some time studying the dictionary's content and style, and this they are disinclined to do. Most guides describe every part of the dictionary article: entry word, syllabication, pronunciation, inflected forms, various kinds of labels, cross-references, variants, etymologies, synonyms, and usage notes. The purpose of the guide is to describe as clearly as possible all the kinds of information included in the dictionary, show the reader how to interpret the data given (i.e., how to read the dictionary's "style"), and provide clues for locating as quickly as possible particular items of information. To put the matter simply, the guide answers the questions, What's in it?, What does it mean?, and How do I find it? Often a sample page from the A–Z section is reprinted with various parts of the entries bracketed and linked to captions that identify each part and refer to sections of the guide where the items are discussed. This is an excellent use of graphics to provide the reader with a simple and clear index to the guide.

The back matter of general adult dictionaries may include sections listing biographical and geographical names—if they are not included in the

A–Z section—and a miscellany of practical guides to writing, covering punctuation, grammar, style, forms of address, and proofreaders' marks. Tables of weights and measures, signs and symbols, lists of abbreviations, foreign words and phrases, given names, and, in college dictionaries, naturally, lists of colleges and universities, are often included. There is no more reason why a dictionary should inform a reader that Allegheny College of Meadville, Pennsylvania, was founded in 1815 than that it should quote the price of gold in 1934 or list the twelve longest-running musical comedies on Broadway. But so it is, with no offense meant to Allegheny College.

In the children's dictionary, and even more so in the ESL dictionary, front matter is much more important. For the child, the guide to the use of the dictionary must not assume any prior familiarity with dictionary use. A children's dictionary guide is really not just to one particular dictionary but a guide to dictionary use. It must therefore be more detailed, yet written in much simpler language than that of an adult dictionary. The task is by no means easy and should be undertaken only by a highly skilled writer familiar both with dictionaries and with school curricula used in teaching dictionary skills.

A children's dictionary guide begins at the beginning, with the alphabet, and instructs the reader how to look up a word and how to use the guide words at the top of the pages. It then more or less covers the same ground that adult dictionaries do, but with numerous examples taken from the A–Z section and sometimes with questions for the reader. Teachers' manuals may be useful in helping the teacher use the front matter for classroom instruction. The front-matter guide, like the rest of the book, is usually printed in large, attractive type, often with a second color to highlight features and to invite attentive reading. Information about the history of the language, etymology, or usage, if included at all, is generally incorporated in the guide, which may run to fifty pages or more.

For the ESL dictionary user, the front-matter guide is integral to the understanding and use of the A–Z material. *Hornby* devotes forty pages to a guide that includes sections on pronunciation, grammar, and style, and a very detailed treatment of verb patterns keyed to verb entries in the body of the book. *Longman* devotes a considerable part of its guide to grammar, in which the ordinary positions of particular words are identified by alphanumeric codes keyed to words in the A–Z section. This device is designed to help the reader place each word in its proper grammatical or syntactic frame.

The back matter of ESL dictionaries contains various linguistic aids specifically for the foreign learner: lists of irregular words, spelling guides, tables of ordinal and cardinal numbers. ESL dictionaries also contain such old standbys as tables of weights and measures and punctuation guides.

117

Much more attention is given to pronunciation, however, than in monolingual dictionaries. I find *Longman*'s "Table of Family Relationships" particularly useful and wish monolingual dictionaries included such a table. It consists of a genealogical diagram of a large, fictitious family with notations explaining the words denoting their relationships, such as "VIOLET is the **grand-niece** of Mervyn (the brother of a grandparent) and of Jessica (the sister of another grandparent). Mervyn is VIOLET's **great-uncle**, and Jessica is VIOLET's **great-aunt**." I can vouch for the fact that it is not only foreign learners who get muddled over such relationships. *Longman,* which has a controlled vocabulary for its definitions, also lists in its back matter the two thousand words that comprise this vocabulary.

Technical and scientific dictionaries usually do not provide full guides to their use. They generally give scant attention to pronunciation even if it is routinely included within the body of the book. Transcriptions of pronunciation may be necessary for competitive reasons but seem to be considered of slight interest to users of technical books. Etymology, on the other hand, at least in medical dictionaries, is given considerable attention in front-matter guides. Curiosity about etymology is widely held to be a sign of keen intelligence. It suggests interest in, if not familiarity with, study of the classical languages, and Latin and Greek strike awe in the hearts of most people. Thus, by giving considerable attention to etymology, the compilers identify their dictionary with the prestige of the classical tradition and with a species of scholarship regarded reverentially by many potential customers.

Technical dictionaries that include subentries usually give the reader some guidance on how entries and subentries are alphabetized, but often it is inadequate and does not account for many exceptions. For example, one medical dictionary sometimes includes subentries with inverted elements, such as *intestinal portal, posterior,* but one looks in vain for any indication of such a practice in the front-matter guide. Yet this system obviously affects alphabetization and can result in the reader's failure to find the term he seeks. Worse yet, it is inconsistently applied, or seems to be, so that the reader is left guessing why some terms are inverted and others not. If the style is really inconsistent, the editors were at least wise not to try to explain it. But a failure of style that contributes to the reader's confusion, as this does, is more serious than an inadequate front-matter guide. (Dictionary style is discussed in Chapter 6.)

Some dictionaries, often called encyclopedic dictionaries, go much further afield than the ones discussed so far. They may include a glossary of mythology, a manual of usage, a selection of quotations, a chronology of World War II battles, or whatever strikes the editor's fancy as a feature that will attract interest and invite purchase. The tradition of including encyclopedic material in dictionaries is as old as lexicography and was one of the practices denounced by Dean Trench in his celebrated paper of 1857. Although separate encyclopedic sections have nothing to do with the dictionary proper, there are no compelling logical reasons for condemning them. Their chief effect on the dictionary is to make it heavier to carry and more expensive to buy. Those who find their dictionaries heavy enough as they are will not rejoice to find biographies of every U.S. president and vice-president contributing to their bursitis.

There is, to be sure, a touch of fraud in many such encyclopedic dictionaries because they usually promise more than they deliver. By attempting to give the reader a bit of everything, they do nothing well, and they encourage the misconception that theirs is a better dictionary because it includes all sorts of aimless irrelevancies. But we must be mindful that we are talking about degrees of irrelevancy, since even the most respectable of commercial dictionaries boasts of certain encyclopedic features. *MW9* proudly displays an index of charts and tables and other marginalia, a device used thirty years earlier by the *ACD*. The *AHD* touts its illustrations, most of which have nothing to do with lexical meaning.

Yet there is a difference between these dictionaries and encyclopedic dictionaries, which are generally sold at substantially higher prices by direct mail (i.e., directly to the consumer via promotional mailings) rather than through bookstores. Encyclopedic dictionaries appeal to a different and on the whole less sophisticated market than the bookstore or college customer, and direct-mail promoters have to have material for a sales pitch for the large flyers sent out by the hundreds of thousands to potential buyers. They want features to itemize, especially those that seem to distinguish their dictionary from all others ever made. No subtleties or qualifications of any kind are allowed to dilute the impact of blunt assertion. The idea that a statement in a mailing piece could be true or false would strike most mass-market, direct-mail promoters as the purest whimsy. They would, like Saint-Exupéry's businessman counting the stars, urge one to be serious.

CHAPTER FOUR

Definition

What do we mean when we say we have defined something? The question, an ancient one, has been addressed by Plato and Aristotle as well as by modern philosophers, especially logicians and semanticists.[1] Although the distinction is not always made, and when made not always observed, logical definition is not the same as lexical definition. Logical definition—Richard Robinson calls it real definition, because it attempts to analyze things in the real world, as distinguished from words—has been the chief preoccupation of philosophers. When Socrates explores the meaning of virtue or truth, he is not seeking to define the words *virtue* or *truth* but the concepts that underlie them and the way people interpret these concepts. Philosophers have also concerned themselves with lexical (or nominal) definition, the definition of words, the subject of this chapter.

The traditional rules of lexical definition, based on Aristotle's analysis, demand that the word defined (called in Latin the *definiendum*) be identified by *genus* and *differentia*. That is, the word must first be defined according to the class of things to which it belongs, and then distinguished from all other things within that class. Thus, *bachelor* is a man (genus) who is unmarried (differentia). Many dictionary entries are not defined this way, however, and even those that are do not exlude all other things within the class. For example, the definition of *bachelor* does not distinguish it from *widower,* also an unmarried man but one who was formerly married and has outlived his wife.

Among other rules sometimes promulgated for definition are that a definition be equivalent to or capture the essence of the thing defined, that the

120

definiendum not be included in any form among the words (called the *definiens*) used to define it, and that the definition be positive rather than negative. Philosophers are not ignorant of the nature of linguistics or dictionary making, but it is remarkable how little attention they pay to the users of dictionaries. By contrast, lexicographers—all of them—pay a great deal of attention to the needs of their readers. For lexicography is a craft, a way of doing something useful. It is not a theoretical exercise to increase the sum of human knowledge but practical work to put together a book that people can understand. The editor of *A Dictionary of the Older Scottish Tongue*—hardly a commercial enterprise—describes his readers, with only very pale irony, as "customers" and identifies them as "philologists, textual editors, literary historians, and general historians and antiquarians."[2] Every lexicographer, like any good author, has his readers very much in mind. Whereas philosophers are concerned with the internal coherence of their system of definition, lexicographers are concerned with explaining something their readers will understand. The methods each uses to achieve his goals only incidentally coincide.

Philosophic descriptions of definition often proffer as a principle what is clearly desirable but what may not be possible or practicable. The space allotted to each definition must be severely limited, else the total number of terms must be reduced. To one who has not struggled to cut two or three words from a carefully crafted definition in order to save a line, it is difficult to convey the intensity of the effort or the misgivings experienced at having to weaken a definition one had worked hard to perfect. But if one considers that in college dictionaries the average number of column-lines allotted to each entry (not each definition) is a bit less than two, one will see why space is at a premium.

To find the average number of column-lines per entry in a dictionary, simply count the lines in a column, multiply by the number of columns on each page, and then multiply that number by the total number of pages in the A–Z section, including any geographical and biographical sections. Then divide by the total number of entries claimed for that dictionary. The result may be slightly over two, but bear in mind that considerable space is devoted to the repetitive pronunciation key, illustrations and tables, and the spaces between the end of each letter of the alphabet and the beginning of the next. By "entries" I do not mean headwords only, but all entries. (See page 84 for a description of entry counting.)

No dictionary is spared the necessity to save space, but scientific and technical dictionaries generally have more flexibility both in the number of entries they must include and in the number of pages to which they can expand. General commercial dictionaries (both monolingual and bilingual) are under severe restraints, regardless of the intended size. An unabridged dictionary indeed has much more space than a college dictionary, but apart from having many more entries it must also give many more illustrative quotations, fuller etymologies and pronunciations, and a more discriminating breakdown of sense, involving a finer delineation of subdivision of meaning within each definition. The task is not rendered easier but more complicated by such treatment, and the need for brevity is no less exigent. The process of determining the size of one's dictionary will be discussed in Chapter 6, but it must be said here that practical considerations do not admit of much adjustment to the projected size of a commercial dictionary once the project is under way. One cannot just add another 128 pages because one needs the additional space—the extra 128 pages of text must be cut to fit the space available. It is precisely to avoid such a disaster that dictionaries should be carefully planned in advance and closely monitored while in progress.

Kinds of Meaning

Before we describe the actual process of dictionary defining, it may be well to examine various kinds of meaning. C. K. Ogden and I. A. Richards pictured the process by which a thing (or referent) is identified as a symbol by drawing a triangle, with Symbol and Referent at each of the base angles, connected by a dotted line, and Thought or Reference at the apex.[3] The idea is that somebody sees a mouse scurrying across the floor and thinks Mouse, which is translated into the word/symbol *mouse*. The dotted line signifies that the animal scurrying across the floor and the word/symbol *mouse* have no direct connection.

Ladislav Zgusta depicts a similar triangle based on the Ogden and Richards model, but his analysis, coming almost fifty years later, is naturally more sophisticated. He calls the mouse/referent the *denotatum* and our perception of the properties of mouse or the class of things to which mice belong (mousedom?) the *designatum* (now and then he slips into English and calls it the designation). Thus his triangle consists of *expression* (form of the word) and *denotatum* at the corners of the base of the triangle connected by a dotted line, and *designatum* at the apex. The word, or *lexical unit* (which may consist of more than one word), "is used to express its designatum and together with it denote the respective denotatum."[4]

Connotation is said by Zgusta to consist of all aspects of lexical meaning that have "contrastive value" with the designation. The designation enables us to say what a thing such as a mouse is, to recognize it when we see it, and to attach a name to it. Although not identical with the lexical definition, it is the chief basis for the definition. Connotation may suggest a degree of formality or informality, or variety of usage, or what the British call register, signifying an adjustment in style or variety of language used for different social situations. The third component of meaning is range of application: how broadly can the lexical unit be applied? *Salary* has a broader application than *stipend* or *honorarium*. Some words, such as *shuck* (corn), have a very limited range of application in modern use.

Zgusta's use of connotation is highly unusual. First of all, it must be distinguished from the logician's use. Richard Robinson, for example, uses *connotation* to mean what Zgusta means by designation. In Zgusta's terms, connotation refers to the difference between "to die" and "to peg out."[5] The antiquity of the latter phrase, evoking the musty smell of discarded bilingual dictionaries, compels me to reject it in favor of *to kick the bucket,* which is comparable in tone and at least distantly recognizable. Zgusta says that *to die* has no connotation, but that an expression like *kick the bucket* does. The real distinction between these two terms is that of variety of usage and range of application.

Zgusta wants to account for those properties of language that are reported by dictionaries but that are not part of their essential meaning. What kind of knowledge are we conveying when we call a word slang or vulgar? Zgusta calls this kind of knowledge connotation. In its more traditional sense, however, connotation refers to the whole store of associated attributes of a word, derived from centuries of use. Far from having no connotation, *die* in the common sense is much richer in connotation than *kick the bucket. Die* suggests grief, pain, suffering, absence, sorrow, and loss. *Kick the bucket* conveys a tone of callous vulgarity, which is what Zgusta means by connotation, but it has no associated affective impact, the traditional meaning of connotation. Dictionaries deal only with certain kinds of meaning and ignore other kinds no less important, and we must not suppose that associated meanings cease to exist because dictionaries fail to note them.[6] Zgusta's use of connotation is so narrowly confined to dictionary practice that in the broader context of meaning it is unappealingly trivial.

Moreover, even if we accept Zgusta's definition of connotation, it is difficult to justify the notion that *die* or any other general word (excluding scientific terms) is always without connotation. To many people it is customary to use euphemisms when consoling someone on a death in the family; the use of *die* or *death* in the linguistic context of a note of consolation might be considered as harsh and vulgar as *kick the bucket* is in other circumstances. All that one can say is that connotation in Zgusta's sense depends upon how the word fits the social context in which it is used, and since *die* fits more contexts than *kick the bucket,* it is more apt to be without connotation.

The Principles of Defining

Zgusta enumerates the following principles of defining:

1. All words within a definition must be explained.
2. The lexical definition should not contain words "more difficult to understand" than the word defined.
3. The defined word may not be used in its definition, nor may derivations or combinations of the defined word unless they are separately defined. But one part of speech may be used to define another, as "to use a crib" if the noun sense of *crib* (in the sense of a secreted copy of notes, etc.) has been defined.
4. The definition must correspond to the part of speech of the word defined.[7]

These are sensible guidelines, but I would like to distinguish between essential principles and good lexicographic practice. Occasionally the criteria of good practice must be compromised, either to save space or for some other compelling reason. But a few basic principles must never be violated, else they defeat the whole purpose of the dictionary. I list these principles in order of importance.

Avoid circularity.   Since the primary purpose of a dictionary is to inform the reader what words mean, anything that absolutely denies the reader the opportunity to find out the meaning of a word he has looked up is the most serious defect a dictionary can have. Mind you, circularity does not just make things difficult—it makes them impossible. No amount of diligence on the part of the reader can penetrate the barrier of circularity.

There are two forms of circularity. One defines **A** in terms of **B** and **B** in terms of **A,** and the other defines **A** in terms of **A.** The first kind is illustrated by these definitions.

	LEXICAL UNIT	DEFINITIONS
A	beauty	the state of being beautiful
B	beautiful	full of beauty
A	bobcat	lynx
B	lynx	bobcat

The second kind of circularity is illustrated by this definition:

LEXICAL UNIT	DEFINITION
fear	the state of fear, one of the basic drives of human beings, the others being . . .

Or, more commonly by

LEXICAL UNIT	DEFINITION
fear	the state of being fearful

when *fearful* is nowhere defined in the dictionary and is perhaps run on as a derivative to the article for *fear*!

The rule may be stated thus: *No word can be defined by itself, and no word can be defined from its own family of words unless the related word is separately defined independently of it.* Therefore, if *fearful* were defined separately without reference to *fear,* the definition quoted above would not be circular, although it would be bad lexicographic practice to define *fear* in terms of *fearful.* In other words, no word can be defined by a word whose own definition depends upon the word it is defining. I do not say that **A**'s definition may not include **B**, and that **B**'s definition may not include **A**. Such a relationship is circular only if the meaning of **A** *depends* upon **B** and vice versa. For example, these two definitions from *The Doubleday Dictionary* are perfectly proper:

	LEXICAL UNIT	DEFINITION
A	lynx	any of several wildcats of Europe and North America, with a short tail, tufted ears, and long limbs; a bobcat
B	bobcat	the American lynx

There is no circularity, because the meaning of *lynx* does not depend on the inclusion of *bobcat* in its definition.

The avoidance of circularity is so elementary that one can be sure its occurrence in any professional dictionary is a simple blunder and not a case of ignorance. No such assurance is possible in many amateurish, special-subject dictionaries or in newspaper glossaries of fad words, where circularity is commonplace. Even in competent hands, however, circularity can creep in when a word's definition is changed and one fails to make sure that the new definition does not introduce circularity.

Dictionaries are often unfairly charged with circularity when their definitions are not circular. As I have pointed out, definitions may include a form of the word being defined, provided the word in the definition is elsewhere defined. The editor of *Webster's Third New International Dictionary*

(NID3), Philip Babcock Gove, has made the point that such treatment must be adopted by dictionaries to enable them to include many more words than they would otherwise have space for.[8] It is not only acceptable but imperative that dictionaries define one part of speech in terms of another. For example, the noun *dream* may be fully defined and the verb may be defined as "to have dreams." There would be no point in repeating the entire noun definition of *dream* in it verbal sense. The reader has only to let his eye pass to the adjacent entry to discover the sense in which *dream* is used. In many entries, as for *bicycle,* where the noun definition may require several lines of description, no purpose would be served by repeating it in the verbal definition, which is best given as "to ride a bicycle." This is an excellent example where the device of defining one part of speech in terms of another is the only sensible policy.

Gove's policy, however, extends well beyond such cases. *Tubbable,* he says, should be defined as "suitable for tubbing," not "suitable for washing." He calls the latter "ostrich-defining." "One function of a dictionary," Gove maintains, "is to rigorously avoid such broadening."[9] This is news to me. I did not think it was the function of a dictionary to rigorously avoid anything that might help the reader grasp meaning better. Gove also argues that the only acceptable definition for *bothersome* is "causing bother"—if the dictionary defines *bother* a few lines away—not "causing trouble or annoyance," since the latter "sweeps up and includes all meanings of trouble and annoyance and adds them to those of bother." But in the next breath, Gove defends the definition for *prank* in *Webster's Seventh New Collegiate Dictionary (MW7)* by the single word "trick." This presents no problem for him, because the "base noun [of *prank*] can be considered synonymous with trick." He is not concerned about *trick* sweeping up and adding all of its meanings to those of *prank* and *prankish* and *prankster* and so on, but he is concerned about *trouble* and *annoyance* adding their meanings to *bother.* I begin to feel like Alice in Wonderland.

Even if Gove were not inconsistent, he would be wrong in demanding that in all cases *bothersome* and like words are best defined by their base nouns. If a reader does not know what *bothersome* means, he is unlikely to know what *bother* means either, and sometimes the grammatically more basic term is less common than the derivative form. Why should the reader be forced to read the entry for a different word (i.e., *bother*) with a different grammatical function, and then have to transfer the sense of that word, if he can, to that of the adjective he wanted in the first place? Even if the entries are a few lines apart, will he really return to *bothersome* and substitute the definition for *bother* in place after "causing"? Or will he just read the definition of *bother* and figure the adjective has something to do with it? More often the latter, I think. If that is so, is not the reader better served by finding at the point of first reference a meaning he can at once understand, such as "causing trouble or annoyance"? *NID3* defines *bothersome*—properly, I believe—as "causing trouble or annoyance," the definition to which Gove would object in a smaller dictionary where *bother* might be a few lines away. By comparison, *MW8,* edited by Gove's successor, Bosley Woolf, defines *bothersome* as "causing bother; vexing." Every dictionary definition is essentially a paraphrase. Why take exception to it in some cases and not in others? Both *MW8* and *MW9* define the noun *bother* as "a state of petty discomfort, annoyance, or worry." Why would it be "ostrich-defining" to define *bothersome* in terms of trouble and annoyance but acceptable to define *bother* in terms of discomfort, annoyance, and worry? Since *bother* is so defined, doesn't the definition for *bothersome,* "causing bother," translate into "causing discomfort, annoyance, or worry"? Which is not so vastly different from "causing trouble or annoyance." Have I nibbled a magic mushroom, or have the editors of Merriam-Webster? To my mind, this is a case (and not the only one) in which *NID3* and its collegiate dictionaries have sacrificed intelligibility to a purity of style bordering on lunacy.

It is one thing to say that one part of speech *may* be defined in terms of another, or even that in many circumstances this is a convenience that does not interfere with the reader's understanding. It is quite another to announce that it is a cardinal principle of good defining. Gove's other examples hardly support his own position. "The basic definition of *occupancy,*" he says, "should be 'the act of occupying.' If it reads instead 'the act of taking or holding possession,' then it will not fit a common usage, as in 'Occupancy by more than 112 persons is unlawful'."[10] True, but *occupancy* cannot be defined by every sense of *occupy.* The very first sense listed in *NID3* is "to engage the attention or energies of." The unsuspecting reader may thus form the sentence, "My occupancy with the TV movie prevented me from hearing the telephone," which will draw blank stares from any native speaker.[11] If the dictionary does not specify which senses of *occupy* apply to *occupancy,* how is the reader to know? One would have to say, "the act of occupying (defs. 2, 3, 5, & 7)," which places a tremendous burden on the user. The definition Gove rejects as unsuitable—"the act of taking or holding possession"—is demonstrably better than the one he endorses, for it at least directs attention to the most common use of occupancy. Some college dictionaries, mindful that there are other meanings of *occupancy* which, though less common, nonetheless should be recorded, add a second definition, "the act of occupying," as a catchall for the miscellany of other senses not specifically defined. This is admittedly a lame tactic, but it is sometimes necessary to save the space that would otherwise be required to define each seldom-used meaning, a policy that no dictionary could afford to adopt.

Gove cites several other noncircular uses of a word used in its own definition. An intransitive use of a verb may be defined in terms of the transitive form, a practice he calls truncated definition. For example, once *impregnate* is defined transitively, the intransitive use may be defined as "to become impregnated." This kind of use is commmplace in all sizes of dictionaries and is essential to conserve space. Once again, however, Gove's advice misses the mark:

> A working rule for the use of the truncated definition is that (*a*) definition should move in the direction of the etymon or the base word rather than away . . . and (*b*) the dictionary user should not be put through more than one rerouting within the family before he arrives at the primary definition.[12]

About (*a*), yes, by all means, *fearful* should be defined in terms of *fear*, not the other way around; but the insistence on defining in terms of older forms rather than more commonly used ones may pose problems for the reader for the sake of a contrived linguistic purity. Gove acknowledges that "exceptions will have to occur, but rarely, as in defining *difficulty* and *pedlar* in terms of the back formations *difficult* and *peddle*." (Back formation refers to the unusual process of forming a new, presumably more basic word from a word that would ordinarily appear to have been derived from *it;* thus, *difficult* was formed from *difficulty*.) What is the virtue of "moving in the direction of the etymon" if it is more puzzling to the reader than moving against the direction of the etymon?

About (*b*), agreed, the user should not be put through more than one rerouting, but unfortunately sometimes he is. Gove cites with approval the definition of *symbolist* as "one who employs symbols or symbolism." If the reader looks up *symbolism,* he will find it defined in terms of *symbol* and thus be rerouted a second time. Though regrettable, the practice is sometimes unavoidable; otherwise the long and complicated definitions of *symbol* would have to be repeated at *symbolism,* a practice no dictionary could countenance.

Gove next discusses modified truncated definitions, in which the base word is qualified by additional definitions that may or may not include the base word. *Builder* is defined as "one who builds or oversees building operations: one whose occupation is to build . . . one who creates something . . ." He says this form is justified when the meaning of the family word includes but "extends beyond the meaning of the base word." In my view the real case is exactly the opposite: the form is used to narrow the range of application of the family word *(build)*. It is a way of saying, "although *builder* can mean 'one who builds' in a great variety of senses of *build*—as a child who is a *builder* with building blocks, or a *builder* of dreams—in most contexts it is used in these senses." The meaning is not extended but restricted. Secondly, Gove adds that "when references back to the base word may involve the dictionary user in an excessively complex analysis"—compare "the act of occupying (defs. 2, 3, 5, & 7)"—"a summary particularization, or a specification, is in the interests of simplicity and clarity." He cites a definition of *beautiful* which, after referring to *beauty,* adds, "exciting aesthetic pleasure: delightful to the sense: strikingly fit or appropriate or especially pleasing." I agree absolutely with Gove's advice in this instance but wonder how it differs from that of *occupancy,* which he insisted upon defining as "the act of occupying." Once again, Gove's stylistic purity leads to hair splitting if not contradictions.

Define every word used in a definition. When using a monolingual, general dictionary, a reader has a right to expect that if he does not know the meaning of a word used in a definition, he can look that word up and find it defined. The Word Not In (WNI, for short) rule is broken more often than the circularity rule, because it is difficult to check the use of every word used in every definition. Computerized files can certainly help to solve this problem, but Words Not In still occur occasionally in most dictionaries.

Two-way bilingual dictionaries generally make an effort to include every target-language word of the first section as a source-language word in the second part, although it is not always possible to do so and is less important than in monolingual dictionaries. Culture-specific words such as *home run* or *grass roots* cannot be directly translated but must be paraphrased. Idiomatic phrases often have no counterpart in another language. Frequently, two different editorial groups prepare the two halves of a bidirectional work, thus rendering concordance of vocabularies that much more difficult. It remains nonetheless a desirable feature, however imperfectly achieved.

Although the circularity rule applies to all monolingual dictionaries, the Word Not In rule applies only with qualification to scientific and technical dictionaries. Since the vocabulary is restricted to a particular subject, only those words pertaining to the subject must be included as entries and defined. General terms used in definitions are excluded from the rule.

Because of the great many variants in some sciences, notably in medicine, it is extremely difficult to ascertain that every scientific term used in a definition is entered in exactly that form. For example, *hyperosmolar hyperglycemic nonketonic coma* may be used in a definition but be entered under *hyperglycemic nonketonic coma* or under some other slight variation. Technically, this is an instance of WNI, but it is not very serious since the reader should be able to locate the relevant term as a subentry under *coma* without much difficulty. More serious is the case where an altogether different variant is used in a definition. The variant is entered, but when the reader looks it up he finds a cross-reference to another term to which he must turn to find a definition. This is bad lexicographic practice but not a violation of the Word Not In rule.

Unfortunately, without a computer check of every word, it is impossible to be sure that every word used in each definition is the preferred form. Frequent checks may be made, to be sure, but the enormous amount of time required to systematically check every word in the dictionary is beyond the endurance of any staff and the patience of any publisher. One must remember, too, that because the entry list in any dictionary in preparation is continually changing, a definitive check for Words Not In cannot really be made until the project has been completed. The time pressures of all commercial dictionary projects preclude such a check's being made at that point, because it would inevitably turn up the need to add or alter many terms, and these would in turn require many other changes. The expense and delay of such far-reaching, last-minute changes could not be tolerated. Therefore, checks for Words Not In must be made while the work is in progress.

Dictionary editors must be vigilant in checking to see how the changes they make affect other definitions. In the early stages of a dictionary, changes can be made with relative impunity; in the latter stages one learns to be reluctant to make any change that alters the status of a word, since the amount of checking this requires may be so onerous that it far exceeds any benefit accruing from the change. One might suppose that computerization has made it possible to carry out major changes at any stage of a dictionary project, but so far this is not the case. No one has yet been able to foresee with sufficient clarity all or even most of the kinds of specific problems that have to be dealt with at every stage of lexicographic work. (See Chapter 7 for a fuller discussion of computer use in lexicography.)

In some smaller dictionaries the Word Not In rule must be deliberately breached. They may have to use some specified derivative words, formed with common suffixes or prefixes, such as *treelike* or *eyeless,* that are not entered. However, *tree, -like, eye,* and *-less* are entered, so presumably any reader could surmise the meanings of the words by consulting their elements. This device, like so many in dictionary practice, is not one lexicographers cherish but one they are compelled to adopt to save space. It is tolerable so long as the particular forms considered acceptable in definitions are clearly specified and the practice is rigidly confined to these forms. For example, the style manual for a children's dictionary of which I was the editor specified that

> The words formed with the following affixes and combining forms may be used in definitions even if they are not entered:
>
> | -ish | as in | greenish, yellowish |
> |------|-------|---------------------|
> | -less | | footless, eyeless |
> | -like | | treelike, shiplike, shell-like |
> | -ly | | chemically, experimentally |
> | -ness | | greenness, cheapness |
> | non- | | nonreligious, nonsocial (sense of "not") |
> | -shaped | | leaf-shaped, balloon-shaped |
> | un- | | unsympathetic, untired (sense of "not") |
>
> Needless to say, all of the affixes and combining forms listed above must themselves be entered and fully defined.

This list was not assembled at the start of the project but only when it was under way, and then it began with three or four forms. Each additional form was added grudgingly when it was clear that it could not reasonably be avoided.

Define the entry word. The definition must define and not just talk about the word or its usage. It must answer the question, What is it?, directly and immediately. There are many other characteristics of a good definition, and different kinds of words must be defined differently, but if a definition fails in its basic purpose of giving the reader enough immediate information to enable him to surmise, at least approximately, its meaning in context, it is of no value whatsoever. Beginning definers tend to say too much and yet often fail to say what is essential. For example, a specialist may define *diagnosis* as follows: "The physician takes the history of the patient, evaluates subjective symptoms, and conducts his own examination to determine objective findings before making the diagnosis."

We see at once that the definition violates the rule of circularity by including the word being defined, but even more important in this case is that the reader is never told what *diagnosis* is. The writer tells him what the physician does but does not say that diagnosis is a judgment about the nature of a disease.

The commonest cause of this error is a confusion between the concept and the word. Specialists sometimes feel that the concept underlying a word is more important than the word itself and merely use the word as a pretext for describing actions or procedures associated with it. It is a natural error for them to make, since they have spent their lives taking these actions and

131

usually only a very short time writing about them. But they must be made to understand that dictionaries are about words, not essentially about the things described by them, and that in dictionaries words are indeed important. Specialists can be given numerous tips on how to define; yet unless they grasp that fundamental point and learn to abide by it, their definitions will never be any good, no matter how carefully they observe the tricks of the trade.

To recapitulate, there are three basic principles of defining: avoid circulatory, define every word in a definition, and make sure that every word's definition says what the word means. Observing these basic rules does not assure one of producing good definitions. Some of the practices described next are almost as important as these three principles; they differ chiefly in that they are matters of craft rather than principle. If one knows the right method, one is not likely to violate the principles even if one is unaware of them. But it is well to be aware of them.

Good Defining Practice

Priority of Essence

The most essential elements of meaning come first, the more incidental elements later. Do not begin a definition with "a term meaning" or "a term referring to" or the like: begin with the definition itself. The definer must put himself in the place of someone who hasn't the vaguest idea what the word means and try to anticipate the kinds of wrong assumptions such a person might make about each draft to his definition, until he has written a definition that cannot be misunderstood.

Substitutability

For many words, the definition should be substitutable for the word in context. Substitutability is often declared to be a principle of defining, but there are so many cases where it is impossible to apply that it is idle to insist that it be universal. As one lexicographer observes, the substitution rule cannot be applied to words like *be, damn, in, it, yes, ought, the, to, tut tut, what?.* and *yes.*[13] More significantly, many thousands of popular meanings of scientific terms, if they appear at all, are not defined in a substitutable way. For example, one looks in vain for a definition of *rose* to fit the context "How sweet of you to give me a rose!" One does not mean "How sweet of you to give me any of a genus (*Rosa* of the family Rosaceae, the rose family) of usu. prickly shrubs with pinnate leaves and showy flowers having five petals in the wild state but being often double or semidouble under cultivation!" (*MW9*, def. 1a) One could mean "How sweet of you to give me the flower of a rose!" (def. 1b), except that it is really "How sweet of you to give me the flower of any of a genus. . . !" We want to know what *rose* means in "How sweet of you to give me a rose!" The other definitions for *rose* in *MW9* don't give us a clue. The common meaning of *feather* in "A pigeon feather fell on my windowsill" is not given in any substitutable way in dictionaries. What we are given are long, precise, scientific definitions, like that for *rose*, and sometimes the catchall, "Anything resembling a feather," which declares that the definer is not interested in wasting much time on a non-scientific use of a precise term. But we do not mean "A pigeon object resembling a feather fell on my windowsill," because we do not have in mind the scientific meaning of *feather;* yet we mean *feather*, not something resembling it.[14]

We must now distinguish between those definitions that are based on examples of actual usage, definitions *extracted* from a body of evidence, and those (like that of *rose* and other scientific terms) that are *imposed* on the basis of expert advice. The experts are not concerned with how scientific words are used nonscientifically, even if such nonscientific use is very common. "Their goal is ease and accuracy of communication between those versed in the language of science."[15]

When we talk about scientific and technical terms and definitions, we are not talking about an odd or uncommon phenomenon. In five pages picked at random from *NID3*, two-thirds of the terms were scientific and technical. I have estimated, probably too conservatively, that over 40 percent of the entries in an unabridged dictionary are scientific or technical and that in college and desk-sized dictionaries the percentage is 25 to 35 percent.[16] Clarence Barnhart, the dean of American commercial lexicographers, has said that "Almost 40 percent of the content of general-purpose dictionaries, such as college dictionaries, consists of scientific or technical terminology."[17] Since college dictionaries now contain from 150,000 to 170,000 entries, Barnhart's estimate translates into more than 60,000 entries, perhaps closer to 70,000. Because imposed definitions are not based, or not based primarily, on a collection of citations of actual usage for the determination of meaning, many of them are not substitutable. One must add to this vast total thousands of encyclopedic entries, such as *Rosetta stone*, that also appear in college dictionaries and to which the substitution rule also cannot apply. It is plain that a substantial percentage of the definitions in most dictionaries do not substitute even approximately for their definienda in context. There is no reason why they should. The substitution rule is often an aid in comprehension and may help the reader learn how to use the word, but definition can be given very well without it, and sometimes the effort to make a definition substitutable impairs its clarity by forcing the definer to use a clumsy or ambiguous phrasing.

Substitution in fact may be of more help to the definer than to the user. As we will see in the next section, when constructing a definition from citations the definer constructs his definitions to fit as many contexts as possible. The meaning, being deduced from a relatively few contexts, should in turn substitute not only for the definiendum in those contexts but for those of a very large number of other theoretical and actual contexts. We can say, then, that whereas substitutability is natural and apt for most extracted definitions, it is incidental to imposed definitions. Always a virtue, it should nonetheless be pursued with discretion and abandoned if it can be purchased only at the expense of clarity or unambiguousness.

Reflection of Grammatical Function

If a definition can be substituted for the word defined, it must be written in accord with the grammatical function, or part of speech, of the word defined. Even if it cannot be exactly substituted, the definition should reflect the part of speech of the word defined. The definition of a noun begins with a noun, that of an adjective with an adjective, and so on. However, as noted in the discussion of substitutability, it is not always possible or wise to make definitions substitutable, such as those of the prepositions *to* and *of.* But in general this rule is faithfully observed and should not be ignored without good reason. (See page 138, "How to Define by Part of Speech.")

Simplicity

"Avoid including difficult words in definitions of simpler words" is a traditional rule that seems to make sense, but like so many lexicographic rules it is often impossible to apply. It is customary, if not obligatory, when citing the rule to quote with great glee Samuel Johnson's definition of *network:* "Any thing reticulated or deccusated, at equal distances, with interstices between the intersections." However, before we all collapse in merriment I should like to quote *MW9*'s definition of *feather:*

> one of the light horny epidermal outgrowths that form the external covering of the body of birds and that consist of a shaft bearing on each side

a series of barbs which bear barbules which in turn bear barbicels commonly ending in hooked hamuli and interlocking with the barbules of an adjacent barb to link the barbs into a continuous vane.

There is no simple way to define precisely a complex arrangement of parts, however homely the object may appear to be. One obvious solution is not to define it precisely; but modern dictionary users expect scientifically precise, somewhat encyclopedic definitions. If one is to criticize Johnson for using difficult words to define a common word precisely, contemporary lexicographers must not be spared for doing the same thing.

What do we mean by "simple"? The word *feather* is simple, but the structure of the thing is anything but simple. What about a simple word like *time?* Saint Augustine said, "What, then, is time? I know well enough what it is, provided that nobody asks me; but if I am asked what it is and try to explain, I am baffled."[18] Unfortunately, definers are baffled too and must resort to more difficult words to try to cope with such difficult concepts. *MW9*'s relevant definition of *time* is "A continuum which lacks spatial dimensions and in which events succeed one another from past through present to future," which would certainly not satisfy Augustine and which is not simple, but is nonetheless an excellent definition. But if one's life experience were so limited that one had no idea what time was and had never heard of the word *time,* this definition would be of no help. However, in that event, what would be of help? How could a concept of this complexity—or those underlying the words *motion, being, life,* and many others—be comprehended in words by anyone who had never heard those simple words uttered? The answer is plain: they could not.

The meanings of many words, including these deceptively simple ones, are seldom learned from dictionaries. A practical appreciation of their meanings is acquired as part of the process of growing up. A child may be unable to define *life,* but he has a sense of what distinguishes living beings from nonliving things. Analogously, many words with concrete referents are learned as a baby learns to associate the physical presence of a dog with the word *dog:* by observing someone pointing at an object or at something happening and uttering a word. This is called "ostensive" definition. Dictionaries define ostensively when they include pictorial illustrations of objects corresponding to the words being defined. All of us learn by the ostensive method all the time. The defect of this method, as Richard Robinson shrewdly observes, is that the level of precision of definition is low. After many repetitions of *dog* when in the presence of the same dog, a child may associate the animal with the utterance and know the word *dog.* But when he first sees a different, much larger dog, he will not associate it with the same word. He will have to be exposed to many kinds of dogs, and also be able to distinguish dogs from cats and other animals, before he has learned the meaning of *dog*. As Robinson says, "No one could learn to apply the word 'dog' correctly from one ostensive definition of it."[19]

When the question is asked, then, "Why can't a dictionary leave out simple words like 'dog' since everyone knows what they mean?" I reply, "It is one thing to be able to recognize dogs, and another to know what *dog* means." Though the lexical definition of *dog* cannot describe what a dog is in words sufficiently simple to one who has never seen a dog, it can, precisely, define the word. It is a commonplace experience for a person to know the meaning of a word but fail to recognize the thing described by the word upon seeing the thing for the first time. We may have studied what a *clerestory* is, but if we have never seen one it must often be pointed out to us in a church before we associate the thing with the word. Does this make the lexical meaning superfluous? Far from it. It is precisely this interplay between lexical and ostensive definition that refines and specifies our knowledge. Lexical meaning cannot always be relied on to give any picture of the real world; but, on the other hand, ostensive definition alone provides only rough clues to the extent and limitations of meaning and is of no help at all in understanding how a word functions as a word, information that is vital if we ever intend to use the word.

We cannot use language either for scientific inquiry or for the play of wit in literature without standards, even if they are only employed as a measure from which to deviate. The standards are not established by doyens of grammar pontificating with pipe in hand. Extracted definitions are determined by an examination of usage. Although usage in scientific terminology is given much weight when it is available, in general imposed definitions are determined by a consensus of experts. The argument against the inclusion in dictionaries of simple words is really based on the idea that because everyone knows how to use these words, their meanings are not important. It is true that their meanings are not important to everyone. Not everyone is interested in sports terms either, and not everyone is interested in religious terms. But every word is a part of the picture of how we view the world, and, as in a pointillist painting, small discrete elements seen on close viewing are not trivial and cannot be omitted without changing the overall impression.

Difficult words invade a definition in direct proportion to the degree of scientific specificity required. Dictionaries that define simply are not necessarily better; their editors have made a policy decision to sacrifice some precision of meaning for increased ease of understanding. The decision depends on how they view their market. Children's dictionaries place a high value on ease of understanding and willingly sacrifice some precision. Scientific and technical dictionaries place a high value on precision and are generally unwilling to compromise the difficulty of their definitions. College dictionaries fall in between the two extremes and vary among themselves, but certainly the trend is toward precision. *Webster's Third New International Dictionary (NID3)*, the only commercial unabridged dictionary, is very much oriented toward precision at the expense of ease of understanding for the generalist. The *OED*, on the other hand, takes an entirely different tack, directing its definition always to the generalist, even though the specialist may be frustrated by what he views as the inadequacy of the definition.[20]

The dictum that every word should be defined by simpler words is gratuitous and misleading. All expository writing should be simple. All definitions should be as simple, direct, and clear as possible. The simple-definition rule confutes simplicity of form and of usage with simplicity of sense, ignoring the fact that an adequate definition often demands exact description or complex statement, which must presuppose familiarity with other, antecedent terms in order to keep the definition from becoming a long textbook essay. Hard words are used not because definers want to show off their vocabularies but because these words have more exact meanings than simpler words; therefore, they do not have to be qualified and they save space. (But see pages 150–151—in technical defining, the rule has some validity.)

Brevity

The need to save space in dictionaries leads naturally to the injunction "Be brief." Dictionary definitions should not waste words. The art of defining depends not only on the ability to analyze and understand what words mean, but equally on the ability to express such meanings succinctly. Robinson writes, "A lexical definition could nearly always be truer by being longer."[21] A good definer learns how to lose the least measure of truth with each shortening of a definition.

The first draft of a definition is almost always too long—and should be. The definer begins by constructing the best definition he can devise. This work is often creative and rewarding, even if it is sometimes exasperatingly difficult. Then the task of cutting begins. Every definition must be pared to say the most in the least number of words. Often it is improved in the process. (Robinson's statement above refers to a definition's "truth value," how well it describes the real world, not its excellence as a definition. It is therefore not inconsistent to say that some definitions are made better by being shorter.) For example, here is an expert's definition of a term used in obstetrics, *trial of labor:*

> allowing labor to either begin or progress with the intention of allowing
> labor to proceed as long as satisfactory progress is being made and as long
> as no complications occur.

It is thirty words long and it is obviously defective, defining a noun phrase
as an adjective, but it does get across the meaning. The definition was
revised to read:

> nonintervention in either the initiation or continuation of labor as long as
> satisfactory progress is observed and no complications occur.

It is twenty words long, clearer and without redundancy, and says the same
thing as the wordier definition.

Avoidance of Ambiguity

Words in definitions must be used unambiguously in the context of the definition. If a word used in a definition has more than one meaning (i.e., if it
is polysemous), the particular sense in which it is intended must be made
clear by the rest of the definition. This problem is most conspicuous in dictionaries that depend on synonyms for definition, such as bilingual dictionaries and short monolingual ones. One cannot define *backyard,* either in
English or its equivalent in another language, by the English word *lot,* since
lot has a lot of other meanings.

How to Define by Part of Speech

Nouns

From a formal point of view, nouns are the easiest of all words to define,
and in scientific and technical dictionaries they are by far the most common.
The defining noun may relate to the appearance, purpose, or composition of
the thing defined, but it should pinpoint that property of the thing that is
viewed by most speakers as being essential to it. If that essential property
were not present, the thing would not be regularly identified by the definiendum. Thus, if *mirror* is defined as "A polished or smooth surface (as of
glass) that forms images by reflection" *(MW9),* one can say that if it were
not a surface it would not be called a mirror. Moreover, the surface must
be polished or smooth. These features describe a mirror's appearance. The
purpose of a mirror is to form images by reflection; this also is essential, but

the definer chose to describe the thing before stating its purpose. If one tries to recast the definition, one realizes why. "An object designed to reflect images from a polished or smooth surface" implies what a mirror is rather than stating it. It is stylistically convenient to put "polished and smooth" first even though these qualifiers are no more integral to the meaning than the mirror's purpose. That mirrors are usually made of glass is indicated by the parenthetical " (as of glass)." Since the word *glass* also means "mirror," this is useful information, but it is only incidental, since mirrors can be made of other substances and still be mirrors.

A noun definition must immediately answer the question, What is it? In order to answer that question it must use a noun, whether qualified or not, in the first part of the definition that identifies the class of things or kind of thing to which the definiendum belongs. If the term to be defined is a phrase, such as *infectious hepatitis,* and *hepatitis* is elsewhere defined, it is perfectly proper to use *hepatitis* as the defining noun, as in "hepatitis characterized by . . ." or "an acute form of hepatitis in which . . ." There is no need to repeat the definition of *hepatitis,* especially in a technical dictionary. The user of a medical dictionary is more likely to know what *hepatitis* means, and the arrangement of entry and subentries places the basic term close to its combinations. In a general dictionary, the extra space required to paraphrase *hepatitis* as "inflammation of the liver" may be worthwhile to spare the reader the effort of looking up a distant entry.

The use of a noun element in the definition of a phrasal entry is not confined to scientific and technical dictionaries but is quite common in general dictionaries. *Student teacher* is defined in *Webster's New World Dictionary (World)* as "a student in a college or university who teaches school under the supervision of an experienced teacher as a requirement for a degree in education." *Puppy dog* is defined in *Webster's Ninth New Collegiate Dictionary* as "a domestic dog; *esp:* one having the lovable attributes of a puppy."

The latter definition illustrates one solution to the problem of conveying connotation. *Puppy dog* is appropriately used in domestic contexts; it is a diminutive and shares the intimate register of words like *daddy, mommy,* or *honey* (as a term of affection). These words would all be out of place in a board of directors' meeting or even in ordinary business conversation. They express a certain attitude on the part of the speaker toward the person or thing described, and for *puppy dog* "one having the lovable attributes of a puppy" is the method used to convey this attitude. The definition might well have read: "a domestic dog: conveying the speaker's affection for puppies." Alternatively, a citation illustrating such an attitude, such as "a cute little puppy dog," might have been included to show a typical use.

139

Adjectives

Every dictionary has its own recommended style for defining adjectives. Style manuals list the particular introductory adjectives that may be used, often for particular kinds of situations, and others that are proscribed. Here are some of the introductory words and phrases used by dictionaries in defining adjectives:

able to	expressing	made of
apt to	expressive of	marked by
associated with	for	of
being	full of	of the nature of
befitting	given to	pertaining to
belonging to	having	producing
capable of	having the quality of	relating to
characterized by	having to do with	resembling
consisting of	inclined to	showing
denoting	indicating	tending to
describing	involving	used (for,
designating	like	with, in,
exhibiting	likely to	etc.)

Some of these should be used with caution or avoided. *Associated with* may be ambiguous; *befitting* is old fashioned; *given to* and *pertaining to* are too formal and stuffy for use in a children's dictionary; and some of the other expressions might also be rejected for the same reason. Sometimes it is convenient to combine two introductory adjectives, e.g., "of or designating the color yellow." But a whole string of introductory adjectives should not be used to combine various senses that have little in common, e.g., "of, for, characterized by, or resembling . . ."

Dictionaries so often use *of* in their definitions of adjectives because it covers a multitude of senses and has the marvelous property of being only two letters long. Its common use depends on strictly observing the substitutability rule. How would one better define *yellow* in "a yellow color" than by "of yellow"? One could say, "denoting yellow," but that does not work so well in "a yellow shade" or "a yellow swatch," whereas "of yellow" works just as well in all three contexts. Almost every defining characteristic common to dictionaries can be traced to the need to conserve space. Indeed, although the principal function of the dictionary style manual (see Chapter 6) is to assure uniform treatment of similar entries, a very important consideration is the need to establish styles, consistent with clarity, that are most economical in expression.

Verbs

Verbs are often considered—justly, I think—the most difficult words to define, in part because many verbs have numerous senses that must be discriminated, and partly because of the complex relationship between verbs and their objects. One could write a long monograph on the question of defining verbs, a disquisition more suitable for a dictionary style manual than for this book. I propose here simply to outline some of the problems and suggest some solutions, but my treatment of this subject must be sketchy.

The definition of a verb begins with the infinitive form, with or without *to,* of another verb. Thus:

> hinder   *vt* **1.** to make slow or difficult the progress of; HAMPER **2.**
> to hold back: CHECK *(MW9)*

Def. 1 refers to slowing the rate of progress and def. 2 to stopping it entirely or preventing it from occurring. Def. 1 might have been phrased, "to make the progress of slow or difficult," but this was likely rejected on the grounds that the unexpressed object should follow the entire definition and not come in its midst. The awkward wording of def. 1 was thus considered preferable to the ambiguity of the alternative.

Both definitions refer to transitive uses. If the sense defined is transitive, the definition must substitute for the transitive use of the verb. The form of the definition should leave little doubt that an object is called for to complete it and should suggest, if possible, the nature of the object. Note also that any verb used as a synonym, such as *hamper,* must also be transitive. In def. 2, the range of application is wider and people are more often among the objects, as in "Shyness hindered him from asking the question." *NID3* gives the useful contextual clue that this sense is often used with *from,* but this is omitted from *MW9. World* gives these meanings in reverse order:

> hinder   **1.** to keep back; restrain; get in the way of; prevent; stop.
> **2.** to make difficult for; thwart; impede; frustrate.

Def. 2 of *World* and def. 1 of *MW9* apply to this use: "Their plan was hindered by irresolution and bad advice."

The two styles of defining are very different. The Merriam-Webster version calls for uninterrupted phrases laid out in logical sequence, however much they may vary from typical English syntax. *World*'s style calls for greater simplicity, marked by reluctance to offend normal syntax and a much freer use of synonyms. *MW9* regards synonyms as a kind of cross-reference and prints them in small capital letters. However, synonyms in the definition of any dictionary can be regarded as cross-references to those words. The implication that *MW9*'s equivalences are more discriminating than those of other dictionaries is apparently one the editors wished to convey by the distinctive type style, but so far as I can determine the only difference between *MW9*'s choices and those of other dictionaries is the type style.

In my sample sentence, *MW9*'s definition substitutes better than *World*'s. First, let us recast the sentence in the active voice: "Irresolution and bad advice hindered their plan." Compare "made slow or difficult the progress of their plan" and "made difficult for their plan." Obviously, the second substitution does not work without the insertion of *it,* as in "made it difficult for their plan." On the other hand, all three of *World*'s synonyms fit the context: "thwarted (or impeded or frustrated) their plan," as does *MW9*'s "hampered their plan." *World* has sacrificed perfect substitutability for readability. Its choice of synonyms (especially *frustrated*) suggests an effort to find words that convey connotations as well as the designation.

In my second sample sentence, "Shyness hindered him from asking the question," *MW9*'s def. 2 works: "Shyness held him back (or checked him) from asking the question," but note that the object falls in the midst of the definitions, which seems to cast doubt on the need to use such an awkward construction for def. 1. *World*'s def. 1 works also, but not as well. "Shyness kept him back (or restrained him) from asking the question" is acceptable, but "Shyness got in the way of him asking the question" needs to be recast as "Shyness got in the way of *his* asking the question." But it is too demanding to expect all parts of a definition to substitute in all contexts. The other synonyms work very well: "Shyness prevented (or stopped) him from asking the question." Once again we see that the fullness and variety of *World*'s treatment leaves it open occasionally to inexact substitution but on the other hand renders its definitions easier to grasp than Merriam-Webster's. Neither style is right or wrong: each emphasizes different qualities.

The intransitive sense of *hinder* is defined as follows:

to delay action; be a hindrance *(World)*
to delay, impede, or prevent action *(MW9)*

An intransitive verb must be defined intransitively. There are two ways to define intransitively: by including the object as part of the definition, or by using another intransitive verb as a synonym. (One cannot use a transitive verb as a synonym for an intransitive verb, because it will not substitute and is therefore misleading.)

Sometimes the objects of transitive verbs are enclosed in parentheses. The *Random House College Dictionary (RHCD)* defines *interpolate* as:

interpolate   **1.** to alter (a text) by the insertion of new matter, esp. deceptively or without authorization. **2.** to insert (new or spurious matter) in this manner . . .

By this device the kind of object usually taken by the verb can be indicated, as well as a restricted range of application. The trouble is that parentheses are used for a variety of information, even in the same dictionary. In some definitions it is not clear whether the parenthetical object refers to the word *as a word* or as a thing. *RHCD*'s def. 2 of *doff* is:

doff   to lift or remove (one's hat) in salutation; to tip.

Is one to assume that the word *hat* is the usual object of *doff,* or that *hat* means "any hat"? Dictionaries should have some way of distinguishing between the word *hat* and "anything denoted by *hat.*" In this instance the object is often "hat" but can be a kind of hat: one can doff a homburg or a high hat. But a parenthetical "one's hat" doesn't make this clear.

RCHD defines *prohibit* as follows:

prohibit   **1.** to forbid (an action, activity, etc.) by authority: *Smoking is prohibited here.* **2.** to forbid the action of (a person) . . .

The objects are specified to distinguish the sense that takes a person as object from that which doesn't. Def. 2 refers to a use such as "He was prohibited from entering by a guard." Clearly, in these cases the parenthetical objects are not to be taken as words but as denoting the things defined by the words. We would hardly ever say, "An action is prohibited here." But the reader is not told this; he must surmise it.

When the indicated object is as vague as "an action, activity, etc.," it serves no useful purpose to state it, especially when an illustrative sentence is also provided. The real meaning of the parenthetical object is: "This sense does not take people as objects." It provides negative information, but the reader is not likely to so interpret it. Rather, the reader will understand that "an action, activity, etc." limits the word's range of possible objects. What does "etc." mean in this context? One can say, "Idleness and absence are prohibited in this school." Are idleness and absence actions or activities? Perhaps they are "etc." The use of parentheses can be defined as a means of indicating collocation and range of application in less space and in less equivocal form than by illustrative quotations. Nonetheless, parentheses are overused in definitions, and their ambiguity is a defect.

143

Other Parts of Speech

Adverbs are defined by other adverbs or by prepositional phrases that substitute in the context of the particular sense. For example, *well* is defined by *The Doubleday Dictionary* as "in a good or correct manner; expertly: to dance *well*." Interjections are defined by other interjections or by explanations of the frame of mind of the user of the interjection or the effect it is intended to have on others. *Nuts* as an interjection is defined by *Doubleday* as "an exclamation of scorn, disapproval, etc." Pronouns are sometimes defined in terms of their grammatical function, sometimes by a substitutable phrase. *Who* is defined in *Doubleday* as "which or what person or persons: *Who* is she? They don't know *who* I am." But *she* is defined as "the female person or being previously mentioned or understood, in the nominative case," which combines designative meaning with grammatical function. *Her* is defined in purely grammatical terms as, "the objective case of *she*." Conjunctions are defined by whatever works in the particular context: other conjunctions, adverbs, or prepositional phrases.

Run-in Phrasal Entries

Phrasal entries are defined according to whether they are considered verb phrases, noun phrases, adverbial phrases, or whatever. *Bring around, bring forth,* and *bring out,* appearing within the entry *bring* as lexical units, are construed as verbs and defined accordingly. *With a rush,* which is part of the article for *rush,* is defined by *Doubleday* adverbially as "suddenly and hastily," because this definition substitutes for its common uses.

Common Mistakes in Defining

One lexicographer lists the following mistakes as the most common in scientific and technical dictionaries:[22]

1. Failure to understand that a textbook type of description is not a definition.

2. Failure to indicate all the meanings of a term in the field covered by the dictionary. The definition should not represent one point of view only.

3. Failure to understand that self-explanatory entries are not legitimate lexical units, e.g., "fractures of the tibia." Hierarchical nomenclatures of scientific terms are seldom of much use in constructing a dictionary's word list because they are based on an arrangement of concepts rather than of words. They include many terms, such as "fractures of the tibia," that are not lexical units though they may be useful conceptual categories.

4. Failure to understand that in scientific usage a synonym (or variant) is a word that is an exact substitute for another.

The fourth point is a very common error, because in practice many pairs of terms that are not exact synonyms are used interchangeably. I am currently engaged in editing a medical dictionary; an obstetrics editor defined *vertex presentation* as a synonym of *cephalic presentation,* which he defined as "a presentation of the fetus in which the lowest part that appears first in the uterine cervix is the fetal skull. This is the most common presentation of a human fetus during labor." Since *vertex* refers to the top of the head, I realized that *vertex presentation* is a *kind* of cephalic presentation, and that other presenting parts of the head—the brow, face, the occiput (back of the head), etc.—are identified as different kinds of cephalic presentations. The obstetrics editor was surely well aware of this fact, but since the vertex presentation is the most common, and since it is cephalic, in ordinary usage when a baby is born vertex first, I suspect that it is often called a cephalic presentation. Thus, "cephalic presentation" is an extracted meaning of *vertex presentation.* But, in a technical dictionary, technical definitions are wanted.

The editor's definition was also faulty because the important fact that *cephalic* refers to the skull or head appeared last instead of early in the definition. I therefore rewrote the two definitions as follows:

cephalic presentation a presentation of the fetus in which the fetal head is the lowest part and appears first in the uterine cervix. This is the most common presentation of a human fetus during labor.

vertex presentation a cephalic presentation of the fetus in which the vertex of the fetal skull is the lowest part and appears first in the uterine cervix. This is the most common cephalic presentation.

I would add to the list of common mistakes a fifth error: failure to realize that the context of a definition may not provide any frame of reference for the reader. An editor who is defining a whole series of definitions about fetal length, for instance, may occasionally neglect to mention that the object being measured is a fetus. But a dictionary user reads one term at a time, and if the context does not specify what is being measured, he will be at a loss to understand the definition. This common error illustrates why dictionary defining is so demanding: each definition is entirely separate from every other definition and must constitute a tiny, discrete essay of its own, providing enough clues to context so that even in the briefest definition the readers know whether we are measuring fetuses or wavelengths, head sizes or reflexes. In an article or book one can skip along from sentence to sentence and presume that the reader will keep pace with one's train of thought. Not so in a dictionary, where every definition must stand by itself.

Many mistakes do not fall clearly into any one category. For example, an expert on measures wrote the following definition of *meter* for a technical dictionary:

meter   the SI base unit of length equal to the distance traveled by electromagnetic radiation through a vacuum in 1/299 792 458 second. Between 1960 and 1983, the meter was defined as being equal to 1 650 763.73 wavelengths in vacuum of the radiation corresponding to the transition between the levels $2p_{10}$ and $5d_5$ of the krypton-86 atom. [SI refers to Système International d'Unités, the metric system of decimal measures.]

It is a marvelously exact definition with one flaw: it gives absolutely no clue to the observable length of a meter! If one said to the expert, "But you have not told us what a meter is," he would reply, "On the contrary, I have told you exactly what it is. Since the meter is the standard by which all other SI measures of length are described, the meter cannot be described by comparing it to any other metric length and should not be compared to any nonmetric length because such measures are scientifically inexact." He is right, of course, yet from a practical point of view—and the lexicographer must always take the practical view—he must be overruled. One must include in the definition, and very early on, the fact that a meter is approximately 39.37 inches, however this pains the metric expert. It will not do to give a pure definition that does not answer the basic needs of many readers. The lexicographer, even of a technical dictionary whose definitions are far beyond his expertise, must insist upon exercising the ultimate judgment of what is useful. The technical data provided by the expert who defined *meter* are certainly useful in a technical dictionary, but because the lexicographer is *not* an expert he is able to recognize the needs of a wider variety of users than the specialist-definer.

The definition of *frog test* in *Butterworths Medical Dictionary* is my favorite medical definition.[23] I quote it in full:

frog test   a test used to indicate pregnancy, in which a frog is used.

This definition has an engaging simplicity and directness that I find charming. But one does wonder how the frog is used. Do woman and frog stare at one another to see who blinks first? (If the woman, she's pregnant.) Is the test positive if the woman's touch turns the frog into a prince? My hopes for such a delightful pregnancy test were dashed and I was dumped right back into a seamy hospital lab with this definition from *Blakiston's Gould Medical Dictionary:*[24]

frog test   a pregnancy test in which urine containing chorionic gonadotropin is injected into the dorsal lymph sac of the male leopard frog *(Rana pipiens).* If spermatozoa are demonstrable in the frog's urine within 3 hours after injection, the test is positive.

Here is an instance in which *Butterworths* defined the extracted meaning and *Gould* defined the imposed meaning of the same term. When *frog test* is used, the context will rarely yield more information than that given by *Butterworths'* definition. In this case it cannot be denied that such a definition is inadequate; *Gould's* definition is more useful, and it is clearly imposed.

Many tests are defined by medical dictionaries by specifying exactly how the test is performed. *Dorland's Illustrated Medical Dictionary* defines *Levinson test* as "(for tuberculous meningitis and other intracranial conditions): one ml. of spinal fluid is placed . . ." and so on, for twelve lines of painstaking detail. *Gould's* definition of *frog test* and *Dorland's* of *Levinson test* are clearly more than definitions. They are instructions on how to perform a test. It may be argued that their extreme specificity is necessary to understand how the test works and hence what it means, but few definitions presume to be detailed enough so that the user can duplicate the action described. The definition of *bridge* does not inform the reader how he can go about building bridges. If it did, the work would be an instruction manual and not a dictionary. Even large and comprehensive medical texts do not provide such exacting descriptions; they cover far too much ground to be able to do so. Why do dictionaries feel they must? Granted that technical dictionaries are more encyclopedic than general dictionaries, I am still baffled by the elaborate specificity given tests, whereas other terms, such as *blood pressure,* are described summarily. Neither *Dorland's* nor *Gould,* for example, describes how blood pressure is read, either under *blood pressure* or *sphygmomanometer* (a device for reading blood pressure). Although there are many types of sphygmomanometer, not one is described, not even the familiar kind with an inflatable cuff that compresses the vessels so that the tester can listen with a stethoscope while the air is slowly released and detect the systolic pressure by the first sound of the pulsation of the blood and the diastolic pressure by its cessation. Still less are we told how to use it. If a test means how it is done, an instrument means how it is used. Isn't *blood pressure* as important as *frog test?*

There is a great deal of following of the leader among all kinds of dictionaries, technical as well as general, and one suspects that some terms are treated fully and others not simply because the most successful dictionary adopted that policy and other dictionaries followed suit. No particular policy informs such uneven treatment of terms; rather, fear of criticism and the safety of conformity are the driving forces behind many conventional dictionary practices.

In a general dictionary, there are many snares for the definer. One must be wary of unintended double entendre. H. Bosley Woolf, editor of *MW8,* cites the early draft of a definition for *Chinese wall:* "a serious obstacle to intercourse or understanding."[25] He also wisely cautions against overspecifying what material things are made of. Nothing dates a dictionary so rapidly as definitions of doors as wooden or of telephones as having dials. Of course, the obsolescence of some definitions is unavoidable. The pace of technological change is so rapid that no one can predict what new materials, designs, and uses will be devised for things. But definers must be well informed and imaginative. They must keep abreast of recent technological advances and be able to guess where they ought to be cautious about being specific.

All definitions of things are compromises between specific accuracy and breadth of inclusiveness. The definition of a door as wooden is not wrong; it just leaves out too many doors. On the other hand, no definition can take in all of the particular things referred to by the word defined. There will always be marginal cases that are not covered by any definition: doors made of blasts of hot air, or doors that do not seem to lead into or out of anything. To include such disparate uses of *door* would so generalize the definition as to weaken its application to the vast majority of doors or so extend its length that it would try the patience of the reader.

The relationship between the definition and the range of actual usages of a term like *door* may be depicted by the diagram here.[26]Every dot represents an actual usage of *door*. The circle represents the compass of the definition. The usages outside the circle are not covered by the definition of *door*. In the future, if such usages increase significantly, the circle may be expanded to include them; alternatively, if the configuration of dots becomes more concentrated, the circle may be contracted to exclude others. One must not assume that the usages beyond the circle of definition are wrong. They are simply not recognized by this dictionary definition. Definition never determines correctness; it merely abstracts meaning from a preponderance of usage. The bigger the dictionary, the more dots its definitions take in, but there will always be some usages beyond the range of even the largest dictionary.

In a general dictionary, specificity is less important than breadth of coverage, but usefulness demands that the definition be as specific as possible consistent with a realistically broad compass of meaning. The challenge of

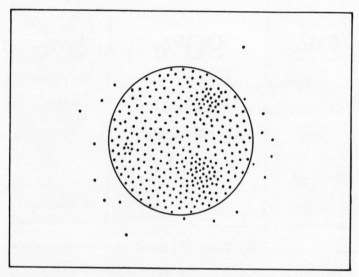

FIGURE 6.   A schematized view of the inclusiveness of definitions.

defining is to learn how to weigh those two goals and intermix them in varying proportions for each novel situation. (This can also be part of the problem of sense division, discussed below under "The Citation File.")

Science editors on dictionary staffs sometimes make the mistake of
demanding specificity even when some ambiguity is part of the meaning.
Many terms, even scientific and technical ones, are flexible in application
by design and serve an excellent practical purpose in defining an area calling
for the user's judgment. For example, *arrested labor* was defined by one
contributor to a medical dictionary as "labor that has failed to progress at
an expected rate, given the particular characteristics of fetus and mother."
The definition was criticized on the grounds that "expected rate" was not
specified. But "given the particular characteristics of fetus and mother"
implies that the expected rate will vary depending on the maternal pelvic
shape, the position of the fetus in the uterus, and so on. The meaning of the
term depends on the judgment of the user as to what the "expected rate"
is, and thus the specific meaning of *arrested labor* will vary too. The critic's
belief that all scientific terms must describe invariable and measurable phenomena is simply not the case. The term *arrested labor* would be applied to

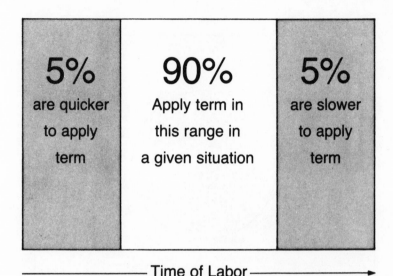

FIGURE 7. The range of usage for the term *arrested labor*.

the same birth at different times by different speakers, but the usage of the vast majority would fall within a moderate range. We might depict the range of usage by this chart.

There is no difficulty in communication of *arrested labor* if this chart is accurate. The difficulty arises when some terms have not 5 percent variation on either side, but 20 to 30 percent variation. Even these terms are useful, but not for the same reasons. Connotation (the affective associations of the word) and the attitude of the speaker generally assume a much greater share of meaning than in terms with less variation. "That's nice" has virtually no meaning except when used in homogeneous cultural groups, such as among business associates, friends, or family members. Indeed, as a word becomes less precise in application it depends more for whatever meaning it has on the similarity of its users and hearers. Scientific terms can be used with the same meaning (or nearly the same meaning) by very different people, but to know what *nice* means with any precision one must know a great deal about the speaker.

Defining scientific terms often involves defining a basic term, or main entry, and a great many subentries that include the entry word, such as the various forms of *nephritis* (inflammation of the kidney). The technical definer should group together all of his terms sharing a common element and construct a hierarchy of definition starting with the basic term, which may be compared to the trunk of a tree, which is gross, encompassing, and profoundly implicit. The branches of the tree, or subentries (forms of *nephritis*), deal with increasingly nice distinctions, are of narrower compass and are progressively more explicit. The flow of elucidation, compass, and explicitness normally goes in one direction only; one must define *acute interstitial nephritis* in terms of *nephritis,* not the other way around.

In dictionary work there are exceptions to every rule, and there are exceptions to this one also. For example, some entry words, such as *ounce,* are really only abbreviations (or *clipped forms*) of specific subentries, and they must be defined with reference to the subentries, such as *ounce avoirdupois, ounce troy, fluid ounce.* The entry/subentry arrangement cannot allow subentry definitions to be repeated under the main entry word, else thousands of definitions would appear twice. One cannot define *ounce avoirdupois* fully as one definition of *ounce* as well as at *ounce avoirdupois.* One must say simply that def. 1 of *ounce* is a variant of *ounce avoirdupois.* But in general the flow of definition does proceed from entry to subentry and from shorter subentry to longer subentry. This may be construed as an example of the rule that difficult terms may not be used to define simpler words, and in the context of scientific terms the rule has a certain validity.

The Citation File

We have been describing the principles and problems of defining, but we have not yet described the chief source of definitions, the citation file. A citation file is a collection of potential lexical units in the context of actual usage, drawn from a great variety of written sources and often some spoken sources, chiefly because the context illuminates an aspect of meaning. Citations are also collected to provide illustrative quotations that will be printed in the dictionary, especially in historical dictionaries or the larger synchronic dictionaries.

There are other reasons for citing a word. Citations provide information about the preferred form of spelling, including whether the unit is written as two words, hyphenated, or as a solid compound. The context can also indicate whether a word is slang, informal, taboo, or used only in one country or region. Some citations contain information about etymology and pronunciation. Citations are often collected simply to show that a particular form exists; this is most often the case with new scientific and technical terms, although general words may also be cited for this reason if no better citation is available or if the term has been previously regarded as obsolete or foreign.[27]

The earliest English lexicographers by and large copied the definitions of their predecessors. Gradually, influenced by foreign-language dictionaries, some eighteenth-century lexicographers began to cite examples drawn from literature as evidence of usage. Although Samuel Johnson is often credited with having originated the use of illustrative quotations, he was not the first to adopt the practice even in English, though he did greatly expand and refine it. Nowadays, general dictionaries depend on citation files primarily to provide them with the basis for defining new words and new meanings of established words. For established meanings of established words, they generally depend on older editions of their own work, acquire the right to use an earlier dictionary, or base their definitions on the definers' own sense of the language with the help of definitions used in other dictionaries. They rely on specialists to define the large percentage of scientific and technical terms. They stock their libraries with specialized dictionaries and reference books on a wide variety of subjects. It can be said with some assurance that the only English dictionary ever created wholly on the basis of citations was the *Oxford English Dictionary,* which took, by the most charitable reckoning, fifty years to prepare. Every dictionary after it has drawn upon its enormous store of information. In spite of other sources, a large ongoing citation file is essential for the preparation of any new general dictionary or for the revision of an existing dictionary.

Here is a sample citation:

```
ITEM       embourgeoisement                    113421
SOURCE     Fortune              PAGE    126
AUTHOR     Herman Kahn          DATE    11/68


    Possibly the most important reason for this waning
    of revolutionary zeal is the growing material pros-
    perity of the Soviet Union--its embourgeoisement--
    and the associated emphasis by Soviet citizens on
    comfort and personal security.
```

Not all citations record the author, but all the other information is essential. Each citation is uniquely identified by a number like that in the upper right-hand corner. Some citation files are typed; others are composed of clippings pasted or taped on slips of paper or lightweight cards, generally 4 x 6 inches. Each system has its advantages and drawbacks. Retyping introduces possible errors. Clippings can become detached from their backings; they will also sometimes be pasted on the wrong slip or with the wrong side out. Nonetheless, one knows at least that the quotation is accurate. Most files are combinations of both types.

Some dictionary citation files are vast, numbering in the millions, but as Clarence Barnhart has pointed out, "Too large a sampling is expensive and serves no purpose if it duplicates information already existing in the OED, the . . . *Century,* the *Dictionary of Americanisms,* and the *Dictionary of American English.*"[28] Furthermore, the definer has only so much time to devote to each definition and it is a waste of time for him to go through a hundred citations when ten will do. Barnhart has estimated that a balanced citation file of 500,000 items supplementing the coverage of the four dictionaries mentioned above is sufficient for selecting new material for a college dictionary.

The number of citations required to define a new word or sense varies greatly. Sometimes a few citations are all one needs for a new word, but often a much larger number is necessary for analyzing new meanings of an established word. One must first decide whether the evidence demands one or more new definitions or whether an existing definition need only be altered to accommodate it. For this sort of judgment, fifteen or twenty or more citations may well be required, though one sometimes has to make do with fewer.

The existence of an ongoing citation file is what distinguishes reputable, general dictionaries from purely derivative works, although far too much is made over the size of citation files. The quality of the citation file and the use one makes of it are at least as important as its overall size. Some citation files are filled with rubbish: nonlexical phrases, advertising slogans, foreign words, ephemeral abbreviations for defunct government agencies, and contexts too brief to case any light on meaning. Although Merriam-Webster dictionaries are excellent, their excellence would not be diminished if their citation files were half as large. I find it hard to believe that Merriam's 12 million citations are duly examined for each new revision. The useful part of their file—the part acquired after the last complete revision—is of much more manageable size.

It is expensive and time consuming to build a citation file by conventional means. Although the use of computers holds great promise in citation

153

collection, it also creates problems that have not yet been fully resolved (see Chapter 7, page 281). The conventional method is to hire and train citation readers to systematically scan various periodicals and books for new words and new senses. The reading material should cover both the general and technical vocabulary, take in a wide range of geographic localities, and include a good sampling of British publications as well as American and Canadian. Some attention should also be given to other English-speaking populations, especially Australia and New Zealand. If one's dictionary is designed for children, juvenile literature and periodicals should be read.

Barnhart asserted in 1962 that his citations cost thirty cents each, and clearly the figure now is much higher. One can see without indulging in higher mathematics that building a file of a million citations is an expensive undertaking.

How to Collect Citations

First of all, it is best to hire as citation readers people who have had experience working on dictionaries. One cannot expect everyone who is fascinated with words to have the necessary judgment to select good citations. Some people, however, who have never worked on a dictionary staff have somehow developed a gift for discerning good citations. Among those without dictionary experience, it is simply not possible to predict who will be good and who won't; one must give a trial to any likely candidate and judge from the results.

To assure that one gets citations of good quality, one must spell out in detail the rules for citation collection. Here are the basic points that should be covered:

· How to prepare citations. The reader must be shown samples and told exactly where to put each item of information. Preprinted slips or cards, such as the one shown on page 152, are helpful. In one citation program I had a fairly large number of readers simply bracket citations in magazines and send the entire magazines to me; clerks on staff would then cut and paste the citations onto cards. It is more usual, however, for the reader to prepare his own individual citations and send them in in rough or exact alphabetic sequence. I have used this method too, which is preferable if one has fewer but highly productive readers.

· Length of citations. It is best to keep the citation as brief as possible consistent with clarity and meaningfulness. As a rule, an entire sentence should be included, occasionally a whole paragraph or more. But nonessential material should be excised. Here is an example of a bracketed citation for "privishing" in an article that appeared in *Publishers Weekly* (May 7, 1982, p. 12):

"Privishing"

Much of the case centered on Gerard Colby Zilg's accusation that Prentice-Hall had not used its "best efforts" to promote "Du Pont: Behind the Nylon Curtain." One of Zilg's expert witnesses, William Decker, testified that ⟨publishers sometimes sign contracts for books and later find that for whatever reason, they aren't excited about the book. As a result, Decker testified, they resort to "privishing," which he defined as "a combination of private and publishing: to publish very private. It is a slang word we use in the trade. 'We privished it, and it sank without a trace' is usually the whole sentence."⟩

Prentice-Hall counsel John Koshel stated: "As far as I know, no court has ever previously discussed the word 'privishing,' and neither I nor anyone at Prentice-Hall had ever heard of the word before it was first mentioned by Mr. Zilg's lawyer several years after this lawsuit began."

This example is unrepresentative of the citation file as a whole in that the article reports the use of a new word, but such articles are by no means rare and are of course an excellent source of citations. It is longer than many citations need be, but all the information within brackets is useful.

• Purpose of the file. Readers must be made to understand that their role is to collect a mass of raw data, not to make judgments about it. One should discourage readers from making many notes or trying to define the term cited. On rare occasions a brief notation is helpful, such as "from a letter to the editor," because this indicates the citation is essentially unedited material. But all too often notes on citations are unwarranted and misleading. If readers begin to imagine themselves editors or definers, their productivity as collectors of citations will decline and the value of the citations they do provide will not be enhanced.

155

• The criteria for selecting citations should be spelled out. If well-established senses of standard forms are not being sought, this should be stated. One should provide numerous examples of the kinds of words to be cited and enclose samples of a variety of citations. Not all the samples should be superb; some should be run-of-the-mill, lest the reader become too selective. The kinds of desired citations should be listed, as follows:

1. New words and phrases that constitute lexical units, such as *nuke* (for "nuclear weapon") or *code word* (for a disguised expression of bias or a controversial opinion)
2. New or unusual meanings and uses of well-established forms, such as *impact* as a verb ("How will the recession impact on unemployment?")
3. Slang, colloquialisms, taboo words, new trade or occupational jargon (such as terms in advertising or computer technology)
4. Special or technical vocabularies (such as new gardening or cooking terms, or terms used in the arts or sciences)
5. Foreign words and phrases if used without translation in predominantly English contexts, thus presupposing the reader's familiarity with them. In articles about a foreign country or a foreign language, foreign terms should not be cited unless the author indicates that they are used among English-speaking people. Foreign terms in English contexts are usually printed in italics (such as *embourgeoisement,* page 152); these may be cited. Any representation of a foreign term in regular roman type is particularly citable, since it suggests the word is well advanced in the process of becoming naturalized.
6. Information on etymology, pronunciation, or grammar. This will be encountered chiefly in articles about language and so is rather special, but as we saw in the citation for *privishing,* it does occur.
7. Information on spelling or form, especially if the term's form is undergoing change, e.g., *legionnaire's disease* vs. *Legionnaire's disease.* However, these must be limited rigorously to specific areas of interest.
8. Americanisms, Briticisms, Canadianisms, Australianisms, etc.: terms whose context reveals a meaning restricted to a particular English-speaking area. Also worth citing are instances of the use of an Americanism (like *hit the sack*) in a British or Canadian publication without reference to its being an Americanism.
9. Trademarks other than in ads, whether capitalized or lower case, when used generically.

This is not an exhaustive list, and readers should be encouraged not to be limited by it once they have proved themselves. They should be provided with a copy of a recent dictionary to use as a basis of selection in questionable cases. As a rule, they should not cite a word in a particular sense if that sense is included in the dictionary provided them. The readers will not have time to check every citation—and indeed should be discouraged from doing so—but they should have it available nonetheless.

Dos and Don'ts of Citation Reading

· Limit the number of allowable citations of the same item from the same source, as, for example, to two citations from any one article in a magazine and to three from any single issue.

· Don't continue citing the same word from the same periodical, even in subsequent issues, unless the word seems to be changing in meaning or the context is especially revealing.

· Don't cite a word unless the context sheds some light on meaning or usage. "A scrumple approach to city planning was recommended by the mayor" gives no indication of what "scrumple" means and is useless.

· Don't cite words in eye dialect (sound spellings), such as *uv* for "of" or *ya* for "you."

· Don't cite proper nouns except when used generically. *Madison Avenue* is acceptable when it means the advertising industry, but not when it refers to a street in New York City.

· Don't cite hyphenated words and phrases unless they have a distinctive meaning as a unit that the separate words would not convey separately. "Easy-mannered," "brown-and-black" (hat), "tired-looking," "light-colored" (hair) are *not* good cites. This practice, incidentally, is the commonest source of poor citations. There are borderline cases, however; an ordinary phrase may be developing a distinctive sense as a compound, such as "self-prescribed" (of a drug or regimen) or "high-risk" (of a group of patients or any group under study).

· If citations are improperly filed, they will never be found when needed. A system for filing multiword items (such as "new kid on the block") must be carefully worked out so that citations for the same item are not filed under two or three different words. In citing inflected forms, such as "nuked," one can convert all to the presumed canonical forms or file them exactly in the forms in which they are cited. Both methods are used. The *OED* used the former. I prefer to file exactly under the form cited, because it is often a matter of judgment whether, for instance, a form should be regarded as the past tense of a verb or as an adjective in its own right. If one lumps these all together, the distinction tends to be lost. Even the choice of the headword for a citation represents an editorial judgment, and unless one has highly skilled citation readers (which was clearly the case with the

OED), the judgment should be deferred. The danger of this method is that when one is using the citations to define, one will fail to notice related forms filed separately under various inflections.

Defining from Citations

"For the lexicographer," says Allen Walker Read, "the crucial question about meaning is how to slice it up into manageable units. . . . [H]e collects large bodies of documented quotations, studies them for similarities and difference, and puts them into various piles."[29] A celebrated baseball umpire once silenced a belligerent player by saying that before he called a player "safe" or "out," he wasn't anything. Before a definer decides whether a collection of usages is one sense or four, it is nothing but a collection of usages. Both are imposing order as they see it on reality and both make errors. Unquestionably, the umpire is more important to baseball than lexicographers are to language, but both are in the business of interpreting behavior, and their interpretations, which are intended to be unbiased and true to the facts, have consequences for the game on the one hand and for the way we perceive the use of language on the other.[30]

The definer's task is not just to say what a word means, but to say whether there is a new meaning to be distinguished at all, or two or three. Bosley Woolf asks, "When do irony and metaphor cross the boundary between rhetorical device and new meaning?"[31] He cites the use of *fat* in "a fat chance" as a case in point. I would suggest that the use of *repression* and *subjugation* in the context of denying women their rights represents a broadening of meaning that may justify additional sense division of these terms. The same process can be illustrated by the word *ghetto*.

Ghetto was first used in English to mean a part of a European city where Jews were compelled to live. The meaning was extended in America to a rundown or overcrowded part of a city where a minority group, particularly blacks, lived. Though not physically confined to the place, their opportunities were so restricted by prejudice or poverty that they were in effect forced to live in that part of the city. Perhaps concurrently with this extension, however, the word was also used to refer to any place of metaphorical confinement; one began to see phrases like "suburban housewives locked in middle-class ghettos," where *ghetto* had no implication of poverty or any relation to cities. Because of a large number of such citations, I added a third sense of *ghetto* to *The Doubleday Dictionary:* "Any community or group separated physically or culturally from the rest of society." But metaphorical uses of this sense, as illustrated by the following citation, suggest an even further extension of meaning:

> Or will the networks simply move these popular characters to later time slots, creating a late-evening ghetto of bigotry and violence where many viewers will fear to tread? (*Wall Street Journal,* April 17, 1975, p. 36)

Ghetto is used here not of a place or people but of a time slot, yet curiously this sense—while completely removed in context from its earlier meanings—has restored part of the earlier meaning, the relation to bigotry. This illustrates how difficult it is to know where to draw the line in defining a new sense when the evidence on which one must base one's decisions is constantly changing.

Take the case of *umbrella.* Consider the following five citations, all from the *New York Times:*

> "Pending the sale, CBS will continue to run Popular Library as an active imprint, one of the six operating under the Fawcett Books umbrella," a CBS spokesman said. CBS, which bought Fawcett for $50 million in 1977, also owns Holt, Rinehart & Winston and W. B. Saunders, hardcover publishers. (June 20, 1981, p. 15)

> There is some question here, however, whether Mr. Arafat is able to control all the factions and splinter groups under the P.L.O. umbrella. (July 25, 1981, p. 4)

> Foreign aid given out of self-interest is "not acceptable," said Leon O. Marion, executive director of the American Council of Voluntary Agencies, an umbrella group of private agencies that supervises foreign disaster relief, redevelopment and resettlement. (August 30, 1981, p. L-11)

> The National Conference of Catholic Bishops, an umbrella group for Catholic dioceses in the United States, and the Apostolic Delegate for the Vatican in Washington refused to comment on the investigation. (September 11, 1981, p. A-16)

> ... charity groups that are not members of the Tristate United Way, an umbrella organization that distributes money to 375 charities in the New York area under the names Greater New York Fund and United Hospital Fund. (November 21, 1981, pp. A-1 and A-19)

One of the first things the definer must ask is, Do these extended senses share some essential part of the basic meaning of *umbrella?* Not so long ago we also heard a great deal about a "nuclear umbrella," an arsenal of nuclear weapons that was designed to protect western Europe. Obviously, "nuclear umbrella" retained the idea of providing a shield or means of protection, as does this illustrative quotation in the *World Book Dictionary* (1981 ed.):

> This is just short of the total 256 million bushels put under the Federal price umbrella for the entire season last year. *(Wall Street Journal)*

But in the five *New York Times* citations, the sense of protection is certainly not prominent. Rather, attention is being drawn to the large area an umbrella covers, and perhaps to the raylike projections of its struts emanating from a central point. Since there are apt to be a good number of citations for this use in any citation file, the sense must be included, and because the meaning differs in a fundamental way from other extended senses (such as that of *nuclear umbrella*), it must be defined separately. When I first included this sense, however, I was not so sure where its meaning was headed, and I had very little space available, so in *The Doubleday Dictionary* I combined the senses:

> umbrella   something serving as a cover or shield, or as a means of linking together various things under a common name or sponsor: the expanding *umbrella* of nuclear power.

But the senses are better treated separately. *MW9* defines the sense of the five citations this way:

> umbrella   something which covers or embraces a broad range of elements or factors ⟨decided to expand . . . by building new colleges under a federation⟩—Diane Ravitch.

Of the other college dictionaries, only *American Heritage (AHD)* has a definition unrelated to protection:

> umbrella   an all-encompassing category, organization, or authority by means of which many different things or groups are linked.

Observe how vague *MW9*'s definition is, using words like "something," "elements," and "factors," whereas *AHD*'s is much more specific, mentioning "category, organization, or authority." Although *AHD*'s definition seems to work well with my five citations, *umbrella* is used in a much broader variety of contexts than these few citations can indicate, and I believe Merriam's large citation files contained many examples that simply did not fit *AHD*'s specific definition. One of the troublesome things about defining this sense of *umbrella* is that whatever is designated an umbrella need not have anything to do with the things it's an umbrella for. This is precisely why the word is useful: it does not imply any structural connection with the things it encompasses. Frequently, the only relationship is that the umbrella entity has a name that subsumes the names of the things within its purview. Often it acts in some way as a sponsor. The key words of my definition are, therefore, "linking . . . under a common name or sponsor." In *MW9*'s definition, the key words are "covers or embraces a broad range." *AHD*'s definition is too specific, and "all-encompassing" is too strenuous a phrase and has too many different meanings to admit of a single, clear sense in this context. The *umbrella* entity in no sense encircles or encloses the things it is associated with. *MW9*'s definition is therefore vaguer but better; so is mine. *AHD2* (published after I had written these criticisms) apparently agreed, since it revised the definition to "something that encompasses or covers many different elements or groups."

Deciding What to Put in the Dictionary

The citation file is vital not just for determining what new words and new senses mean, but for providing evidence that they exist in sufficient numbers to warrant inclusion in a dictionary. Clarence Barnhart estimates that eight hundred or so new words come into the "common or working vocabulary" of English each year, and that of these about five hundred find their way into dictionaries of various sizes and types.[32] What are the criteria for deciding whether to put new words and new senses in a dictionary?

The number of citations for a word or sense collected over a period of time from a variety of sources determines whether it will be included. A single citation proves very little, but even two citations from different kinds of publications may prove a great deal. They prove that it is not a "nonce word"—a term coined for a particular occasion. If a term pops up in *Rolling Stone* and in the *Wall Street Journal,* one can conclude that it is not restricted to a small clique of speakers. Likewise, if a term appears in a recent American novel and in the *Manchester Guardian,* one can surmise it is not limited to provincial use. As Laurence Urdang points out, the occurrence of a technical term ten times in a highly specialized monograph tells us less about its exposure than a single use in *The New Yorker* or the *New York Times.*[33] Therefore, we are less concerned with the sheer number of citations than with the number and diversity of sources. Only thus can we know whether a term is still confined to technical contexts or is part of the general vocabulary, or whether a term is restricted in usage to one region of the country. We want to know whether the word belongs strictly to the idiom of young people, or rock-'n'-roll musicians, or sports lovers, diplomats, or salespeople.

Next, we want to know that a new word, even if used with great frequency over a short period of time, is not obsolete by the time the dictionary is published. Fad words may have enormous density of usage for a period of months and then disappear except for an occasional nostalgic use. When in the early 1970s young men took to racing through public places after shedding all their clothes, the event was dubbed *streaking*. As the number of such events multiplied, so did the word's use in its various manifestations. At the time, I was editing a dictionary that was just about ready to go to the printer, and I astonished my publishers by wondering aloud whether it ought to be included. I had more citations for it than I needed, but they were all from the very recent past, and I was unsure how long the word would remain current. (It took no sociological genius to realize the event would soon die out—but that did not mean the word would die out.) In the end I decided to put it in, and in this case it was the right decision, since *streak* is still used in this sense. But at that point it was little more than a guess.

Unfortunately, dictionary editors have everything to gain and nothing to lose by inserting every new word, faddish or not, that comes along, since the popular view is that the ultimate test of every new dictionary is that it has the very latest words. No attention is paid to the older words and meanings it has omitted to make room for the current crop of ephemera. But those words don't sell dictionaries, and *streak* does. Most reviewers appear to be ignorant of the fact that dictionaries occupy a finite space and assume that whatever is not included in a dictionary was overlooked. Although exceptions occasionally must be made, as a rule no word should be included unless it has been in use for at least five years and shows signs of remaining in use.

In summary, the four basic considerations in evaluating whether the citations justify the inclusion of a word are their number; the period of time covered; their geographic distribution; and the diversity of sources. One can compromise on one of the four criteria if the term in question meets the other three. For example, *streaking* lacked a sufficient period of time but was widely distributed, occurred in diverse sources, and existed in profuse numbers.

Given the impact of television and weekly news magazines in picking up some current subject of popular fascination, a new word today can gain wide currency in an amazingly short time, but many such words fizzle out after a few years. Remember *hula hoops* and *teenyboppers?* It is a lot easier to fill a dictionary with novel words than to prune it of obsolescent ones. Because a particular item is not collected in one's citation file does not prove that it does not exist. As Zgusta rightly observes, it is always difficult to draw negative conclusions from a citation file.[34] No one's file is perfectly comprehensive; many usages will be missed. There is no reliable way to determine when a word has become obsolescent. Thus, those dictionaries that have the most liberal policy of inserting new terms are precisely those most likely to be filled with antiquated slang and fad words of another generation. They lie buried like calcified fossils amidst the living words around them, awaiting some word geologist to hack them out and preserve them properly in a period dictionary.

How Useful Are Citation Files?

The underlying presumption of citation files is that, though infinitesimally small compared to all the uses of language, they truly represent the state of the language. Even the largest citation file represents only a tiny fraction of the immense volume of speech and writing that occur every single day. Since speech occupies a much greater role in the use of language than writing, and since citation files are based predominantly on writing, it is fairly certain that traditional citation files do not accurately represent all uses of language. (One wonders whether they should even pretend that they do, since dictionaries are used chiefly by people who are concerned with the written word.) In spite of *Webster's Third New International Dictionary (NID3)*'s promotion of itself as an innovator in recognizing the primacy of the spoken language, its files and its definitions were largely based, much as its predecessors were, on the written word.

In a seemingly simple but brilliant study in 1940, Kemp Malone tested the assumption that citation files are representative of actual usage by assembling a much larger sample for a single word, *mahogany,* than any dictionary had to date. He and his associates collected fifteen hundred citations for *mahogany;* even the *OED,* he pointed out, averaged only ten citations per term. His analysis of the citations showed that the chief meaning of *mahogany,* attested by 70 percent of the citations, was for a sense not included in *NID2. NID2* had included the term only in its scientific sense, and defined it primarily as a species of *Swietenia,* particularly *S. mahagoni.* Malone asks, "But what of the man who speaks of mahogany wood without having in mind any particular botanical species or genus?"[35] There are many kinds of wood called "mahogany," as Malone demonstrates. *NID2*'s definition was not based on the facts of English usage but on scientific sources or earlier dictionaries. Malone's analysis bears directly on the inability or unwillingness of dictionaries to define scientific terms on the basis of ordinary usage.

The definition for *mahogany* that Malone constructs from the preponderance of his citations does not mention any particular species:

A more or less hard and heavy wood derived from various related and unrelated tropical trees; the wood usually has interlocked or crossed

163

grain, varies in color between reddish brown and brownish yellow, seasons well, and takes a high polish; it is much used for fine cabinet work and in making other articles of luxury or superior quality, as yachts and fine furniture.[36]

Whether this sort of definition is more helpful to the reader than the more precise botanical definition, which indeed covers some of the same information as this one, is beside the point. That question merely has to do with the most helpful mix of encyclopedic and lexical information. (Malone's article evidently did not persuade *NID3* to adopt his strategy, though it modified *NID2*'s definition considerably.) The point is that Malone's article presents evidence for doubting that citation files fairly and fully represent even the written language, let alone the spoken language. We must face the fact that citation files are flawed, particularly in their representation of technical words in widespread popular use. Their usefulness is limited by the impracticality of coping with thousands of citations for every word, even if such large numbers of citations could be assembled. The files are collected by many different people who necessarily applied different standards at different times and who were influenced by their own biases as well as those of their sponsors. The collection of citations is subject chiefly to the availability of certain written materials, which are overrepresented compared to other written material and all speech.

The written materials forming the core of citation files tend to be those of the educated and upper classes. *NID3* tried to broaden its scope and was roundly denounced for having done so, but the enlarged breadth of its coverage, though more than token, did not change its bias in favor of educated writing. I am not proposing that it should; I merely state the fact. Dictionaries act as a conservative force on the language because they tend to overrepresent the volume of conservative speech and writing, which is that of the educated classes, and underrepresent the volume of speech and writing by and for people who are relatively uneducated. I believe this imbalance serves most dictionary users better than a more balanced coverage would, but certainly the point is arguable. Dictionary users are not necessarily educated or of the upper class, but they are most interested in the usages of this class. *NID3* was criticized because it dared to give—*boasted* about giving—some attention to the usages of the less well educated. Its innovation was mild and utterly benign, about as threatening to established usage as New York City's latest antinoise campaign is to taxi drivers, which is to say, for those unfamiliar with New York, of no consequence whatever. From this point of view, citation files should be weighted to some extent in favor of educated usages. But certainly the larger dictionaries should make an attempt to cover a broad variety of usages, and in this respect *NID3*'s coverage, however imperfectly it may have been presented, must be applauded as a step in the right direction.

Some of the objections to the competence of a citation file, as we shall see in Chapter 7, can be at least partially answered by a computerized system, but others cannot. Nonetheless, with all of its imperfections, the citation file remains the best and the only original source for new general terms and senses.

We have seen already how important collocational aids are to foreign learners of English. Traditional citation files are of limited usefulness in providing information about collocations of words. Far more useful are computerized studies such as the Survey of English Usage. However, citation files are used for ESL dictionaries just as they are for any other dictionary: to provide information about new words and new senses. They also suggest common illustrative phrases that can be used in the dictionary to exemplify meaning. In ESL dictionaries, illustrative phrases are generally invented by the definer rather than quoted from actual usage. Illustrative quotations are too wordy and often miss the exact point one is trying to make. The pedagogical end of ESL dictionaries is better and more economically served by illustrative phrases and sentences crafted deliberately to exemplify a particular usage, as a drawing is compared to a photograph. The same is true of children's dictionaries.

Children's dictionaries are much shorter than adult dictionaries and tend to be revised abridgments of adult dictionaries, to which a specialized citation file focused on children's literature is considered a useful supplement. There is really no point in laboriously constructing every sense of *get* from a citation file when one is concerned with brief, simple definitions. The assumption, however, that the supplementary citation file should be based on books designed for children, even if one includes classic works as well as comic books, needs to be questioned. I have discussed in Chapter 1 (see pages 15–16) the error of the assumption that a frequency count for a children's dictionary need consist only of words occurring in textbooks designed for children. The same criticism would apply to the preparation of a citation file. Indeed, a citation file for a children's dictionary must take in much of the same material collected for an adult dictionary, for a child is exposed to extended senses of common words, like that of *ghetto,* just as an adult is. If the aim of a children's dictionary is simply to help children understand the words used in their textbooks and other assigned school reading, a specialized citation file will meet the purpose admirably. If, however, a children's dictionary is designed to represent the language of children, a specialized citation file will fail utterly. The file for such a work would have to monitor television, movies, and the words of popular songs as carefully as it scrutinized the language of *Huckleberry Finn* and *David Copperfield.*

Illustrative Quotations

The illustrative quotations or invented phrases that exemplify meaning are a critical part of the dictionary definition and should not be regarded as mere appurtenances. Illustrative quotations can convey a great deal of information about collocation, variety of usage (degree of formality, humorous or sedate context), connotation (affective implications), grammatical context (if a verb, does it take an indirect object?), and, of course designative meaning. Often there is no better way to provide this information than by an illustrative quotation. Short, invented phrases are frequently essential to tell the reader how the definition is actually used in ordinary contexts. For example, in the verbal sense of *mean, MW9*'s definition "to have an intended purpose" hardly suffices without the illustrative phrase, "he *means* well." Zgusta argues that in larger dictionaries quoted examples are to be preferred over invented ones.[37] He is right, but often there is no available short quotation that exemplifies the usage as well as an invented one. In dealing with actual quotations, one is constantly frustrated by their inclusion of words that are needlessly difficult or irrelevant to the usage being illustrated but that are integral to the quotation. Thus, even an unabridged dictionary such as *NID3* commonly uses invented illustrative phrases as well as quotations. (Part of the genius of Samuel Johnson lay in the artfulness with which he abridged his quotations.[38] Sometimes he altered the wording of quotations to get his point across more economically, a practice that would not sit well with modern standards of scholarship.) There are many times when the only sensible way to amplify meaning is with an invented phrase. However, this hardly suggests that in such cases the citations are of no value. On the contrary, they provide the essential evidence for constructing a short and apt illustrative phrase.

Whenever actual citations can be used, especially in larger dictionaries, they should. Actual usage has the weight of authority behind it. It provides documentation for the definition, which is really only an interpretive claim made by the lexicographer. He says the definition means thus-and-so based on the citations available, of which the one or two quoted are presumably exemplary. The reader is free to form his own conclusions as to whether the citations are apposite and justify the definiton. But the illustrative quotation does more than support the definition; it can indicate its range of application and show whether it is used metaphorically as well as literally. Judiciously selected quotations can substitute for part of a definition by indicating, to the reader who knows how to interpret them, what the limits of literalness of a definition are. For example, here is *NID3*'s def. 2 of the adjective *suspect:*

suspect (adj.)	having the nature or status or a suspicious person or thing: provocative or worthy of suspicion: SUSPICIOUS ⟨hold one ∼ until his innocence is proved⟩ ⟨treat all innovations as ∼—A. T. Quiller-Couch⟩ ⟨he has been ∼ to many members of his own party —*Time*⟩

The first citation, which is invented, gives the most common literal usage, that relating to legal guilt. The second citation illustrates that *suspect* is not confined to people but may be used abstractly, and in this sense the word suggests skepticism on the part of the person suspecting rather than culpability of the thing suspected. The third citation is again of a person but illustrates that it can be applied metaphorically to suggest that the person suspected is untrustworthy, unreliable, or unfaithful; the metaphor equates the official party position with right behavior and stigmatizes dissent as morally culpable. These citations do more. No two are alike in collocation. *Suspect* in the first and third is followed by prepositional clauses introduced by *until* and *to,* respectively. We see that someone can be "held suspect" in the first citation or "treated as suspect" in the second, and we see from the second that *suspect* need not be followed by a clause. One of the quoted citations is British, the other American. Such considerations are not accidental but were weighed by the definers to convey as much information as possible.

The Definition of Names

The decision as to whether a name is generic or not is often difficult to make, even with the help of a citation file. As one English lexicographer asks, "If musicians say 'What this country wants is a Bayreuth,' does that amount to generalization?"[39] The question may be resolved, one would suppose, by an analysis of the citation file to see whether the generic usage of *Bayreuth* meets the criteria for any term's inclusion. If it does, it should go in. But it is not that simple.

What does one do with terms like *Chomskyan* and *Kafkaesque?* Randolph Quirk has argued that such words are properly the material of an encyclopedia rather than a dictionary because their "semantic interest . . .

resides in the work of Chomsky and Kafka."[40] I disagree, and have written in response:

> Some [eponymous words] belong in dictionaries and some do not. *Chomskyan* is specialized, appears usually in linguistic contexts, and therefore does refer to the man and his work. Not so with Kafka. *Kafkaesque* (like *Freudian*—would Professor Quirk exclude that from dictionaries?) is used, or at least is understood, by many people who have never read a word of Kafka.

I quoted the following three citations:

> It is symptomatic of the Kafkaesque atmosphere which currently prevails at the highest levels of the Administration that Mr. Agnew.... (*New York Times* editorial, August 2, 1973)

> ... involvement in mysterious clan rivalries, Kafka-esque in their complexity. (*Punch,* September 6, 1972)

> The case involved George Whitmore, Jr., ... who for the past nine years has been entangled in a Kafka-esque web of criminal charges. (*Newsweek,* April 23, 1973)

and continued:

> A similar situation exists with place names. I have not put *Watergate* in the Doubleday dictionary because I could not find any evidence that the word has been used without reference to the original event, e.g., "it was another Watergate" still refers to the unique event. Yet recently published dictionaries include it. If one is going to define *Watergate* as a symbol of governmental dirty work, on what grounds exclude *Vietnam* ("Will Angola become another Vietnam?") as a symbol of undeclared, unpopular war? ... But compare *Watergate* to *Disneyland*—rather a charming comparison, I think. *Disneyland* is used generically for any fantasy land. *Time* magazine (May 13, 1966): "The Johnson Administration's 'War on Poverty' is a churning Disneyland of administrative chaos." Note the distinction between "another Watergate" and "a Disneyland." This use of *Disneyland* has nothing to do with the Disneyland of Los Angeles, California.[41]

To which Professor Quirk responded:

> If a dictionary has such an entry as "*Chomskyite, n* a follower or admirer of A. N. Chomsky, b 1928," it is to my mind little less vacuous linguistically than an entry "*taxes, n* the plural of *tax*" would be—and pretty unhelpful encyclopedically into the bargain. The lexical point would be catered for by something like "*-ite,* affix denoting a follower or admirer." ... [¶] Now, if *Freudian* and *Kafkaesque* had no more reference than to

168

Freud and Kafka, the same would apply, mutatis mutandis. But this is not so. *Freudian* also means (roughly) "revealing a significant unconscious bias," and *Kafkaesque* likewise has an additional meaning, (roughly) "nightmarish." These are true "dictionary" meanings, in respect of which Freud and Kafka are of only etymological relevance. To take a more obvious example, we would not want an entry for *mesmerize* like "to apply the theories of F. A. Mesmer, 1734–1815": and if that were all *mesmerize* meant, we would rightly question its presence. . . .[42]

We are dealing, I think, with three different uses of names: first, the generic meanings of words like *Freudian* and *Kafkaesque* as cited by me and by Quirk; second, the vacuous lexical meanings (pertaining to Freud and his theories and Kafka and his works); and third, allusive meanings, such as those of *Watergate* and *Vietnam* cited in my letter, or of *Bayreuth,* cited by R. W. Chapman. The third use depends upon knowledge of the particular place or event alluded to (the denotatum); the name (or designatum) of the place or event is used to trigger the connotations that are the heart of the lexical definition. The meaning thus depends upon associations the user of the word expects the listener will share with him upon hearing the name.[43] Dictionaries do pay attention to words that are almost purely connotative *(nice, damn!, Hey!, uh-huh),* but are uneasy about them and try to steer them toward designative meanings.

The trouble is that allusive meanings tend to be unstable. As the impact of the events associated with a person or place fades, the use of the name can no longer be counted on to conjure up the feelings of outrage, dismay, or derision that attended its earlier use. To the extent that this happens, the word becomes more encyclopedic and less lexical. One must be cautious about including such terms prematurely, since they can have tremendous exposure for a few years and then vanish as quickly as they appeared. Nonetheless, dictionaries of college size and larger ought to include this third type of meaning if it meets the citation-file criteria for inclusion. (But they ought to flag such terms for eventual excision when the connotations have disappeared.) They should be entered frankly as encyclopedic terms with a brief description of the events that have made them lexically significant.

The attempt to force an essentially encyclopedic note into the procrustean bed of lexical meaning, as current college dictionaries do, is misguided and artificial. For example, *AHD* defines *Watergate* as follows (*World*'s treatment is similar):

Watergate   a scandal that involves officials violating public or corporate trust through perjury, bribery, and other acts of abuse of power in order to keep their elective or appointive positions.

169

This defines *Watergate* generically, and I have yet to see evidence that the word is used generically rather than allusively. The definition thus defines hypothetical rather than actual usage. A better treatment would be to define Watergate with *AHD*'s etymology: "a building complex in Washington, D.C., housing the Democratic Party headquarters, burglarized in June, 1972, in accordance with instructions issued by government officials," and to add, "The ensuing scandal involving the Nixon administration included allegations of perjury, bribery, and other acts of abuse of power by high public officials." Exactly this sort of treatment is accorded an older scandal, *Teapot Dome,* in the same dictionary:

Teapot Dome   a region near Casper, Wyoming, set aside in 1915 as a naval oil reserve: the subject of a scandal during the Harding administration (1922).

This is the only sensible way to handle allusive meaning.[44] *Teapot Dome* is yesteryear's *Watergate,* and to all but elderly readers who remember the event, its dictionary entry is purely encyclopedic.

About the first use of names, the generic use, there is no doubt. These must be included with definitions based on the record of usage; the identification of the eponym is properly part of the etymology, as Quirk said. About the second use of names, whose meaning Quirk finds vacuous, what shall I say? Much of what we define is vacuous, or may look so at despondent moments, yet in it must go. If *Chomskyan* satisfies the four criteria for inclusion with respect to its occurrence in a citation file, it must be included, however bleak and uninspiring its meaning may be. Dictionaries cannot afford to say more than "pertaining to Noam Chomsky or his theories"; they cannot discourse on Chomsky's linguistic theories. There is no space for that, and the information would be purely encyclopedic, irrelevant to a dictionary's purpose.

Other Sources of Definition

As we have seen, no citation file can provide the right kind of data for all dictionary entries. Most scientific and technical terms must be defined by specialists on the basis of their judgments about preferred scientific usage. (The difficulties of determining preferred scientific terms have been discussed in Chapter 3.) Moreover, the pedagogical purpose of ESL dictionaries and children's dictionaries calls for greater flexibility in the choice and presentation of material than a rigorous dependence on citations could accommodate. In the case of children's dictionaries, the advice of educators and teachers must be sought. In the case of ESL dictionaries, the advice of linguistic scholars familiar with the problems of foreign learners must surely outweigh a numerical totting up of citations of one form against another.

Citation files cannot be relied on to turn up new scientific and technical terms in any systematic way. They provide a great many scientific terms for dictionaries of neologisms, such as the Barnhart dictionaries of "New English," but they will not provide adequate or consistent coverage of various scientific fields for a general dictionary. For that one needs specialists, who compile lists of terms in their own subjects that they regard as essential. Existing dictionaries often have their scientific and technical terms already categorized and coded by subject. In preparing a new edition, each subject's list is sent to the respective specialist with the old edition's definitions. He is asked to review and revise them, if necessary, deleting obsolete terms and proposing new ones for inclusion. The same practice is employed for terms of many other special subjects such as law, business, sports, the theater arts, music, and so on. However, the prudent reader will regard a dictionary's inclusion of long lists of special advisers on everything from archery to zither playing with a certain skepticism. Many experts, even some prominent ones, are not averse to having their names listed for a modest fee. The practice was begun in 1658 in Edward Phillips's *The New World of English Words* and has continued without let-up ever since. It is not known whether Phillips paid his prominent consultants anything, or even whether they knew their names were to appear in his dictionary. Modern consultants are paid, though meagerly, and if they have sinned, we may at least have the satisfaction of knowing they have not profited much by it.

Another important source of new words and new senses is reference books, including other dictionaries. Dictionary makers acquire every significant new dictionary as soon as it is published. One's direct competitors' works are examined with due care to see what new terms they have included—or failed to include. Though definitions are protected by copyright, the listing of new terms and new senses is fair game for all comers. Once having discovered the existence of new words by seeing them in another dictionary, nothing prevents one from seeking more information about them from other sources and writing one's own definition. Facts cannot be copyrighted, only the specific way in which they are represented. Another dictionary's definition must be considered along with other citations for the word being defined. In Johnson's day and long afterward, dictionaries openly cited other dictionaries in print as the source for certain terms, quoting their definitions as illustrative quotations. Historical dictionaries still do, but commercial dictionaries are now loath to admit to having relied on a competitor. For marketing reasons, every dictionary is represented as being unaffected by every other. Nothing could be further from the truth. I doubt that anyone has the time to go through a competitor's dictionary entry by entry, or that such an exercise would be worthwhile if one did. Rather, the dictionary is examined under key terms, as a physician who from long familiarity with a patient knows where to look and what to look for. Copies of the new dictionary are kept close at hand and used by several staff members, for from such use new terms and senses will be found.

Dictionaries of new words and new word supplements are a good source of potential new entries and senses. The criteria for inclusion in such works are, however, much more lax than those for a general dictionary, so they are not quite as rich a source as one might suppose. If one has an ongoing citation file, one should already have some record of many of the terms listed, and the chief benefit of dictionaries of neologisms may well be the chance to see additional citations and compare the definition given with one's own.

When one defines a new term one is truly on uncharted grounds. The intellectual effort is analogous to that employed in deciphering a message in code, except that, unlike the cryptographer, the definer never knows whether he has the message right. Therefore, he seeks what aid and comfort he can get by comparing notes with whatever else is available. When working from citations, one should compose one's own definitions before looking at comparable definitions in other dictionaries. Otherwise, one is likely to be too much influenced by the other dictionaries' definitions. However, it is wise to check. Sometimes on reading another's definition of a new sense one may see that one's own has missed the essential point. Every definer has had this experience. It is for this reason, as we shall see in Chapter 6, that each definition passes through a number of critical reviews before it is adjudged to be final.

When there are gaps in the record of citations, as when one is revising a dictionary that has been allowed to become far out of date, other recent dictionaries are consulted as a matter of course. The *OED* and its *Supplements* are essential sources to any such revision. Often the definer must construct his own definition based on the facts conveyed in other dictionaries' definitions. The definer cannot use the wording of another dictionary's definition. His own knowledge of the language, his familiarity with the word and its use, and his *Sprachgefühl* (feeling for the language) play a decisive part in framing his own definition in his own words. (See Chapter 8 for a discussion of plagiarism in lexicography.)

Specialized dictionaries and encyclopedic works are also useful to the definer. They are not a primary source of new words and senses but are valuable as a means of checking to see whether "new" technical words or senses turned up by the citation file are really new, or whether they are well established in technical nomenclature but only now beginning to enter the general vocabulary. Slang dictionaries are valuable for the same reason: words that at first blush seem novel may turn out to have been in use for half a century in the argot of a particular group, such as among southern black jazz musicians. Current citations still determine current meaning, but the word's earlier uses may contain important clues about more recent usage. Without a good reference library, one might easily mistake mere extensions in meaning or variations in form of an existing word for an entirely new word.

I have been speaking about the citation file and the defining process as though definition depended simply on following a set of rules, and I hope I have not given the impression that anyone willing to faithfully follow the rules can learn to define. The qualities of a good definer are discussed in Chapter 6, but it must be made clear that aptitude in defining is an uncommon skill and that it cannot always be taught, even to those with excellent formal educations. The best citations, the finest specialists, and the most exhaustive reference library will go for nought if the staff is unable or unwilling to use them. Good definers are precious; one puts up with their foibles and eccentricities as impresarios put up with those of their leading performers. They are not replaceable. It takes years of training and experience to make a really good definer, and without a small cadre of such people no dictionary of quality can be produced.

CHAPTER FIVE

Usage

Usage refers to any or all uses of language, spoken or written. Usage bears the same relation to other aspects of language as the bloodstream does to the endocrine hormones. As the bloodstream circulates the hormones, which affect every aspect of growth and development, so does the vast flow of words in sound and writing constitute the medium through which speech is perceived as intelligible, meaning is discerned, and grammar is understood. But *usage* is used in another sense as well: the study of good, correct, or standard uses of language, as distinguished from bad, incorrect, and nonstandard uses. *Usage* may also take in the study of any limitations on use, whether geographic, social, or temporal. This chapter deals with those aspects of usage (in its broad sense of all uses) that are singled out by dictionaries as being limited to some part of the universe of speakers or writers, past or present, either by special notes or labels or by qualifications within definitions.

No discussion of usage can be meaningful without giving some attention to why people regard certain usages as good or standard and others as improper or ignorant. Controversies over "good usage" have a long history in English and continue to the present day. I will therefore devote a considerable part of this chapter to a discussion of attitudes toward usage. Finally, I will propose methods that might be employed in the future to determine standard usage and usage that needs to be qualified in dictionaries. We shall see that an examination of usage cannot easily be confined to an examination of language and its contexts but turns us around toward the world of behavior in general, where our grounds for making assertions often leave us feeling uncomfortable and uncertain and sometimes even a bit foolish.

Here are the most common kinds of usage information given by general dictionaries, along with typical dictionary labels:

1. Currency or temporality: *archaic, obsolete*
2. Frequency of use: *rare*
3. Regional or geographic variation: *U.S., British, Canadian, Australian;* sometimes regional areas within a country are specified.
4. Technical or specialized terminology: *astronomy, chemistry, physics,* etc.; these are called *field labels.*
5. Restricted or taboo usage: *vulgar, obscene*
6. Insult: *offensive, disparaging, contemptuous*
7. Slang: *slang*
8. Style, functional variety, or register: *informal, colloquial, literary, poetic, humorous*
9. Status or cultural level: *nonstandard, substandard, illiterate.*

The Kinds of Usage Information Given in Dictionaries

Currency and Frequency Labels

When a word has completely disappeared from use but is retained for historical purposes it is labeled "obsolete," such as *purchase* in the sense of pillage or plunder. "Archaic" is applied to words that are no longer in regular use but may occur occasionally in contexts deliberately historical or humorous, such as *damsel.* General monolingual dictionaries, which must be selective in their choice of entries, have relatively few archaic words and fewer still obsolete ones. An unabridged dictionary, even one synchronically focused like *Webster's Third New International Dictionary,* must pay considerable attention to older forms, as *NID3* does in reporting all usages from 1755. In bilingual and ESL dictionaries, accurate currency labeling is essential, since the user with limited familiarity with the target language might otherwise use a word in altogether inappropriate contexts. Some bilingual lexicographers try to match the currency of the translations with the terms in the source language; if this can be done accurately, no label is necessary.[1]

Dictionaries with large, historical citation files can document reasonably well that a word or sense is archaic or obsolete. If no occurrence of a particular sense has been found in two hundred years, we can say with some assurance that the sense is obsolete. If we have none for the last fifty years, we cannot be so sure, and we might call such a sense archaic. Some dictionaries include the label "obsolescent" for borderline words that appear to be fading from use.

Specialized dictionaries have particular difficulties in applying currency labels accurately, because no large historical citation files of technical terms exist. Yet it is of great practical importance to label archaic and obsolete usages to alert the user that these terms should not be naïvely employed in a present-day scientific paper. One must therefore rely on the rather subjective and variable experience of experts and try the best one can to convey a consistent message regarding what constitutes obsoleteness and archaism. When dealing with a large number of specialists, some of whom may have only a primitive grasp of dictionary practice and little intuitive feeling for the use of language, uniformity of treatment of currency is impossible.

Frequency of use is usually indicated by the label "rare." Although frequency is related to currency, the distinction is worth preserving, since a word may be rare and still be current, a principle that the *OED* consistently recognizes by doubly labeling those words that are both obsolete and rare, such as *registery* as a form of *registry*. The inclusion of rare words is confined by and large to unabridged, historical, and technical dictionaries. General monolingual and bilingual dictionaries have little space for such oddities, and they would be positively harmful to include in ESL dictionaries.

Occasionally one finds definitions labeled "rare & poetic" or "archaic & poetic" in general dictionaries, especially in older editions. I have never understood what the style label "poetic" meant, or what it was doing mixed up with rare or archaic words. One bilingual lexicographer maintains that the label "poetic" works all right "if you are willing to say that English poetry stops with Tennyson. . . ."[2] There are perhaps a dozen words like *o'er* and *even* (for *evening*) that have traditionally been called poetic because it was felt that they required some kind of restrictive label and nobody could think of anything better. *Poetic* is merely confusing, however, and a slander against poetry. It should be quietly dropped and forgotten.

Regional Labels

Forms of expression and pronunciations limited to a particular region have long been regarded as objects of contempt and ridicule. Harold B. Allen cites Edmund Coote's *The English Schoolemaster* of 1596 as providing "the first wholesale indictment of provincialisms." Although Nathan Bailey included dialectal terms in his *Dictionarium Britannicum* (1730), Johnson did not. "Even the scholarly acceptance of the legitimacy of dialect studies in the last third of the 19th century did not affect the general notion that dialectalisms are substandard if not plainly incorrect."[3] One is exempt from such aspersions only if one's regional speech happens to coincide with that of the prestige dialect of the country or the part of the country where one lives. *Prestige dialect* refers to a dialect widely accorded respect by all social levels in a community because it is identified with well-educated people of high social and economic standing.

Prestige immediately calls into play social and economic considerations of class. Randolph Quirk points out that uneducated speech is more closely identified with regional dialect, while educated speech conforms more nearly to a national variety.[4] In Britain, educated speech is identified with "BBC English," in the United States with "network English"—that is, with national broadcasters of radio and television. The observation is more apt for Britain than for the United States, where there is no national standard, rather a different prestige dialect for each of the main dialectal regions of the country.

Dialect, states one linguistic scholar, is "neither crude nor quaint speech; it is a natural variety of a base language, possessing characteristics that may identify the speaker with a region, an era, another language in his background, or even . . . his social class or his race."[5] This discussion is confined to regional dialect, but it is well to be reminded that dialect is any feature of speech that serves to identify the speaker as a member of a particular speech community, past or present.

Dictionaries have had an indifferent record in reporting regional usages. *Webster's New International Dictionary,* Second Edition, *(NID2)* often labeled definitions as "dial." or "illit.," as did college dictionaries after it, thus perpetuating the notion that dialectal forms were an illiterate form of speech. Moreover, many of the forms labeled dialectal were not in fact regional, and others labeled "illiterate" or "nonstandard" were actually dialectal. In part, the poor performance of dictionaries was due to the dearth of available studies. Regional literature is unreliable, since authors tend either to misrepresent or grossly exaggerate regional features of speech. But scholars have complained with some justice that even those works that were available were not fully utilized: the *Linguistic Atlas of New England* (1939–1943), *Word Geography of the Eastern United States* (1948), and *Pronunciation of English in the Atlantic States* (1961). In 1976, the *Linguistic Atlas of the Upper Midwest* was completed.[6] As Audrey Duckert has pointed out, however, up until recently the atlas records were not indexed, thus making their material difficult to use. Moreover, the data recorded in

177

the atlases often cannot be concisely and accurately represented in a dictionary; the picture is often too complicated for simple labeling. How much space can a general dictionary afford to give to the usages peculiar to a particular region?

The purpose of linguistic atlases is to chart dialects by exemplifying divergences in use. They are not designed to serve lexicography. Thus their coverage of vocabulary is only one aspect, and usually not the chief one, of their effort. They are not concerned with recording a vast number of usages but in finding just enough differences to draw meaningful conclusions about regional dialects. Valuable as they are, atlases are not ideal sources for determining which words, among the hundreds of thousands that may be included in a dictionary, should be labeled with respect to region, or for determining what the labels should be.

Happily, the forthcoming *Dictionary of American Regional English* (abbreviated *DARE*) edited by Frederic G. Cassidy is likely to go a long way toward providing systematic guidance both for identification and labeling of vocabulary items. This work is based on a vast collection of regional materials and on painstaking interviews with over 2,700 informants in 1,002 carefully selected communities in all 50 states. Each questionnaire contained 1,847 questions, and nearly 2.5 million responses were obtained. Each informant was categorized by age, type of community, race, education, and sex. It is estimated that when *DARE* is published it will contain about 100,000 entries and include 2,000 maps showing the regional distributions of vocabularly items. By plotting each variable on a computer-generated map of the United States, the *DARE* editor can see at a glance the distribution of the responses. The maps are intentionally distorted to reflect population densities; thus New York and Massachusetts appear larger than they are and many of the western states much smaller (see Figures 8 and 9). Figure 8 identifies each state on the *DARE* map. Figure 9 shows the distribution of *gesundheit* and *scat* in answer to the question, "When somebody sneezes, what do people say to him?" One can see that *scat* is widespread in the entire southern half of the United States except for the far west. It does not occur at all north of southern Missouri, nor does it occur west of the Rocky Mountains.

There is no doubt that *DARE* will become the basic source for regional labeling in American dictionaries for many years to come. It is the first substantial American *dictionary* to employ unassailably objective, scholarly methods for assembling a vast quantity of data on regional differences in vocabulary. Its publication should see a significant improvement in the coverage of regionalisms in all reputable American dictionaries.(For further discussion of *DARE,* see page 221.)

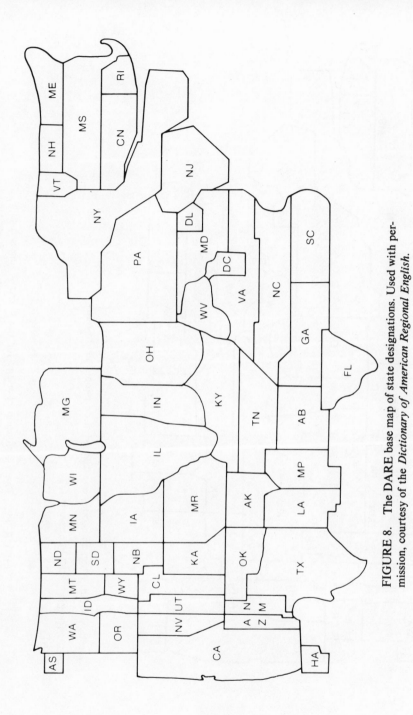

FIGURE 8. The **DARE** base map of state designations. Used with permission, courtesy of the *Dictionary of American Regional English*.

179

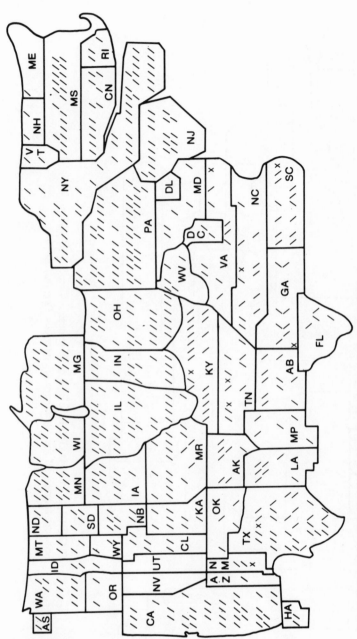

Question NN18: When somebody sneezes, what do people say to him?

GESUNDHEIT   467 Informants (/)

SCAT   95 Informants (\)

BOTH   (x)

FIGURE 9. The distribution of usage for the words *gesundheit* and *scat*. Used with permission, courtesy of the *Dictionary of American Regional English*.

Field Labels

Every general dictionary contains some words that have special meanings in a technical field or science. Field labels such as *astronomy, physics, engineering,* and *law* are applied to terms that are important in the field and in such widespread use that they have appeared in popular articles or in specialized magazines for the amateur rather than for the professional. Science digests, financial newspapers, health magazines, hobbyist publications of all sorts include a great range of technical terms, terms like *DNA, pulsar, antimatter, macroeconomics,* and *toxic shock syndrome.* Some dictionaries use field labels abundantly, others sparingly. Some incorporate the label within the definition with an introductory phrase, such as: "In astronomy . . ."

The profligate use of field labels has the effect of fragmenting knowledge and presenting each definition in the narrow terms of a specialty instead of simply letting it stand for what it is. Many scientific terms that were regarded forty years ago as strictly chemical are now seen as having profound biological importance, and to label them *chemistry* would be misleading. The use of multiple labeling is no solution, because one would soon find oneself adding a third and fourth label to the series. If one can craft the definition to reveal the context clearly, no field label is necessary, and in most cases it is preferable to have none. One is often embarrassed at the way scientific progress confounds our penchant for making neat distinctions in definitions. Suddenly a new use is found for an article that takes it entirely out of its original frame of reference. A highly technical term that no one but an elite group of specialists had ever heard of is suddenly a familiar topic to millions because it is discussed on a TV talk show. Such events make the assignment of field labels seem presumptuous and short-sighted. In a general dictionary, the best definition takes in the broadest possible range of application consistent with meaningfulness. Though a label has the virtue of immediately placing the definition in its customary context, it has the defect of restricting it to that context even when it might be applied in the same sense to other contexts. Nonetheless, if a definition cannot conveniently establish the context, a label or brief introductory phrase announcing the subject is far better than a wasteful preamble to provide background. A label or qualifying phrase is essential when a word is used in two or more different disciplines with different meanings, or if it is used in one sense technically and in another popularly, such as *parameter.*

NID3 was severely taxed for dropping many of the field labels used in *NID2.* Critics missed seeing the copious use of such labels as *civil engineering, metallurgy,* and *manufacturing,* but they should have reflected that the changes in many fields over the years had made such labels arbitrary and would have dated *NID3*. On the other hand, in its zeal to use few labels, *NID3* sometimes omitted one when it could have spared the reader confusion by including one. For example, def. 4 of *nothingness,* unlabeled, is as follows:

> nothingness   the conceptualization or reification of the affective content in an emotional experience (as of anxiety) that is negatively colored ⟨∼ is ... a distinctive metaphysical entity —J. A. Franquiz); also: MEAN- INGLESSNESS ⟨the utter ∼ of not being—Jean Wahl⟩.

The first illustrative quotation is supposed to tell us that the definition is a philosophical one, but the reader who innocently encounters this definition is likely to be baffled by it. A simple label or introductory phrase, such as "In existential philosophy ... " would have immediately made the definition intelligible and rendered the illustrative quotations, which are singularly unilluminating, superfluous. The introductory phrase would thus have saved space as well as clarified the definition.

In technical dictionaries, the broader the scope of the work, the easier— and more essential—is the application of field labels. Popular dictionaries embracing all or many of the sciences or the arts can distinguish one subject from another without too much difficulty, since each designation is apt to be broad. The more specialized the work and the more professional the intended audience, the more difficult it is to label by field. It is the difference between cutting large wedges from a whole pie and dividing one piece into smaller pieces. The simpler definitions of the more popular dictionary can be served perfectly well by limiting them to a broad field, whereas the more specific and fuller definitions of a professional dictionary tend to branch out and intersect with other subdisciplines.

Taboo

Offensive and taboo words are usually grouped together, but I have distinguished between them because they represent two different situations.

Until the *American Heritage Dictionary (AHD)* was published in 1969, no general American dictionary in this century had included the basic taboo words, those four-letter terms dealing with sex and scatology that once had the power to shock. Thus, when two New York University students wrote in that year to ask me what the origin of *fuck* was, I took the opportunity of answering them according to the credo that had informed lexicographic practice for the previous century. My answer (except for changing the names of the correspondents) is as follows:

October 16, 1969

Dear Misses Crawley and Schmidt:

I presume you are referring to the word f**k, since we have no record whatever that any word spelled "fuck" has ever existed or been used in the English language. You are probably confusing it with the word *fluck*, a seventeenth-century blend of "flood" and "muck," as illustrated by this quotation from a Cornish manuscript found in 1633 by Bishop Arkney:

> the fluck and slime sucked down our boots . . . advance was par-
> lous in th' extreme

F**k is of fairly recent coinage, probably being a blend of *f*** and *k*, although some authorities insist that f**k was used at least as early as the fifteenth century. Queen Isabella is said to have uttered it upon learning that the *Santa Maria* had foundered off the coast of the New World. Be that as it may, there is no doubt that the word is of English origin. The most likely explanation attributes the coining of the word to Lord Byron. While penning a letter to his mistress, in which he had the intention of inviting her to drop a fork under the table at which they would soon be supping, wherewith to converse with her in private as they both leaned low to retrieve it and perhaps arrange an assignation at his apartments, Byron, while making the word "fork," spilled two star-shaped inkblots over the medial letters. Byron failed to notice the blots and sent the epistle as it was. From then on it was only a matter of time until every seedy rake about town was making similar inkblots, and forks were dropped all over England when men and women supped together.

Sincerely,
Sidney I. Landau
(signed)

Allen Walker Read's classic article entitled "An Obscenity Symbol" never once specified the word, but it took considerable courage in 1934 both on his part and that of the editor, Cabell Greet, to print the piece. Read gives a somewhat more credible history of the word than mine and observes that its first occurrence in a dictionary was in John Florio's work of 1598. He also speculates on the nature of taboo. Neither sex nor excrementary functions are obscene, Read says. Attitude determines obscenity.

> [O]bscenity is any reference to the bodily functions that gives to anyone a certain emotional reaction, that of a "fearful thrill" in seeing, doing, or speaking the forbidden. Thus it is the existence of the ban or taboo that creates the obscenity. . . .[7]

But what is the origin of the ban or taboo? Allen Read distinguishes between the taboo of thing (the sexual act) and the taboo of word (*fuck*). Attitudes toward taboo, he says, have been fostered by others' attitudes,

183

engendered by punishment from parents and the thrill and hushed sense of daring and naughtiness from one's childhood peers. Taboo fulfills a deep human need, he argues, and societies preserve its usefulness as taboo by objecting to it. Doubtless Read is on firm anthropologic ground for making these assertions, but I question whether taboo of thing is really quite separate from taboo of word. In a survey of the definitions (or lack of definitions) of *sexual intercourse* in American college dictionaries, I found that "the tabooness of *fuck* exists not so much in the supposedly coarse contexts in which it is used ... as in the essential meaning which every modern man and woman professes to find entirely wholesome: sexual intercourse."[8] Uttering "sexual intercourse" in a crowded restaurant would turn more heads today than uttering "fuck." Dictionaries, even those that include *fuck,* generally do not define *sexual intercourse,* preferring to abandon the basic principles of lexicography and tiptoe back and forth between aseptic scientific and veterinarian substitutes. If included at all, it is defined tersely as "coitus" or with the legalistic and baffling "sexual connection." These words are often defined circularly as "sexual intercourse."

> One could more easily excuse such inadequate treatment of a term of immense importance and broad currency if it were in accord with the treatment given other terms. Here is AHD on *transformer:* "A device used to transfer electric energy, usually that of an alternating current, from one circuit to another; especially, a pair of multiply wound, inductively coupled wire coils that effect such a transfer with a change in voltage, current, phase, or other electric characteristic. See step-down transformer, step-up transformer." (The same dictionary needed but four words to define *sexual intercourse!*) ... We should all learn things we'd never dreamt of if we were told half so much about sexual intercourse.[9]

The *Random House College Dictionary (RHCD)* is the only college dictionary that actually defines *sexual intercourse.* Among smaller dictionaries, *Doubleday* is the only general work to define it. The *Scribner-Bantam English Dictionary* defines it as "sexual connection between humans," but *sexual connection* is nowhere defined, and *coitus* and *copulate* are defined in terms of "sexual intercourse."[10] The *Oxford American Dictionary* defines it as "copulation," which is run on to *copulate,* which is defined as "to unite sexually as in the act of mating." Yet one sense of *intercourse* and the entire definition for *coitus* is "sexual intercourse."[11]

If the tabooness of sexual intercourse inheres in the obscene word for it and not in the act itself, what are we to make of this record of gross violation of the basic rules of lexicography? Will anyone seriously allege that the expression *sexual intercourse* is an obscene term? No dictionary labels it as vulgar. If the term is not obscene, why this peculiar reluctance to define it? The conclusion is inescapable that the expression of its meaning is taboo, if not the meaning itself. The tabooness of word and thing are more closely intertwined than Read suggested.[12]

A number of seventeenth-century dictionaries contained taboo words, and Nathan Bailey included them in his *Universal Etymological English Dictionary* (1721). Johnson included some vulgar words, such as *bloody,* but by and large omitted them. In 1785, Francis Grose's *A Classical Dictionary of the Vulgar Tongue* appeared. In the nineteenth century, consciousness of taboo was stronger than ever, and Read reminds us that in America *leg* was not uttered before ladies. (If necessary, *limb* was used.) One of the few consistencies in Noah Webster's behavior was his determination to exclude all vulgarities from his dictionaries, and the compass of vulgarity then was much greater than it is now.

The decision whether to include or exclude taboo words in a dictionary relates directly to the purpose of the work. If one conceives of a dictionary as purely descriptive, every word that can be documented as being in sufficiently wide use should be included, no matter how abhorrent. If a dictionary has normative or pedagogic aims, one must question whether taboo terms are useful. For an ESL dictionary for adults, they may well be; a foreign learner should be made aware of common taboo words to avoid the embarrassment of using them inadvertently. In a children's dictionary, the inclusion of taboo words would probably cause much less harm to children than is commonly supposed, but there is no doubt that it would cause a great deal of hardship for their teachers. Young children cannot be expected to understand the dictionary's principle of objective selection of entries based on usage. Teachers would be confronted on the one hand by puzzled and titillated students and on the other by outraged parents. Life is too precious for sacrificial heroism to so little purpose; let us acknowledge the undesirability of including taboo words in children's dictionaries.

Difficulty arises in deciding whether to include taboo words in general adult dictionaries that may be used in schools. Educators view such dictionaries as normative; lexicographers usually do not. Even if the dictionary publisher is willing to compromise and omit those few taboo terms that are deemed most offensive, the educational censors are unlikely to be appeased. In 1976 the education commissioner of Texas refused to list any of the four major college dictionaries or *The Doubleday Dictionary* for purchase. It was not just the inclusion of the four-letter words that disturbed the commissioner. *Webster's New World Dictionary* did not include them yet was banned anyway, because the textbook committee and the commissioner also objected to terms like *bed, clap, deflower, john, G-string, slut, bastard,* and many others.[13] Newspaper accounts of dictionaries being banned from the school libraries and classrooms of small towns are commonplace.[14] The real decision facing a lexicographer who is asked to omit terms on the grounds of taste is not a matter of leaving out *fuck* and half a dozen other words. If that were the issue, its resolution would be fairly trivial—scholarship will not languish because dictionaries omit *fuck*. But the moment the lexicographer accedes to the principle of excluding any words on the grounds of someone else's taste, he has relinquished control of his dictionary and turned it into an instrument of privileged propaganda, like an American history text that omits mention of slavery. Once he acknowledges that any criterion overrides that of use, how can he object to the exclusion of countless other words deemed objectionable to one group or another? For like other categories of usage, the offensiveness of various words is a continuum from the most objectionable sexual or scatological terms to mild profanities.

Even today, *hell* and *damn* are objectionable to a great many people for vague or specific religious reasons, though not, to be sure, to those who write for mass-circulation magazines or for television or movies. The use of *hell* in a rural fundamentalist family may be more shocking than that of *fuck* in a suburban upper-middle-class family with weak religious inclinations. Shock value depends on circumstance and the attitudes of the audience. Nonetheless, as a rule, oaths, whether euphemistic or explicit, mild or savage, perform a different function from that of the sexual and scatological obscenities. The purpose of oaths can hardly be described better than in this passage from *The Golden Bowl* by Henry James:

> His wife had once told him, in relation to his violence of speech, that such excesses, on his part, made her think of a retired General whom she had once seen playing with toy soldiers, fighting and winning battles, carrying on sieges and annihilating enemies with little fortresses of wood and little armies of tin. Her husband's exaggerated emphasis was *his* box of toy soldiers, his military game. It harmlessly gratified him, for his declining years, the military instinct; bad words, when sufficiently numerous and arrayed in their might, could represent battalions, squadrons, tremendous cannonades and glorious charges of cavalry. It was natural, it was delightful—the romance, and for her as well, of camp life and of the perpetual booming of guns. It was fighting to the end, to the death, but no one was ever killed.

Insult

Terms of insult—*wop, kike, nigger, mick*—are also offensive, and the lexicographer is subject to the same pressures about omitting them. However, he is usually under no pressure to omit equally offensive terms like *white trash, hillbilly,* or *redneck; queer* or *fag; cretin* or *retard* (as terms of abuse). These epithets are not addressed to members of groups that can exert pressure on state commissioners of education; hence they are unimportant and considered to offend no one. Most are not even labeled by dictionaries as offensive. The question that arises is, To whom are they not offensive?[15]

No aspect of usage has been more neglected by linguists and lexicographers than that of insult. Although off-the-cuff comments about *ain't*— "improper in polite society," for instance—are ridiculed as *ipse dixit* declarations, exactly the same kind of comments when applied to *frog, kraut,* or *canuck* are customarily praised as sensitive and precise judgments. For example, a review of the *OED Supplement,* Volume II, in a professional library journal asserted, "Derogatory ethnic words and expressions have received an exacting treatment, with appropriate designations such as 'vulgarly offensive' or 'deliberate and contemptuous ethnic abuse.'"[16] But there are no agreed-upon criteria for finding some usages vulgarly offensive or contemptuous or abusive. There are few studies that shed any light on the degree of offensiveness of specified terms under specified conditions. Such studies would have to take into consideration these vitally important questions: Did speaker and listener belong to the same or different groups? The same term uttered with a laugh to a member of one's own group might be deeply offensive if uttered to a member of another group. The intonation patterns (patterns of rising and falling pitch) and loudness will be quite different in the two utterances, as will paralinguistic features (gesture, nonmeaningful sounds accompanying speech, facial expression). Even between members of two different groups, supposedly offensive words are not necessarily offensive if the two people know each other very well or if the situation is one where certain male ritualistic behavior is considered appropriate. Insult can be affectionate. In short, there is no basis for asserting that terms of insult are vulgarly offensive or contemptuous, but because ethnic slurs are politically important and *ain't* is not, one opinion is accounted reliably scientific and the other dismissed as backward prejudice. None of us wants to be taken for a racist or bigot, but we are very willing to be taken for egalitarians for whom social distinctions based on language are a matter of indifference.[17]

Of course, we *know* that terms of insult are usually taken to be offensive under certain conditions, and it is important that these words be labeled to warn those unfamiliar with them that the may be offensive. But there is nothing scientific or exacting about these warnings. They are simply prudent, like telling someone not to say *ain't* to a teacher. Few lexicographers have actually been witness to the use of many terms of insult or had the opportunity to observe the offended reactions of listeners or bystanders. The decision to label a word offensive is rarely based on reasoned discussion of what one or a group of people have actually experienced. It is based on the editor's judgment of society's norm for the limits of reputable public behavior. As in dress and manners, so in speech there is considerable freedom, and the range of freedom varies greatly from one group to another, but there are limits that all but a few dissenting groups would agree to. The advice is only about *public* behavior, since many reputable members of society routinely use terms of insult in private among like-minded people to whom these words are not in the least offensive. It is only when they miscalculate and use such terms when not among like-minded people that they offend.

The editor arrives at his judgment of the norms for permissible speech chiefly by consulting slang dictionaries and other written sources rather than spoken ones. Citations for terms of insult in a citation file are apt to occur mainly in fiction and in journalistic glossaries. Many citations for terms of insult in fiction do not at all support the judgment that they are offensive, since they are often used among intimates who share the same prejudices. The citation file is thus of limited use in providing a basis for determining which words are offensive. The lexicographer is compelled to use his own experience, moderated of necessity by his own moral views, whether consciously or not.[18]

Labeling of insult, then, is essentially political and moral. The lexicographer is taking a stand on the side of those who deplore racial and ethnic bigotry. He is also deflecting criticism for including offensive terms by showing his repugnance for them. This is a position with which we can sympathize, even while it must be acknowledged that the warnings are given selectively, as already noted. People who are deformed or of low intelligence, for whom terms of abuse exist by the score if not by the hundreds, are not recognized as being important enough to warrant labeling the words they might find offensive. Since the number of abusive words in English is vast, any attempt to label systematically all the words used for insult would be an immense and ultimately hopeless assignment. One would have to know much more than it is possible to know about the social contexts in which each word was used. One would have to be alert to many groups that one had not previously considered offendable: people of short stature, fat people, forceful women, timid men. English has terms of abuse for them all, as well as for atheists, scholars, children, old people, poor people, and many other groups. Labeling of insult must be selective. It must slight certain groups and recognize others, however much we may wish we could be perfectly disinterested. Traditional dictionary practice, as we have seen also in connection with definition, reflects the prevailing norms and prejudices of the dominant culture.

Slang

Slang deserves a category all by itself. It is sometimes grouped with the style labels ("formal/informal") and sometimes with the status labels ("standard/nonstandard"), but it does not comfortably fit with either. Slang does not represent a vocabulary that one can adopt to suit a social situation, as one can with terms on the "formal/informal" index. In fact, when slang is used appropriately it is on the way to becoming standard speech. Unlike other words restrictively labeled, slang is deliberately nonstandard. Much slang has been introduced by criminals, hucksters, and gamblers; how shall we characterize the cultural levels of these groups? They are off the beaten track, but are they necessarily of low cultural level because their occupations happen to be antisocial? Much slang derives also from the cant of musicians and soldiers and other groups that feel isolated or beleaguered. Their private vocabulary percolates through layers of language to become tomorrow's slang, then routinely peppers the conversations of young people everywhere. Some dictionary users mistakenly suppose that slang is in the category of taboo words. Although much slang deals with off-color subjects, taboo words are not necessarily slang and most slang words are not taboo. There is only an incidental correspondence between the categories.

Jonathan Lighter, who is compiling a dictionary of slang, has said:

> Slang denotes an unorthodox, nontechnical popular vocabulary composed especially of novel-sounding synonyms for standard English words and phrases: it is primarily associated with youthful, raffish, or otherwise undignified speakers, who are presumed to use it for its often striking connotations of impertinence, irreverence, or rejection of polite conventionality.[19]

His is a more exclusive definition than some would give. Note that he distinguishes slang from both technical language and standard English, and proposes that the intention for using it and the kind of people who normally use it are essential properties of its meaning.

Although most slang is novel sounding, it is not necessarily new and can even be archaic or old fashioned. *Longhair* and *egghead* were two contemptuous slang words for intellectuals much in use in the early 1950s but now gone quite out of fashion. Nothing dates a person so quickly as using old slang in the presence of his children. Most slang is ephemeral, and often the same meaning is reincarnated anew with each generation, although the connotations may differ, as with *hep, hip, cool, with it,* and *laid back.*

Dictionary labeling of slang is notoriously inconsistent, as a number of critics have observed. In 1949, James B. McMillan compared five dictionaries with respect to the words *movie, razz, tycoon,* and *plug* (in the sense of a promotional mention). In no case did they all agree. *Movie* was called slang by one, colloquial by three, and popular by the other. *Plug* was called slang by one, colloquial by one, cant by a third, and unlabeled by the other two.[20] Similar inconsistencies, particularly noticeable in the treatment of slang, were found by Thomas J. Creswell in his analysis a quarter of a century later of ten dictionaries. He compared their treatment of 318 specific items in the *AHD,* and concluded:

> Every analysis presented in the preceding pages shows that as far as the 318 items under study are concerned, the ten modern dictionaries studied are far, far more often in disagreement than they are in agreement. As there is no well developed external criterion or bench mark currently available to evaluate dictionary judgments on usage, the dictionaries' claims of objectivity and authoritativeness in the treatment of usage must be rejected.[21]

Although I agree with Creswell's conclusion, the evidence he presents does not necessarily support it. If ten physicians arrive at ten different diagnoses of the same patient, we have no basis for impugning either their objectivity or their authority. The evidence available to each may have differed, as the linguistic evidence available to each dictionary certainly differed, and their interpretations of the evidence, even had it been the same, may have legitimately differed. We can conclude only that medicine and lexicography are inexact sciences and that some patients and some words are hard to diagnose.

The failure of *NID3* to label many of its words as slang was the focus of innumerable protests and derisive newspaper editorials following the dictionary's publication in 1961. Whatever criteria *NID3* used to determine slang status has never been made public, and some of the inconsistencies pointed out by critics are hard to explain. The policy of labeling very few words as slang has been continued in *NID3*'s collection of supplements, *6,000 Words* (1976), which defines *ape* in *go ape* without comment: "being beyond restraint: crazy, wild ⟨went ape over another girl . . . ⟩." Nor does it label *bag* in any of the following senses: "something suited to one's taste . . . an individual's typical way of life . . . a characteristic manner of expression." Its reluctance to take a stand on slang infuriated many critics, who felt the absence of a label stamped a word as approved and fit for use in all contexts. In this respect the critics were misguided. Inclusion of a word in a dictionary connotes no approval, and illustrative quotations were designed to show typical contexts. However, the absence of any qualifying label did suggest that the word was in standard usage, and one may wonder that if *go ape,* which appears to fit perfectly the definition of slang proposed by Jonathan Lighter, is not slang, what is?

The controversy over *NID3*'s judgments merely highlights the difficulties confronting every dictionary editor. Creswell is right that there are no agreed criteria for making usage judgments, and it is this assertion, rather than the inconsistencies he found in dictionary treatment, that supports his claim of the lack of objectivity and authority in the treatment of usage. (Medicine, on the other hand, does have benchmarks for making diagnoses, in spite of which diagnoses differ.) How do editors decide what to label slang? They examine citations and see if the context is slangy. (The alert reader notes some circularity, I hope, and begins to fidget in his chair.) They look in other dictionaries and see what *they* have done. They look up the word or expression in slang dictionaries, but without much chance of finding it. Slang dictionaries inevitably miss many slang expressions, and slang changes so rapidly that recently coined locutions will not be found in any slang dictionary. Even if the word sought is included, it does not necessarily merit being labeled slang. As Lighter has pointed out, slang dictionaries have universally fattened their coverage by including many terms that are by no conceivable definition slang.[22]

One is tempted to throw up one's hands in exasperation, utter some loud, irreverent slang of one's own, and forget the whole business. Nothing elaborates theory so much as the need to justify practicality. It is easier to spend one's time constructing theories to explain why there is no such thing as slang than to identify and harness its peculiar energy and spice and stick a label on it. But that is what the dictionary editor must do, like it or not, for slang is a useful concept. Since there are no external criteria for identifying slang, we must support efforts to establish them; but in the meantime we must rely on subjective criteria lacking in any authority save that of informed and educated people trained to be sensitive to language style. In day-to-day decisions, words are labeled slang by lexicographers or their advisers because the words are deemed to be extremely informal. This is unsatisfactory; slang is not simply very informal usage. But until we have agreed criteria by which to judge them, slang and informal words will appear in more or less free variation in dictionaries (see also page 24).

Style and Status: An Introduction

In 1948, John S. Kenyon drew a distinction between cultural levels, usually identified by the labels "standard" and "substandard" or "illiterate," and functional varieties of English, describing the degree of formality or informality of a word or expression. He argued that whereas the degree of standardness depended on the social status and education of the speaker—his cultural level—the use of familiar or formal speech depended on the social situation in which it was used. He said it was wrong to stigmatize informal usages as a "level" because that suggested a norm comparable to that of nonstandard usage. It was perfectly appropriate to use informal speech in informal situations. Moreover, both standard and substandard levels of speech had formal and informal varieties.[23] He also pointed out, as Charles C. Fries had in his introductory essay on usage in the *American College Dictionary,* that the label "colloquial" in dictionaries was widely misinterpreted to mean a localism, hence inferior to standard usage.

Although the label "colloquial" was intended to mean "more often used in speech than in writing," in practice it was often used to mean "informal," and the next generation of dictionaries replaced "colloquial" with "informal." In fact, dictionaries had never had any evidence for labeling some words as "more often used in speech than in writing," since they were almost entirely based on writing, and no studies of frequency of usage in actual speech had been made. The decision to label some words colloquial was strictly a matter of the editors' own impressionistic sense of what was more appropriate to speech than to writing. In view of recent studies that show how inaccurate are the perception and reporting of our own speech as well as the speech of others, one cannot have a great deal of confidence in the accuracy of these labels. Perhaps those who thought "colloquial" meant "Don't use this word in standard formal contexts" understood the lexicographer's judgment better than the lexicographer himself.

Kenyon's article was instrumental in changing dictionary practice. What had been called "levels of usage" was from then on divided into a normative category (standard/nonstandard) and a stylistic one (formal/informal). In 1967, Martin Joos, in a short but important book, elaborated five styles that he compared to five clocks, each of which recorded a different time. Using another metaphor, he compared shifts in styles of speech (or *registers*) to the changes of clothes appropriate to different situations: "pajamas and overalls and committee-meeting suit . . ."[24]

The five styles Joos specifies are, in order of decreasing formality: frozen, formal, consultative, casual, and intimate. The *consultative* style is used when it is assumed that one will not be understood unless one provides background information. The listener is treated like a stranger, though he participates fully, interrupting when necessary to ask questions or offer comments. The consultative style is normally used in business situations in America, where a degree of informality is common. In the *formal* style, "participation drops out," either because the assembly of listeners is too large or the speaker is too much given to command or too self-absorbed to tolerate listener participation. The formal style is also used for the first exchange between "urbane strangers," which Joos says, somewhat waggishly, lasts about six seconds. However, there are very few urbane strangers in America, and even this estimate may be too long. Bergen Evans and Cornelia Evans are much closer to the mark in saying (in 1957!):

> Forty years ago it was considered courteous to use formal English in speaking to strangers. . . . Today it is more flattering to address strangers as if they were one's intimate friends. This is a polite lie, of course; but it is today's good manners. Modern usage encourages informality wherever possible and reserves formality for very few ocasions.[25]

Joos's formal style is used to inform, and it is more detached (employing "one" rather than "I," for instance) and more cohesive in sentence structure than the consultative style. (This book is written mainly in the formal style, though now and then I lapse—as right now—into the consultative mode.) The *frozen* style is entirely written or declaimed without intonation. It is used between social strangers and has all the warmth of a railroad timetable or a summons to jury duty.

On the informal side, the *casual* style is used among friends and, unlike the consultative, requires no background information. If used with a stranger or acquaintance, it is an invitation to be on closer terms. It is studded with slang and with such ellipses as "can't find him" or "over here." The *intimate* style is virtually in code, depending upon long familiarity, and is not often used to convey information. Whereas slang is used in the casual style to signal that both listener and speaker are insiders and are attuned to the same restricted vocabulary, slang is not used in the intimate style, because intimates do not have to be told they are insiders. "Each intimate group must invent its own code," or jargon, that individualizes it.[26]

While Joos's descriptions of the five styles are full of insights, they cannot be translated directly into criteria for labeling dictionary entries. The intimate style is unwritten and unrecorded and is peculiar to the particular set of people—who may number all of two—using it. At the other extreme, the frozen style in most written contexts cannot be distinguished from the formal: almost any word used in a context of the frozen style could be used in a formal context. In practice, the styles that dictionaries can distinguish correspond to some extent with Joos's formal, consultative, and casual styles. The casual style, which corresponds closely with what used to be called "colloquial," is now represented by "informal" and "slang" labels. The consultative and formal styles are usually unmarked. A few dictionaries, notably the *Longman Dictionary of Contemporary English* (for ESL learners), label formal usages, but general dictionaries for native speakers do not.

The difficulty in determining style and status (standard vs. nonstandard) is that the criteria are not strictly linguistic but depend to a considerable extent on social context. This is the meaning of Joos's comparison of styles

193

of speech to pajamas, overalls, or business suits. Neither lexicographers nor linguists are equipped to evaluate social contexts reliably. Philip Gove cites the example of Leonard Bernstein "in full dress" at the dedication of Lincoln Center in New York, asking Mrs. Bernstein, Mrs. John F. Kennedy, and Aaron Copland, "Can you sweat it out?" Although Gove acknowledges it as conversation, the fact that television was carrying it coast to coast disposes him to ask, "How much more formal in time and place can conversation get?"[27] But such a rigid standard for determining style suggests that no public utterance by any high government official or anyone in formal dress can be other than formal. That is to say, the president of the United States cannot speak publicly and informally. Certainly the social situation, including dress of the speaker, influences our perception of linguistic style, but no single criterion can be used to determine it. Gove's standard would preclude the possibility of deliberately mixing varieties of style—as Bernstein did in the instance cited—to relax others by conveying the warmth of informality or for humorous effect. Much humor depends on the unexpected contrast of normally incompatible stylistic varieties.

What, then, determines style? The answer, even a partial, tentative answer, cannot be proffered without backtracking to review the historical forces that have shaped our attitudes toward usage, specifically to the status levels of standard and nonstandard. For although Kenyon's distinction between functional varieties and cultural levels is accepted today by virtually all dictionaries, the public and some well-known critics still argue that style and status are related, and some recent linguistic studies suggest that they are not wholly wrong.

Attitudes Toward Usage and the Notion of Correctness

The teaching of English grammar in the seventeenth century was intended to prepare students for the study of Latin grammar. English was considered inferior to Latin, and approximations of Latin grammatical forms in English translation were used to drill students in Latin. Those English constructions were considered to be correct if they corresponded to the Latin equivalents and incorrect if they did not. For example, the rule of not ending a sentence in a preposition stems from analogy with Latin grammar. As Karl Dykema observes, the eighteenth-century grammarian was thoroughly conversant with classical grammar but had no basis for analyzing English in its own

194

terms.[28] The tremendous interest in grammar in the eighteenth century is exemplified by the publication of about fifty grammars in the first half of the century and more than two hundred in the second half. The prevailing theories governing instruction in English grammar assumed that there was an ideal English, now debased, and that English was a corrupt descendant of Latin and Greek.[29] Nineteenth-century textbooks were collections of rules based on these assumptions; they ignored actual usage. Many of the early grammarians were retired clergy, well versed in Latin, who expressed their disapproval of deviations from correct grammar in strongly moral terms. Popular commentators on usage in America are now more likely to be newspaper or television journalists, authors, literary critics, or professors of literature, but the tone of moral outrage has not changed. Verbal solecisms are frequently denounced as if they were morally indecent, not just trivial errors but fundamental assaults on dignified communication and the tradition of human civilization. This section will seek to explain why this is so.

Historical Treatment of Usage in Dictionaries and Grammars

Edward Phillips's *The New World of English Words* (1658) used symbols to mark certain words considered "hard words" or technical, and in later editions Phillips compiled a list of words "to be used warily, and upon occasion only, or totally to be rejected as Barbarous, and illegally compounded or derived; the most notorious of which last are noted with an Obelisk."[30] Nathan Bailey's supplementary volume (1727) to *An Universal Etymological English Dictionary* (1721) employed a symbol to distinguish questionable usages from standard ones. Although Johnson proposed in his *Plan* (1747) to use a variety of symbols to denote questionable usages in his dictionary, in practice he appended a warning or brief notation, such as *low, barbarous, cant, ludicrous,* or *coarse.*

Robert Lowth's *Short Introduction to English Grammar* (1762), published in England seven years after Johnson's *Dictionary,* was based on the presumption that English grammar had been neglected and was in a state of disorder that needed correction and standardization, much as spelling had been before Johnson's *Dictionary.* He accused even the "best authors" of making mistakes and set about affirming rules and illustrations of proper use.[31] Although Lowth, later Bishop Lowth, recognized the principle that usage governs correctness, he held with other eighteenth-century grammarians that logic, analogy, and his own sense of proper form—moderated by Latin models—overrode the dictates of usage. His book was widely read and extremely influential.

195

For Americans, the most influential grammar of the early nineteenth century was that of Lindley Murray, an American living in England. His *English Grammar,* closely modeled on Bishop Lowth's work, appeared in England in 1795 and in Boston in 1800. It was enormously successful, going through more than three hundred editions and selling 2 million copies in Britain and America. As Edward Finegan observes, Murray was a devoutly pious man with a sense of mission. He tended to view linguistic propriety as a matter of right and wrong. Like Bishop Lowth, he saw his grammar not simply as a work of linguistic guidance but as a moral instrument for correcting bad behavior. He adopted the unfortunate practice of illustrating the usages he deplored with invented sentences that no native speaker would ever use. For the rest of the century, millions of schoolchildren would have to endure the examination of countless illustrations of bad grammar in wholly fantastic sentences, such as "Never no imitator ever grew up to his author" and "The fields look freshly and gayly since the rain."[32] Two other important grammarians of this period were Goold Brown and Samuel Kirkham, both of whom, like Murray, viewed their grammars as morally inspired. Both included copious examples of proscribed usages, often from passages of each other's work that were not intended to illustrate error: they were bitter rivals. Goold Brown's voluminous *The Grammar of English Grammars* (1851) delighted in pointing out putative errors of other grammarians. The petty and mean-spirited nature of the work—Johnson would have called it "peevish"—is apparent on every page, as in this quotation:

> Dr. Webster gives us explanations like these: "CHINESE, *n. sing. and pl.* A native of China; also the language of China."—"JAPANESE, *n.* A native of Japan; or the language of the inhabitants."—"GENOESE, *n. pl.* The people of Genoa in Italy. . . ." —"IRISH, *n.* 1. A native of Ireland. 2. The language of the Irish; the Hiberno-Celtic." According to him, then, it is proper to say, a Chinese, a Japanese, or an Irish; but not, a Genoese, because he will have this word to be plural only! Again, if with him we call a native of Ireland *an Irish,* will not more than one be Irishes? If a native of Japan be a Japanese, will not more than one be Japaneses?[33]

Brown continues, at great length, to expound the proposition that all such words are adjectives only, except in reference to languages. Here is the principle of analogy carried to the point of madness; yet Goold Brown, while not equal to Murray in influence, was widely read and respected. Brown cites innumerable examples of actual "incorrect" usages from Lowth's and Murray's grammars as well as from the great writers of English literature, such as Addison. From any rational view he would seem to have collected a vast body of evidence to refute his own argument, but to Goold Brown, the usage of the greatest writers was of no account compared to his own peculiar appreciation of the logic underlying grammar.

There were nineteenth-century grammarians who disputed the views of Kirkham, Brown, and like-minded authors, but they were greatly overshadowed by the traditionalists and comparatively little known by the general public. Joseph Priestley in *Rudiments of English Grammar* (1861) accepted the principle that language change is natural and that current custom determines correctness. Noah Webster's views wavered between those of Priestley and those of Lowth; he endorsed usage in theory but in practice prescribed what was correct, with little regard for usage. William Dwight Whitney, the great Sanskrit scholar who would later assume the editorship of *The Century Dictionary,* wrote *Essentials of English Grammar* (1877), a school text, in which he maintained that the function of grammar was not to set rules but to describe actual usage "in an orderly way." This is the view of grammar now universally accepted by linguists. The grammarian seeks to uncover the principles and organization that underlie naïve speech and make it coherent. Whitney defined good usage as the usages of the best speakers and of the best educated, and poor usage as the usages the best speakers disapproved of. He did not say how one would determine who the best speakers were. The definition thus appears to be circular, but it is still the one most commonly used. Nearly a century later, Morris Bishop, writing in an introductory article in the *American Heritage Dictionary,* states that those best fitted to determine good usage are "the enlightened members of the community . . . those professional speakers and writers who have demonstrated their sensitiveness to the language and their power to wield it effectively and beautifully."[34]

If we can tell who the best speakers are only by examining the quality of their usage, and if we cannot evaluate the quality of usage without knowing who the best speakers are, where are we? Clearly, there must be some independent means for determining either quality of usage or quality of speaker; they cannot be interdependent, no matter how cleverly one phrases the equation. Some scholarly studies, which we shall examine in the following section, have attempted by various means to address this question. The teaching of English has, however, until recently followed the traditional pattern of Bishop Lowth and Lindley Murray in viewing all usages as either right or wrong. Thomas Pyles has written: "[The] inadequately educated, unsophisticated teacher of the near past . . . has to a large extent fostered the layman's confused notions about English usage, his belief that there are many rules governing English which must not be broken by those who aspire to write and speak well." The teacher is unfairly called upon to resolve trivial questions of usage in conformity with the popular notion that he (or, more frequently, she) is an expert arbiter of right and wrong usages. If she demurs, she is apt to be thought incompetent or disobliging. In short, if she wishes to retain the confidence and respect she must have to carry on her work effectively, she must "falsify the facts of usage as [s]he knows them from first hand observation."[35]

Studies of Usage by Linguists

Four major linguistic societies were organized in the United States in the fifty-year period beginning about 1870. The American Philological Society was founded in 1869, the Modern Language Association in 1883, the National Council of Teachers of English in 1911, and the Linguistic Society of America in 1924. Collectively, these groups would have a major impact on shaping scholarly attitudes toward usage and changing the way English would be taught, although change has been much slower in the secondary and grade schools than linguists had hoped. The general public and some scholars in other branches of the humanities have been much less affected by and often hostile to the recommendations of linguists. The National Council of Teachers of English (NCTE) has been in the forefront in trying to change the attitudes of English teachers, but all have collectively strengthened the professional standing and influence of the linguist in lexicography as well as in education at all levels of instruction.

One of the earliest studies of usage to attempt an objective approach was that of J. Lesslie Hall, whose *English Usage* (1917) analyzed 125 disputed usages by consulting 75,000 pages of English and American literature. His determination as to whether a usage was acceptable was based on whether reputable authors used it.

Sterling Leonard's *Doctrine of Correctness in English Usage 1700–1800* (1929) not only presented a wealth of information about eighteenth-century grammars but suggested that their rules were intended to maintain distinctions of social class between gentlemen and the lower classes. It was not foreseen, he said, that the lower classes would imitate the usages that had been prescribed for their betters. It is hard to say whether usage guidance expressly for the privileged is any more elitist than the approach used by the *American Heritage Dictionary,* in which "the ordinary user . . . can discover just how and to what extent his presumed betters agree on what he ought to say or write."[36] In *AHD2,* William Buckley identifies one of Bishop's presumed betters as Willmoore Kendall, a close colleague, who exemplifies those "expertly trained and congenitally gifted." This instance of modern elitism recalls the demands of Swift and other eighteenth-century men of letters for an academy to "fix" usage.[37] Now, as in the eighteenth century, the emphasis is on preserving the significance of differences in usage that are linked to social class; but the market for usage guidance has broadened considerably. One must be forgiven for suspecting that mixed with the concern for the ordinary user that underlies present-day attention to correct usage is the awareness that insecurity about usage is good business. If nearly everybody thinks his speech needs to be monitored and corrected by "his presumed betters," nearly everybody is a potential customer. In Britain, where linguistic insecurity is less prevalent than in the United States, the market for usage guidance is much smaller.

Leonard next devoted himself to taking a survey of linguists, teachers, authors, editors, and others, and asked them to rate 102 usages. They were asked not for their own opinions but rather for their observations of actual usage. Nonetheless, as several critics have pointed out, the responses often reflected the opinions of the respondents. The study, sponsored by the NCTE and published in 1932 under the title *Current English Usage,* was undertaken to show that actual usage was less conservative than had been represented in textbooks. Ironically, the Leonard study set the precedent for soliciting the advice of presumed authorities about usage that *AHD* would adopt forty years later with the aim of showing that good usage was more conservative than commonly believed.

Although *Current English Usage* is widely viewed as a pioneering advance in the study of usage, it is seriously flawed in many respects. The presumption that those polled had enough facts at their command to give a meaningful response was unwarranted, and the assumption that their judgments would be uncolored by prejudice or the appeal of prestige forms was unjustified. In 1938, Albert H. Marckwardt and Fred Walcott's NCTE study, *Facts About Current English Usage,* was published. It attempted to objectify Leonard's data by comparing his conclusions with the recorded evidence of usage in various published sources, including the *OED* and *NID2.* Leonard had said that dictionaries tended to lag behind informed opinion of usage, but the Marckwardt and Walcott study shows that, on the contrary, the conclusions based on the opinions of Leonard's respondents lagged far behind the record of usage as reported in dictionaries. The actual usage reported by these dictionaries was far less conservative than Leonard's experts said it was.

Marckwardt and Walcott decline to label any usages as "illiterate," as Leonard had, even if the dictionaries they consulted so labeled them. They say, "when an expression was labeled in the dictionaries as 'dialect and illiterate,' it was classified here as dialect; when it was labeled 'illiterate' in present use but had obviously been in current use at an earlier period, it was classified here as 'archaic.'"[38] They argue that no usages are really illiterate and that "nonstandard" is a more suitable label for slang and dialect terms.

199

This may well be true, but it weakens the methodological purity of their study since they have allowed an extrinsic conclusion to color their use of dictionary data. For this reason, although they succeed in showing that Leonard's study was misleading, their own study does not directly controvert his findings. Rather, it demonstrates a better way of evaluating actual usage.

Charles C. Fries's study of usage, *American English Grammar* (1940), is the first attempt to establish independent social criteria for categorizing style of expression.[39] It is one of the most original and thoughtful studies of English usage ever made. Fries obtained the right to use two thousand hand-written letters and parts of another thousand letters addressed to the United States government, chiefly involving complaints and requests for some bureaucratic action to alleviate financial or other distress. Because the correspondents evidently had had to complete applications about themselves, Fries was able to identify most correspondents by age, schooling, occupation, place of birth, and in some cases by a confidential report describing the domestic conditions of the letter writer. All letters were those of native Americans for at least three generations. He was thus able to classify the writers by social class before examining what they wrote. He divided them into three (noncomprehensive) groups: many people did not fit into any of the three groups.

Group III consisted of people with less than an eighth-grade education whose occupations were those of manual or unskilled laborer. Their letters showed a pattern of misspelling of simple words, no punctuation, and the violation of elementary conventions, such as the failure to capitalize the personal pronoun *I*. The writing of Group III was called "vulgar" and considered nearly illiterate.

Group I, at the other end of the scale, consisted of graduates of reputable colleges, members of professions, and army officers above the rank of lieutenant. (Anyone who has ever been an enlisted man in the army and worked for officers above the rank of lieutenant must smile at the presumption underlying that classification.) Their letters showed a pattern of observing the conventions of spelling, punctuation, and capitalization. The writing of Group I was called "standard" and considered socially acceptable.

Group II, the majority of the correspondents, fell between these extremes. Their schooling consisted of from one year of high school to one year of college; their occupations, neither manual nor professional, included those of salespeople, skilled laborers, nurses, and noncommissioned officers in the army. Their letters conformed to the ordinary rules of capitalization and end punctuation and did not have misspellings of very simple words, but otherwise misspellings and departures from conventional form were tolerated. The writing of Group II was called "popular" or common.

200

It may be objected that Fries's use of the observance of formal rules of spelling and punctuation involved linguistic and not social criteria, thus impeaching the integrity of the study. But if the linguistic features used as group criteria are unrelated to the grammatical constructions under study—and that was the case—there can be no objection to their use. Indeed, the inclusion of a set of linguistic criteria unrelated to the linguistic data being studied is an ingenious tactic and may well be the single most important contribution of Fries's work to the future study of usage. One sign of standard English is a standard way of writing the language, "accepted (with some slight variations) all over the world as the 'right way' to spell, no matter what the English it represents sounds like."[40]

By placing each correspondent in a group, Fries could analyze statistically the differences in particular grammatical usages between one group and the next, and could thus call certain usages "vulgar" and others "standard" or "popular" without circularity. Fries does not imply any derogation of usages labeled "vulgar." He accepts the position that grammar is purely descriptive and that if any locution is in general use it is by definition grammatical. Usage and only usage, he says, is the basis of correctness. He defines standard English as that form of English used to conduct the important affairs of the people, whether political, social, economic, educational, or religious. He recognizes that to the extent that those who are socially acceptable use the standard variety, standard English has become a social or class dialect. Fries felt that it was the responsibility of the schools to teach this variety, since it was the means by which students could aspire to gain acceptance and prosper. In spite of all the hullabaloo over *NID3* and the supposed permissiveness of linguists, the great majority of linguists and linguistically informed educators still endorse Fries's position, though they may have differing views about the best way to teach standard English.

Fries's definition of standard English is unfortunately no better than definitions referring to reputable speakers. What constitutes "important affairs"? What is important to one person may be of no consequence to another. If Fries means to restrict the sense to matters of government or public officialdom, the definition is much too narrow. On the other hand, an illegal drug transaction involving millions of dollars would be regarded by most people as an important affair yet involve very few words that Fries would have called standard. One cannot detach standardness from social acceptability, and social acceptability is a very broad and elusive category.

Largely as a result of the pioneering work of Fries, it was gradually realized that if we were ever to be able to make judgments about style or status we must know a great deal more about the social conditions in which language is used.The need for linguists versed in sociological techniques led eventually to the creation of a new branch of linguistics called sociolinguistics, which developed to record and analyze social rather than regional dialects—that is, dialects of social or economic class, ethnic background, or race.

William Labov's *The Social Stratification of English in New York City* (1966) employed much more sophisticated sociological criteria for establishing distinctions of social class than Fries had used.[41] Each informant was graded on a four-point numerical scale according to education, occupation, and income. The resulting numerical index placed each person in one of three groups: lower class, working class, or middle class, which was in turn subdivided into lower middle class and upper middle class. Each informant was tested and recorded on tape recorders for five styles: casual, careful, reading, word list, and "minimal pairs." Labov's styles were selected along a continuum of self-monitoring, addressing the question, To what extent is the speaker aware of the style of his own speech? Casual speech defines a style used in relaxed conversation; careful speech is typical of a formal interview. The other three styles refer to reading a narrative, a list of words, and selected pairs of words (such as *guard* and *god* or *source* and *sauce*) designed to reveal particular phonological features (such as the pronunciation of *r*).

Through ingenious techniques, Labov was able to test informants in all three categories. In one part of his study he spent hours pretending to be lost in three New York City department stores—catering respectively to the wealthy, the middle class, and the lower class—and asking employees where he could find an article that he knew to be on the fourth floor. When they said "Four" or "Fourth" he pretended not to have heard them to see whether the emphatic repetition—no longer casual—duplicated the feature being tested. He became friendly with black and white teen-agers and young men and women who habitually socialized on the streets in poor sections of New York, and after being accepted as a familiar could engage them in casual conversation as well as subject them to more formal study. This took a great deal of time, tact, and the gift of a manner that would invite trust rather than suspicion. Whereas Fries worked from handwritten, unedited materials exclusively—the closest thing to speech he could get—Labov worked directly with people and recorded their speech. As important as Fries's work was, therefore, Labov's method cut away an intermediate step in the examination of usage. The recording of speech itself was nothing new; it had been used for many years in studying regional dialect. What was new was Labov's use of the technique for describing style variation by social class. Methodologically his work was far and away the most soundly crafted study of its kind.

One of the more interesting findings of his study is that the New Yorkers' report of their own usage is very inaccurate. What they actually report, he shows, is their norm of correctness. Labov suggests that the informant is not consciously lying. Rather, his "audio-monitoring norm" perceives his actual speech as if it were the norm. He hears the norm, not the speech. But Labov had the speech on tape and could verify that it was not what the speaker said it was. A series of words was read to the informant. Each word was pronounced several different ways. The informant was asked to circle the number corresponding to the way he pronounced the word; he could circle more than one number if he chose. Labov then checked the informant's choices with recordings previously made of the ways he had actually pronounced these words. If his choices corresponded to his actual pronunciations more than 50 percent of the time, he was considered to have accurately reported his usage. By this standard, few informants reported their usages accurately.

In another ingenious test, Labov determined the index of linguistic insecurity of his informants: "[T]he respondent is presented with a test which measures his tendency to consider his own pronunciation wrong, and to accept a pronunciation which he does not use, as right." It is a very simple test. Each of a series of words is pronounced two ways and the respondent is asked to circle the number of the pronunciation he thinks is correct. Then he is asked to mark the pronunciation he actually uses. "The number of items in which the respondent circles one form and checks another is the index of linguistic insecurity."[42]

Labov found that linguistic insecurity was highest among the lower middle class and much less among the upper middle class. About half of the lower and working classes had no measurable linguistic insecurity; they used the forms they regarded as correct. But the other half showed greater linguistic insecurity than the upper middle class. The working-class group was less insecure than the lower class. Women had a much higher index of linguistic insecurity—50 percent higher—than men. Labov also showed in another test that women exhibit "a more extreme range of stylistic variation than men—a much greater degree of correction in formal style."[43] When we remember that the great majority of schoolteachers in America in the nineteenth and early twentieth centuries were drawn from the ranks of lower-middle-class women, Labov's findings help to explain the exaggerated emphasis on correctness taught in most traditional schools during this period.

Dictionary Treatment of Usage Since 1947

Clearly, the traditional approach to correctness in usage inherited from nineteenth-century grammarians was incompatible with that of twentieth-century linguists, and the two were bound to come into conflict. Dictionaries had always relied on scholars for guidance in etymology, but the *American College Dictionary* broke new ground in 1947 by relying on a team of advisers who were among the most prominent linguists in the nation. Its editorial advisory committee consisted of Leonard Bloomfield, Charles Fries, Cabell Greet, Irving Lorge, and Kemp Malone. The *ACD* was an enormously successful dictionary, and no college dictionary after it could afford to ignore modern linguistics.

In 1952 a commission of the NCTE published *The English Language Arts,* which presumed to advise teachers about modern linguistics. It specified five basic principles:

1. Language changes constantly.
2. Change is normal.
3. Spoken language *is* the language.
4. Correctness rests upon usage.
5. All usage is relative.

It adopted the definition of "good English" of Robert C. Pooley, who had defined it as " . . . that form of speech which is appropriate to the purpose of the speaker, true to the language as it is, and comfortable to speaker and listener. It is the product of custom, neither cramped by rule nor freed from all restraint. . . ."[44]

It was the apparent adoption of these dicta by *NID3* in 1961 that so enraged many critics and set the stage for a public controversy that has been well documented and needs no repeating here.[45] Criticism by Dwight Macdonald in *The New Yorker,* Jacques Barzun in *American Scholar,* and Wilson Follett in *The Atlantic* was often singled out for quotation in contemporary accounts. On the one hand, Merriam-Webster's aggressive and misconceived promotional efforts had aggravated the problem by exaggerating the degree of linguistic innovation in *NID3.* On the other, many of the criticisms were based on ignorance of the actual content of the dictionary or on misunderstandings of how dictionaries are prepared. But even when one has hacked away the luxuriant overgrowth of tangled misconceptions, biases, jealousy, spite, glory seeking, and plain muddleheadedness, there remains a kernel of truth in some of the criticisms. Here is Philip B. Gove, editor of *NID3:* "Not putting a label on a word even with hundreds of citations suggesting what the label might be does not mean that a reader is unable to do so mentally for its use in a particular context."[46] In spirit, this seems uncomfortably close to the abdication of responsibility with which *NID3* was charged. The reader does not have hundreds of citations at his disposal; the lexicographer does. Dictionaries had always assumed that their editors were better able to make decisions about usage than their readers were. If they weren't, what were they doing editing dictionaries?

What caused *NID3* to take this position? Why, to be specific, did it originally insist on not capitalizing any entries (except *God*), on labeling very few words as "slang" or "nonstandard," on omitting the "informal" label entirely? Why did it generally forbear to provide usage guidance for the reader?

First of all, it must be remembered that older textbooks, often called derisively "Dick and Jane" textbooks for their stereotyped descriptions of white, middle-class America, were the near descendants of the highly moralistic textbooks of an earlier generation. Dictionaries were following the trend of other educational books by dropping—or at least moderating—traditional middle-class biases in evaluating behavior. Second, general adult dictionaries have never come to terms with what their primary purpose is. Is it to describe the language objectively, with special attention to the spoken language? Or is it to be useful to the greatest number of people who are apt to consult dictionaries? The two goals are in conflict, for the general reader expects dictionaries to recognize standards. The descriptive and normative goals of dictionaries demand different approaches. The influence of modern linguistics subordinated the goal of greatest possible usefulness to that of objective description, especially for an unabridged dictionary such as *NID3*. However, promotional campaigns for all dictionaries continue to emphasize usefulness as if it were the only goal; but while it is certainly a major goal, it may not always be the chief one. It is not surprising, then, that some readers felt they had been deceived when they discovered that *NID3*, formerly advertised as "the supreme authority," often failed to note whether a term were informal or slang, standard or nonstandard, in contexts that suggested that some qualifying label was called for. It often seems as though *NID3* would rather be unhelpful than wrong. This is a wholly defensible scholarly position, and it must be tempered by certain compromises that *NID3* did make. It did include some slang labels; it did give some usage guidance. By no means did it altogether reject the goal of usefulness. To be fair, we can say only that its attitude was ambivalent and that it failed to work out any satisfactory method for resolving the apparent conflict of the priorities of usefulness and objectivity.

The question of usage in dictionaries is, however, not simply a matter of conflicting goals. It involves the more fundamental question of whether the description of attitudes toward usage is or can be factual. One group may regard a particular usage as informal or nonstandard, whereas others may use it and regard it as entirely natural for any conceivable circumstance. When we talk about disputed usages, or what I should rather call "class markers," we are not marking the class of those who use them so much as those to whom their usage is objectionable. For example, the record plainly shows that most people of all classes customarily make no distinction between *disinterested* and *uninterested* or *nauseated* and *nauseous,* yet critics continue to note the alleged differences in urgent or melancholy tones.[47] Such a fastidious attitude serves to mark the critic as belonging to a high social class. The situation is analogous to that of a guest remarking on transposed forks in the place settings at a dinner table. As Dwight Bollinger puts it (a bit too contentiously): "The *lie-lay* distinction is fragile and impractical, and the price of maintaining it is too high. But that is exactly what makes it so useful as a social password: without the advantage of a proper background or proper schooling, you fail."[48]

We cannot say that the principal motive of those people who pass judgment on others' usage is to mark their own class as higher than those they criticize, but their criticism certainly has that effect. When an action always produces certain results, it is safe to say that some people will perform the action to produce the effect. Indeed, since American society is in theory egalitarian, the evident superiority of usage critics must be formally denied even while it is patent. Thus, usage critics commonly confess that they themselves have been guilty of many of the same infractions they deplore in others. (Just so, the dinner guest may laugh and say, "Oh, I always forget which way the forks go too!") It is a way of lessening the severity of the charge, of *noblesse oblige,* a token acknowledgment, even though both parties know it to be false, that speaker and critic are of the same social class. The difference between critics of table settings and usage is that critics of usage often act as though their objections were mainly moral rather than a matter of social grace. The dinner guest may or may not be a snob. The mere recognition of a social error does not make anyone a snob; it merely reflects breeding. It is the importance one attaches to the error and the way it affects one's behavior toward the culprit that makes one a snob. Likewise, the mere recognition of stigmatizing usages convicts one only of having had an old-fashioned education or of being sensitive to language use. But to accuse those whose usage differs from one's own of corrupting the language or of being sloppy thinkers, as the panjandrums of correctness routinely do, is quite another matter.

If usage cannot be determined without reference to social class, which class will be the standard? Pooley had described the informal style as one including words and phrases used by people "in their more informal moments, but which are generally excluded from formal public address, social conversation with strangers, and formal social correspondence."[49] Apart from the difficulty of determining socially informal moments, the very wording suggests a strong bias toward the upper class and upper middle class. Except for listening to an occasional formal public address, such as a political speech on television or an educational lecture, most people do not hear any formal speech. Social conversation with strangers in the United States is not usually formal except among the very privileged and in elegant shops or restaurants that cater to the wealthy. For most people, formal social correspondence is mainly a matter of weddings, graduations, and deaths, and when compared to their overall use of language plays no role whatsoever. There is no real distinction between formal and informal usage except among the privileged and the highly educated. To the extent that dictionaries of the past were created by and for this class, the distinction was possible and meaningful.[50] But if dictionaries are to be directed toward a wider—though still exclusive—group, they cannot in good faith mark out some usages as informal without saying to whom they are informal. Informal actually means "informal for those of the higher social classes, especially older, well-educated authors and professors in the humanities." We ought not then to be surprised that dictionaries differ so in their treatment of this label, since their estimations of the attitudes toward usage of a loosely defined educated class are also apt to differ.

Perhaps we can now understand why *NID3* omitted the "informal" label. The editors may have felt they could not define or know the attitudes of the class of people to whom some usages would be informal. They also knew that the proposed definition of *informal* as "more often used in speech than in writing," i.e., colloquial, is entirely specious. No one knows what usages are more often used in speech than in writing, since no one has made or could make an exhaustive comparison of speech and writing. And they knew that "informal" was often used interchangeably for "slang." In deciding not to use the "informal" label, *NID3* simply declined to represent a particular social class. For an unabridged dictionary committed primarily to describing the language fully, it was a sound decision, though unpopular with critics who belonged to the social class thus disenfranchised.[51] For college dictionaries, however, usefulness must outweigh descriptive purity, and the "informal" label is probably still justified, though it needs better definition. (See page 216, "Some Proposals for Improving Dictionary Treatment of Usage.")

NID3's original policy of entering every word in lower-case letters was a rather sophomoric misreading of the linguistic principle "Spoken language *is* the language." It was a way of pretending that the entry word wasn't really a written word but only an alphabetic artifact to be used to find the spoken form. This, of course, is nonsense. Dictionaries, *NID3* included, are not based on the spoken language; they are preeminently records of the written language. They are loath to admit this overwhelmingly obvious fact because they claim to represent "the language," and if the spoken language *is* the language—don't you see?—then dictionaries must represent the spoken language.

In fact, we have no dictionaries that represent the spoken language, though such dictionaries are possible. (Current pronunciation dictionaries simply list how certain forms are, or ought to be, or have been pronounced; they do not define the word forms they include and their entry list is very limited.) One can conceive of a large dictionary with all the elements of a general adult dictionary whose entries consist solely of spoken forms. Such a dictionary need not and probably would not be arranged alphabetically, but by an arbitrary sequence of phonemes. Written forms might be included, just as pronunciations are included in our orthographic dictionaries, but they would serve the subsidiary purpose of linking various orthographic forms with the speech sounds corresponding to dictionary entries.

Status labels present some of the same difficulties as style labels, but it is more important to know when one is using a nonstandard usage than an informal one. Labov has said that all speakers shift styles depending upon the relation of the speaker to listener, the social context, and the topic. Contrary to Kenyon's assertion that functional varieties and cultural levels are entirely distinct, Labov showed that there was a relation between them. For example, the use of /d/ for /th/ in words like *this* and *then* varied both by class (lower, working, lower middle, and upper middle) and by style (casual speech, careful speech, reading style, word list reading). The use /d/ occurred in all classes in casual speech, though more frequently in the lower classes than in the upper. It occurred in all classes with decreasing frequency as the style became more formal. Labov remarks that if Kenyon's view were right, "no matter how casually an educated person spoke, we would have no trouble in recognizing him as an educated person," since all of his usages, formal or casual, would be standard usages. But this is not the case. "In actual fact, the same variables which are used in style shifting also distinguish cultural or social levels of English. . . ."[52]

For years lexicographers have been assuring dictionary users that style labels like "informal" suggest no animadversion against such usages. Informal usages are perfectly standard, they said and reiterated whenever possible. Well, they are standard—but not perfectly, for if Labov is right, the more informal the variety of style, the more likely it is that the style will include nonstandard usages *in every social class*. We cannot simply say, as many have, that standard English is the usage of the better-educated, higher social classes of a community, for at least in their casual speech these classes too use forms—though less frequently than lower classes—that are widely regarded as nonstandard. In the most formal style—the reading of word lists—the nonstandard form /d/ tended to disappear entirely in the lower middle and upper middle classes and diminished sharply in the lower class and working class. Informal speech is thus more apt than formal speech to include nonstandard forms. The degree of self-monitoring is greater as formality increases and usages perceived as incorrect are suppressed. As Martin Joos remarks, "Since usage differences call for efforts to keep them under control, there must be rewards for the efforts. They must have survival values."[53] Indeed they must.

Since all social classes use nonstandard forms casually, we cannot rely on the actual usage of any social class for determining standard English. Rather, we must rely—as with style levels—on the attitudes toward usage of a particular range of social classes. *NID3*'s modest and probably futile attempt to enlarge the range of its coverage of social classes was interpreted by critics as a rejection of any standard. The critics were right to assert that by including without comment a greater range of social and educational classes than had previously been recognized by *NID2, NID3* was broadening its definition of *standard,* but *NID3* was right to do so. The world had changed since 1934 when *NID2* was published. Radio and television had vastly increased the penetration of forms that would previously have remained local. Standard English could no longer be based on the elitist writing approved by authors of usage handbooks. If tens of millions of people heard and used certain locutions, aparently without disapproving of them, by what right could a dictionary charged with the responsibility of describing usage say they were wrong?

It is a mistake to regard standard English as a rigidly definable category. As Pooley has observed, standard usage describes a range of acceptable variations. What may be standard for one social context would be improper for another.[54] Moreover, even within the same social context, the point at which standard usage becomes nonstandard usually cannot be detected. A cultural level represents a continuum and its divisions, like the arbitrary divisions of taxonomy, are merely a human convenience imposed upon nature. Standard usage is an artifical construct that is immensely helpful in teaching English and in guiding people who are ambitious to adopt forms that are more generally acceptable among those people who have the power to reward them. But it is not heaven-sent truth.

The sciences too are largely composed of concepts that upon close analysis have no beginning and no end but, like standard English, are useful because they are of great practical importance. The more fundamental the idea, the harder it is to define. Dr. J. L. Burton, writing in a dermatological journal, had occasion to make these remarks on the nature of *disease:*

> It is difficult to define the general concept of "a disease." J. G. Scadding has given considerable thought to this problem . . . and he now defines the term as follows: "in medical discourse, the name of a disease refers to the sum of the abnormal phenomena displayed by a group of living organisms in association with a specified common characteristic by which they differ from the norm of their species in such a way as to place them at a biological disadvantage." . . . Dermatologists may be interested to note that, according to this definition, acne vulgaris is not a disease. Acne patients do not differ from the norm since the majority of the age-matched population suffers from the same condition. Moreover, those individuals who never get any sign of acne are more likely to have a decreased level of androgens and a correspondingly decreased libido. If one regards a tendency to decreased reproductive activity as a biological disadvantage, therefore, it is the lack of acne, rather than its presence, which constitutes a disease.
>
> Homosexuality on the other hand, by this definition is a disease, and considering homosexuals do not reproduce, it is amazing that there are so many of them! The desire to go rock-climbing would similarly be a disease, unless the increased mortality of the rock-climber is counter-balanced by his increased fecundity, and so a homosexual rock-climber who had never had acne would be suffering from three diseases. Fortunately such a patient would be unlikely to seek dermatological advice for his diseases, and so we will confine ourselves to the question of diagnosis of disease in those patients who do seek our advice.[55]

In spite of such criticism, the medical profession is not likely to abandon the notion of disease, nor should we abandon the notion of standard usage because it cannot be defined precisely.

Nonstandard varieties of English, notably Black English, have been studied by sociolinguists so that teachers might be better able to teach standard English to inner-city black children. If teachers could be made to understand that the black child's speech is not random or "illiterate" but conforms to grammatical rules that differ, often slightly, from standard grammar, they would not regard that speech with contempt and the children themselves would not regard their speech as inferior. Such, at least, is the theory underlying the sociolinguistic study of Black English, eloquently and persuasively presented by Labov in *The Study of Nonstandard English*. Familiarity with the structure of Black English can minimize conflict between teacher and student, such as that caused by confusing a difference in pronunciation with a mistake in reading. Some differences are typical of most southern rural speech and others are apparently unique to Black English. But because most studies so far have dealt principally with pronunciation and grammar rather than with vocabulary, the study of Black English has had little impact on dictionaries. The situation is likely to change as the techniques for studying social dialect grow more sophisticated.[56]

Usage Books

Usage books are the twentieth-century descendants of the eighteenth- and nineteenth-century grammars discussed earlier in this chapter. They purport to instruct and caution us on the proper usage of language and are largely an American phenomenon, even though the greatest of them all, H. W. Fowler's *A Dictionary of Modern English Usage* (1926), is British. Fowler's work is distinctive because he brought to it a background in lexicography, considerable writing skill, and, at least occasionally, a sense of humor. He does not seem to believe that the fate of the world hangs in the balance of disputed usages, and his work is noteworthy for the large number of illustrative quotations shown for both "right" and "wrong" usages. He was the editor, with his brother, F. G. Fowler, of the first *Concise Oxford Dictionary* (1911) and the sole editor of the second edition (1929). Writers on both sides of the Atlantic have found his engaging style and the sheer volume of material encompassed irresistible, and his admirers are legion. In spite of a few instances where his interpretations can be called progressive, he remains a defender of the attitudes of the well-educated, upper-class Englishman. The usages he recommends, however, do not reflect the usages of educated people in America or Britain today, and various attempts to update and Americanize the work, which are on the order of converting a redundant cathedral into a Howard Johnson's restaurant, have mercifully failed.[57]

The popularity of usage books in the United States reflects the great degree of insecurity Americans feel about their use of language. We have seen in Labov's study that linguistic insecurity is felt most intensely among the middle class, the class most characterized by ambition to move up both socially and economically. The mastery of a particular kind of language use is perceived, correctly, as important and perhaps essential for upward movement. Since American society is more fluid than British and movement between classes is more common, Americans are naturally more highly motivated to acquire the skills that will help satisfy their ambitions. In Britain, pronunciation alone (received pronunciation or an approximation of it) still serves to mark off the better-educated, privileged classes from others;

but in America, every region has its own variety of standard pronunciation. Thus, the distinctions that Americans look for and that usage books help them find must depend on an arbitrary set of conventions dealing with particular items and involving chiefly diction (the choice of words) and grammar, with attention to pronunciation confined to a relatively few items.[58]

While linguists may deplore the attitudes expressed in usage books, there is no doubt that usage books are popular, and with good reason. The attitudes of others toward one's own use of language must be considered seriously by anyone who hopes to achieve practical goals. To deplore such attitudes, to argue that such attitudes ought not to exist, is to indulge in fancy and usually means that one is fortunate enough not to need ambition but wants to show one's sympathy for those who do. Since those who are ambitious and insecure are the great believers in prescriptive attitudes and buy the usage books that perpetuate them, scholars who are scornful of such attitudes must realize sooner or later that they are addressing only each other.

Most usage books are akin to the publishing genre known as "how to" books, a genre that is arguably the most profitable of all kinds of books published. Such books appeal to various kinds of insecurities and ambitions—social, economic, moral, sexual, health related, religious—and purport to tell the reader how to win friends, be more self-assertive, get promoted on the job, invest money to advantage, be more attractive to the opposite sex, and so on. They appeal directly to personal interest, are often sold by direct mail, newspaper advertisements, or through book clubs rather than primarily through bookstores, and generally promise immediate, practical results. The reader who believes in the book's promise has great incentive to lay out a comparatively piddling amount of money, since the promise is that his life will be dramatically changed. (Direct-mail selling reaches many people who are not normally book buyers and who have little experience in evaluating books and nothing to compare the book in question with.)

Although "how to" in spirit, usage books are in the form of reference books, hence are often called dictionaries. Some, like Fowler's, are more clearly reference books than others, but all share the implied promise that if one takes their advice one will have made oneself linguistically acceptable to a higher class of society than one's own. They cannot be reasonably criticized for giving advice any more than a book of etiquette or a guide to personal beauty can be criticized for giving advice. The difficulty, as John Algeo has noted, is that usage books usually fail to specify even vaguely the group whose norms they seek to represent.[59] Furthermore, the authority of usage books must depend ultimately on the presumption, whether stated or not, that the usages recommended are actually used by educated or cultivated speakers. For if they are not typical of educated usage, the book becomes a linguistic memoir rather than a how to book. It makes no promise but says, "This is the way I do it, and it is right!" (If applied to any other form of behavior, such an attitude would be considered infantile, but in linguistic behavior it is often represented as devotion to high principle.) Yet for the vast majority of the usages dealt with there is no evidence to support the judgments made, and where there is evidence, it often flatly contradicts the conclusions drawn. Some usage books try to get around the point. Wilson Follett's *Modern American Usage* states: "This discussion draws its authority from the principle that good usage is what the people who think and care about words believe good usage to be."[60] This comes very close to being an *ipse dixit* declaration, since we must depend upon the authors to reveal to us the thoughts of those who "think and care about words," and the suspicion deepens that it is the authors themselves who constitute the only secure group in that category.

William Morris and Mary Morris's *Harper Dictionary of Contemporary Usage* is dedicated to correcting usages regarded as improper or substandard by "careful users of the language" and to showing by right example the "standards of linguistic usage adhered to by those who use the language well."[61] To assist in this enterprise, the Morrises collected the opinions of 136 writers, editors, educators, journalists, TV and newspaper personalities, and others in the public eye. Who are the "careful users" and "those who use the language well" other than the 136 consultants? On what basis can we believe that their views of how other people speak are any more reliable than those Sterling Leonard queried in 1932 or those of Labov's informants in his study of New York City speech? Those studies do not give us much confidence in the discriminating judgments of 136 people whose comments are often passionate or moralistic. "No!" is a commonly expressed short opinion, and "No, no, no, no" its pregnant amplification.

Writing from a different perspective, Richard A. Lanham criticizes usage books for their pettiness and shrill vocabulary of dos and don'ts.

How do you cultivate an "ear" [for language]? [Jacques] Barzun [who completed Follett's book] knows the answer as well as the Harper panelists—wide reading. You cannot memorize rules, you will not even want to try, until you have an intuitive knowledge of language, until you have cultivated some taste. Now usage dictionaries, if you browse through them, can help you confirm and sharpen your taste, but they are unlikely to awaken it. They move, again, in the opposite direction, argue that intuitive judgments are not intuitive but conceptual, codify them, render them a matter of rules. They would keep us perpetually on our "p's and q's," and a love for language does not lie that way. The perpetual single focus on correctness kills enjoyment, makes prose style into one long Sunday school. Usage dictionaries, that is, can teach us only what we already know. They tend to be the affectation of, well, of people specially interested in usage. They are most useful as the central document in a continuing word-game played by sophisticated people.[62]

How often have we not heard a usage expert taken to task for using in his own writing one of the very usages he inveighs against? For example, Stuart Sutherland reviews John Simon's *Paradigms Lost,* a traditional lament that language use has gone to hell; in the course of the review he upbraids Erica Jong for having written, "Everyone lies about their feelings." Three weeks later in the same periodical, a correspondent points out that Sutherland, in the same review in which he had criticized Jong, committed the same solecism by writing, "When someone seeks to tell others how to use words, the temptation to expose their own verbal sins is strong."[63] Can anyone doubt that this sort of pastime is played by people who have the leisure to indulge endless whimsy or who, like Goold Brown, are grimly committed to humiliating their peers?

Bergen Evans and Cornelia Evans's *A Dictionary of Contemporary American Usage* is often cited, justly, as one of the few books that takes a moderately permissive approach. The Evanses define their recommended usages as "respectable English," "the kind of English that is used by the most respected people, the sort of English that will make readers or listeners regard you as an educated person."[64] This is a rather less restrictive standard than the Morrises' or Follett's. It is based on the presumed effect such usages will have on "readers or listeners"—not necessarily *careful* readers or listeners, or readers or listeners who "think and care about words"—just "readers and listeners." Ordinary people will regard you as educated if you follow our recommendations. This is what the Evanses promise. Their book is not essentially different from other usage books; it merely represents the norms of a different class. But it is informed throughout with good humor and good sense and a much keener appreciation than that of other books of the history of language use, with special attention to differences between British and American usage. Follett's work and Fowler's represent the attitudes of older, well-educated, upper-class, academically oriented people, with particular attention to usages of the established British writers.

Margaret Bryant's *Current American Usage* is exceptional, though slight in coverage, in purporting to be based on actual studies of usage rather than the opinions of the authors or a stable of consultants. Much of its data was collected by the distinguished scholar James B. McMillan for a committee on English usage of the NCTE. Standard English is defined as "the type of language employed by leaders of our society, those who command respect and esteem, such as important journalists, statesmen, political figures, scientists, and business and professional people."[65] The definition is really not so different from the "careful users" of Follett and seems somewhat more restrictive than the guidelines of the Evanses. It is no more scientific, although Bryant does state that there is no clear line between standard and nonstandard usage. Further, the attempt made to lend scientific substance to the judgments misfires. "Formal English" is defined as that English "used in serious writing" and "not much used in speech," but no negative statement about usage can have credibility. Margaret Bryant's declaration that an expression is not much used in speech is no more verifiable than one by Wilson Follett that a usage is avoided by careful writers. Neither statement has any justification other than the author's intuition. Bryant's definition of informal English is also suspect. She says that the sentences are shorter than the sentences of formal English, but I know of no study that confirms this view, and in fact the contrary seems as probable to me.[66] Nonetheless, in spite of its deficiencies, Bryant's work is the only reasonably current guide to usage even to attempt to draw upon the results of actual research, and for this it commands respect.

There are numerous other usage guides, such as those of Theodore M. Bernstein *(The Careful Writer)*, Roy H. Copperud *(A Dictionary of Usage and Style)*, the Reader's Digest (*Success With Words*, which in spite of its mass-market title is in some respects more sophisticated than many of the other works cited), and many other lesser works. But as John Algeo truly remarks, "Anyone who compares usage books will recognize that they propagate by inbreeding."[67] Copperud's *American Usage and Style: The Consensus*, a distillation of the treatments in nine usage guides and a number of dictionaries, merely makes explicit what most of the usage books he surveys have been doing clandestinely for years.[68] The consensus of usage books reminds one of the consensus the top sergeant gets when he gives an order and asks if anyone objects.

The basis for most judgments in modern usage books has not changed very much from that of the nineteenth-century grammars. Analogy, logic, and etymology are still favorite determinants of correct usage. One also reads a great deal about the value of clarity in writing and the supposed truism that the chief purpose of language is the communication of ideas. Language, however, is not used chiefly for the communication of ideas. It is more often used for "calling someone to get up; morning greetings; singing to oneself in the bathroom; asking if breakfast is ready; grumbling about the weather or about where that other sock has disappeared to; teasing someone; appealing for help with a ticklish job."[69] Much writing and talk is designed

215

to be obscure. Advertisements seldom communicate ideas. If one examines Joos's five styles, one finds that only the formal style often involves the communication of ideas. The intimate style never does and the casual hardly ever, the consultative style only rarely, and the frozen style only in such formulaic expressions that few people would realize ideas were even intended. For the beginning writer, clarity of expression is an undoubted virtue; but, as Lanham points out, most usage dictionaries are not for beginners. Usage books often make sweeping statements about good usage without acknowledging that speech and writing have many different purposes.

Usage books could perform a valuable service if they were more honest about their aims and more humble about their judgments. They ought to specify the particular kind of writing their advice is meant to improve. As already noted, they ought to define for whom their advice is intended and spell out the benefits to be acquired by adopting the strategies they recommend. They ought, in other words, to make clear what social, economic, and educational class they identify themselves with. The promise to the reader can then be understood to be an invitation to imitate the usages of this class. But let it not be supposed, as usage books so often do, that the usages of any one class are correct and all other usages wrong. The resentment sometimes felt by linguists for usage books is not caused by the stated aim of usage guides—to improve communication—for linguists themselves as teachers have the same goal. It is caused by the usage-book author's smug assurance that the usages of his own class are the best and a fit model for all others.

Some Proposals for Improving Dictionary Treatment of Usage

If the reader is wondering why dictionaries are not subject to the same criticisms I have made against usage books, let me set his mind at rest. They are, but only to the extent that they function as how to books. Fortunately, dictionaries are much more than "how to" books, in spite of some attempts to represent them as being chiefly that. The *American Heritage Dictionary* was designed to emphasize its how to aspect by drawing attention to its usage panel's advice. The *AHD* tried to sell the promise of usage books in the guise of a dictionary. In spite of its advertising, however, *AHD* remains primarily a dictionary, with its usage guidance a comparatively minor part. The failure of its promise to correct one's usage is made harmless by its irrelevance, as an inept thug with the worst of intentions is incapable of hurting anybody.

Whereas usage books are primarily how to books in the form of dictionaries, dictionaries are primarily reference books dealing with all the kinds of information I have been discussing in previous chapters, and only incidentally including usage guidance. Although some readers may take all dictionary data as if they were authoritative guides on how to spell, pronounce, or interpret meaning, they are not, as we have seen, so intended. Whether accurate or not, they are intended to be descriptive. In this respect usage labels and notes are unlike all other kinds of information given in dictionaries.

There are marked differences in the way dictionaries and usage books present information and guidance. Dictionaries generally do not make flat statements that a usage is right or wrong and, apart from the *AHD* panel's comments, are not in the habit of suggesting that people who use particular expressions are ignorant or contemptible. In fact, most try to suggest by the phrasing of their notes that the editors are neutral about usage but feel it important for the reader to know that some people will regard him as ignorant if he uses the locution in question. For example, *Webster's New World Dictionary (World)* says of *hopefully* (used to modify an entire clause): "regarded by some as a loose usage, but widely current." Granted that the scientific basis of such statements leaves much to be desired: we really do not know who or how many regard *hopefully* as a loose usage, apart from writers of usage books. The need to specify the class for whom the norm exists applies to dictionaries no less than to usage books. But the tentative manner in which much usage guidance is presented in dictionaries contrasts sharply with the confident if not strident tones in which it is presented in most usage books. Furthermore, dictionaries usually do have some basis for making certain assertions about usage. When the editors of *World* say that *hopefully* is "widely current," they *know* it is widely current, at least in writing (and probably much more so in speech), because they have umpteen citations from all kinds of sources to prove it. When a usage book makes a factual statement of that kind, we have reason to be skeptical of the basis for its authority. Dictionaries may also have citations in which dismay is expressed at the usage in question. While this kind of evidence is inadequate for making sweeping assertions, it may provide justification for including a note of caution for the reader. As we have seen with respect to terms of insult, however, citation files are not usually of much help in determining attitude.

How can usage information be more reliably represented in dictionaries and still be helpful to the person who seeks guidance? First of all, it would help if dictionaries abandoned the pretentious claim that they represent the current state of the language and admitted that they represent chiefly its written form. Although they should try to expand their coverage of speech, they should also use the devices of the written language to represent its usage better. For example, many words are enclosed in quotation marks with special meanings. In the following sentence, note the different meanings of the interior quotation marks: "From the point of view of getting meaning from a statement, 'dig' is perhaps a better figure of speech than 'stand under.' At this point I hope you 'dig' me."[70] The quotation marks around the first *dig* mean: "I am talking about this word as a word and not using it with any of its usual meanings." The quotation marks around the second *dig* mean: "I do not normally use this word with this meaning, but use it now for special effect." Quotation marks are also used for words used in a novel sense and for words about which the writer feels insecure; they can thus mean "I do not care for this word but cannot think of a better one." Or they can express contempt for those who do use the expression and mean "I refuse to accept responsibility for using this word; its use here is to be taken as a quotation of other, inferior writers."

In spite of these and other uses of quotation marks, many of which convey attitude, dictionaries have not attempted to report which words often appear in quotation marks. A large citation file could demonstrate that certain words and expressions appear significantly more often than others within quotation marks. Although, as we see, quotation marks can mean many different things, even a simple statement, such as *often quoted,* or *sometimes quoted,* or abbreviations or symbols for these labels, would be helpful in alerting the reader to the prevalence of attitude shaping the connotations of the word in question. Illustrative quotations showing the word in context might suggest the particular meaning of the quotation marks. If space did not allow that, the lexicographer might be emboldened to characterize the predominant meaning of the quotation marks, again by some abbreviated statement or label. If, to begin with, the chief meanings of quotation marks were categorized so that their uses could be broken down into one of several categories, a simple and meaningful label could be devised for each meaning. Such categorization is not so very different from the normal process of extrapolating meaning from citations. There is a vast body of information about attitudes toward usage locked within quotation marks, which has been until now entirely neglected by dictionaries.

One of the major problems in the selection of a dictionary word list is determining whether a loan word, like *barrio* (in American usage meaning a part of a town or city largely occupied by Spanish-speaking people), has been naturalized or not. Since it is customary to print foreign words in italics, the appearance of a loan word in roman type (like this, as opposed to *this*) is evidence of its acceptance as an English word. Although the contrary is not necessarily so—that it, the appearance of a loan word in italics does not necessarily prove that it has not been accepted into English—citation files could be used much more effectively than they are if notation were made whenever a cited word or expression were italicized. Dictionaries should report that a particular word is *usually italic* (or *often* or *sometimes italic*), just as they now note whether a particular word is often capitalized. Italic type is, of course, variously used: for emphasis, to mark out a word as being used in other than in its customary meaning, and so on. But italics are not used so variously as quotation marks, and surely numerical tabulation will quickly establish which words have been occasionally italicized for emphasis and which are italicized 25 percent of the time or more. The latter will include the loan-word or foreign-word categories, as well as some traditionally italicized expressions. The editor would then have a basis for including the term and labeling it accordingly. The italic label would provide the reader with a useful guide to the degree to which writers regard the term in question as naturalized.

Second, dictionaries have never confronted the basic question of whether a style of usage is characterized as formal or informal because of its use or because of the people to whom it is addressed. We have seen this confusion in children's dictionaries, where books written for children are regarded as the stuff of a children's dictionary. Similarly, when we regard the writing of the *New York Daily News* or London's *Daily Express* as informal, and the writing of the *New York Times* or *The Times* (of London) as rather more formal, are we making a judgment about the use of language or about the intended audience of each newspaper? How can we presume that the readers of the *News* or the *Express* speak in the same vernacular with which these newspapers are written? Or, indeed, that the readers of the *Times*es do? The styles are intended to reflect, we presume, the uses of their readerships. But do they? If they do not, but merely represent the misconceived journalistic traditions of a relatively few people, are we not giving such usages weight out of all proportion to their due? Is a usage informal because it is directed at working-class people, and not informal because it is directed at middle- and upper-class people? Does widespread exposure to a particular style of writing imply widespread use?

If a computer program could compare the vocabularies of *Rolling Stone*, the *Reader's Digest*, and the *Times Literary Supplement*, we might have a statistical basis for citing certain terms as characteristic of one style of writing and certain terms as characteristic of another style. We might then have a basis for calling some words *informal* or *popular* and others *formal* or *literary*, but we would then have to make clear that the distinction were one of intended audience rather than widespread usage. If we wish to establish

criteria for determining styles of actual usage, on the other hand, each citation counts as one, whether it appears in the *Readers Digest,* with a circulation of 13 million or in a twelve year old's personal diary. But dictionaries
are not based on entries in diaries. Just as I do not believe that children
habitually use the vocabularies in children's textbooks, I am skeptical that
any particular class of people habitually use the vocabularies of the publications they habitually read. The disparity between exposure and use is liable to be greater among the less educated, since a higher percentage of the
better educated write the materials that dictionaries pay attention to. We
simply do not know what the habitual usages of most people who are not
writers are. Dictionaries would be improved by openly admitting this fact
and making the best of what they do know.

Third, the editing process has a tremendous and incalculable impact on
dictionary treatment of usage. Copy editors, like teachers, are devotedly
conservative in matters of usage; they are paid to be. It is safer to observe
every ancient quibble about usage than to risk an outcry among one's customers. The *Reader's Digest*, for example, a prototype of middle-class linguistic conservatism, is extraordinarily "well" edited. Every questionable
usage and every characteristic of individual style is edited out. (For this
reason the *Digest* is a poor source of citations for new words or new senses.)
The extent to which dictionaries are dependent on the artificial intervention
of editors has never been publicly acknowledged by dictionaries and ought
to be. Some unedited sources are available in letters to the editor and tran-
scripts of radio shows and interviews; although valuable, these sources play
a very small part overall in a dictionary's citation file. What has this to do
with usage? Just this: The fact that dictionaries are dependent on edited
copy rather than impromptu speech or unedited writing presents a distorted
picture of actual usage, which is far less uniform and far less standard than
dictionaries ordinarily represent it to be. Dictionaries should try to segregate
their representation of usage information based on edited material from that
of unedited sources or naïve speech. Any usage judgment based on an edited
source might be designated as "edited," so that "informal edited" words like
teeny or *chintzy*, which are readily found in edited material, might be distinguished from words like *yuck!* (an expression of disgust). The distinction
would be based strictly on the nature of the sources for each term, not on
the editor's intuition.

Fourth, many terms, especially informal and slang usages, are age
related. As we have seen, one part of the definition of slang may be its association with young people, but we should not assume that this is always the
case. Slang dictionaries such as Wentworth and Flexner's *Dictionary of
American Slang* often specify "student use" or "teenage use" or the like,
although it must be acknowledged that such usage notes become dated very

220

rapidly. Nonetheless, if the information is reliable, it is worthwhile including it in a general dictionary. Some expressions are used in direct address and typically by older people to younger people with a tone of condescension, such as *young man* or *young lady*.[71] When the respective ages of the speaker and listener are customarily linked to particular usages, the fact should be noted. A similar situation may apply to sex: we intuitively feel that many terms are used chiefly by women and many chiefly by men. But in practice it would be very difficult, short of assembling vastly greater citation files than now exist, to determine any reliable statistical frequency, based on the sex of the speaker or listener, of one set of terms over another. Given the limited resources of any dictionary, the effort involved in such a study would not warrant the expense. Age related terms, on the other hand, being relatively few in number, would be easier to quantify reliably, especially with the help of slang dictionaries and other published sources.

The Dictionary of American Regional English

We have already noted the importance of the *Dictionary of American Regional English*. *DARE* will provide a great deal of general usage information apart from regional usage.[72] Differences in usage based on community, age, education, race, and sex may be reliably distinguished for the first time. Apart from the actual data that dictionaries will be able to draw upon, the methodology employed by *DARE* is one they would do well to imitate. The percentages of informants falling into each subdivision of the five criteria were tabulated and recorded. For each question, the percentages of informants responding were compared to the percentage of that group giving a particular answer. For example, if 30 percent of a sample responding to a question are young, and 60 percent of those giving a particular response to that question are young, one can infer that usage differs according to age and that the particular response given is used chiefly by young people. "Eskimo kiss" (the affectionate rubbing of noses) was established on this basis as a usage predominantly of the young. See Fig. 10 for a representation of the ages of informants responding *talkfest* when asked to describe "a meeting where there's a lot of talking." From the widespread geographic distribution it is clear that this usage is not regional but is a usage predominantly of older people. Likewise, of the informants who called "eggs ... taken out of the shells and cooked in boiling water" *dropped eggs*, 83 percent were old, significantly higher than the proportion of old people responding to the question, and also higher than *DARE*'s overall proportion of old informants, 66 percent.

Equally usefully, *DARE*'s method provides evidence that certain usages suspected of being old fashioned or uneducated are in fact not so restricted. The description of a sandwich big enough to be a meal in itself as a *dagwood* was not age related: of those who called the sandwich by this name, 67 percent were old, compared to the *DARE* norm of 66 percent in this age group. The assumption that the use of *borrow* is an uneducated usage in the sense of "lend," as in "Will you borrow it to me?" was not borne out by the results. Twenty-seven percent of the informants who used this expression had had at least two years of college, as compared to 31 percent in the study as a whole.[73] Moreover, *DARE*'s method can even specify two variables as significant, being able to demonstrate, for example, that certain usages are restricted largely to blacks and older southern whites or predominantly to rural people of limited education. Of all the informants responding to the question, "Words used for a bull?", 72 percent were old, 44 percent were of community type 5 (rural), and 67 percent were male. But of those informants who responded "animal," 84 percent were old, 58 percent were of community type 5, and 76 percent were male. The inference may be drawn that the usage is chiefly that of older, rural, male speakers. *DARE*, apparently cautious about labeling a usage that of older people because of its large percentage of older informants, labels this response "euphem., esp among rural and male speakers."[74]

Figures 11 and 12 show the geographical distribution of *ever* for *every* in "everywhere." Figure 11 shows the regional distribution by the type of community of each informant, Figure 12 by educational level. In Figure 11, one can see the preponderance of 4s and 5s—small-town and rural use— and the distribution in the south and south midland states. In Figure 12, the picture is not as decisive, but 53 percent have fewer than two years of high school.[75]

I have discussed *DARE*'s methodology at length because it represents an enormous breakthrough in technique in the analysis of usage. It has brilliantly adapted the framework of Fries' pioneering *American English Grammar* to long-standing dialectal methods to produce a reliable system for evaluating usage. But since its attention is directed to regional usages, it covers only a small part of the material that dictionaries are expected to evaluate. It remains, then, for general dictionaries to employ the methods of *DARE* to inquire about other aspects of usage. Clearly, this is a long-term goal, and such a study is quite beyond the means of any individual publisher to finance. In 1973, at a conference of the New York Academy of Sciences devoted to lexicography in English, several speakers called for a central archive for lexicography.[76] A large-scale study of usage modeled after *DARE*'s techniques can only be accomplished in a far-ranging program of citation collection on a grander scale than any so far attempted.

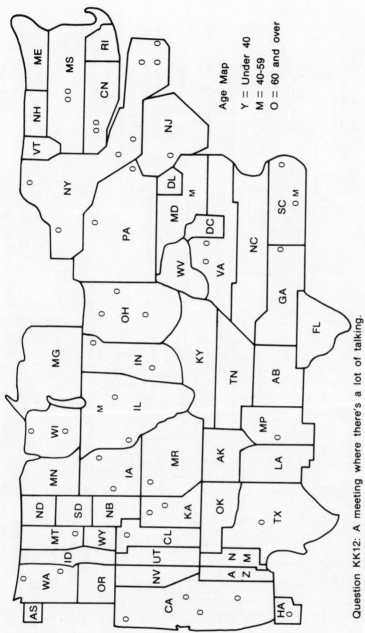

Question KK12: A meeting where there's a lot of talking.

TALKFEST   47 Informants

FIGURE 10.   Geographical versus age distribution of usage of the term *talkfest*. Used with permission, courtesy of the *Dictionary of American Regional English.*

223

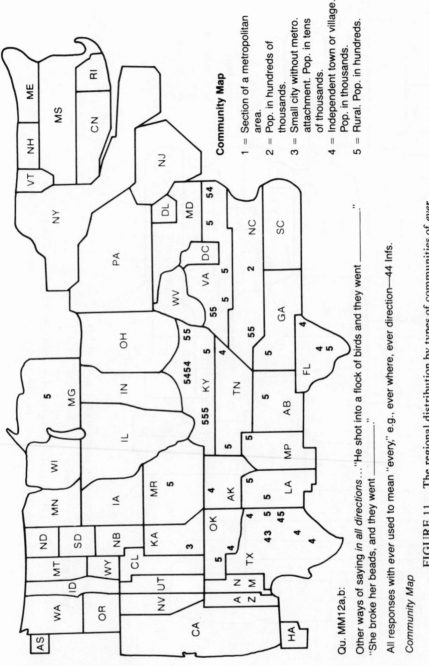

Qu. MM12a,b:

Other ways of saying *in all directions*.... "He shot into a flock of birds and they went _____."
"She broke her beads, and they went _____."

All responses with *ever* used to mean "every," e.g., ever where, ever direction—44 Infs.

Community Map

FIGURE 11.   The regional distribution by types of communities of *ever* for *every*. Used with permission, courtesy of the *Dictionary of American Regional English*.

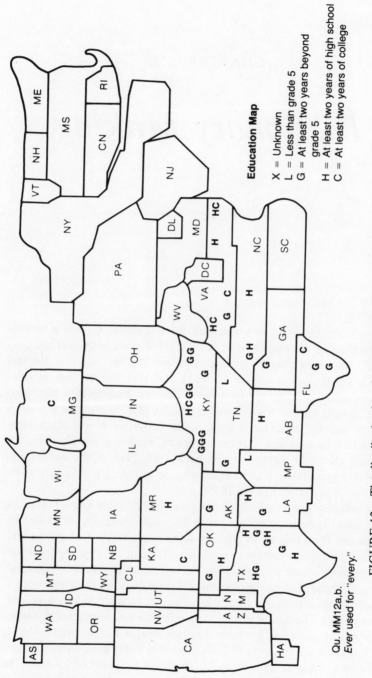

Qu. MM12a,b.
Ever used for "every."

Education Map

X = Unknown
L = Less than grade 5
G = At least two years beyond
    grade 5
H = At least two years of high school
C = At least two years of college

FIGURE 12.   The distribution by education level of the usage of *ever*
for *every*. Used with permission, courtesy of the *Dictionary of American
Regional English.*

CHAPTER SIX

Dictionary Making

Dictionary making is nothing less than the attempt to fashion a custom-made product on an assembly-line basis. Each dictionary project is unique and calls for its own set of specific rules, but the vast reach of the task demands rigorous organization to make the best possible use of one's resources and staff. The common belief that the making of a dictionary starts with defining words is as naïve as the idea that the erection of a building starts with the purchase of construction materials. If one can imagine ordering tons of steel girders, cement, bricks, window glass, plumbing fixtures, and electrical wiring without having any plan of the building for which these materials are to be acquired, one will see the absurdity of the notion that dictionaries begin with defining.

The architect commissioned to design a building must know, first of all, to what uses the building will be put. A hospital requires an altogether different design from that of an office building or a church. Just so, the lexicographer is commissioned by a publisher to design a dictionary for a particular purpose or, as we should say, for a particular market. A general, adult monolingual dictionary demands different qualities than one for children, for foreign learners, or for a special market such as physicians or electrical engineers. The design of a building reflects a vast number of decisions, some practical and some aesthetic, that are unique to that project, but it depends also on a large body of knowledge that every competent architect is expected to have at his command. These are the tools of his trade. In lexicography, too, a knowledge of the tools of the trade is crucial to meet the particular demands of each project.

226

Every dictionary has essentially three stages: planning, writing, and producing. The planning stage usually requires about 30 percent of the entire duration of a commercial project, the writing stage at least 50 percent, and the producing stage the remainder. In noncommercial historical projects, the writing stage can take much longer. We turn our attention now to the planning stage.

Planning the Dictionary

In general commercial publishing, the first consideration in evaluating any proposal is identifying the market: Who will buy the book? This is the first consideration in dictionary publishing as well. Once it is established that there is a market for the dictionary, the size of the market is estimated and one's likely revenue from the dictionary's sale projected. The particular features of the dictionary must be worked out to fit within that financial framework. In practice, the budget is neither a simple nor invariable calculation, since it depends on many assumptions subject to change.

The size of the dictionary is one of the earliest and most basic decisions to be made. How big is the book to be? How many entries should it contain? Dictionaries competing in the same market are compared, potential users are surveyed, and advice is sought from people who know the needs of the group to which the dictionary is addressed. Entry count is more important in some kinds of dictionaries than in others. College dictionaries generally vie with one another, at least in the United States, to claim more entries than their competitors. On the other hand, in children's dictionaries the size of the entry count is probably less important than clear and simple definitions, attractive illustrations, and large type. In technical dictionaries, too, matching a specific number of entries is less important than up-to-dateness and quality of the definitions.

When the type of dictionary, size, and approximate budget have been established, the next major decision is scheduling, which in turn demands that one address the fundamental question of how the dictionary is going to be put together. On what materials will it be based? Who will write and edit the work? Will it be written entirely by an in-house staff of dictionary editors, or by free-lance editors, or in part by each? What role will outside experts play in providing definitions in special fields?

Sources

Once the size of the dictionary has been established, the word list must be selected and sources for definitions must be identified. Dictionaries are compiled from a variety of sources, as we have seen in Chapter Four (see pages 151–161 and 170–173). Whether the predominant source is another dictionary or a collection of citations makes an enormous difference in the time required to do a dictionary. All commercial dictionaries are based to some extent on preexisting works. As James R. Hulbert notes:

> We have noticed that Johnson used Bailey and that Webster used Johnson. . . . For commercial reasons it is natural that customarily dictionaries should minimise or even deny their use of competing books. . . . Whether . . . explicit acknowledge is made or not, anyone who consults a dictionary can be sure that its editor has considered what appears in preceding books of the kind and in his competitors, and used as much of it as seemed to him desirable for his own book.[1]

No one would dare risk overlooking an important sense because of having failed to check other dictionaries. However, citation files must supply new terms and new senses unless the new dictionary is to rely entirely on existing works. Citations grant the work an independent validity but are vastly more time consuming to collect and use than other sources. The mix of old and new material is therefore of crucial importance in determining the dictionary's schedule.

Experts, whether on staff or not, can be called upon to draw up definitions in special fields, such as law, music, sports, or cooking, and to prepare definitions for scientific and technical terms. If the definitions are written by outside contributors, the schedule is vulnerable to the failure of one or more of the contributors to produce their material on time—or to produce it at all. There is little one can do to make outside contributors meet their commitments, since in many cases the fees are small and the threat of non-payment would have little effect other than to suggest that the contributor resign. This is the last thing the lexicographer wants, since replacing such specialists would mean a much longer delay than tolerating some tardiness. If someone resigns, the dictionary editor has not only to find a competent replacement—no small task in itself—but also to teach him to follow the dictionary's style, a process he has already gone through with the former contributor; at the end of it, he has no guarantee that the new contributor will meet his commitments any more faithfully than the last.

Reference books other than dictionaries are also used for various purposes, such as the assignment of usage labels. With respect to definitions in general dictionaries, reference works are used mainly to supplement or confirm information rather than as a primary source. In specialized dictionaries, on the other hand, reference books and textbooks often play a key role in assembling a word list, and in some fields they may provide standard definitions.

Scheduling and Estimating Expenses

Scheduling of dictionaries is notoriously inaccurate, most dramatically in the preparation of scholarly dictionaries but also of commercial ventures. Zgusta remarks, "I certainly do not know all lexicographic projects past and present; but of those I know not a single one was finished in the time and for the money originally planned."[2] He cites a Dutch dictionary that was planned to take twenty-five years but took sixty-five, and Swedish and Danish works, planned for a dozen years, that required sixty-five and forty-nine years, respectively. When James A. H. Murray assumed control of the *New English Dictionary* (later the *Oxford English Dictionary*) in 1879, it was expected to take ten years to complete. It took nearly fifty, the last volume appearing in 1928, thirteen years after Murray's death. The chief reason the *OED* took so long to write was its requirement that all of its vocabulary entries and definitions be based on original citations. If one counts the years during which the Philological Society collected citations, the work took seventy years to complete. No purely commercial dictionary could, of course, tolerate such a protracted period of preparation.

Why are predictions of scheduling so bad? Zgusta lists the "fragility of human nature," the difficulty of organizing teams of workers, and the mistaken idea that lexicography is simple and mechanical, whereas, on the contrary, "nearly . . . [every] context has something particular that defies generalization."[3] This is very true. In the context of commercial lexicography, I have offered these observations:

Usually the publisher is ignorant as to what's involved in preparing a dictionary, and the lexicographer is quite irresponsibly optimistic. I have often thought that no new dictionary would ever be undertaken if all parties knew in advance just how long it would take to do it. . . . [L]exicography is truly the *writing* of a lexicon, and a major part of it happens on company time. And writing cannot be rushed without penalty. Moreover, dictionaries are not easy to write, and they are very long. The average college dictionary has close to three million words—about the equivalent of 30 good-sized novels. It is written simultaneously by a great many people who must be trained and supervised and persuaded to follow a set of consistent rules; it includes thousands of cross-references that have to be checked; artists and art directors must be cajoled or bullied into using the proper weight of line in their drawings and into suppressing their instincts for individual expression; production people, who are used to doing things their own way, must be made to understand why *you* should be involved at all with the selection of type. . . . [I]t's an awful job getting *any* dictionary written, even a bad one. The idea that all of that work by so many different people will one day be neatly compressed

229

into one oblong book and look as though it just fell out of a tree—that is really a wonder. . . . [4]

Scheduling is by far the most difficult aspect of planning a dictionary because it involves many factors that cannot be foreseen or properly evaluated in the planning stage: the rate at which definers, etymologists, and others will produce copy; the quality and stability of the staff; in the computer age, the time required to write the computer programs (the complexity of which is often greatly underestimated by computer people) that will process dictionary copy at each stage of its development, and to work out the "bugs" that such programs inevitably have; technological changes, such as new computer hardware or composition equipment, that necessitate reediting or additional programing to convert to the new system; the quality of the composition (hence the number of proof stages that will be required); changes in the publishing management that may precipitate sudden changes in the policies of the dictionary; and, finally, the need to take time to defend and promote the dictionary within one's own company.

Apart from the few publishers of major dictionaries, most book publishers have no idea of the costs or complexity of producing a dictionary. Dictionaries are unlike any other book they have ever published. They do not fit into the usual pattern of financing; from an accountant's point of view dictionaries behave quite bizarrely. Most books cost comparatively little to prepare (the plant cost, in publishing argot) but a great deal to produce (paper, printing, and binding costs). The opposite is true of dictionaries, where the cost of production, though hardly negligible, is small compared to the huge development costs, which must be amortized over a much longer period of time than book publishers are generally familiar with. Composition costs and data-management costs (systems analysis, computer programing, and processing of information) are also much higher than they are for other books. Most publishers would simply stare in disbelief at a lexicographer who announced that with a staff of twelve he could produce a dictionary in eight years.

The pressure is great to make the schedule of commercial dictionaries as lean as possible. The lexicographer who values continuous employment makes concessions, even some he may have deep misgivings about, while he clings to the cherished idea that he is not compromising his integrity, not, to be blunt, lying to keep his job. For he has his vision set on a distant goal— one that his publishers cannot see and that they suspect will not occur, but one that he knows is worth reaching. It is almost a matter of faith, because at times it is quite impossible to see how the end of the task can ever be reached, even if all concerned work as hard as they are capable of working.

David B. Guralnik, the editor of *Webster's New World Dictionary (World)*, made the same point in speaking about the preparation of his dictionary's first edition of 1953: "There were times when ordinary prudence, good common sense, dictated the abolishment of the whole project. I am happy to report now that in this instance common sense did not prevail."[5] It must be added that *World,* like many another dictionary that was almost abandoned before its completion, has proved to be immensely profitable in the years since its first publication. But the editor of a dictionary has to be absolutely bound and determined to finish the dictionary, or it will never be done.

> If from one end, he has the publishers tugging at him to finish more quickly, from the other he has people tugging at him to slow the pace to make certain improvements. These counter-pressures come sometimes from contribuing scholars, but almost always from the staff itself—the people writing the definitions and all the other elements of each entry. . . . The editor in chief is placed in the untenable position of appearing to defend a lower quality of work than his subordinates demand. But he must cope with the knowledge that unless he compromises to some extent by setting quotas, there will be no dictionary at all, and he and all of his staff will be out of a job. . . . In short, the role of the editor in chief is perhaps best viewed as a political one: that of balancing opposing interests. He must satisfy his creditors, on the one hand, that work is proceeding as fast as possible, and his craftsmen, on the other, that work is proceeding as slowly as possible. In no small way, how well he accomplishes this feat will determine how good his dictionary is.[6]

The situation has close parallels in other businesses, where considerations of quality must always be tempered by cost and by the price the customer is willing to pay. But it is not widely appreciated to what extent these factors apply also to articles having intellectual properties such as dictionaries. The commonplace idea that dictionary definitions are discussed leisurely by groups of scholars puffing pipes could hardly be more mistaken. Definitions are composed by definers working alone under the pressure of time to meet daily quotas. Every definition calls for scores of small decisions that the definer has little time to ponder but must make promptly. Dictionaries take so long to do not because they are done by perfectionists but because there is so much to be done. Certainly, care is taken at every step, and no good dictionary editor tolerates sloppiness in thought or execution of a definition; but the degree of care is always measured against the time required to employ it.

How does one go about estimating the time required to compile a dictionary? One breaks down each step that can be foreseen, estimates how many definitions each editor can do per day, and calculates how many editor-days, -weeks, -months, and -years will be required to complete the job. An editor-week—the amount of work that one editor can do in one week—is the unit most often used. Two editor-weeks equal the amount of work that two editors can do in a week or that one editor can do in two weeks. Of course, remembering the parable about the number of men needed to dig a ditch, we will not suppose that the work thirty editors can do in a week equals the work one editor can do in thirty weeks. In fact, no dictionary staffs have more than a handful of senior definers, though they may have as many as forty preliminary definers for temporary periods. There are two opposing philosophies that obtain in dictionary work. One argues for a relatively small, stable staff that may add a few people when burdened with the toughest part of its schedule but never numbers more than a dozen or so. The other strategy calls for a very small nucleus of top editors, perhaps three or four, but for vast additions and subtractions during heavy and light periods of the schedule. Each method has its advantages and disadvantages in both practical and human terms.

After one estimates the optimum rate of defining per editor week, one divides this number into the total number of terms to be defined, then inevitably finds that the dictionary can be done in something like 12,432 editor-weeks, which means that it would take 20 editors working 52 weeks a year (with no vacations or illness, and of course no turnover) almost twelve years (12,432 divided by 20 = 621.6 weeks divided by 52 = 11.95). If the editors averaged $20,000 per year, the editorial cost would be $400,000 per year or nearly $4.8 million overall. One turns pale, sits, asks for a glass of water. "Well," one says, after a time of limp reflection, "maybe they can work a little faster." Later, one may try working from the other end, that is, deciding how much money can be spent, how many editors can be afforded, and how fast each will have to work. But the result may prove to be an impossibly fast rate of work. Ultimately, one works from both ends and seeks a compromise between what budget and time constraints allow and what editors can physically and mentally do every week, week after week.

As an aid to this exercise, many years ago I elaborated the accompanying Editorial Expense Chart. Once one is used to the process, it may no longer be necessary to use it, but as a reminder of what is involved in planning a schedule and budget it may be useful to consider now. Under each step, one calculates the rate per editor-day and editor-week, and on this basis fills in, on the line above, how many editors will be used for how many weeks to perform that task. Suppose one determines that the first defining rate will be 15 entries per day or 75 per editor-week. If there are 15,000 entries to be written, 200 editor weeks will be needed (15,000 divided by 75). One must decide how many editors will be employed in that assign-

Editorial Expense Chart

Title _____ Date _____

PRELIMINARY: _____ eds. x _____ wks. = _____ ed.-wks.
    I. Style Book: _____ eds. x _____ wks. = _____ ed.-wks.
    II. Word List: _____ eds. x _____ wks. = _____ ed.-wks.
    Rate per ed.-day _____ ; per ed.-wk. _____
    III. Consultants:
    Duration _____ Staff eds. _____ Expense _____

PREPARATION OF MANUSCRIPT: _____ eds. x _____ wks. =
                                      _____ ed.-wks.
    I. First Defining: _____ eds. x _____ wks. = _____ ed.-wks.
    Rate per ed.-day _____ ; per ed.-wk. _____
    II. Special Assignments: _____ eds. x _____ wks. = _____ ed.-wks.
    Specify:
    III. Contributing Editors (nonstaff):
    Duration _____ Staff eds. _____ Expense _____
    IV. Review: _____ eds. x _____ wks. = _____ ed.-wks.
    Rate per ed.-day _____ ; per ed.-wk. _____
    Duration _____ Staff eds. _____ Expense _____
    Duration of Prep. of MS. _____ ; Expense _____

PREPARATION OF ART: _____ staff eds./artists x _____ wks. =
                                        _____ ed.-wks.
    I. Selection: _____ eds. x _____ wks. = _____ ed.-wks.
    Rate per ed.-day _____ ; per ed.-wk. _____
    II. Research: _____ eds. x _____ wks. = _____ ed.-wks.
    Rate per ed.-day _____ ; per ed.-wk. _____
    III. Artwork: Total units _____ ; Total Expense _____
    Unit cost _____ x _____ pieces; Expense _____
    IV. Editorial Coordination: _____ eds. x _____ wks. = _____ ed.-wks.
    Duration _____ Staff artists/eds. _____ Expense _____

COMPOSITION: _____ eds. x _____ wks. = _____ ed.-wks.
    I. Proof 1st gals.: _____ eds. x _____ wks. = _____ ed.-wks.
    Rate per ed.-day _____ ; per ed.-wk. _____
    II. Proof 2nd gals.: _____ eds. x _____ wks. = _____ ed.-wks.
    Rate per ed.-day _____ ; per ed. wk. _____
    III. Proof pages: _____ eds. x _____ wks. = _____ ed.-wks.
    Rate per ed.-day _____ ; per ed.-wk. _____
    IV. Other:
    Duration _____ Staff eds. _____ Expense _____

SUPERVISION: Editorial _____
    Art _____
    Expense for Supervision _____
Total Duration _____ Begin: _____ End: _____
Total Editorial Expense _____ Total Art Expense _____
Total Expense _____ ; Ed. Staff: _____ Art Staff: _____

ment. Four editors could complete it in 50 weeks, or 8 in half the time. Any combination of factors whose product equals 200 can be used. The chart also allows one to estimate the expenses of these and other stages that cannot be calculated by this method, such as the cost of artwork and supervision. However, it does not include most of the planning-stage costs (staff salaries and data management).

Staffing

To what extent should one rely on a free-lance editorial staff rather than an in-house group? The attraction of free-lance editors is mainly financial. The cost of office space, equipment, administration, and employee fringe benefits makes in-house staffs many times more expensive than free-lance staffs. A staff worker who turns out to be a poor editor or have personal problems that interfere with his work performance must be tolerated for a considerable period, whereas a free-lancer who does not measure up is easily dismissed. Moreover, when work is slow the staff member must be paid nonetheless, and when the project ends the employer may be forced to discharge part of the staff, a prospect neither side views with any satisfaction.

On the other hand, because one has less effective control over free-lance editors, the rate and quality of work are variable and the schedule more vulnerable to delay. A free-lance editor can decide to take a vacation whenever and for however long he wishes, and there is nothing one can do about it. Whereas the staff editor has all the incentive that his ambition can fuel, the free-lancer is relatively uncommitted. He is probably engaged in several projects and will not be crushed by any single loss. If a better-paying opportunity comes along, he may quite naturally seize it, no matter what the consequences to one's project. The daily personal contacts between in-house staff and supervisor correct errors as soon as they occur, and the sense of teamwork and mutual respect of a staff can certainly inspire better work than that of an equal number of editors working independently, even if both groups are able and conscientious.

The use of free-lancers versus in-house staff depends upon the nature of the project as well as on the size of the budget. The more complex the work, the more essential it is to have in-house editors. Work on a thesaurus, however large, is straightforward and simple compared to dictionary work, and much of it can be done perfectly well by competent free-lance dictionary editors. Abridgments of relatively small dictionaries may also be done by free-lancers, but at considerably greater risk. Large, original dictionaries cannot be done principally by free-lancers, though they may contribute major elements, such as etymologies and pronunciations, which are more or less independent of the defining work. Even smaller, specialized dictionaries, such as children's dictionaries and dictionaries for foreign learners, must be done mainly by an in-house staff or risk blatant inconsistencies and long delays while improperly done work is redone.

It is very difficult to find highly skilled general definers. Such people are about as rare as good poets. Discounting those who have left or retired from the field of lexicography, there are probably fewer than a hundred experienced general definers in the whole of the United States. Training new definers, which anyone who seeks to build a large staff must do, takes much of the time of the skilled staff who act as teachers, thus cutting down sharply on their own productivity. It usually takes about a year to train someone with aptitude to be a definer, and even then he cannot be trusted, as a rule, to work without supervision. Of course, some learn faster, but many never learn. Of a group of ten carefully selected candidates, several may contribute usefully to the project in various ways, yet one is fortunate if two develop ultimately into good definers capable of independent work.

In speaking of the lexicographer as "he," I follow the policy stated in the Introduction, but it is particularly unfortunate with respect to staffing, since it may give the impression that lexicographers are predominantly men. I have never polled the industry, but in my own experience there have been quite as many women as men active in all aspects of the field. Today at least one major dictionary staff—and after all there are not that many—is headed by a woman. Prejudice against women has hurt not only women; it has undoubtedly hurt lexicography by discouraging many a good female lexicographer to the point where she left the field. But certainly there are far fewer obstacles in the way of a woman's achieving the editorship of a dictionary now than in the past.

What are the qualities of a good definer? First and foremost, he must be able to write well and easily. A definer is primarily a writer, whether we call him an editor or not. Second, he must have an analytical mind that seeks to chop things up into parts that can be understood separately and reassembled to fit his purpose. Poets are like that—good poets make good definers—but defining is not creative in the sense that writing verse is creative, and defining would bore most poets to death. Third, the general definer must have a broad, but not necessarily deep, fund of information; he must read the newspapers and be interested in the world. The special definer, on the other hand, who may handle, for example, only biological subjects for a general dictionary, needs to have a deep knowledge of that field but may know next to nothing about other subjects. Lastly, the definer must have a feeling for the language, *Sprachgefühl,* a sense of aptness of expression, an appreciation of nuance, style, and idiom. This is to some

235

extent implicit in the ability to write well, but not all good writers have it in equal measure. For example, many foreign-born authors write English well but lack an appreciation of style, such that their writing may seem a bit heavy-handed even when they intend to be casual. Any such gap in intuitive understanding of style is disastrous in dictionary defining, and for this reason definers for general monolingual dictionaries are almost always native-born speakers. Bosley Woolf, former editor of the Merriam-Webster dictionaries, has said that it is a basic requirement that a definer be a native speaker of English.[7]

A word is in order about what definers do not have to be. They need not have enormous vocabularies or be polymaths. They need not be linguists; in fact, knowledge of linguistics is of no particular help in dictionary defining. I say this from my own experience in working with definer trainees, and it is confirmed by the experience of other lexicographers. Patrick Hanks remarks, "I have not found that people with a sound theoretical understanding of current linguistic theory make good definition writers. It is a literary, not a scientific activity."[8] Bosley Woolf states that graduate study, while it may give the new definer an initial advantage, does not ultimately make him more fit for the job than "last year's college graduate."[9]

Woolf also says that defining requires humility. To those who have not worked on a project as vast and complex as a dictionary, the remark may be puzzling. But nothing cuts one down to size as quickly and finally as dictionary work. There is so much one doesn't know, and more, so much of great importance that one doesn't know, that one soon gets a proper estimation of one's own place in the universe. One's own place in the world of words is perceived as the traditional Chinese landscape artists perceived man in the world of nature, that is to say, as a speck lost amidst miles of mountains, valleys, and distant rivers. So much does each of us know of our language. Novice definers with advanced degrees, whether in linguistics or another field, are apt to be overconfident, especially if those teaching them know far less than they about the academic subjects they are freshly acquainted with. Such beginners often imagine that their academic training qualifies them for advanced work in lexicography and are chagrined and hurt when they discover that it doesn't.

The lack of humility of contributing specialists in a technical dictionary can be an acute problem. Medical specialists, for instance, have a great deal of confidence in their knowledge. The system of medicine as practiced in the Western world is designed to ensure that patients respect the knowledge of their physicians; a doctor's judgment is rarely challenged by a patient. Thus the medical specialist believes—he *must* believe—himself to be authoritative. Fine, one wants authoritative specialists. But they must also appreciate their relative ignorance of the vast majority of medical nomenclature, past and present. They must not, for example, exclude words from the dictionary simply because they have never heard of them; yet most medical experts would do just that unless countermanded by a nonexpert lexicographer. Apart from all other reasons, this illustrates why a general lexicographer must be in charge of a specialized dictionary: he knows enough about language to be humble.

Most dictionary staffs are run by an editor-in-chief and a managing editor. The editor-in-chief has the ultimate responsibility for producing the dictionary on schedule and within budget. He often selects the policy advisers and takes an active part in the discussions that help to shape the decisions determining the dictionary's scope and market. Whether the editor-in-chief is invited to participate in the business decisions affecting the profitability of the dictionary—its pricing, production costs, and so on—depends more on his particular situation within the company than his position as editor-in-chief. In any event, much of his time is spent in monitoring costs. If the dictionary is a contributed work, he deals with the contributors and is responsible for telling them what to do and for getting them to do it. He is also responsible for the quality of the work and does as much editing as time permits.

The managing editor's position varies greatly from publisher to publisher and from project to project. In some projects with an in-house staff, the managing editor, apart from doing his own editing, makes individual assignments, supervises their quality, sees that they are completed on schedule, trains new definers, keeps statistical data on the work's progress, and, if the work is computerized, has a large hand in shaping the data-management program. The managing editor is thus turned inward toward the staff and the daily routine, while the editor-in-chief, Janus faced, has to look inward and outward at the same time. In some cases the editor-in-chief is little more than a figurehead, with the managing editor doing most of the planning and all of the staff supervision. In other cases where the in-house staff is very small or nonexistent, the managing editor may be in fact little more than a staff editor who occasionally supervises a few free-lance editors. In short, "managing editor" can mean a lot or a little, depending on the particular situation.

Selection of the Word List

After the policies, scope, and market of a dictionary have been established and its schedule and costs estimated, the next step is the selection of the word list: all those terms to be included as dictionary entries, whether main entries or not. Although it is popularly believed that unabridged dictionaries contain all the words in the English language, as we have seen in our discussion of types of dictionaries, even an unabridged dictionary must have principles of selection and must exclude many thousands of words and expressions because they are obsolete, rarely used, or too specialized for a general dictionary (see pages 17–18). Considerations of available space always place practical limits on the number of entries that can be accommodated, especially in a one-volume dictionary. Clarence Barnhart has succinctly stated the practical necessity for selectivity in deriving the word list for a college dictionary.[10] If a college dictionary did not limit its entry count, it would run out of space somewhere in the letter **D**, about one-fourth of the way through an unabridged-sized lexicon. But there are other compelling reasons why a word list must be selected before defining begins. As we have seen, one of the cardinal principles of defining is the rule that all of the terms used in definitions must themselves be entered in the dictionary. But how can this rule be observed if there is no word list? How can a definer know when he is using a Word Not In in his definition? Furthermore, he will have no way of ensuring that parallel terms are defined in comparable ways, or that all the terms in a semantic cluster of equivalent or opposite meanings are included at all. His dictionary, if ever completed, will be a hodge-podge of inconsistencies and random omissions. The compiler of a glossary can afford to include whatever he feels will cause the reader difficulty, but a dictionary is self-contained, and within its stated scope it should be comprehensive and balanced in its coverage of comparable terms. This can be accomplished only by having a word list.

The time required to select a dictionary's word list may constitute a significant part of the entire project. Barnhart writes, "On my first high-school dictionary a staff of ten editors spent over five years combing the OED. Out of this mass of material we selected the meanings that were to be included in our high-school dictionary."[11] Barnhart also drew upon a large citation file for senses that appeared after the *OED*'s publication. Frank Vizetelly stated that the compilation of the vocabulary for the Funk & Wagnalls *Standard Dictionary* (an unabridged work published in 1893) took twenty compilers a year. In my own experience, the compilation of the word list usually takes from 20 to 25 percent of the entire duration of the project, from beginning to bound books.

The particular selection of terms depends chiefly on the presumed user. There is no need to belabor the point made earlier that the vocabulary needed for a children's dictionary will be different from that for adults, and that an ESL or specialized dictionary will have vocabularies different from both. However, a few comments may be in order on difficulties of selection that apply to almost all kinds of dictionaries.

What constitutes a legitimate dictionary entry? What is it, specifically, that makes a multiple lexical unit worth including? Two criteria have been cited. First, it must function like a unit so that its meaning inheres in the whole expression, as in *guinea pig,* rather than in its separate elements. No part of it can be replaced without the loss of its original meaning: one cannot call a *guinea pig* a *guinea hog.* The existence of semantically comparable one-word units (*rat, rabbit,* etc.) is further evidence that *guinea pig* is a unit.[12] Second, the stress pattern of multiple lexical units is frequently that of compounds (two words functioning and often written as one, such as *blackbird* or *ladybug*), with the primary stress on the first element and very little pause, if any, between the two elements. If one says aloud *guinea pig* and *large pig,* or *ladybug* and *green bug,* one will perceive that both elements of the second expression receive equal stress (large′ pig′, green′ bug′), which is the more noticeable because the pause between the two words is slightly lengthened as compared with *guinea pig* and *ladybug.*[13]

Although much attention is given to determining the lexical validity of multiple lexical units, every dictionary includes many phrasal entries that are not lexical units. The obvious cases of biographical and geographical entries need no elaboration; these are clearly encyclopedic terms. Less obvious, but bountiful in numbers, are terms like *Copernican system* and *listed building* (in the *Collins English Dictionary*) or *Jefferson Davis's Birthday* and *Riemannian geometry* (in *MW9*). Open a dictionary to virtually any page and one will find terms such as these, which are included for a variety of reasons but principally because the reader expects to find them. *Copernican system* and *Riemannian geometry* provide useful historical and scientific information, but their status as lexical units is arguable. *Listed building* is an official designation in the United Kingdom and of national importance, but it is part of a nomenclature rather than a vocabulary based on usage. When one gets into the realm of nomenclature, where volume of usage is not a factor, one is hard pressed to find any theoretical basis for including one or a few elements of the nomenclature and omitting all others. Yet clearly one cannot admit more than a few, else one's dictionary would rapidly turn into a nomenclature.

The difficulty of distinguishing between lexical units and items in a nomenclature is especially nettlesome in specialized dictionaries, which are by their nature more encyclopedic than general dictionaries. For example, medical nomenclatures may include many different terms for kinds of *agenesis* (absence of a part or organ resulting from its failure to develop in the course of embryonic growth) or *atresia* (congenital absence of a normal opening in a body vessel or part). It so happens that it is possible for virtually every part normally open to be closed at birth. We could thus have hundreds of *atresias* and thousands of *agenesis* entries. Some kinds of atresia and agenesis are more common than others and some are identifiable elements of complex genetic disorders; medical dictionaries try to confine their selection to terms that meet either of these criteria, but in many cases the decision is borderline if not arbitrary. Many diseases such as tuberculosis can afflict virtually every organ in the body. We may therefore reject *prostatic tuberculosis* along with many other like terms, but what about *pulmonary tuberculosis?* Logically, it should be omitted, yet no medical dictionary does so, even if the definition given is simply "tuberculosis of the lungs." In a specialized dictionary, the determination of whether a term is a lexical unit must depend on whether it is used often enough in preference to other phrases that mean the same thing to distinguish it as a name rather than as a merely fortuitous description. Unfortunately, few people are in a position to make that judgment, and those who do frequently disagree.

The selection of entries depends very much on the compiler's sense of what is wanted, and if what is wanted occasionally violates theory, so be it. My illustration of nonlexical terms in the *CED* and in *MW9* was not intended as criticism. Surely it is no fault to serve well the needs and expectations of the reader, provided one is faithful to the overriding purpose of a dictionary: describing the use of language. When the inclusion of nonlexical units becomes promiscuous and haphazard, merely serving the ends of marketing the dictionary rather than the needs of the user, we may fairly object to the practice. But dictionaries are *the* basic reference book in many homes, particularly in the United States, and it is hard to believe that the public would be better served by denying it nonlexical items in order to conform to a theoretical construct of a proper dictionary. The leitmotif running through Johnson's *Plan* of 1747 is that his dictionary beyond all else must be useful; to my mind that is still the first rule of good dictionary making.

In former years, the word list was compiled in a card file, with each proposed lexical unit on a separate card. This allowed space for other information, such as the source from which it was obtained, its part of speech, its status as a main entry or run-on derivative, an indication as to whether it was a general or a specialized word (and if the latter, what specialty), and perhaps a symbol representing its degree of importance to the dictionary. Optional words could then be cut to conserve space at a later time. Nowadays, editors usually store this information in a computer and many operations formerly done manually, notably alphabetization, can be done mechanically. Statistical data, such as the ratio of main entries to total entries or the number of entries in each part of speech, can also be obtained more easily.

To provide guidance in selecting dictionary word lists that accurately reflect the distribution of lexical units throughout the alphabet, Edward L. Thorndike prepared a study of the lexicon in the 1950s for the Thorndike-Barnhart dictionaries. On the basis of his study he divided the alphabet into 105 approximately equal units, called blocks[14] (see the table on page 242). One can see that in English there are far more words that begin with S—which has thirteen blocks—than with any other letter. The letter C, with ten blocks, is next. It is a truism in dictionary work that one is in sight of the end of the project on finishing S, but not before. The block system is helpful in providing a check on the criteria used by various compilers working in different parts of the alphabet. If one's word list shows that E has as many entries as S, for example, one should suspect that whoever selected the terms for E was far more permissive than the selector for S, and adjust the word list accordingly.

Language changes, of course, and the distribution of words according to their initial letters may have changed since this table was prepared and may change in the future; but I doubt that the overall distribution changes rapidly. I have used Thorndike's block system for several different dictionaries, adult and children's, and found it to be a very helpful guide in fashioning the word list. It will not work for every kind of dictionary, most obviously for specialized dictionaries, nor for dictionaries of every size. (It would probably not work for very small dictionaries.) But for intermediate to large, general, monolingual English dictionaries—say between 30,000 and 200,000 entries and perhaps more—it is a fairly reliable guide to the alphabetic distribution of the lexicon. One should not be rigid about the equivalence of all the blocks. For example, the J block is actually somewhat shorter than any of the thirteen S blocks, but it was given its own block for simplicity's sake. Likewise, one will find that the XYZ block does not measure up to the usual size of other blocks. Frequently, too, the last block in a letter will comprise fewer terms than other blocks within the letter. But in spite of these minor imperfections, the block system is a valuable tool not only in entry selection but in organizing the assignments to definers. Each definer can be given one block with the knowledge that it represents a fixed percentage of the entire work. Of course, some blocks contain words that are harder to define than other blocks, or words with many more definitions, so that the the work involved in doing two different blocks is not strictly comparable. But the system does provide a rough guide to equivalence, and in assigning deadlines to individual definers the editor-in-chief or managing

Thorndike's block system of distribution of dictionary entries by initial letters

A-1	a–adk	F-36	fore–fror	P-71	post–prh
A-2	adl–alh	F-37	fros–fz	P-72	pri–prot
A-3	ali–angk	G-38	g–geq	P-73	prou–pz
A-4	angl–arak	G-39	ger–gord	Q-74	q–qz
A-5	aral–ath	G-40	gore–grouo	R-75	r–recn
A-6	ati–az	G-41	group–gz	R-76	reco–renn
B-7	b–basd	H-42	h–hav	R-77	reno–rhn
B-8	base–benf	H-43	haw–hh	R-78	rho–rotd
B-9	beng–bld	H-44	hi–horr	R-79	rote–rz
B-10	ble–bouq	H-45	hors–hz	S-80	s–sat
B-11	bour–buc	I-46	i–inam	S-81	sau–sd
B-12	bud–bz	I-47	inan–infn	S-82	sea–seo
C-13	c–caq	I-48	info–intn	S-83	sep–shio
C-14	car–cel	I-49	into–iz	S-84	ship–sinf
C-15	cem–chim	J-50	j–jz	S-85	sing–smd
C-16	chin–cled	K-51	k–kz	S-86	sme–sors
C-17	clee–col	L-52	l–ld	S-87	sort–spln
C-18	com–conf	L-53	le–lil	S-88	splo–stas
C-19	cong–coo	L-54	lim–louh	S-89	stat–stov
C-20	cop–cq	L-55	loui–lz	S-90	stow–sucg
C-21	cra–culs	M-56	m–marb	S-91	such–swar
C-22	cult–cz	M-57	marc–med	S-92	swas–sz
D-23	d–defd	M-58	mee–mil	T-93	t–tel
D-24	defe–deteq	M-59	mim–monn	T-94	tem–thq
D-25	deter–discol	M-60	mono–mz	T-95	thr–too
D-26	discom–dold	N-61	n–nif	T-96	top–trh
D-27	dole–dt	N-62	nig–nz	T-97	tri–tz
D-28	du–dz	O-63	o–oo	U-98	u–unl
E-29	e–elk	O-64	op–ou	U-99	unm–uz
E-30	ell–en	O-65	ov–oz	V-100	v–vim
E-31	eo–exb	P-66	p–par	V-101	vin–vz
E-32	exc–ez	P-67	pas–peq	W-102	w–wess
F-33	f–fem	P-68	per–picj	W-103	west–wis
F-34	fen–flah	P-69	pick–plea	W-104	wit–wz
F-35	flai–ford	P-70	pleb–poss	XYZ-105	x–zz

Courtesy of Robert K. Barnhart.

editor should make allowances for the degree of difficulty of each block and adjust the deadline accordingly.

The Style Manual

Most publishing houses have a company style manual that sets forth suggested rules for manuscript preparation, rules concerning capitalization, punctuation, spelling, footnote references, and so forth. But dictionaries are so specialized that they require their own style manuals, for many of the rules of regular manuals have no application to dictionaries (such as footnotes), and literally hundreds of situations that must be resolved for dictionary work are not addressed at all, or not in sufficient detail, in regular style manuals. Moreover, etymologies have such a different set of problems that they often require a separate style manual, especially for large dictionaries. The etymological style may differ substantially from that used elsewhere in the dictionary.

The dictionary style manual is an alphabetically arranged reference guide to every aspect of editing dictionary copy. Though called a style manual, it is in fact also a teaching manual. It discusses the general defining style to be employed, with illustrations of various kinds of definitions. It explains, often in great detail, how particular grammatical forms (such as transitive and intransitive verbs) are to be treated. It illustrates how each part of the definition is to be type-styled or, in the age of computerization, coded. The more problems the editor-in-chief can anticipate by dealing with them in the style manual, the better off he will be later on. He is well advised to discuss the issues thoroughly with his top associates and to make his manual as comprehensive as possible. It is very difficult to find and impractical to correct inconsistencies once the defining stage is well under way. Dictionary style manuals are frequently amplified and refined as novel situations are encountered by definers. The variety of linguistic situations in which the rules must be applied cannot possibly be anticipated. Every dictionary has unique problems; there can be no generalized manual that suits all dictionaries. Because of the frequent changes and additions required, a looseleaf binder is the best way to maintain a dictionary style manual.

A style manual I prepared for a children's dictionary ran to over eighty pages in typescript. College or unabridged dictionary manuals are often printed, and because of their complexity they may be considerably longer. As an example of the range of material covered, see the main headings covered in my children's dictionary style manual in the list on pages 244–246.

This style manual, like most, was designed for the use of in-house staff editors. The situation is complicated when one must depend on outside con-

In-house Children's Dictionary Style Manual

Abbreviations
1. As main entries
2. Used in the dictionary

Acronyms

Act of . . .

A.D.

Adjectives
1. Comparative degrees
   a. When to include
   b. When to separately enter and pronounce comparatives
   c. Variants
2. Introductory phrases used in the def. of adjectives

Adjective Uses of Nouns and Verbals

Archaic and Obsolete Defs.

Australian

B.C.

Biblical References

British
1. Briticisms for which there is either an exact American–English synonym or a parallel word or phrase
2. Words describing something peculiar to Britain
3. Pronunciation and spelling
4. For multi-def. entries in which all defs. are British . . .

By (use in measures)

Canadian

Capitalization
1. What to capitalize
2. Capitalized main entries
3. Lower-case main entries
4. See Order of Entries

Center Period (used in pronunciations)

Chemical Elements

Color Terms
1. Adj. + color ("light blue wall")
2. Adj. + adj. ("light colored")
3. Color + color ("blue-green")
4. Use of black-and-white, etc. (set phrases)

5. Colors as main entries

Combining Forms

Compare (use of)

Compass Points

Contractions

Cross-References
1. As main entries
2. As run ins
3. X-refs to particular defs.
4. Geographic x-refs
5. When to use
6. Including more than one part of speech

Dates

Defining, Techniques of

Division of Words

Especially (use of)

Etymologies

Examples

Foreign-language Labels

Formerly (use of)

Geographic Entries

Geographic Variants

Homographs

Hyphenated Words

Illustrations (pictorial)

Illustrative Phrases and Sentences

Inflected Forms
1. When to include
2. Where to include
3. X-refs
4. Inflected forms in phrasal main entries

Inverted Entries

Italics (use of)

Main Entries

Main Entry Variants

Mythological Entries

Names

Nouns
1. When to show the plural as an inflected form
2. Form of the plural as an inflected form
3. When to pronounce plurals as inflected forms
4. Variant plurals as inflected forms

244

5. Plurals as main entries
6. Nouns ending in *-ics*
7. Methods of defining nouns
Numbering of Definitions
Numbers
1. When to write out and when to use numerals
2. Ordinal numbers beyond ten
3. Dates
4. Use of commas
5. In hyphenated unit modifiers ("five-toed")
Offensive Words
Old-fashioned Words
Or
1. Typeface
2. When to use
Order of Definitions
Order of Entries (i.e., alphabetic system: Do capitalized forms precede lower-case forms? Do forms written solid precede hyphenated forms?) A listing of theoretical possibilities in proper order should be included here, such as: sc, sc-, sc., s/c, s.c., -sc, Sc, Sc-, etc.
Ordinal Numbers
Parentheses (use of)
Part-of-speech Labels
1. Entries taking part of speech labels
2. Entries having only one part of speech
3. Entries having two or more parts of speech
4. Entries showing inflected forms
5. Parenthetical information
6. Defs. having more than one part of speech
Phrasal Entries
Prefixes
Pronunciations
1. Pronunciation key
2. Form of typescript (i.e., how to represent pronunciation symbols in typescript)
3. Placement of pronunciations

4. Variants
5. Optional syllables or sounds
6. Order of pronunciations
7. Foreign names and words
8. When to pronounce a main entry
Qualifying Words (i.e., "usually," "chiefly," etc.)
Rare
Regional Labels
Run-on Derivatives
1. Suffixes used to form run-on derivatives (a list of suffixes that may be used)
2. When to pronounce
3. When to include as derivative, when as main entry, when to omit
4. Phrasal run-ons
5. Variants
Run-ins (defined phrasal entries "run in" to other articles: usually idioms)
Sample Entries (actual samples shown in each category)
1. One def., one part of speech
2. Multiple defs, one part of speech
3. Multiple parts of speech (Many different situations are exemplified.)
See (use of)
See under (use of)
Semicolon
Series Entries (Sometimes called *category entries,* these entries include series of terms that comprise semantic sets and hence can all be defined according to the same or similar formulas. In practice some members of the series require individual treatment, but the identification of series entries and the establishment of a uniform style for each series is an important time-saver as well as a way of maintaining consistent

treatment of like terms. Normally, one definer will be assigned to define all the members of a series. Dictionaries differ in how many kinds of entries they regard as belonging to series. Some common series entries are listed below. Each series entry is exemplified with one or several prototypes.)

1. Alphabet, English and Greek
2. Notes of musical scale
3. Musical directions
4. Musical instruments
5. Numbers, cardinal and ordinal
6. Units of measure
7. Days of the week
8. Months of the year
9. Compass points and directions
10. Countries
    (Many other geographic entries can be placed in series.)
11. Colors
12. Nationality designations
13. Military ranks
14. Chemical elements

Signs and Symbols
Small caps (use of)
Stress in Pronunciations
1. How shown
2. When to show stress
Suffixes
1. As main entries
2. Form of definition
Syllabication
1. In main entries
2. Inflected forms
3. Run-on derivations
4. Pronunciations

5. Variants

Synonym and Antonym Lists
Synonym Discriminations
Taxonomic Classifications
Technical Entries
That and Which (use of)
Time
Trademarks
U.S. (as label and nationality designation)
Usage Labels
1. Which will be used
2. Placement
Usage Notes
1. Kinds of notes
2. Information conveyed by usage notes
3. Idiomatic use of prepositions and adverbs
4. Words referring to a particular thing ("said of")
5. Words with contemptuous or offensive connotations
Variants
Verbs
1. Style of defining
2. Principal parts
3. When to separately enter (and pronounce) principal parts
4. Pronouncing principal parts within an entry
5. Archaic or nonstandard variants of principal parts
6. Treatment of transitive and intransitive verbs
Words Not In (list of prefixes, suffixes, and combining forms that may be used to form words in definitions even though they are not separately entered, e.g., *-ish, -like, -shaped*)

tributors, as for a specialized dictionary. The specialists may need to know some of the items covered by an in-house manual, but certainly not all. One must therefore prepare a simplified version of the style manual for contributors, omitting many of the finer points of style while leaving in most of the teaching aids. It is best to tell specialists only as much as they need to know to do their work. One must curb one's open-handedness not because of any proclivity for secrecy but because people unfamiliar with editing procedures tend to misinterpret the simplest editorial directions. The same person who can separate and suture microscopic blood vessels of the eye with perfect assurance falls into a state of mental collapse when instructed in the proper use of parentheses.

One of the chief differences in style between British and American dictionaries has been the British practice of clustering or nesting (to use Zgusta's term) related entries within the same article. Under this system, compounds, idioms, and other multiple lexical units, as well as some derivatives, are embedded within a consolidated paragraph alphabetized under a word with which they share a common element or from which they are derived. Thus, in *Chambers Twentieth Century Dictionary,* the entry for *eye* includes entries for *eyelash, eye-wash,* and *eye-witness,* as well as for *in one's mind's eye,* etc.[15] An American might have difficulty finding *popcorn* in the *Concise Oxford Dictionary (COD),* since it appears within the entry for *pop,* not as a main entry in its own alphabetic position. American dictionaries also assign different numbers to each sense (usually in boldface type), whereas dictionaries modeled after the *COD* designate only major sense divisions by number and divide definitions within each numbered category with semicolons. That is also the style most commonly employed by bilingual dictionaries. *Chambers* goes one step further and dispenses with definition numbers entirely.

The clustered style is more compact, but it can be argued that some entries and meanings are harder to find than in the typical American method. It appears that the trend in British lexicography now favors the American approach. The *Collins English Dictionary,* for example, does not employ clustering and numbers individual definitions, as do the leading ESL dictionaries, *Longman* and *Hornby.* On the other hand, the recently published *New York Times Everyday Dictionary* breaks with the American tradition in using the clustered-entry approach of *Chambers* and the *COD* but combines it with the American practice of individually numbering definitions.[16] Typographically, individually numbered definitions are more striking, and the practice seems to encourage a finer breakdown of sense division, since each definition is easily distinguished from the others. From a different vantage point, this system sometimes encourages an artificial proliferation of senses that could be amalgamated at no great loss to understanding. There is some merit to both points of view. On balance, the effectiveness of each method of presentation depends on the value one places on conciseness. If one wants to be as comprehensive as possible in the least amount of space, clustering makes sense. But there is a price to pay in terms of ease of access to the information. In very small dictionaries, in which definitions are often little more than synonyms, definition numbers are a waste of space. Numbering senses in a "vest pocket" dictionary is little more than a conceit.

Controlling Length

We have all read of dictionaries and encyclopedias abandoned after twenty years of labor upon the completion of the first four volumes, constituting the letter **A**. Such works were not, we may presume, perfectly planned, chiefly because no effort was made to control the length of individual entries. Accurate projections of the length of an entire work cannot be made unless one monitors the length of individual entries and calculates the average number of lines each entry requires. Since most dictionaries are printed two or three columns to the page, the basic measurement is the ratio between entries and column-lines. If each entry takes an average of two column-lines, and one's dictionary has 150,000 entries, one can expect to have 300,000 column-lines in one's dictionary. The calculation is not based on main entries only, but all entries. (See page 84 for an explanation of what constitutes a dictionary entry.) Let's suppose that the design for the dictionary calls for 80 lines to the column or 160 column-lines per page. Such a book would have to have 1,875 pages to provide space for that many entries (300,000 divided by 160). However, if the average number of column-lines per entry could be cut to 1.7, the same number of entries would fit into fewer than 1,600 pages (1.7 $\times$ 150,000 = 255,000 divided by 160 = 1593.8). Saving 280 pages of text in the huge print runs of most dictionaries represents an enormous saving of money. The dictionary could thus be sold at a cheaper price than would otherwise have been possible. Of course, one could also cut the number of entries or reduce the size of the type so that more column-lines fit on each page, but there are drawbacks to each of those options. The size of the book cannot be greatly altered without losing the market for which it was designed. A dictionary with small type is apt to be less appealing than competing works, and its sales may suffer as a consequence. For these reasons, the space allotted to individual entries must be watched closely to see that no space is wasted, and to make sure that the expected ratio of lines per entry is maintained. When a definer is assigned a block of terms, he is not only given a deadline but is allotted a certain number of column-lines in which to produce the requisite definitions. Editors are instructed as to how many typewriter characters correspond to one column-line in print. Definitions are typed to this measure.

One can now see why the lexicographer must be involved with the design elements of the dictionary. Since he is responsible for ensuring that an enormous amount of material fits into a given space, he must have a hand in designing that space to accommodate the maximum amount of copy. As a matter of fact, college dictionaries average fewer than two column-lines per entry, generally between 1.5 and 1.8. As dictionaries compete with each other by adding entries, the ratio drops, since they seldom add pages.

Most production people, like most publishers, have no idea of the amount of material that must be compressed within the covers of a dictionary. They have never dealt with a book in which the editor felt he had not only an interest but a right to be involved, and involved he must be, or risk disaster. To a large extent the dictionary staff handles its own production. It evaluates copy, sends it out to referees if necessary, edits it, proofreads it, and, in controlling its length, performs the production task of copy fitting. Nonetheless, the lexicographer certainly needs knowledgeable production people to advise and collaborate with on the selection of type and the design of an attractive but efficient page layout. The lexicographer should be open to all proposals to make the dictionary page more appealing; but he must insist that the design be economical of space and he should have the decisive say in what the final design is to be. He certainly cannot afford to regard typography and page layout as none of his business, because it is he, not the designer, who will be held responsible years later if the book runs hundreds of pages too long.

Apart from the design characteristics of the type page, the type chosen must often accommodate an unusually large number of typefaces and special characters. Elegant style must be sacrificed for readability and conciseness in setting, a factor determined by the widths of the individual letters in print. Some readable typefaces can set more characters per line than other faces. If one gains 1.5 characters per column-line over 300,000 column-lines, one has gained 450,000 characters, or the equivalent, at 5.5 letters per word, of over 80,000 words, the size of a modest book.

What steps can be taken if a lexicographer does misjudge the length and finds it necessary to cut back? The lines per entry ratio is closely related to the ratio between main entries and total entries. As we have seen in Chapter Three, in college dictionaries between 44 and 48 percent of the total entries are main entries. By converting main entries to run-on derivatives, the ratio of lines to entries will drop, since run-on derivatives take up very little space. But a dictionary with too many derivatives is not serving its readers well. Another way to save space is to leave out definitions in polysemous words. Clarence Barnhart has estimated that college dictionaries have on the aver-

age two definitions for every entry, and definitions, of course, do not contribute to entry count.[17] Finally, definitions can be cut in length. Each of
these steps diminishes the value of the book and is demoralizing to editors
who must undo their own carefully wrought definitions in order to save
space. But to avoid them, strict planning and control of entry length and
design features are essential.

In contributed works, controlling length is problematical at best. It is
virtually impossible to get a large number of specialists to confine their definitions to a set length. First of all, some subjects must be defined at greater
length than others, either because the subjects themselves are more important and central to the purpose of the dictionary or because they are more
complex than other subjects. Second, contributing specialists, no matter how
expert in their own fields, are not experienced definers and lack the judgment required for a sense of proportion in definition length. Inexperienced
definers often treat a pair of terms of equivalent importance and complexity
quite unequally. One is analyzed in enormous detail: particles of matter are
weighed and described, conditions that might influence them are assessed,
theories that account for their behavior are cited. The other, of quite the
same rank, is dismissed with a genus and differentia statement, such as "a
Herpes virus." Why? The two terms were defined at different times, and by
the time the second one's turn came around the contributor had grown for-
getful, weary, or careless. Or the simpler definition was written at an early
stage before the contributor had developed a better idea of what was wanted
or the confidence to be expansive. Although the dictionary editor can sometimes cut lengthy definitions, they may be too technical for him to rely on
his own judgment and he must have recourse to another expert. Similarly,
he must ask other experts to expand definitions that are too sketchy. But in
spite of these efforts, the results are often uneven. In a contributed dictionary, it is necessary to be flexible as to the overall length.

In a large work, one can form a fairly reliable estimate of the overall
length when one has between a fourth and a third of the projected number
of entries in hand, provided they represent a broad range of subject matter
and types of entries. For shorter dictionaries, one may need half of the total
entries. One's task then is copy fitting: determining the size and typography
of a book that will accommodate that volume of material. Of course, if the
volume of material is far above or below one's expectations, it is not too late
to change one's guidelines and implore one's contributors to contract or
enlarge their forthcoming definitions. One can exercise much greater control
over the length of an abridgment, regardless of the kind of dictionary, than
of an original work. For this reason large abridgments are often better balanced and often, in fact, better dictionaries than the works from which they
were derived.

Technical Vocabularies and Glossaries

As an aid for those preparing technical vocabularies and glossaries, Alexandre Manuila has written a practical step-by-step outline, originally prepared for the World Health Organization, that is summarized here.[18]

1. Define the field to be covered by the vocabulary. The mere statement of a subject area or the selection of the title is not enough. Fields to be included and omitted should be carefully delimited.
2. Identify the group to whom the vocabulary is to be addressed.
3. Decide on its size (i.e., the approximate number of terms).
4. Decide whether a classified arrangement or alphabetic order is to be used.
5. Even if alphabetic order is selected, draw up a scheme for classifying the entire vocabulary. This step is essential to ensure that important concepts are not omitted and that contradictory definitions are not drawn up.
   Example: The preliminary classification scheme for a vocabulary of air pollution might be as follows (in practice, more divisions would probably be used, and certainly many more subdivisions; only a few are given here as an example).

   air pollutants
       gaseous pollutants
       particulate pollutants
   processes that cause air pollution
   meteorological phenomena that affect air pollution
   methods for measurement of air pollutants
       gravimetric methods
       volumetric methods
       electrical methods
           amperometric methods
           conductometric methods
       optical methods
           spectroscopic methods
   effects of air pollution
       effects on health
       effects on materials, structures
   methods for reduction of air pollution

6. Select the concepts to be defined. List the preferred terms for these concepts under the appropriate divisions and subdivisions of the classification scheme. Under each heading, list the terms in a logical sequence, not alphabetically. Do not invert the terms.
7. Circulate the completed classified list of terms to a number of experts for comment. These experts should be representative of (a) the dif-

ferent disciplines covered by the vocabulary; (b) different geographic areas; (c) (if the glossary is multilingual) different mother tongues.

8. After adjusting the word list and the classification scheme in the light of the comments of the experts, draw up an entry for each term, using cards. At the top of each card, list the preferred term; then give the definition and other pertinent information. The only way to avoid contradictory definitions is to draw up entries for a group of related concepts *as a group*.

9. If the vocabulary is to be arranged alphabetically, go through the completed cards and invert the preferred terms, if necessary. Write the inverted term at the head of each card. Change all the cross-references to reflect the inversion of terms, and arrange the cards in alphabetic order. Check carefully several times to make sure that the order is correct.

10. If the vocabulary is to be in classified order, number the entries.

11. Type the manuscript. Each entry heading (preferred term) should be written in lower-case letters (initial capitals are used only for proper names) and should be marked for boldface type (usually indicated by a wavy underline).

12. Carefully proofread the manuscript.

13. If the vocabulary is arranged alphabetically, carefully read the manuscript again, this time solely for cross-references. Check the reference of every cross-reference to make sure that it is included.

14. If the vocabulary is in classified order, prepare an alphabetic index that will refer to the number reference identifying each entry in classified order.

15. Submit copies of the completed manuscript to a number of experts for comment (see paragraph 7 above). A glossary of air pollution, for instance, should be submitted not only to air pollution experts but also to chemists, meteorologists, engineers, etc., who may have specialized knowledge of air pollution. If the manuscript is in alphabetic order, it should be submitted together with a copy of the final classified list of terms so that it can be checked for adequacy of coverage. Revise the manuscript accordingly in the light of the comments received.

Writing the Dictionary

The Use of Staff

Assuming that one has an in-house staff, there are essentially two ways to dispose them. Each reflects a different philosophy, or at least a different emphasis. One can have a staff of generalists who define all but the most specialized terms and who have the final say over all definitions, or one can have a staff of specialists with very few generalists.

The first method reflects an older tradition, in which lexicography is seen essentially as an application of humanistic scholarship and in which the ideal lexicographer, modeling himself after Johnson, is the supreme generalist. The Oxford dictionaries still employ this method, with obvious success. The editors of the *OED Supplements* not only define terms but write their own etymologies and prepare their own pronunciations. Science terms are defined by science graduates of Oxford but are reviewed by general editors.[19] Such dedication to the tradition of the broadly educated humanist as a master of every field is rare and has its drawbacks. The *OED* was notably deficient in its coverage of scientific terms. (This is one of the chief gaps the *Supplements* are expected to fill. Robert Burchfield estimates that 20 to 25 percent of the terms in the *Supplements* are scientific.) Although the *OED*'s etymologies have been justly admired, its pronunciations are simply the transcriptions, inherited from older works, of what received pronunciation is supposed to be. Little or no attention is paid to actual speech.

Implicit in an extreme generalist approach is the idea of what an educated person is. In this view, a narrowly educated person is not truly educated. He is half formed, suspect in his grasp of fundamental facts and ignorant of refined taste; the responsibility for compiling a dictionary should not be placed in the hands of such a person. Clearly, whether admitted or not, from this vantage point the role of status and authority lurks only slightly beneath the surface. The generalist view willingly tolerates certain deficiencies, such as a summary treatment of pronunciation, for the overriding benefit of placing the ultimate authority of the work in the hands of generalists. The absence or scant treatment of specialized terms has not always been regarded as a serious defect, for it was implicit that the dictionary was not only *by* but *for* broadly educated people.

The generalist approach, historically British, has long been modified in America by the introduction of special editors assigned to special tasks. Etymologies are almost always done separately by special editors or by outside contributors. (The danger of relying on a generalist for all aspects of lexicography is perhaps best illustrated by the rejection of many of Webster's etymologies by C. A. F. Mahn for the 1864 edition of Webster's dictionary.) Pronunciations, too, are routinely done by specialists in American lexicography, as are biographical and geographical entries. Increasingly, British lexicography has also begun to employ specialists for many of these assignments, as well as for definitions of scientific and technical terms. Usage labels are usually written by the general staff in the course of defining; usage notes are normally assigned to a designated general editor in addition to his defining duties. (Although the *American Heritage* usage panel has received much attention, many of *AHD*'s usage notes were staff written, and even those submitted to the usage panel had to be interpreted and written by a staff editor.) However, national or regional labels for varieties of English may well be applied by outside experts to whom certain terms are submitted.

Some American dictionary staffs appear to be highly specialized, with each editor assigned one or several subjects, not just broad areas like the biological or physical sciences but subjects such as sports, cooking terms, horticulture, ornithology, and so on. Some staffs have one editor who is particularly adept at defining verbs and who therefore defines the most difficult ones. But in point of fact, editors who specialize in several fields are little more than generalists with some particular strengths or weaknesses in their educations, and an editor who can define all general terms having a particular grammatical function is not so very specialized, in my view, unless the function be interjection. It is nonetheless true that specialists are playing an increasingly significant role in dictionary preparation, particularly in the sciences. Dictionaries differ on how independently special editors work. Traditionally, in America as in Britain, the final decisions on all definitions, whether general or technical, resided with general editors. Some American dictionaries still adhere to this practice; others do not.

The philosophy underlying an approach emphasizing specialization endorses the importance of doing as opposed to understanding. The specialist has greater practical experience than the generalist; he has actively studied the subject of his definition and therefore writes from the viewpoint of one engaged in the occupation of which he writes, in a word, as a professional rather than as an informed amateur. A dictionary composed entirely by specialists is often a collection of special points of view with no unity of approach; its usefulness may depend on whether the reader's particular interests coincide with those of the specialists.

As I hope Chapter Five made clear, the dictionary staff cannot turn to outside experts for reliable help in reporting varieties of style or status. It must rely on its own resources.

The differences between British and American practice are outweighed by their similarities. Though the Oxford dictionaries may still rely on their editors for all particulars of each entry, I doubt that any other British dictionary publisher does so, and it is safe to say that no major American dictionary publisher follows such a practice. Most general dictionary staffs are a mixture of generalists and specialists. The differences are those of proportion and emphasis rather than an absolute commitment to one philosophy or another, and this is all to the good. No modern dictionary staff can afford to be without a complement of specialized editors to handle its scientific and technical definitions. But the nucleus of almost all dictionary staffs is composed of generalists. My own view is that general editors should retain ultimate control of every element of the dictionary entry. They should rarely overrule a specialist acting within his own competence, but the authority to decide what goes in a general dictionary should be theirs, for they are free of the narrow focus that may blind the specialist to the needs of the nonspecialist user.

The Stages of Defining and Editing

In a general monolingual dictionary, defining always requires at least two stages: preliminary or *first-run* defining, and review or final editing. The first run may involve a large staff of relatively inexperienced definers or a small staff of experienced definers. In either case, first-run definitions must be carefully reviewed by senior definers, in no case by the same editor who wrote the original definitions. The review, moreover, is not simply critical; the second definer actually redefines the word, using the preliminary material however he will. Only rarely does the preliminary definition pass unchanged; more often it is considerably altered, sometimes entirely rewritten. The existing definition serves as an impetus to hasten one's absorption of the particular problems of the word's meaning. Often the very mistakes of the first definer are of immense help in pointing up these problems. A good first definer does not have to be polished; but if he has enough insight to address the real difficulties inherent in his definitions, he will speed the work of the second definer and contribute no little to the dictionary's ultimate merit. A definition can be wrong in so many ways and right in so few that it cannot be left to a single writer, no matter how experienced a definer he may be. (For a discussion of definition, see Chapter Four.)

Following the two defining stages, the former practice was to set the copy in type, usually in the form of galley proofs, which were proofread and corrected before page proofs were prepared. In practice, a considerable amount of editing apart from the correction of typographical errors occurred in every dictionary after it had been set in type. This was the bane of publishers, since it is very expensive to make many changes (called "author's alterations" or AAs) once a book has been composed, and it is even more expensive than usual to make them in a dictionary. Most standard book contracts contain a clause specifying that any author's alterations exceeding a certain percentage of the work, usually 15 percent, will be paid for by the author. In a dictionary, however, the authors are employees of the publisher, and dictionaries, as the reader is probably tired of hearing, are not like other books. The complexity of the relationships between the various parts of a dictionary is such that omissions, inconsistencies, ambiguities, and even errors cannot be discovered entirely in the manuscript stages. Poor definitions find their way into print and must be revised. Missed cross-references must be inserted. Style changes that were overlooked must be corrected. An occasional new term may have to be included. The sense of an existing term may have undergone rapid change since the early stages of the work and necessitate rewriting. Many a dictionary's AAs have totaled 100 percent of the cost of the initial composition; that is, it has cost as much to make changes once the manuscript was set as it did to set the copy in the first place. (This does *not* mean that the entire work was reset. The alteration of a printed character requires much more time than initial composition. AAs are made one at a time and the initial setting is a massive, streamlined operation involving many people.) This percentage is unheard of in connection with any other type of book, yet the AA rates of some new dictionaries have run to 200 percent and more. For an original dictionary, as distinguished from an abridgment, an AA rate of 50 percent of the cost of initial composition is good (abridgments may have considerably lower AA rates). AAs are obviously a major cost of dictionaries, and to the extent that they can be avoided or minimized, as by providing editors with an on-line computer system for making their own changes, a great deal of money could be saved. Of course, setting up such a system and training people to use it also costs money. (See more on computerization in Chapter Seven.)

Most large dictionary projects today have an intermediate stage between manuscript and type that enables the editors to make changes far more cheaply than after type has been set. In traditional practice the typesetters or compositors were, as the names imply, those who actually keyboarded the copy sent them. It is now common, however, for a computer company (which may or may not also be a compositor) to keyboard the copy and insert the various codes that will identify particular components of each entry. Once the dictionary has been entirely keyboarded, the editors may thus be provided with a final alphabetic copy of the file that includes the computer codes. (Some of these codes will be converted later to composition codes to instruct the typesetter's computer in what fonts to set copy so marked.) Although it may be less than ideal to have to read copy with computer codes, this stage does give the dictionary staff a comparatively inexpensive last chance to make corrections before typesetting; in other words, before the tape is converted to meet the compositor's needs.

The proofreading stages of a dictionary are numerous and exacting. A college dictionary contains about 3 million words or in the neighborhood of 16.5 million characters, each of which must be proofread. The type is small and the typography complicated. It includes pronunciation and etymology symbols and an uncommonly large variety of type styles. According to Frank Vizetelly, the Funk & Wagnalls *Standard Dictionary* of 1893 went through at least eleven proof stages.[20] It is doubtful if any dictionaries go through eleven proof stages today, but for college dictionaries two or three galley proof stages and two page proof stages are not uncommon. Even so, the first edition of every new dictionary is bound to have a number of errors.

In a specialized dictionary in which definitions are contributed by outside experts, the editors' task is quite different. Many of the problems confronting the specialized dictionary editor are problems of nomenclature rather than definition. For example, few specialists have any sense of the distinction between a lexical unit (e.g., *hypopituitarism*) and its generic equivalent (e.g., *anterior pituitary hormone deficiency*), which is in fact a brief definition. They will quite commonly represent the two expressions as variants, leaving it to the nonexpert lexicographer to sort things out. This he does on the basis of analogy with similar sets of terms, by analyzing the way the specialist himself uses these expressions in other definitions, by consulting other dictionaries and reference books, and by his own sense of how the language works. It comes as a surprise to many people that a dictionary editor can quite competently edit a specialized dictionary in a field in which he himself is not an expert. Of course, some familiarity with the terminology helps, but it is much more important that the editor of a specialized dictionary know the principles of lexicography than that he be an expert in the subject of the dictionary. Long before he has finished editing the dictionary he will be expert enough in the terminology; but if he has not begun with an understanding of lexicography, he will not learn it from his editing, and the dictionary will suffer as a result.

I referred earlier to the deep knowledge of a subject required by a special definer for a general dictionary. The reader may be perplexed as to why the editor of a specialized dictionary needs no such knowledge, or at least much less of it. The explanation is simple. The special definer is *writing* definitions from scratch, and he is writing them for a general audience. The definitions in a specialized dictionary are written by outside contributors, and though the editor frequently must rewrite, this is quite a different matter from that of creating one's own definition. It is also harder to write a technical definition for a lay audience than for another group of specialists, since in the latter case one can assume that ordinary technical terms will be understood. For a lay audience nothing can be assumed. The writer must therefore understand the theoretical basis of the term so that he can have a number of options at his disposal for recasting it in simple language.

In most general dictionaries, as we have said, while the defining stages are under way the pronunciations and etymologies are being written independently by specialists. Synonym discussions and encyclopedic material such as biographical and geographical terms are also prepared independently, as are lists of abbreviations, foreign terms, various tables and charts, and the illustrations.

Illustrations

The importance of illustrations varies greatly from one dictionary to another. The *American Heritage Dictionary* is exceptional among college dictionaries in devoting an enormous amount of space to illustrations, but the selection and preparation of illustrations is no small matter for any illustrated dictionary. For children's dictionaries, in particular, it is of prime importance. One of the early decisions to be made by the advisory committee and the editor-in-chief (with the understood approval of the publisher who pays the bills) is how much importance—and how much money—is to be assigned to the illustrations.

Once that has been decided, the main question to be answered is, What will be illustrated? Although one would like to have the definers' advice, one cannot afford to wait until each definer comes to a term that would benefit by being illustrated. Certainly a few illustrations can be added along the way, but essentially the choice of what to illustrate must be made early on. The best arrangement is to have a picture editor whose chief responsibility is to select—in cooperation with the art director, the editor-in-chief (or the managing editor), and the defining staff—those terms that will be illustrated and to determine *how* they will be illustrated. Dictionaries are usually illustrated by line drawings. (For a discussion of the comparative advantages of drawings and photographs, see page 112.) If there are a great many illustrations, the picture editor may need one or two subordinates, including a picture researcher who assembles illustrative material (called scrap) from which the artists work. Many of us have a vague idea of what an aardvark looks like, but how many could draw one without having an actual likeness, preferably a photograph, before us? The picture researcher digs out photographs or high-quality drawings of aardvarks, lacewings, cogwheels, bend sinister diagonals, Egyptian pyramids, and anything else that is to be drawn. In many projects the picture editor must do his own research. He (or she) should maintain a constant liaison with the dictionary staff and the art director to make sure that the terminology used in labeling the parts of an automobile engine, for example, is not only included in the dictionary but is given the preferred terms. Although he may solicit definers' suggestions, some definers do not have a keen visual sense, and they often lack the knowledge as to what can practically be illustrated. The picture editor must be free to reject any definer's suggestion, but definers should be shown preliminary sketches and asked to comment on them.

Attempts to economize by piecing together artwork from various older sources are never satisfactory. The weight of line, style, and scale differ greatly from drawing to drawing, and the effect is all too obviously makeshift. All drawings should be made to the same scale, usually twice or three times as large as they will actually appear in the printed book, and there must be agreed guidelines for indicating perspective and comparative size. Squirrels must not look immense when compared to elephants. The picture of the squirrel may be quite as large as that of the elephant, but it must be drawn in such a way, with reference objects such as leaves or twigs, that the squirrel's comparatively small size is clearly portrayed. The elephant, on the other hand, is drawn with reference objects like trees or people. Such referents, incidentally, are more useful and probably truer than conventional statements such as "9 ft. high at the shoulder" or "12 in. long including tail." Individual specimens of each species, like man, differ greatly in size, and such supposedly standard representations of length are based on dubious, often exaggerated data. The point is that, in a pastiche, reference objects of comparable kind will not exist in all pictures, if they exist at all, and comparative size will not be indicated.

Weight of line is also of great importance. The manner in which the dictionary is printed affects the choice of line weight. Some methods will accommodate a lighter, more sensitive line than others, but as a rule the weight of line must be heavier than most artists would like it to be, and many fine details must be omitted because they simply will not reproduce clearly when the art is reduced to the small size in which it must appear in the dictionary. Many an artist has had to white out exquisite details that he or she had labored hard to perfect because the art director knew they would appear in print only as a muddy blotch.

Consistency of style is likewise important. Even though a number of different artists may draw the pictures that go into one's dictionary, their styles must be compatible. One must not be fancy and the others plain, nor one devoted to shading and the others, of similar objects, dependent wholly on line. Criteria must be set on when, if, and how to show a groundline. Will a simple abstract line do, or need one show a hint of shrubbery? Must horizons be shown in panoramic views? Just how detailed should machinery be? Can it depict, even if it does not label, parts that are not defined in the dictionary, or must it be no more specific than the dictionary is? A great many questions of this sort arise in the course of illustrating a dictionary.

259

A good art director anticipates many such questions that would not occur to dictionary editors and establishes guidelines to encourage uniformity among the various artists who will contribute to the work. Whereas the picture editor is primarily an editor/researcher representing the dictionary staff to the artists, the art director is an artist who is in the business of managing other artists. He (or just as frequently she) must be expert in typography as well as illustration and should have experience in illustrating reference books. The illustrations for a children's dictionary, for example, are drawn in a different style, with a more relaxed and freer quality, than those for an adult dictionary. The children's dictionary should avoid the cuteness that may be suitable for children's storybooks but is jarringly discordant in a reference book. It is the art director's responsibility to determine just how to tread the fine line between a fresh, informal look and a cloying condescension, and to prevail upon the artists to follow his or her instructions. Whereas the picture editor is responsible for the choice of illustrative content, the art director is responsible for the clarity, style, and consistency of the art, as well as for seeing that the job gets done in time.

Although some fairly expensive encyclopedic dictionaries, such as those of the Larousse line, have long had color illustrations, it is only in comparatively recent years that the practice has spread to moderately priced general dictionaries, especially those for children. The *Harcourt Brace School Dictionary* (1968) was the first authentic dictionary, as distinguished from alphabetic storybooks or vocabulary builders (many of which are called dictionaries), to include a second color in its illustrations. Color enhances the appeal of a children's dictionary but is difficult to use effectively. If it is to have one color other than black, which color will be chosen and how will it be used? If the second color is used invariably to highlight the particular part of the illustration corresponding to the entry word, any particular color will sometimes be inappropriate. Red, for instance, can be misleading if used to highlight anatomical parts, because of its association with blood. Some depicted objects, such as a stethoscope or a monkey wrench, are never actually red. The same objection applies to any other color that might be chosen. Ambiguity results from not knowing whether the second color is intended to be taken as representing that color in real life or whether it is intended as a means of drawing attention to a particular feature. In practice, color is used for both purposes in different drawings and sometimes, less ambiguously, in the same drawing. On the other hand, if the second color is used simply as a background to make the drawing visually appealing, it fails to serve any useful purpose; a colorful background merely distracts the reader, especially a child, from perceiving the information the illustration is meant to convey, without adding any positive aesthetic quality to the picture. Such use is purely a marketing device intended for parents and teachers, who may feel that any use of color is better than none. Recently, dictionaries with multicolor illustrations have appeared on the market, notably the Macmillan dictionary series for children.[21] These are undeniably attractive assets, particularly from a marketing point of view, but whether they succeed in conveying any more information or conveying it more clearly than with an additional nonblack color, or none, is open to question.

Some dictionaries have set words or text features in a second color: running heads, for example, that indicate the first and last words on the page, or ruled boxes around special features, or symbols to highlight usage notes or synonym discussions. Graphically, all such uses are unwise, since the page begins to look as if it has chicken pox and, in point of fact, no color stands out as well as black. Many people find colored type hard to read, especially when the impression is lighter than intended, and it is difficult to control the intensity of some colored inks. One also has to realize that a substantial number of children, especially boys, are color blind and cannot distinguish certain hues easily.

Producing the Dictionary

Design Specifications

We have already alluded to the editor's involvement in the typographical design of the dictionary. The art director, often with the help of outside consultants, should prepare sample pages based on specifications outlined by the editor-in-chief. In former times, once the design was set it was virtually unchangeable. The manuscript was immediately set in type, and that was that. Any design change after a considerable amount of setting had occurred was enormously wasteful. Nowadays, however, the manuscript is keyboarded with computer codes, as we have seen, that will eventually be translated into composition codes that determine point size and style of type. Since the computer codes are arbitrary, they can be converted to whatever directions one wishes. Thus, if one's dictionary is running shorter than predicted, one can add more leading (spacing) between the lines, or slightly increase the size of type, or take a contrary action if one's work is running too long. This is a great advantage, but changing the typography drastically once the book is well under way is never a good idea. One should not abuse the privilege of modest flexibility lest one introduce a host of unforeseen problems. It is therefore no less necessary, even with computerized typesetting, to have all the type specifications fully laid out in the planning stage. Modifications may have to be made during the writing stage, but the design should be settled before a substantial amount of typesetting has been done. Nonetheless, provided the programing and coding have been properly planned, uniform typographic changes can be made even in the proof stages.

The typography must not only be readable but must not be wasteful of space, as noted. "Readable" does not mean readable compared to novels but compared to other dictionaries. Most college dictionaries, for example, are set in a point size ranging from 5½ to 7. (Type is measured in picas, of which there are 6 to the inch. Each pica is divided into 12 points; thus there are 72 points to the inch.) Many novels (and this book) are set in 10 point type and 2 points of leading between the lines (known in the trade as 10/12), whereas even a readable dictionary may be 7/7 (that is, 7 point size with no leading between the lines). A knowledgeable typographer can play tricks with type to give the appearance of greater size and legibility than one would suppose to be possible. The spacing between particular clusters of letters, for example, can be adjusted automatically by computer to set "tighter" or "looser" in order to save as much space as possible without compromising legibility. Also, various styles of type of the same point size differ greatly in their apparent legibility. The dictionary editor clearly needs a style that has maximum legibility and apparent size even in very small point sizes. This requirement limits his choice, especially when it is coupled with the demand for tight setting to save space and the need for a font with many different styles, sizes, and special characters.

In choosing the size of type one must also be mindful of column width. A type size of 7 points or less becomes unreadable if the line is too wide; the eye cannot easily make the transition to the next line. In unabridged dictionaries, however, which are usually set in three narrow columns, the point size can be quite small (5½ or 6 points, with minimal leading) and still be readable. Larger type is always used for children's dictionaries on the grounds, one supposes, that in comparison with adults their keener eyesight is more than offset by their greater penchant for distraction. I am not sure this is so, and think it equally defensible to argue that whereas children's dictionaries might be set in very small type, their myopic elders need much enlarged print. The dictionary marketplace being what it is, however, a small-type children's dictionary, unless it has several remarkably promotable features, is bound to be stigmatized by reviewers as unattractive and rejected by teachers as pedagogically unsound. (Many a good dictionary, let it be noted, has failed because its appearance did not measure up to the preconceptions of the reviewer; see more about reviewers in Chapter Eight.) Therefore, though I question the need for large type in children's dictionaries—or at least for type quite as large as it usually is—on practical grounds I endorse it.

The type size of the larger children's dictionaries, those for grades six to nine or above, is usually 8 points and may have a point of leading. In our computer age it is possible to have intermediate point sizes as well, so that an actual type size may be 8¼/9½ or 7.8/9.1, or whatever. Dictionaries for younger children have commensurately larger type and more leading between the lines.

If one's dictionary contains many illustrations, as children's dictionaries do, page layout requires the close attention of the art director to see that each picture falls on the same page as the term associated with it. This is not as easy as it sounds, since in children's dictionaries pictures occupy a much greater proportion of the total space available than in adult dictionaries, and if a picture happens to fall at the very beginning or end of a page, one may have to rewrite definitions, adding or subtracting lines in order to get the picture to fit on the right page. With very large pictures this may be impossible, and a cross-reference from the entry to the illustration may be necessary; but wherever possible the picture should be adjacent to or at least on the same page as the entry to which it refers.

In determining the design specifications of a dictionary, one must evaluate the need for printing an abbreviated pronunciation guide (or pronunciation key) on every two-page spread, a practice that takes up a great deal of space. Children's and college dictionaries routinely include pronunciation keys, but ESL dictionaries generally do not, presumably because grammatical and semantic information is considered more important and because the highly motivated foreign learner can be expected to refer to the front-matter explanation when in doubt about pronunciation. Technical dictionaries and bilingual dictionaries rarely include pronunciation keys throughout the text.

Proofreading

In former times when one's dictionary was typeset either in hot metal (especially Monotype) or by photocomposition, one received printed galleys set exactly according to one's type specifications. It was easy to determine whether the style had or had not been followed. Because the typesetting went much faster than the writing or editing of a dictionary, one waited until one was far advanced with the writing stage, at least half finished, before typesetting began. As first galleys arrived for the letters **A** and **B**, one might still be writing definitions for **R** and **S**. After the initial proofreading of **A** and **B**, one would receive corrected second galleys for **A** and **B**, along with first galleys for **C** through **E**, while still writing definitions for **T** and

U. At any given time, one might have first and second—perhaps third galleys—and even first page proofs, while the basic manuscript had not been completed. The mere logistics of handling so many overlapping stages of proofreading required an elaborate bureaucratic apparatus and the personnel to keep track of it. There are only so many simultaneous things a dictionary staff can do, and it therefore makes sense to handle some stages sequentially even though, with a larger staff, they might theoretically have been handled concurrently. (This is one of the reasons it takes so long to publish dictionaries.)

Computerized typesetting has contributed to greater flexibility of design and brought numerous other advantages, but it has also made proofreading more complicated. The price of greater flexibility is that one may have to read and interpret computer coding embedded in the text. That is, ?61 may mean, tentatively, "What follows is to be set in italic type." One can later change one's mind, as we have seen, and make ?61 mean "Set in roman type," but the proofreader must be able to identify the situations in which ?61 should occur. Some computerized systems have embedded codes also for certain other characters, such as accent marks, Greek letters, and superior and inferior figures. Proofreaders must therefore learn the language of the computer system—not an insurmountable problem, but a complication to be reckoned with. In practice, the coding systems for dictionaries are far more complicated than I can indicate here, and no two dictionary programs are the same. Whatever the form of the initial proofs, eventually the embedded codes will be translated into composition codes, and the resulting proofs will have all the characters and type styles that will appear in the printed books. These proofs must be proofread carefully to catch errors overlooked at the earlier stage.

Dictionaries should be proofread as many times as the schedule and budget permit. The manuscript should be checked carefully for errors before being sent for composition. As noted, there are usually a large number of AAs to be made in the early proof stages of a dictionary and, if the compositor is not experienced in setting dictionary copy or highly technical material, there will be a large number of printer's errors (PEs) as well. In choosing a computer keyboarding company or compositor, one should give great weight to previous experience in dictionary composition since, as we have had occasion to remark so many times, no other book is like a dictionary, and the untried compositor who is eager to get the contract—often worth hundreds of thousands of dollars—is apt to exaggerate his shop's expertise and vastly underestimate the complexity of the task at hand. Giving a dictionary manuscript to a compositor who has only set straightforward text is rather like giving a chess set to a first grader and expecting him to learn the game all by himself. There may be, somewhere, a first grader uniquely gifted with the talent to do just that, but betting on the event is no way to run a business. Even experienced compositors of technical copy find dictionary work unusually demanding and can be expected to charge for it accordingly.

The number of changes that are made in the early proof stages makes each succeeding proof stage that much more likely to have errors and therefore requires repeated proofreading. Normally, first galleys should be read by two different editors, at least one of whom is a senior editor. If time permits, second galleys should also be read by two editors, both of whom should be senior. In many cases, however, there isn't time to have two complete proofreadings of second galleys and one proofing must be selective, focusing only on certain kinds of errors such as misalphabetization, errors in the pronunciations, and the like. Some parts of the dictionary, depending on the extent of changes in the earlier stages, may require a third set of galleys. Specialized, contributed dictionaries must be proofread first of all by the individual contributors, since only they can catch many technical errors that would elude the general editor. Proofs must also be read, however, by general editors, not only to correct errors the experts missed but to correct errors of style they may have introduced.

If a dictionary is not illustrated or if it has few illustrations, the pages can be *cast off* rather than *dummied.* In a castoff, the lines on the galley proofs are counted and an indication is made wherever a column-line ends. This used to be done manually, with pages numbered directly on the galleys, but is now more often done automatically by the typesetter's computer. A dummy, on the other hand, is a page-by-page paste-up of each dictionary page, showing the layout of type and pictures. Prepared either by the art director or by someone working under his or her supervision, a dummy takes much more time and costs more money than a castoff. But if there are many illustrations or charts and tables, it must be done. The task of dummying is made much smoother if all illustrations are drawn to scale, to one or a few sizes such that when reduced for printing they can be categorized as "A size," "B size," and so on, indicating fixed percentages of reduction. If they are not, and each drawing has to be separately measured and its reduction calculated, mistakes are more likely, the dummying will take much longer, and the resulting page layouts are likely to be less attractive.

Paper, Printing, and Binding

The final stage of any book is its manufacture, commonly referred to as paper, printing, and binding. Since a dictionary has a comparatively large number of pages and, if a commercial dictionary, must be competitively priced, the paper must be of light weight but sufficiently opaque so that type on the underside of a page cannot be seen. The inclusion of illustrations, and especially of halftones, influences the choice of paper. Some lightweight paper of high quality may actually have to be rejected, not so much because of price as because the dictionary appears too insubstantial if it is used. The *bulk* of the book—the breadth of the compressed pages measured at the spine—makes the dictionary appear too slight when compared with other dictionaries of similar size. Unfortunately, the public and reviewers judge dictionaries principally by their apparent size, not by an informed examination of their contents. If two otherwise identical dictionaries of different bulk are presented to book buyers, nine of ten will select the dictionary with the greater bulk, even though the slimmer volume may actually have paper of superior quality. To market a dictionary successfully, it must not only *be* comprehensive; it must look comprehensive.

Many dictionaries are produced with thumb indexes supposedly to provide easier access to alphabetic sections. These are quite expensive but are popular with most dictionary users. In the college market, the vast majority of dictionaries sold are thumb indexed. Whether to include thumb indexes or not is strictly a marketing decision, like the choice of color of the cover or the design of the jacket. Index tabs lend the volume a tone of elegance and breadth of content lacking in a book with a plain front. They are popular principally because they appeal to the public's view of what a dictionary ought to look like, not because they are of any intrinsic value. For the same purpose, some dictionaries, like Bibles, are provided with a tipped or stippled edge, to give the impression of permanence, authority, and dignity. Dictionary publishers are not unhappy to have their books look like Bibles.

The preferred cover and jacket design emphasizes the title of the work, in particular the word *dictionary*. Design elements are usually subordinated to the words of the title and descriptive material, and the typography is usually bold but neither subtle nor fancy. It may have a certain elegance, though that is more often due to placement of the type on the cover or spine than to unusual typography. Dust jackets may be of somewhat freer design than covers and are of brighter colors. Academic dictionaries often do not have jackets, but commercial dictionaries do. There have been dictionary jackets (and covers) that sought to project an image of newness rather than dignity, and that forsook the time-honored biblical approach in favor of brilliant colors and vibrant design. Since there is no single factor that determines a dictionary's ultimate success or failure, it is impossible to say whether such an approach, which has seldom been attempted, has helped or hurt. Although newness and up-to-dateness are powerful selling points for a dictionary, it seems likely that attempts to capitalize on these qualities by innovative design deter some people from buying the book because the design offends their sense of the dignity a dictionary should have. Of course, much depends on the particular market the publisher has in mind. If the market for a slang dictionary, for example, is thought to be predominantly young people, the absence of dignity may not be considered a defect; but most general dictionaries have a much broader market than any particular age group.

Revising a Dictionary

Making a dictionary is like painting a bridge: by the time one coat of paint has been applied, the bridge is in need of another. Just so, before a dictionary has been published one should start making plans for its revision. In spite of all the care that goes into its preparation, the first edition of any dictionary contains numerous errors. Some of these errors will have been detected in the page proof stage, but unless they are very serious corrections must not be made in pages. The expense is prohibitive, and provoking delays in production for minor corrections makes no sense. Every change made renews the possibility of introducing fresh errors, necessitating still further changes. At some point in the process the editor-in-chief must simply issue an edict: no more changes unless they are absolutely essential. A misalphabetized or misspelled entry will always be corrected on the spot, but an omitted comma or period, or the occurrence of a word in roman type when it should be in italic must at this time merely be noted for future correction. Such notations should be made in a card file, called a correction file, to be implemented at the earliest practicable time in a subsequent revision. Every dictionary should have its ongoing correction file, where no error is too trivial to be noted. Occasionally users will draw one's attention to an error, but most errors and omissions are observed by the dictionary staff itself.

College dictionaries are revised every ten years or so, but they are updated every year or every other year, chiefly in order to provide themselves with an up-to-date copyright date. Commercial publishers tend to feel that their dictionary's copyright date must be as current as that of their competitors, and thus demand frequent updatings, some of which are merely cosmetic, involving only a few-score minor changes and perhaps updated population figures. On the other hand, some updatings are far more extensive, consisting of several hundred significant changes and including the insertion of many new words and new senses. Even such a revision, however, would be quite invisible to most dictionary users who compared the old edition with the new. Updatings, whether comparatively extensive or trivial, do not involve a resetting of the entire dictionary or a redesign of the dictionary's style. They consist of selective changes on certain pages, even if called extensive, and compared to the volume of material that is unchanged, the amount of altered material is minute.

A genuine revision is another matter.[22] A revision, as I use the word here, implies a complete reexamination of the previous edition, an entirely new typesetting of the whole, and frequently the alteration of some design elements. The new edition ordinarily does not have the same number of pages as the old edition, and the title usually indicates that the dictionary has been completely revised. This does not imply that every entry of the new edition is entirely different from the corresponding entry of the old; far from it. It implies only that every entry has been critically reexamined, exactly as I have described how the review editor reexamines the work of the first definer. In this instance, the work of the "first definer" is often finely polished and in need of nothing more than a slight shift in emphasis or a modernized phrasing. Sometimes it cannot be improved and is best left alone. The important point is that it *is* reexamined in light of current citations and modern usage.

Why cannot dictionaries be continually updated instead of being revised? As I wrote in the Introduction (page vii) to *The Doubleday Dictionary*,

> Dictionaries may be updated by the substitution of some new entries for old entries, and for the first few years after publication, such a procedure may work very well. But when a dictionary passes the ten- or fifteen-year-old mark, updating takes on a desperate character. Substituting a few new entries for old entries in such a book is like bailing out a swamped boat with a sieve. The language has accumulated too many new meanings and new words; too many of the definitions in the dictionary have taken on new emphases or passed from slang to informal usage or from informal to standard; too much of the book is written with a vocabulary and in a style that seems odd or baffling to a new generation of readers. Only a fresh examination of the entire range of possible entries, with careful attention to examples of current usage and the assistance of special consultants in the sciences and other fields, can provide an adequate basis for a thoroughly up-to-date dictionary.

Revisions follow much the same process that I have outlined in this chapter for new dictionaries but are made immensely more manageable by having a solid basis from which material may be selected and used or rewritten. Nothing is more difficult to predict or control than a dictionary begun from scratch. Adding new meanings or words to a revision is no different from adding them to a new dictionary, but the revision of existing definitions is infinitely easier than creating them anew. Still, the work is exacting, often long term, and demands skills of the highest order; witness the *OED Supplements*. Each new edition of Merriam-Webster's unabridged dictionary is more on the order of a new dictionary than a revision, as I use the term here. The magnitude of the differences between *NID3* and *NID2* in definition, pronunciations, usage, etymology, and illustrations is so great that in spite of being called a new edition it cannot be thought of merely as a revision.

Abridging a Dictionary

Abridging a dictionary follows the same steps outlined, but abridgment is less demanding than revision and simpler than creating a new dictionary. However, in practice, abridgments of very large works such as unabridged dictionaries also involve a considerable amount of revision, since the larger work has already become somewhat dated by the time the abridgment has begun. Many new words and new senses are included along the way. The compass of a major abridgment, such as a college dictionary reduced from a larger work, gives room for a considerable degree of invention. Such abridgment is neither simple nor plainly derivative, but allows for many departures and improvements on the original.

One begins an abridgment by having the larger dictionary cut apart and pasted up, one column to a page, or by having one's printer provide equivalent galley proofs. The word list selection for the abridgment is made from the paste-up or proof. If one can devise a system for relating the column length of the larger dictionary to the projected column length of its abridgment, one can predict with reasonable accuracy how many column-lines of the larger work must be cut. One seeks entire categories of definitions and other elements to cut, since any such policy saves time and can be implemented by relatively inexperienced editors, thus freeing senior editors for more demanding work. For example, one may delete all abbreviations or obsolete terms, or make all nationality designations run-on derivatives to the countries to which they apply. The more space-saving policies of this sort that can be set initially, the easier the task of abridging will be.

Apart from cutting definitions, etymologies must also be reduced or deleted entirely. If pronunciations are not lengthy, they are often left unchanged. All other elements, such as usage notes and synonym discussions, are subject to omission or reduction in size. Illustrations are dropped entirely or omitted selectively. Individual illustrations are not photographi-

269

cally reduced in size, a practice that would be expensive and impractical for the meager amount of space saved. Though drawings may occasionally be cropped, as a rule they are either used or not used as is.

The chief difficulties of abridging, apart from that of getting everything to fit in the space available, are readjusting the cross-reference system and checking Words Not In. If the entry list of a dictionary is reduced, some of the omitted words may be the object of cross-references; others may be used in definitions. It is essential that every cross-reference be checked to make sure its referent has been retained. It is also essential that every editor have an up-to-date copy of the new word list close at hand, to be referred to as he rewrites each definition. The editor must be especially wary of recasting definitions in technical or specialized words that may save space but are not defined elsewhere in the dictionary.

Abridging without revision calls for somewhat different skills than those needed for writing definitions. Though the abridger must know a good definition when he sees one, he need not be capable of creating one from citations. His skills are mainly critical: he must know how to reorder words, deleting as many as possible along the way, until the definition is stripped to its essence. He must, however, no less than the definer, be a good writer. Space limitations in an abridgment dominate the quality of the editing. The commercial imperatives that govern abridgments call for comparatively large entry counts in a much smaller space than the original volume. Typically, one has to retain two-thirds of the entries of a larger dictionary but fit them into one-half the space. Clearly, this means a low ratio of lines per entry, often 1.5 or fewer. There is a law of diminishing returns in defining: after one has cut a definition to a certain point, it cannot be cut further without making it nonsense, and one would be better off using the space to list a few synonyms. Synonym definitions are not necessarily a mark of lazy or inept editing; they may be the best solution to the problem of too little space.

In most cases, the decisions that led to a dictionary's inadequate definitions were made in a corporate boardroom six years earlier by a group of men who hadn't the slightest idea how dictionaries were compiled and who wouldn't dream of consulting anyone who did. This is not meant to excuse the editor from responsibility; if he chooses to write dictionaries, he must take his share of the responsibility. The editor-in-chief must be loyal to his dictionary even though he is well aware of its shortcomings, not just because of his self-serving fidelity to the company that sponsored it but because he owes it to the many people who worked long and hard on the book. At the beginning of this chapter I compared the making of a dictionary to the construction of a large building. Just as a large building demands the attention of many different people of varying levels of education and skill, so does a dictionary. We have spoken only of the definers and art directors and other highly skilled people who prepare the work; but there are also a legion of typists, mail clerks, file clerks, secretaries, and many other people in comparatively low-level jobs who process the work, and who often know the system so well that they are indispensable to it. Their contribution cannot be measured in definitions produced, yet it is as real as that of any definer. It is well to remember, too, that no building is constructed by architects, and no dictionary is produced by lexicographers. The contributions of computer analysts, compositors, and printers are often major factors in the success or failure of a dictionary. It is always a shock to the lexicographer, no matter how many dictionaries he has supervised or worked on, to learn again how many other skills are required to produce "his" dictionary. If he is honest, he must realize it is their dictionary too.

CHAPTER SEVEN

Computer Use and the Future of Dictionary Making

For some years we have been told that books are becoming obsolete and will soon be preserved as ingenious and quaint mementoes, like box cameras or slide rules, of a bygone era. We will derive our intellectual nourishment from television screens hooked up to computers. To some people today the prediction is a reality, and the growth of the personal or microcomputer business, along with that of word processors, is a fact with major implications for the entire book industry. Some books will be replaced in time. The makers of telephone directories, for example, or inventory catalogs for automotive parts, or mail-order catalogs like that of Sears, Roebuck, may soon find it more economical to equip households with the means of access to their electronic databases than to continue to publish catalogs in print. Although printed dictionaries are not likely to become obsolete in the foreseeable future, the development of cheaper and better computers has profound implications for the preparation of dictionaries, if not for the distribution of their contents. It is inconceivable that any major dictionary could be undertaken today without planning to store the material in a computer.

272

Current Computer Uses in Lexicography

Computers are now well established in many aspects of dictionary making, especially in the use of coded material to provide access to particular elements within the file, such as all terms dealing with a given subject or all etymologies. Computer use has progressed well beyond this stage, however, to include word list preparation; the acquisition and arrangement of citation files; the checking of conformity to style of various features (as of formal punctuation within definitions), and sometimes their correction if in error; the generation by computer of certain editorial elements, such as cross-reference entries; and even the creation of entirely new dictionaries, thesauruses, and other language reference works from elaborately encoded databases.

In Britain, the Longman dictionaries have used computers extensively to produce other dictionaries, the most innovative example being in the ESL market. The *Longman Dictionary of Scientific Usage* is a conceptually arranged thesaurus of basic and scientific words culled from the Longman database.[1] Each word is identified by an alphanumeric code, such as MG024. An alphabetic index to each listed term links it to the code so that the reader can have access to the material by subject or by the alphabet. The traditional *Roget's Thesaurus* (even the earliest editions) included an alphabetic index too, as do its many modern imitators, but the Longman thesaurus has been created entirely by pulling forth from a larger file definitions coded for a particular subject and then re-sorting the terms alphabetically with their identifying alphanumeric codes.

Other publishers have used computerized systems to produce thesauruses, but some early efforts seem to have been produced more for the convenience of the computer than for the reference book user. For example, the alphabetically arranged *Webster's Collegiate Thesaurus* includes entries for *immaleable, immedicable, immingle, immix, plummetless, prodigalize, proemial, profusive, programma,* and many others of similar rarity. One wonders who in the world would require synonyms for such words; surely a person to whom these words sprang to mind would need no thesaurus. It is apparent that the entry list and synonyms were created to some extent from a database and that the work was prepared with insufficient editorial intervention.

The *Longman Lexicon of Contemporary English,* another work produced automatically from a database for the ESL market, includes fifteen thousand general (chiefly nonscientific) terms arranged by subject and with an alphabetic index (which includes pronunciations) along with an alphanumeric reference to each sense covered.[2] It remains to be seen how useful such a work will be, but it is innovative in many respects. Unlike a thesaurus, which assumes that the reader knows the meanings of the included words, the *Longman Lexicon* is designed for people who do not know the meanings of related words and has set up an apparatus to teach them what they are. It is essentially a vocabulary builder divided into hierarchies of meaning, with definitions drawn from the *Longman Dictionary of Contemporary English* and with many composite pictures (as in those of a pictorial Duden) in which implements, kinds of apparel, and the like, are labeled. A number of other features common to ESL dictionaries are also included. Its vocabulary of 15,000 terms may not be sufficient, and the system by which meaning clusters are arranged may be challenged; but the *Longman Lexicon,* together with the *Longman Dictionary of Scientific Usage,* are important evidence that computers can be used to produce substantially new language reference works if the database has been carefully programed. Though the success or failure of these works will be of interest mainly to the Longman company, the fact that they are here at all should be of immense interest to all who are interested in lexicography.

Selecting the Supplier of Computer Services

When analyzing the need for computer assistance, the dictionary editor should ask himself first of all whether his need is basically for the input of a large amount of data—as for a word list—or for a complex program for the manipulation of data. There are companies that specialize in each of these areas, and one of the worst mistakes that can be made is to hire the wrong kind for the job required. By the time one realizes the mistake, it may be very difficult and expensive to extricate oneself and start afresh. To oversimplify and so make the distinction clearer, there are keyboarding services (which I shall call Type A companies) that employ large numbers of keyboard operators, modestly paid in comparison to programers but often highly competent at typing technical material. Type A companies have few programers and very little programing capability. Type B companies, on the other hand, provide a wide range of file manipulation services and are frequently also compositors, with their own computerized typesetting equipment. Type B companies also provide keyboarding services, though at a much higher rate than Type A companies, because they have the expense of more elaborate computer and typesetting installations and more highly paid personnel: systems analysts, programers, customer service representatives, and salespeople.

Type B companies tend to be older and bigger than Type A companies and are often a division of a large corporation. Type A companies, by contrast, tend to be independent and entrepreneurial, with a sales staff represented usually by the president and perhaps vice-president of the company. The continued solvency of Type A companies is of more than sympathetic interest: a mid-course bankruptcy would be almost as much of a disaster for the dictionary house depending upon the company as it would be for the computer company itself. Yet dealing with a small company has its rewards. A small company is apt to give one more attention than a big one, simply because it needs the business more. For the same reason a small company is more likely to exaggerate its programing expertise. Type B companies tend to have high turnover, frequent internal reorganizations of personnel, and sometimes a too complacent confidence in the ability of their company to do whatever one wants.

Designers of computer programs invariably say that they can do whatever one needs to be done. This should be taken as a philosophical and rhetorical comment rather than as a practical statement of intention. No doubt one's needs *can* be met, but only by people who are capable, intelligent, experienced, dedicated, and imaginative, and unfortunately such attributes are no more common among computer people than among others. It is not easy to find someone who can really do what the computer is theoretically capable of doing. It is important to realize that the penalties for complex programing can be profound if the programing is not done well. The errors of a computer program, unlike human errors, cannot be guessed. They conform to computer logic and cannot be traced to familiar human carelessness.

I have oversimplified the differences between Type A and Type B companies. Many Type A companies are in various stages of becoming Type B companies by upgrading their programing capabilities. But the distinction at bottom is valid, and one must evaluate one's needs carefully and try to match them with the company offering the most economical services of the kind required. The advice of a disinterested computer expert may be helpful.

Suppose one needs both a massive input of data and, at a later time, an elaborate set of programs. All other things being equal, it is better to go with a Type B company so that the programing can begin earlier and be better coordinated, and the problems of transferring the file from Type A to Type B can be avoided. But if all other things are not equal—namely, if budgetary restraints loom large—one may well decide to go with a Type A company for the initial keyboarding of a massive word list. The difference in cost can be great—and do not believe Type B salesmen who insist that only their keyboarders are trained to record technical material accurately. Many Type A companies can do as well. However, one should make sure that the Type A company has adequate checks on the accuracy of its typing, including in-house proofreading. Its output should be compatible with the

275

systems generally in use by Type B companies; one wants to avoid intermediate stages of conversion if possible.

Whatever the choice, one must take the time to investigate (or seek expert advice about) the computer company one plans to do business with, and be certain in one's own mind just where it stands in the Type A–B continuum. If one will eventually need programing, one will have to decide whether the company chosen will have the capacity to do it or if one will have to transfer the file. The transferal should be a routine matter, but one should nonetheless take the precaution of putting the principals of both companies in touch long before the transfer is scheduled. For large dictionary projects, the programs must indeed be sophisticated, generally more complex than anything most programers have ever been asked to handle. For this reason, and because the designers of his programs are apt to know nothing about dictionaries and very little about editing in general, the dictionary editor must keep in close touch.

A good programer or analyst often helps to clarify the dictionary editor's own cloudy thoughts by insisting on understanding exactly what each program is supposed to do. In the course of trying to explain the specific purpose, the editor frequently finds that the kind of program he recommended will not accomplish it, or that the object he originally thought vital to the entire enterprise because it is traditionally so viewed is actually unnecessary in a computer system. It is as helpful to the editor as to the programer to be as explicit as possible about every step in the programing. The editor often begins these lengthy discussions with the idea that because the computer analysts are ignorant of dictionaries he must go through a tedious period of instructing them; but after several days of talks, he realizes with a jolt that he is the one being instructed, and not just in computer logic but in the logic of his own lexicographic ideas. It is humbling yet in the long run a beneficial exercise.

The Advantages and Disadvantages of Using Computers

A computer database can give one the power to reorganize the material on file in many different ways. Think of the difficulty of going through an enormous card file or manuscript and recording every sense of every transitive verb, or every definition dealing with astronomy or cooking or philosophy, or all definitions labeled "obsolete." A properly coded computer file can sort and print such material simply and fast. In preparing a revision, it is an immense advantage to be able to pull out word lists and definitions of particular subjects so that they can be sent to specialists for review. All etymologies can be printed in a separate list and can be further divided by language groups, if need be, so that words of Germanic origin can be sent to one expert and those derived from Latin or Greek to another.

In abridging a work, the computer file can automatically omit particular sets of items, such as illustrative phrases or technical definitions. But this can only be done if such items were previously coded. If they were not, it is usually impractical to add computer codes to facilitate a computerized abridgment; one might just as easily abridge without the aid of computerization. Thus, a computerized file demands considerably more planning than conventional files, since one must plan not only for the current dictionary but for its subsequent revisions, abridgments, and derivative works, and at a time when these offshoots seem remote and problematical. If one does plan for such eventualities, however, they will be infinitely easier to do when the time comes to do them. For example, it is possible to prepare a dictionary and its abridgment at the same time by deciding what parts of each entry and each definition will be omitted from the abridgment and coding the material to be omitted. Even if the resulting abridgment requires substantial emendation, as it probably will, one will have saved many steps compared to those required in conventionally abridging a work.

All of this sounds wonderful, yet it is seldom done. The problem is not computer technology but capital financing and corporate management. Dictionaries are expensive, and few companies are willing to commit themselves to spending millions of dollars to produce a line of dictionaries that will not generate revenue for many years. Although programing for several different dictionaries saves money when compared to doing each independently, it is still more costly and time consuming than programing for one dictionary. Frequently one simply cannot predict, years earlier, exactly what the size or qualitites of an abridged or derivative work should be. Programing done too soon may have to be undone if the marketplace or one's ideas about it change.

What makes dictionary coding so complex is the necessity of linking every definition—not just every entry—to a set of identifiers one has elaborated. These may include, for example, subject, source (where obtained, i.e., from a citation file, another dictionary, a specialist's list), currency, usage information, and geographical range as well as formal data, such as part of speech, number (if a noun or pronoun), transitive or intransitive status (if a verb), and numerous other facts. Nouns may be classified as to whether they are count versus mass, adjectives according to whether they are only predicative. How elaborate a program one has will depend on the uses to which one intends to put the information recorded. An ESL dictionary requires far more complete grammatical and syntactic information than a work for native speakers. If the program is not elaborate enough, one will have to waste time later doing manually what might have been done more efficiently by computer. If the program is too elaborate, time and money will also be wasted, and the likelihood of programing errors that may lead to further delays will be unnecessarily increased. For example, although it is feasible for a computer to check for Words Not In in any dictionary, the difficulty of distinguishing between particular senses of polysemous words is a formidable problem, and in my view the Words Not In check is best confined to small dictionaries or to those utilizing a fixed defining vocabulary. (Even then the check is not perfect.) The expense of repeatedly checking a very large file against a very large word list can be prohibitive, and one wonders if this is the best use to which such money can be put.

Always, in evaluating whether or not it would be wise to add a particular program, the question is not, Would it be helpful to have this program? The answer is invariably yes. The relevant question is, Does it make sense to take the time, hire the people, and pay the costs to perform this particular operation? One could construct a computer program to calculate how to sink a difficult billiards shot, but it would be a very complicated program for a trivial purpose, and on the face of it the idea appears ridiculous. Yet it is precisely this sort of judgment that has to be made in deciding what aspects of an editorial effort should be computerized. One must weigh the cost— not just monetarily—of doing an operation oneself against that of having it done by computer. Most of all, one must think hard about how important each step of a project really is and decline to computerize steps that are relatively unimportant unless the programs for such steps are routine. An operation simply done by human beings may be extremely complicated to program for a computer. For example, the distinction between main entries and subentries in a large medical dictionary is one that can be made in a second by any editor familiar with the project, but a program that would answer every case would necessarily be extremely complex. One may decide to have a simpler program that would be right 98 percent of the time and rely on human editors to intervene to correct the 2 percent of errors.

Certainly, computerization does not make sense for a small project, but it does not follow therefore that the larger the volume of data, the more advantageous the use of computers. In one sense this may be true: a computer might as well do a million operations of a given kind as one. Our goal is, however, not to maximize the efficiency of the computer but to make things easier for us. In many cases, the human work that must be done to prepare material for use by a computer—chiefly the coding and sequencing of information—varies directly with how much data are to be processed. It is naïve to suppose that in computerized projects apart from computer time there is no penalty for increasing the volume of data. It all depends on the nature of the data and what the computer has been programed to do.

Word List Preparation   A computer can be extremely helpful in building word lists, categorizing them by subject or other criteria, and alphabetizing them. If one wishes to assemble a technical dictionary, for example, one can key all of the terms found in various technical glossaries and dictionaries, code each by subject field, and have the computer alphabetize them by subject and delete duplications. The alternative manual process of handling a large card file is much more cumbersome and time consuming.

However, even the compilation of a word list can involve extensive pre-editing (inserting symbols by hand so that specific items in the file can be identified by the program). In compiling a very large list of multiword lexical units for a medical dictionary, we had to identify the "sort word," the word under which the term would subsequently be automatically alphabetized, with an asterisk. The sort word would not invariably fall in any given position, such as at the end of a lexical unit, because in many Latin anatomic expressions (e.g., *arcus aortae*), the sort word is the initial word. In others it is medial, as in *anterior arch of atlas,* sorted under *arch.* Our staff had to identify each sort word, since the computer keyboarders could not be expected to make this kind of decision. We also had to write the singular sort word whenever the term was plural. Thus for *aortic arches,* [*arch*] had to be inserted in square brackets. Identification of the sort word was also necessary in plural Latin expressions like *rami tracheales* [*ramus*] and *vasa vasorum* [*vas*]. Many terms acquired from existing medical dictionaries had to be reviewed by editors and assigned a subject specialty. Since our file comprised initially over 220,000 terms, the staff editing was no small task.

One should not assume, therefore, that computerizing a file means that all tedious work is at an end. On the contrary, at despondent moments, usually on Monday mornings, the sole effect of computerization can appear to be the substitution of unfamiliar kinds of tedious tasks for familiar kinds. In part the attitude is fostered by the truism that the more powerful the system at one's disposal, the more one expects it to do. Before xerographic copiers were invented, most of us were content with one copy, if that. Now we are accustomed to making half a dozen copies by pressing a button. Many projects would never have been undertaken had it not been for the availability of computers. Even in compiling a word list, one must resist the temptation to make the file larger than it has to be on the mistaken presumption that the computer will do all the work.

Computerized Corpora Used in Lexicography   A number of computer files have been created by assembling excerpts of writing from a variety of published sources. The assumption is that if such a collection is large and diverse enough it will—like any citation file—more or less accurately reflect the way the language is used. One enduring value of such a computer-generated file for lexicography is, theoretically, to provide a solid basis for reexamining the definitions of the standard lexicon. It can also be a treasure of information on word frequency, punctuation, preferred written form (spelling, capitalization, and compounding), word order, verb patterns, and other grammatical data. A broadly based computer-generated file may, however, be beyond the means of any one publisher and may depend upon the creation of an archive supported by a consortium of publishers, perhaps with government support.[3]

Computers have already been of value in compiling counts of word frequency, as we have seen, and in providing representative corpora of edited English, the most important of which is the *Corpus of Present-Day Edited American English,* assembled by W. Nelson Francis and analyzed by Nelson Francis and Henry Kučera. (See page 15 for a discussion of *The American Heritage Word Frequency Book.*)

The Brown Corpus, as it is called—the original work was done in 1963–64 at Brown University—consists of five hundred passages of two thousand words each, representing different categories of writing. The corpus thus totals slightly more than 1 million words (or tokens) in which about fifty thousand different words (or types) are used. Every major dictionary house has a copy of the Brown Corpus in some form; most have used it to provide confirmation of word frequency or to add citations to their files. But it is preposterous to say, as one commentator does, that dictionaries "derive their definitions" from the Brown Corpus or from any other computer-generated corpus.[4] Of the fifty thousand types in the Brown Corpus, twenty thousand occur only once, seven thousand twice. As Richard L. Venezky points out, among those words occurring twice are *abysmal, checkup, landslide,* and *rap.* Those occurring once include *ballistics, gnaw, invert,* and *radiate*—hardly rare words! To get ten examples of the latter group, Venezky speculates that we would need a corpus ten times as large as the Brown Corpus, that is, one of at least 10 million words.[5] The Brown Corpus may be a useful adjunct to a citation file, since it is already programed with a Key Word In Context (KWIC) format, but it is no more than that. I personally found it to be of only marginal use with respect to new senses and words, since the vast majority of its material deals with standard usages and many of the citations are not particularly illuminating of meaning. For lexicographers, the word frequency count is more useful than derived citations.

It hardly needs to be said that the Brown Corpus is an extremely important model for linguistic study apart from lexicography. Indeed, a British study, the Lancaster Corpus, was undertaken by Geoffrey Leech on the American model and completed by the University of Oslo. In Chapter One we discussed the Survey of English Usage (begun before the Brown Corpus), a corpus of spoken and written English prepared by Randolph Quirk at University College London; the spoken portion has been computerized by the University of Lund, in Sweden, under the direction of Jan Svartvik.

Computerized Citation Files   The real revolution in assembling large bodies of texts on computer has been brought about by the growth of computer-assisted photocomposition. Previously, type had to be "read" by optical scanners to be converted to computerized form, and much material was not machine readable. As I wrote in the 1960s, "Until machine readable equipment (optical scanners) are available that are far more clever and cheap than now seems possible, the sources will depend on a very limited number of places of origin. Ten million words from *Time* magazine do not fully represent the state of English in this country."[6]

If the material is typeset with the help of a computer, the computer tape that generates the shape of each character in one system can be used to generate a computer tape that will conform to a different system. This process makes optical scanning unnecessary. However, a corpus consisting entirely of composition tapes would hardly be representative of the written language, let alone the spoken. The relative inaccessibility of smaller-sized photocomposition tapes from offbeat sources would limit the range of uses exemplified by the corpus. It is much easier and cheaper to load up with 10 million words from *Time* magazine or from the *New York Times* than to obtain material in machine-readable form from a large variety of sources. As pointed out in Chapter Five (pages 219–220), the volume of exposure to a particular usage is not necessarily equivalent to the volume of *use*. It is questionable to assume that because *Time* reaches millions of people, citations from that source are vastly more important than citations from sources with much smaller circulations. How many readers of *Time* ever use the neologisms they read?

Though people are quick to take offense over trivial variations of usage, the gross distortions of usage committed by poorly programed computers are regarded with indulgence. We are not in the habit of protesting when electronically driven elevator doors close just as we are about to pass through them, but accept the act docilely as the work of God. Just so, we have come to accept word divisions like these:

> begins with words or phrases like "Ah, you reply ...", "So you see ...", "Look", "No sir", "Fair enough", and "Well ...". His repeated use of the last word becomes extremely tiresome.

(*Times Literary Supplement,* October 23, 1981, p. 1,239)

> Mrs. Carter issued a statement from
> her home in Plains, Ga., saying that she
> and former President Carter were "sho
> cked by Rita Merthan's untimely
> death."
>
> (*New York Times,* December 5, 1981, p. 50)
>
> Some of
> these are often mentioned: for inst-
> ance, the dual personality theme in
> Robert Louis Stevenson's *Dr Jekyll
> and Mr. Hyde* (1886).
>
> (*Times Literary Supplement,* December 25, 1981, p. 1,504)

I would suggest that such word divisions, examples of which could be multiplied endlessly, have done more to obscure sense and encourage poor writing habits in students than any number of presumably illicit uses of
hopefully.

If lexicographers unfamiliar with English were somehow engaged in preparing an English dictionary and had collected a sufficient number of citations indicating that *shocked* were divided after the *o,* they would be justified in concluding that *shocked* were a multisyllabic word. The example
illustrates a danger of using one or few sources, even so rich a one as the
New York Times, for too large a proportion of one's citations. One's files
may then become a measure of the quality of *programing* rather than a
measure of how writers and editors use the language. The widespread use
of computerized composition has resulted in many oddities more subtle than
sho-cking syllabications, and the lexicographer may not be able to distinguish these from deliberate editorial decisions.

Although editing oversights have always occurred, the transfer of a computerized file to typesetting equipment occurs *after* the main editing process,
and errors that appear then, especially in hastily prepared publications like
newspapers, are not likely to be corrected. These errors are fundamentally
different from editing errors. How is the lexicographer to distinguish
between programing errors, which he does not want to record, and writing
or editing errors, which may reflect eventually a change in the use of language? If his file is simply a matter of transferring a magnetic tape or disk
from one computer to another, there is no basis for such a distinction.

Can computerization be of significant help in the compilation of a dictionary
citation file? There is no doubt that it can, but the file would have to be
much larger and more diversified than any now in existence: it would have

to include at least 50 million words and be drawn from many different sources. Given the capacities of modern computers, this staggering total is by no means impracticable, but it is expensive to store and process such a large file. The *Trésor de la langue française,* a massive historical dictionary dealing with the period from 1789 to 1960, under the editorship of Bernard Quemada, has a computerized file of 90 million occurrences, all drawn from literary sources.[7] It remains to be seen whether so large a file is manageable.

Too large a file can bury significant facts beneath mountains of trivial variation, redundancy, and irrelevance. It may take as many years to wade through such extraneous material as it would have taken to handwrite only the pertinent facts and file them manually in cardboard boxes. Certain devices exist, however, for coping with redundancy. Common words like *of, the,* and *a* can be filtered out. Since the commonest one hundred words comprise about 48 percent of the vocabulary in use, such a filtering system could be relatively efficient, and the true frequencies of the remaining vocabulary items could be calculated. Nevertheless, many problems would remain. Novel uses of existing words could not be discovered without first identifying the words or their immediate contexts. Citation readers would still be needed. Once the items to be tracked were identified, there is a serious question as to whether a computerized collection would be a cost-effective way to find such occurrences. The program for citations would have to be sophisticated enough to recognize some grammatical and syntactic features. It would have to recognize that *boy* and *boys* and *say* and *said* were related terms. It would have to give enough context to render citations intelligible, which often involves more than the immediate sentence in which it appears or a set number of characters on either side of the item sought (the KWIC format). It would have to recognize criteria for citing or not citing proper names and be capable of citing multiword lexical units. Such systems can be generated, but they are not perfect, and they require a great deal of study, trial and error, and expense. The question is not, Can they be done? The question is, Is it worthwhile to create and manage such a system on a vast scale?

Opinion differs. On the one hand, Thomas Paikeday, a Canadian lexicographer who has spent considerable time developing a microcomputer system for lexicographic research, claims conventional citations files are now obsolete:

> I cheerfully consigned my citation collection of 20 years to the back burner. I was now able to have citations displayed . . . on my video screen and printed out as hard copy for close study. I could search idioms and phrases as well as terms such as "Catch-22," "state-of-the-art," "toxic shock syndrome," "unitard," and "videotex." By entering "get" followed

by "her," for example, I could find citations for "get it together," "get it all together," and "get one's act together." [get . . . (toget)her] [8]

Paikeday has publicly maintained that he can find citations for new terms beyond the scope even of the largest conventionally assembled citation files. On the other hand, Robert Burchfield, the editor of the *OED Supplements,* while acknowledging that computers have much to contribute, tends to dismiss such claims as exaggerated, and holds to the view that traditional citation files are as irreplaceable as ever. [9]

Computerized Access to Conventional Citation Files   If we acknowledge that conventionally assembled citation files are still necessary, the problem remains how best to store them for efficient retrieval. Conventionally, they have been placed on slips of paper or lightweight cards and filed in cabinets. This, of course, takes up a great deal of office space and demands the attention of people to file and retrieve citations. An apparently promising development is the use of computers for quick retrieval and display of microfilmed documents. Citations, microfilmed in random order and identified by a key word or phrase, can be retrieved after a few seconds. Computer-assisted retrieval may represent the best interim solution—until something better comes along—to the problem of storing vast numbers of citations obtained from diverse printed sources. Given the enormous variety of type styles and sizes in which conventional citations appear, optical scanning for computer storage is impractical and expensive.

Microfilming is comparatively cheap, and a computer-assisted retrieval system might cut down greatly (though not entirely) on the number of clerks and cabinets needed. Best of all, it should speed the retrieval process and still enable the editor to print out citations for extended study. Whether such a system could cope with the enormous size of a large citation file, however, has not to my knowledge been demonstrated. But in theory, computerized access to microfilmed documents seems the most efficient and economical way to use a citation file without limiting one's sources to machine-readable documents.

Computer-assisted Editing   In addition to the ordinary word-processing functions, a computer can save the editor time in many significant ways. For example, if all the citations used in constructing definitions are in the computer database, those slated for inclusion as illustrative quotations in the printed work can be specially designated during the editing process, and all other citations will be suppressed during the conversion to a composition tape. This is of great benefit in historical dictionaries, particularly those with a limited corpus of citations.

Many elements of style can be automatically implemented if the text is properly coded. Designated elements can be made to begin with a capital letter and end with a period, or be placed in a particular type style or placed within square brackets. If the coding becomes as complicated as the style editing would have been, one has not simplified the editing function but simply shifted it back a step and interposed a computer process between the editor and the compositor. Even this is of potential benefit, however, since the interposition of computer codes enables one to alter the physical appearance of the material at any stage: to change, for example, the size and style of type, or the style rules that demand initial capitalization or numbered definitions. Even more important, the interposed computer codes enable one to reorganize the material so as to abridge or revise it, as we have seen. Therefore, even if the editing is more complicated than conventional editing, the advantages of a computer database often justify the extra effort. Editing for a database is as a rule no less demanding of dictionary skills than conventional editing, and it is not without its subtleties; but it does—or should, if the program is any good—save the editor a great deal of repetitious work.

Style Checks, Data Summaries, and Other Useful Features What can programing do for the dictionary editor? If each element is properly coded, it can provide checks of omitted or incorrect cross-references. If term **X** is a cross-reference to term **Y**, and **X** should appear following the definition at **Y** after the word *also* (or a code that designates the word), the computer can check that it does so appear, and if it does not, print a list of all those **X** terms that do not appear following *also*. Conversely, it can check to see that all those terms following *also* at **Y** terms appear in their own alphabetic positions as **X** terms. By this means it can catch many simple typographical errors, because unlike the human eye a computer will never be fooled into thinking that *pavilion* and *pavillion, état* and *etat*, or *worldwide* and *worldwide* are identical. It will never fail to notice when a term having a numbered definition 1 has no definition 2.

The computer can give one frequent and accurate statistical summaries, as of the average number of characters in each definition or each entry, or of the number of terms and definitions in each subject. Such data are of great help in planning and monitoring the size and balance of coverage in a dictionary. Of course, lexicographers have always kept such data but often had to extrapolate from small samples; thus their estimates were often unreliable. Computers are much better counters than people—and indefatigable. Being freed from the necessity of counting, humans can now devote themselves to what they do better than computers, that is to say, the writing and editing of dictionaries.

The editor always has the option of using codes that are strictly instructions to go into a particular type mode, but they are used only in special cases. Let us say that !sc means "Go into small capitals." If one means eventually to put cross-references in small capitals, why not label them all !sc? One should not because, since other elements will also be in small capitals and therefore introduced by !sc, one could not then uniquely identify cross-references and design a program to check to see that they are also included as variants following their preferred terms. It is best, therefore, to label them in some arbitrary and unique way, such as !VR, for this can later be converted to mean "Go into small capitals" after it has outlived its usefulness as a means of checking cross-reference style. Thus, except in special circumstances (which unfortunately occur all too frequently), composition codes should be avoided in the initial input stage of dictionary preparation. A set of arbitrary codes should be developed to represent every feature that one may need to have access to at later stages. At a minimum, the following individual elements should be uniquely identified: the entry word, each definition, the pronunciation, etymology, special notes for usage or synonymy, and variant terms.

Here is a definition of the combining form *levo-*, edited with computer codes for entry in a technical database:

> !E L *laevus* (from Gk *laios* left) left, to the left !D91 a combining form meaning left, to or on the left. !03 in stereochemistry, a combining form designating the levorotatory enantiomer of a substance. !L laevo- ?90 (British spelling). !C dextro- !M (?nm) ?EP

Translation: !E introduces the etymology. The !D codes refer to different definitions applying to different subjects. !L means "Also." !90 means "Do not use the normal type style following !L but style exactly as shown." !C means "Compare." !M means "Symbol." ?nm symbolizes the minus sign. ?EP means "This entry exceptionally does not end with a period." Each ! symbol introduces a computer code that must be inserted by an editor, as must the ? codes.

The chief complication that occurs in preparing a dictionary database is that in many cases the systematic rules governing particular computer codes must be violated and one must devise codes that provide a means of making exceptions, as we have seen in this example. Suppose one's definition code automatically puts the initial letter in capitals. In the great majority of instances this is a useful feature, but what does one do with abbreviations? One may not want the definition for *p.m.* to appear as *Post meridiem* but as *post meridiem*. One needs an exception code, a code that means "Hold everything! All systematic rules are rescinded; style exactly as you see." One can then write *post meridiem* following that code and it will appear with an initial lower-case letter. Of course, the best program is that which requires the fewest exceptions; but a dictionary is such a vast and complex undertaking that in the course of the entire project many exceptions are bound to occur. There are always means to address them, yet it may require a high level of sophistication on the part of a dictionary staff to master the coding apparatus of an elaborate dictionary program.

A computerized database can be helpful in many ways in updating a dictionary. For example, one of the most taxing and generally fruitless tasks in updating is that of locating the names in etymologies of those people who may have died since the last revision. I was able to solve this problem by identifying each living eponym with a distinctive computer code. Before each revision I can obtain a list of these names and verify whether any of the people designated has died. This, like so many other computer functions, was strictly an editorial invention. No computer person would ever have dreamed of identifying living eponyms. The editor must learn to use the computer creatively to serve his needs, and when it does not serve his needs he should not use it. It is not simply a means of gathering data or of inserting type specifications into a manuscript, useful though those functions are. It is a means by which the editor can gain better and continuous control over his manuscript. No one can tell him how to do it. Computer people can tell him what is possible and what is impossible, but only he can decide what is desirable and, if he knows a little about computer logic, propose a system for making his goal practicable. An elegant solution to an editorial problem is no less satisfying for having been solved with the aid of a computer.

The advantages of computer use are manifest, but the drawbacks are often belittled or ignored. In former times the compositor was frequently an educated person who took a proprietary interest in the accuracy of the material he set. Many a compositor's timid inquiry has kept editors from looking very foolish, and the compositors seldom received any credit in return. But the computer keyboarder is of a different breed. Computer keyboarding is a massive and cheap operation, and the keyboard operator is simply filling in for an optical scanner, keying exactly what is written down. No inquiries will be made, timid or otherwise. The burden of getting everything right is entirely on the editor; even major and obvious mistakes will not be caught, because the keyboarder is now a specialist who has no understanding of a particular subject.

In contributed works, providing too much information can be a real disadvantage of computer use.

287

What are the practical human limitations in implementing time-saving, computer-based, systematic efficiencies? Put another way, there is a point of diminishing returns between the sophistication of a system and the attention span of one's contributing editors. Before computers, the slow and slovenly apparatus of dictionary-making was finely attuned to the carelessness and indifference of many contributors. The system worked, if not well, at least adequately. Now that we have the capacity to give editors more information, the problem is, How much information is it wise to give them, and how much to withhold?[10]

In contributed dictionaries, one must have in effect two style manuals: a simple one for one's contributors and a far more complicated one for the staff editors. The contributors' manual will have few or no codes and focus entirely on content, with little attention to form. (A good program enables one to do that, since the program should handle the basic styling functions.) The staff manual, on the other hand, should describe the coding in detail, explaining the purpose and standard use of each code as well as its exact form and placement.

The Future of Dictionary Making

On-line Dictionary Editing

In the long run, perhaps the most promising development of computer use is on-line editing of dictionaries, as of other kinds of data. *On-line* means "having direct access to the computer file," usually by means of a video screen with an attached keyboard. Although on-line editing has been and is being employed in some dictionary projects, it is still not widely used, which is why discussion of it has been delayed until now.

In on-line editing, the editor can summon to the display unit any identified element of the current file in order to see it, change it, transfer it to another part of the file, or delete it. The great advantage of on-line editing is the immediate availability of the very latest file data. In ordinary editing, no one editor can know what other editors have done to other parts of the file without some delay—often a long one—and without laborious checking of card files or manuscript. Without knowing what is in the file, the editor may make mistakes or duplicate work already done. On-line editing makes style checking easier and has many other advantages.

Up until very recently, however, attempts to prepare dictionaries on-line have been plagued with difficulties and have seldom materialized on a large scale. The *Dictionary of American Regional English,* for example, which as we have seen uses computers extensively, was originally planned to have been written and edited on-line, but it was found to be easier to write it conventionally, while using information produced by computer on video screens. In the United States, the *Random House Dictionary* was one of the first major commercial dictionaries to utilize computers to store and categorize word lists, but the dictionary was not written or edited on-line. Neither was the *American Heritage Dictionary,* which used computers even more extensively to help produce its citation files. A scholarly historical work, the *Dictionary of Old English,* is, however, being edited on-line at the University of Toronto.[11]

However slow it has been to become incorporated in the editorial process, on-line access to the dictionary database is certain to become an accepted practice in dictionary making in the near future. Dictionary editors may choose to continue to compose their definitions with pencil and paper, but they (or trained computer keyboard operators) will then transfer the information directly from the editorial office into the file. Longman has already employed such a system in preparing some of its dictionaries, which will undoubtedly be adopted and improved upon by other dictionary houses in the years ahead.

In the future we can look forward to the increasing use of speech synthesis for proofing pronunciations. The computer will be programed to interpret phonetic symbols and record them in audible speech. Possibly, some day, one may be able to bypass the written form entirely and utter a word, wait a second or two, and hear in response the word's definition in one's own language, or its equivalent in another. An aural dictionary for the blind recently developed by the Library of Congress consists of audio cassettes and a voice index that the user must play at accelerated speed to find the word he wants, but we may look forward to the day when the sound of a human voice will by itself elicit an aural response of dictionary information about the word spoken.

Semantic Analysis and Machine Translation

A number of studies have been funded over the past fifteen or twenty years to explore the use of computers to assist or even replace the definer of monolingual and bilingual dictionaries.[12] Although computer studies of stratified meaning elements have provided linguists with material for scholarly research, they have not to my knowledge been of any practical help in monolingual lexicography. Still less can computers write definitions.

More promising, especially in technical fields, is the development of machine translation. If two languages have a number of direct counterparts, clearly a computer can be of service in translating terms from one language to the other. There are, in fact, a number of bilingual dictionaries that have been created by programing a computer to link morphologic elements in one language to that of another.[13] However, even in closely related languages, two words seldom mean the same thing in all contexts; their connotations or degree of formality may differ also. Technical terminology, as we have seen in Chapter Four, is characterized by meaning that is designed to be the same in all contexts; it therefore lends itself ideally to the vehicle of machine translation. Scientific and technical terms are also supposed to be unambiguous, and in many cases there are standard translations in various languages to facilitate international communication. Even in this area there are many difficulties, but much progress has been made. In the general vocabulary, however, progress is slower and more problematical, although increasingly we can expect to see software packages—whether in the form of floppy disks for microcomputers or in self-contained units—provide competition for printed bilingual dictionaries. In any case, the human bilingual lexicographer need not fear for his livelihood, since whatever the means of dissemination his work will still be in demand.

Electronically Published Dictionaries

Encyclopedias, and more recently several dictionaries, have been made available in databases that provide on-line service of their full texts. Plans are under way to make the entire *OED* and the *OED Supplements* available on-line.[14] Assuming that the user knows the exact form of the dictionary entry word, or that the program is sufficiently sophisticated to pick up a large number of possible variants of it, the user keyboards the term, or enough of it to identify it. Is this really easier than looking up the term in a book?

A book is a marvelous device for random access to short entries. If the amount of information it yields is often slight, the time and effort needed to find the information is likewise insignificant. But if one has to keyboard *oscillation* or *indefatigable,* let alone *plexus venosi vertebrales anteriores,* is it worth it? Most search systems have shortcuts. The computer might display, for example, a number of terms similar to the one keyboarded and one could then select the very term desired. But this takes additional time. On the other hand, on-line access to a dictionary corpus enables one to avoid having to look up two terms, if the first should be a cross-reference, to find a definition. The computer can present the definition and its preferred term regardless of the variant under which it is first sought. There are also systems employing phonetic search for desired items. One might write, for example, *plecksus,* and still find *plexus*—an obvious advantage for the poor speller. This feature is of particular value when one is dealing with an unfamiliar language.

Although the full-text, on-line use of commercial dictionaries may be less practical than their use in print, the on-line use of dictionary material together with much larger files of full texts may be another story. In the latter case, the dictionary is ancillary to other material; one can "look up" the meaning, let us say, of particular words that appear elsewhere in the text. All such words may be distinctively marked if they appear also in the dictionary file, and the user therefore knows that he can obtain a definition (or a pronunciation or an etymology) of any such word. In technical files, dictionary information might be a valuable adjunct to full-text use.

The Declining Role of the In-house Staff

From 1890 to the 1930s, dictionary houses sometimes assembled very large in-house staffs, as well as large groups of outside consultants, to write, proof-read, and compose their major dictionaries. When highly skilled labor was plentiful and comparatively cheap, it was possible to have staffs of forty or fifty people. Although a few dictionary houses on both sides of the Atlantic have maintained permanent dictionary staffs, most have tended to let their staffs go once a project has been completed. From a lexicographic view, the practice is foolish, since without continuity no dictionary can be well maintained. Preparations for the next revision will languish or be handled improperly. Gross changes in the dictionary's style will be inadvertently introduced by those unfamiliar with past practice or ignorant of the basic principles of lexicography. Unfortunately, many a fine dictionary has been allowed to decay with age; repairs were made too late and in too slipshod a way to do more than call attention to the neglect they so feebly were meant to address. Such a dictionary resembles a cathedral in ruins, without worshipers, visited only by passing tourists or specialized historians.

But the simple fact is that maintaining a permanent dictionary staff of any size has become prohibitively expensive. Labor is no longer cheap, and the skills necessary for writing and producing dictionaries are much less ordinary than they once were. They therefore demand a higher price. Even a small dictionary staff costs well over $100,000 a year. For a large staff, the costs are huge and could not be justified unless it were kept busy producing a steady stream of dictionaries and other reference books. Very few companies, if any, are willing to devote their resources year after year to such a program, which demands heavy investment in specialized marketing staffs and promotion. The more usual practice nowadays, as noted, is to maintain a small cadre of experienced lexicographers and to enlarge the staff temporarily as the need arises. Often the cadre is very small indeed, that is, a cadre of one; and all too often not a single experienced dictionary editor is retained following the publication of a dictionary.

What of the future? Will unabridged dictionaries be allowed to age without revision because staffs large enough to cope with them cannot be assembled? This is a distinct possibility. If it does happen, we can be sure that dictionary publishers will try every means at their disposal to conceal the fact. They will say that their marvelous computers enable them to update their dictionaries continuously and that no large-scale resetting of the work is therefore necessary. This, as the now-dated expression has it, is a copout. No dictionary can be adequately maintained by fidgeting with it, whether it is on-line or in the form of paper and ink. Computerization does not make major revision superfluous. It can indeed make it easier, but the work must still be done, and it is not done by nibbling at an occasional entry but by tearing the book apart and redoing it.

I tend, optimistically, to believe that major revisions and major new dictionaries will still be done, but not in the same way they have been in the recent past. We are likely to see fewer and fewer large dictionary staffs except in nonprofit, academic ventures. Qualified people will be too hard to find and too expensive to bring to one working place. Instead, the working place will be brought to them. Microcomputers or their technological successors will be placed in the homes of each dictionary editor, who will have direct on-line access to the dictionary file. He (or she) will have the convenience of working at home, whether he lives in California or Missouri or New York, and will have immediate knowledge of the current status of the file. He may compose his definitions or etymologies or pronunciations on paper just as he has always done, or he may compose them on a word processor, but in either case they will be put directly into the file. Equipped with printers, home computers could provide each editor with printed versions of particular parts of the file that he might wish to examine at length. The single greatest value of computer use in lexicography (and in other large reference projects) is its capacity to make use of the contributions of widely dispersed people.

With such an arrangement, the in-house staff might consist only of an editor-in-chief and managing editor, two or three assistants to check cross-references and style, and secretarial help. Yet the working editorial staff might be very large. Just as a great deal of keyboarding of computer material is done today by home workers rather than by compositors working in a plant, so will editorial work of all kinds increasingly be done in the home rather than in the office. Obviously, such a trend has implications far beyond the publishing industry, and just as obviously it will not extend to all industries. But for dictionary work and other projects that depend on collective intellectual effort, it is made to order. The technology for such a system exists today, and when technological advances reduce costs sufficiently, we can expect large editorial projects of all kinds to take advantage of its many benefits. Not the least of the advantages is that the old and infirm, now prevented from making arduous trips to an editorial office, will be able to contribute. The editor will be able to adjust his working hours to suit his convenience. Publishers will save money by not having to have large offices in prime locations. (They can have small offices in prime locations.)

Computer programs are already used to make style and spelling consistent, and to some extent such programs can be more fully utilized in dictionary work to replace elements of the dictionary style manual. But there will always be many points, too subtle or variable for any program, that must be addressed by the editors. With instantaneous communication between all editors, the editor-in-chief can make changes in the style manual, confident that every editor will be aware of them. For example, as soon as each editor presses the button to turn on his home computer screen, he could be reminded to check the style manual key to be informed of any style changes or other memoranda from the editor-in-chief. Periodically, it would surely be advisable for all editors to meet to discuss problems in their editing or in the computer system itself. Human projects will still progress more smoothly if all concerned know each other personally. But on the whole the advantages of having a large staff work in their own homes are manifest.

CHAPTER EIGHT

A Miscellany

Letters to the Editor

A dictionary editor soon learns that once a dictionary is published, letters start to arrive. Almost everybody has ideas about language and the way it should be used, and a great many people have ideas, though usually charmingly eccentric or naïve, about how dictionaries are made. The letters they write fall generally into three categories: the helpful, the critical, and the ambitious.

An astonishing number of people believe that new words are invented by individuals, and in an effort to be helpful they devise a list of neologisms of their own, which they kindly make available for inclusion in the next edition of one's dictionary. Because these letters are so commonplace and so well intentioned, a brief but informative pamphlet describing how words get into dictionaries is a worthwhile investment for any dictionary publisher. (One also receives a number of inquiries on this subject from schoolchildren fulfilling homework assignments, and such a pamphlet would serve them as well.) Some correspondents are quite proud of the new words they have devised and feel that the dictionary editor owes them a debt of gratitude. I have received letters from correspondents who offered to sell me their neologisms at ten dollars each and were much aggrieved when I declined to purchase them.

People have all sorts of ideas on how dictionaries might be improved. Many have devised their own conceptual system that they believe would be superior to the alphabetic arrangement. Others have ideas, often completely unrealistic, as to how to convert monolingual dictionaries to bilingual or multilingual use. Many are fascinated by etymology, though few are familiar with its principles, and one receives numerous letters offering fantastic suggestions for the etymologies of words.

The critical letters deal predominantly with two issues: omitted words and questions about usage. Very often one is challenged with the omission of a common word, only to find that it is entered; the correspondent simply could not find it, usually because he did not know how to spell it or because the word sought was an inflected form and did not appear as a main entry. People of particular religious persuasions, such as Christian Scientists, define certain terms precisely according to the dictates of their religion and object to the omission of these senses in their dictionaries. Other letters cite words that are extremely technical or rare or that have not been naturalized in English and are therefore excluded for good reason. However, a few letters do identify terms that are credible candidates for inclusion, even words one may have agonized over before deciding to omit, and letters of this sort serve the useful purpose of disposing one to take another look at the issue and seek to find more citations for the term—the letter writer may be right. Rarely (one hopes very rarely), a common term has inexplicably been left out of one's dictionary—deleted by mistake from a galley proof at some stage—and never discovered. Such letters are especially dreaded upon the first publication of any dictionary, for it sometimes seems that our vigilance in catching minor mistakes of all sorts has been matched by our failure to notice conspicuous blunders, such as a headword misspelled or placed out of alphabetical order.

There is scarcely any aspect of usage about which someone does not feel strongly. Some people are irate if one includes taboo words and terms of insult, others irate if one doesn't. Many accuse one of being racially or religiously biased for including words of this sort, or for including ordinary words with pejorative senses that appear to be directed at the group with which they identify. Dictionary editors are accused of being antiblack or anti-Semitic because they include definitions that express prejudice toward blacks and Jews. The lexicographer can only claim to be objectively reporting usage. The language expresses bias toward these and other groups because large numbers of people over protracted periods of time have felt the need to express these biases. The inclusion of offensive terms in a dictionary is a record of this fact.

Some people are concerned about the inclusion of any word having sexual significance. (See the discussion of taboo in Chapter Five, especially pages 185–186.)

Many object to the inclusion of slang terms on the ground that they are "not really words." They believe that words are accepted as part of the language by linguistic authorities and that dictionary makers exercise this authority. If a word appears in a dictionary, then in their view it has been legitimized, and the dignity of the language is diminished by a relaxation of standards that permits the inclusion of slang words they deplore. Others criticize the choice of usage labels applied to particular terms, or the absence of any usage label. Sometimes these criticisms have merit; but more often one is reminded that few people bother to read the guide to the use of the dictionary, for in a great many cases the answers to the questions asked and criticisms made are to be found plainly stated in the front-matter guide.

The third and last kind of correspondent is the person who wants to compile a specialized dictionary, or has compiled such a work and asks one to underwrite its expenses or publish it. I have no wish to discourage would-be lexicographers, but I must say candidly that few dictionary publishers regard such submissions favorably. First of all, the great majority are amateurish and are composed by people who, though often intelligent and informed in the discipline relating to the proposed dictionary, lack the writing skills or knowledge of lexicography necessary for compiling a dictionary. Second, if a dictionary publisher were to decide that such a specialized work were worth doing, he would have his own staff do it or supervise the doing of it. In this way it would be compatible with the other dictionaries published by the house. Third, most specialized dictionaries are not profitable. Specialists in particular fields always overestimate the sales of their projected work. If there are ten thousand specialists in the field, they assume all ten thousand will buy the dictionary, when in fact perhaps 538 will buy it. Such specialized dictionaries are printed in relatively small quantities and are therefore expensive to produce and must be sold for a high price.

Legal Considerations

Plagiarism and "Fair Use"

Dictionaries have always copied from one another, but no reputable dictionary today would dare take over entire sections of another work and print them verbatim, a practice common in the seventeenth century. If one makes a definition-by-definition comparison of a number of competing dictionaries, one will find very few identical definitions apart from the short, formulaic ones of the "of or pertaining to" variety. There are only so many ways one can define *bovine* or *reptilian.* On the other hand, one will find few sharp discontinuities. Although phrased differently, the definition of a given sense usually covers the same ground in all major dictionaries. Dictionary editors look at each other's books, and though each editor may form his own opinion about what ground should be covered, he dare not depart too far from the area laid out by his competitors. To be fair, the definition quality of American college dictionaries is very high, and in the vast majority of instances any major variation in treatment would be foolish. In this respect, the Merriam dictionaries, as befits the leader in its field, are less influenced by other dictionaries than those works are by each other or by Merriam's books. All American and British dictionaries, however, owe a great debt to the *OED,* and one can find numerous similarities in wording as well as in sense division between the *OED* and its successors. When does similarity became plagiarism?

It must first be understood that neither facts nor ideas can be copyrighted—only the particular form in which they are presented. If one defines a word representing an object by saying what the object is made of, how it is used, and what it looks like, anyone can define the word with reference to those same three criteria, provided the new definition is written in different words. Moreover, the second definition can also agree entirely as to the particular facts describing the materials, use, and appearance so long as they are not described in the same words as the original definition. In very short definitions, two definitions may be identical without implying plagiarism. One should not have to contrive awkward circumlocutions simply to avoid charges of plagiarism when straightforward definitions can be given.

On the other hand, odd metaphors that crop up in definitions of two different dictionaries suggest that someone copied from someone else, or perhaps both copied from a third source. Though technically this might be plagiaristic, no dictionary is entirely free of occasional, too close correspondences with antecedent works. They are surely to be avoided and should be weeded out when discovered, but as a practical matter occasional lapses of this sort could not be the ground for a legal action: it would be next to impossible to prove the origin of the disputed passage. For proof of plagiarism, one would have to show a pattern of close correspondence between two works. If two dictionaries consistently shared the same or closely similar wording of a large number of definitions, and if these definitions were of a complexity and size that suggested there might have been many ways to treat them, plagiarism might be provable.

It behooves all dictionary editors to take an indulgent view of the pilfering of ideas, since no one is innocent. Ideas are sometimes expressed similarly not from want of imagination but because any major alteration of form would use too much space. With this understanding, it can be asserted that none of the major dictionaries in the United States or Britain engages in plagiarism, but use each other as sources or checks against their own work.

In the United States, the legal concept of "fair use" governs the use of quotations of copyrighted work as illustrative examples of definitions. There is no numerical guide to how many words or characters may be quoted without infringing another's copyright, and any reasonable use of quoted material in a dictionary seems secure against legal action. In practice, no more than a sentence or two is usually required to render the sense. Longer quotations may be justified if the quotation actually defines the term or if it illustrates a variety of usage. However, the dictionary editor should adopt the policy of never requesting permission to use any quotation in his dictionary. If he does so, his request can be used as evidence that the use of the material was not subject to the fair use doctrine. If his request is denied and he uses the quotation anyway, he might be liable for infringement of copyright. Even if his request is approved, the request itself establishes an unfortunate precedent should he be challenged for the use of other material. In short, if the use is covered by fair use, don't ask.

Generally, in order to win a suit for infringement of copyright, the copyright owner has to show that he has suffered some material damage by such infringement. If the quotation is so long that potential customers might decide not to buy the book in which it originally appeared, the author has been materially hurt and deserves to be recompensed for his injury. Obviously, this possibility is extremely remote in dictionary use. Nevertheless, lexicographers should be prudent in their use of copyrighted material and strive to keep their quotations as brief as possible, consistent with the purpose for which they are used. We should not assume that because one is unlikely to be sued, profligate and unnecessary use of copyrighted material will be ignored. If dictionaries abuse the privilege of fair use to the point where the doctrine is narrowed or rescinded altogether, all dictionaries would suffer immeasurably. Readers would no longer have the opportunity to see how different senses are actually used, and their grasp of meaning would be much impaired.

Trademarks

A trademark is a symbol or name used by a maker of a product to distinguish the product from others of its kind. *Coca-Cola* is a trademark, or trade name, for a brand of soft drink. Trademarks usually are written with an initial capital letter. Trademark owners are naturally protective of the exclusive use of their trademarks, since their business often depends upon the public's recognition of their trademark. When a trademark is commonly used, however, as if it were an ordinary (or generic) term, not for a brand of a kind of thing but for the kind of thing itself, it enters into a never-never-land and is subject to various interpretations. To the lexicographer, the word has become generic, even if trademarked, and should be included in the dictionary and defined. If it is written generically with an initial lower-case letter, he may enter it in this form, although he usually identifies it as a trademark. To the trademark owner, such generic uses are illegal, based on ignorance of the term's protected status or contempt for his proprietary interest. He therefore views the dictionary's inclusion of his trademark as a compounding of the infringement of his protected name. Some trademark owners are extremely vigilant in challenging any alleged infringement of their trademark. Many trademarks have been lost because they were not adequately protected.

If a competitor uses someone else's trademark as his own and is thereupon sued by the trademark owner, his defense may be that the trademark is actually a generic word in common use. As evidence in support of his position, he may adduce dictionary definitions and other examples of generic use. If these are sufficient to persuade the judge that the term, however trademarked it once may have been, is now a generic term, the trademark will be declared invalid, at potentially enormous cost to the original owner. Thus, *aspirin* was lost as a trademark in the United States by the Bayer Company, though it is still a trademark in Great Britain. Many other once-valuable trademarks, such as *windbreaker* and *tabloid,* have also lost their protected status.

To the trademark owner, the case is clear and simple. He asks the lexicographer to omit his trademark from dictionaries. It's not generic, he says. It is a protected name, like *General Motors* or *U.S. Steel.*

But is it? When the lexicographer reviews his citations and sees numerous uses of *kleenex,* both capitalized and not, to mean a facial tissue; of *xerox* used both as noun and verb to refer to a xerographic duplicate; of *band-aid* to mean a makeshift and usually inadequate remedy—what is he to do? They are as much a part of the language as any other term. If his charge is to represent the language so that people unfamiliar with the meanings of words can find those meanings in his dictionary, is he not, by omitting them, subordinating the interest of dictionary users to that of the trademark owners? By what right should trademark owners or anyone else be empowered to dictate the facts of usage? If the facts so warrant, any term can be generic, and any generic term is subject to inclusion in a general dictionary. The lexicographer has no intention of depriving a trademark owner of the exclusive right to use a term; he merely argues that his overriding obligation is to dictionary users, and he cannot allow any special-interest group to determine what he can or cannot put in his dictionary.

As a hedge against the sometimes importunate demands, even threats, of trademark owners, some dictionaries have taken to including a statement on their copyright page disclaiming any intent to affect the copyright status of words they include. The *Random House College Dictionary (RHCD)*, for example, states:

> A number of entered words which we have reason to believe constitute trademarks have been designated as such. However, neither the presence nor the absence of such designation should be regarded as affecting the legal status of any trademark.

The *American Heritage Dictionary (AHD)* has included a veritable essay disclaiming any responsibility for affecting the trademark status of its entries. These nervous disclaimers are probably futile, in any event, since the fact and form of inclusion could be used as evidence regardless of such statement. For whatever good it might do, it would be quite sufficient to include such a disclaimer within the explanatory guide in the front matter, but obviously some publishers are afraid that they will be drawn into lawsuits over trademarks. However, so long as there is documentary evidence to support the form of a dictionary's inclusion of trademarked terms, I see no reason why publishers should be so abjectly concerned.

In the past, dictionaries took a distinctly more standoffish approach to trademark owners. But now that many dictionaries are published by subsidiaries of huge companies—frequently companies that have no direct interest in or knowledge of book publishing, much less of dictionaries—the influence of corporate legal counsels is more apparent. Large companies have their own trademarks to protect and are naturally more solicitous of those of others. Often the corporate vice-president overseeing a dictionary publisher cannot understand why the dictionary, which in comparison to the entire corporation is a tiny part, should take any unnecessary risk of legal action. The dictionary editor must do battle to include any trademarks, and he is under great pressure to distort the facts of usage by entering all such terms only in capitalized form, even though the record clearly shows they are often written in lower-case letters.

By far the most weaselly nonrecorders of generic meanings of trademark terms are the Merriam-Webster dictionaries. *MW9* defines *Band-Aid* as "trademark—used for a small adhesive strip with a gauze pad for covering minor wounds." But what about these uses?

> And, while the old pedagogy has failed for many reasons, clearly one of them is that its fundamental principles are wrong. It has mistaken a band-aid for the science of medicine.

(Richard A. Lanham, "The Abusage of Usage," *Virginia Quarterly Review* 53:1 [Winter 1977], p. 49)

Arofsky continues: "Everything the Knicks [a basketball team] try is a Band-Aid remedy. There's no real vision of the team concept. . . ."
(*New York Sunday News Magazine,* January 1, 1982, p. 20)

"From my point of view, I've seen no change how we're doing business to get qualified controllers," Mr. Thorstenson added. "I don't see any light at the end of the tunnel. All we've had is a helter-skelter, Band-Aid, stop-gap type of approach. There's seemingly no plan to deal with the situation."
(*New York Times,* April 30, 1982, p. A-10)

By now, most persons who suffer with knee problems have heard about the marvels of "band-aid" surgery on the knee, surgery which may avoid the pain and recovery time associated with more traditional knee surgery.
(*Harvard Medical School Health Letter* 7:5 [March 1982], p. 1) [This sense differs from that of the other three citations.]

How can it be that the G. & C. Merriam Co., which boasts of having over 13 million citations, has insufficient documentation to include these and many other comparable senses? Even *AHD,* with its lengthy disclaimer and its fulsomely conservative approach to language, included a second definition for *Band-Aid:* "Any superficial or temporary remedy or solution." (This was, however deleted from *AHD2.*) The Merriam-Webster dictionaries consistently fail to meet their responsibility to define trademarked terms in common use. Instead, they employ the formula, "used for . . .", in defiance of the basic lexicographic rule of substitutability, and they include only the official reference approved by the trademark owner. The Merriam-Webster dictionaries have sacrificed the needs of their users in this respect for the goodwill of corporate trademark owners.

If a lexicographer hopes to stay honest, he should keep his company's legal counsel at arm's length or persuade him that he needn't turn into jelly every time a trademark owner complains about the treatment of a term.

In the United Kingdom, if a draft resolution of the European Economic Community (EEC) is enacted, publishers of dictionaries will be subject for the first time to a legal obligation to identify as a trademark any word that happens to be registered as a trademark. Dictionary editors, among them Robert Burchfield, editor of the *OED Supplements,* have protested strongly, and other sympathetic commentators have joined forces with them, but at this writing all efforts by dictionary editors to discuss the issue with the EEC legislators in Brussels—who have obviously been in close touch with trademark owners—have been unavailing. As one correspondent to the *Times Literary Supplement* puts it: "It is . . . an inadmissible introduction into

English law of a vested interest distorting the function of a dictionary, which is to reflect actual use of words rather than their legal status."[1] It is to be hoped that the EEC will not allow its promotion of commerce to lead it to ignore the value of freedom of expression and require dictionaries to misrepresent the facts of usage. American lexicographers can scarcely afford to regard this dispute as a matter of no concern to them, for surely if the EEC directive is put into effect it will not be long before U.S. trademark owners propose similar legislation in various state legislatures in the United States, if not in the Congress. The ramifications of such restrictive legislation on the free expression of facts and ideas are alarming.

The Dictionary as a Reflection of Social Values

The relative length accorded some kinds of words, compared to that accorded other kinds, provides us with a rough index of the values implicit in a dictionary's treatment of the lexicon. (A notable exception is that of taboo words, which are often defined with extreme brevity not because they are unimportant but because their meanings are considered offensive.) The guide is far from infallible, especially in the specialized lexicon, in which some basic terms can be simply defined and some less common terms (for example, in medicine, a rare syndrome) may require lengthy treatment. But even if a basic term can be defined simply, it is often amplified with encyclopedic material in recognition of its importance. Although one cannot say that any particular term has been adjudged important because it is defined at great length, a pattern of extraordinarily long definitions of a particular class of terms is significant. In regarding a dictionary of religion, which is necessarily somewhat encyclopedic, we are justified in concluding that the terms defined at greater length than others are considered by the editors central to the study of religion. The treatment of terms in a general dictionary is usually less deliberate.[2] Often unacknowledged even to the editors themselves, the disparity of treatment of different kinds of terms reflects an implicit judgment, just as the choice of front-page stories in a newspaper reflects a judgment of what is important.

The assumption that there is objectively more of importance to be said about one class of terms than another can hardly be justified by any reasonable criteria or by broad consensus. Some terms are nonetheless routinely given more encyclopedic treatment than others. For instance, *MW9* devotes fully eight column-lines to the theory of *relativity* (def. 3), but two lines apiece to the basic senses of *trust* (def. 1) and *piety* (def. 1). The editors would defend this treatment by asserting that it takes that much more space to explain a complex idea like relativity. Compared to other college dictionaries, *MW9* is a paragon of conciseness—*RHCD* takes fourteen lines and *World* all of twenty-one lines. Their entries subsume the *general theory of relativity* and the *special theory of relativity* and are in fact encyclopedic entries, explaining the concept of relativity as used in two fundamental theories. I do not mean to criticize this treatment; I merely wish to draw attention to it. In a society with a different set of values it is conceivable that words like *hope* and *piety* would be considered so important, and indeed so complex, that explanations at least as full as that for *relativity* would be essential. Simplicity is in the eye of the beholder. If we scrutinize any word sufficiently, like a patch of apparently unblemished skin under high magnification, we will find a new world awaiting investigation. In our world, scientific and technological words are considered worthy of such scrutiny; other words are not.

The length of a definition has nothing to do with the commonness of a word. *Relativity* is not heavily used in the general vocabulary and *hope* is. If commonness were the criterion, the longest definitions would be for *the, of, and, a, to,* and *in,* and dictionaries would be even more boring to read than they already are. Common usage cannot be considered in determining definition length. The definer may think that the peculiar demands of each word determine definition length, but this is only partly true. Although people who make dictionaries come from various classes, dictionary definitions represent the views and prejudices of the established, well-educated, upper classes, generally speaking.

It is no conspiracy. No one is in league to distort meaning to keep the poor and uneducated oppressed. The upper-class bias of dictionaries stems partly from tradition: the earliest dictionaries were intended to help the educated classes understand difficult words. The pedagogical attitude remained even after dictionaries became broader in purpose and included a wide assortment of words. Although contemporary dictionaries generally disavow any intention to improve or correct anyone's speech, they are nonetheless powerful forces for the preservation and dissemination of a distinctly cultivated form of expression. They give it such attention both in the choice of entries and in the language used in their definitions (called metalanguage, because it is language about language). Dictionaries are not written in informal, chatty style. They employ a sophisticated and formal diction for maximum content in the least amount of space. This use of formal diction is not wholly accounted for by the need for brevity. Although it is considered by dictionary editors to be the style most fitting for a dictionary, there is, however much it may be denied, an element of social judgment in its use.

Another explanation of the upper-class bias of dictionaries depends upon the nature of the work and the conditions of employment. The skills of lexicography call for highly educated people who have themselves been exposed over a long period of time to the formal language of instruction. There are definers who were born in poverty as well as those who began with every advantage, but all acquire a respect for formal education and for the values that make the development of the sciences and the arts possible. Editorial evaluation of the importance of particular terms is likely to reflect this, which coincides to a great extent with the established, upper-class view.

I must now pull back a bit and issue qualifications. Upper-class usage and values are much more evident in British dictionaries than in American. The upper classes in America are more diffuse and are populated with a variety of people, some of whom are not well educated and have little use for formal education. There is no identity between educated class and upper class; rather, there is an amalgam of different classes and different degrees of education.

Nonetheless, the views of the upper and better-educated classes do differ, as a group, from those of the middle and lower classes. For example, the degree of specificity of most scientific definitions in popular dictionaries goes far beyond what most users need or want. The pronunciation systems, though not very complicated, are largely misunderstood. Yet dictionaries persist in being very specific in their scientific definitions and in using pronunciation systems that are not widely understood. They do so as a matter of policy. They do so because to be specific about scientific terms represents a view of the world they endorse, and they insist upon using pronunciation systems that do justice to the sounds of the language because to them an objective standard of accuracy must take precedence over the widespread inability of dictionary users to appreciate it. These policies are defensible, even noble, but they are seldom defended because they are not widely recognized as policies.

Criticism of Dictionaries

General dictionaries are usually reviewed in the popular press by popular authors, literary critics, or professors in the humanities. It is assumed that because such people use dictionaries regularly, they are qualified to be dictionary critics. However, few would argue that because we work or live in a building we are qualified to judge the architectural quality or structural integrity of other new buildings. Without practical experience in the building trade, knowledge of structural engineering, or training in architecture or its history, we could address only those superficial aspects of a building that happened to coincide with an accidental awareness or particular interest of our own. We might see, for example, that the windows were small and that little light was admitted, but fail to realize whether small windows were a design element or a structural necessity imposed by certain conditions of the site or by the purpose of the building. In other words, knowledge about architecture is essential for evaluating new buildings and knowledge about lexicography is essential for evaluating new dictionaries. Though this may seem so obvious as to be insulting, in practice it has been widely disregarded, especially in the United States. (Reviewing in Britain is distinctly better.) As a result, the great majority of popular reviews of dictionaries serve chiefly as vehicles for displays of irrelevant learning or amusing word play. Such reviewers, however well intentioned, intelligent, and in command of the use of language, lack the basis for making informed judgments about dictionaries because they do not know why certain decisions were made (why the windows are so small). They do not even know what questions should be asked, much less how to answer them.

Often, new editions of major dictionaries are scarcely reviewed at all, even in library and academic journals. Robert L. Chapman, in a survey of dictionary reviews from 1900 to 1975, notes that "several good dictionaries apparently went unreviewed," and cites five such. The second edition of *World*, he notes also, was hardly reviewed at all, and new school dictionaries were often ignored.[3] It is easy to see why. Reviewing a dictionary properly is hard work: it involves making a systematic analysis and comparison of a number of dictionary entries. Chapman suggests that a team of advisers collaborate to review dictionaries in their respective technical fields. This might be a sensible idea, but only if the advisers were conversant with dictionary practice or the reviewer free to reject unrealistic criticisms. Experts almost always find definitions in their own specialties inadequate; they usually expect encyclopedic essays for which few dictionaries have space.

Most reviews in academic and library journals, while generally written by those with long or practical familiarity with dictionaries, are also unsatisfactory. Short reviews tend to take the form of uncritical recitations of the publisher's claims (number of entries, illustrations, usage notes, etc.). Long reviews follow no coherent pattern of emphasis; they merely reflect the reviewer's particular interest or bias. It is easier to cite a specific alleged deficiency, such as the absence of taboo words, than to spend the time required to analyze the overall worth of a dictionary. Library reviews tend to be more balanced and complete but are often bland and uncritical, whereas academic reviews are often idiosyncratic, unpredictably critical of minor faults and indifferent to or oblivious of major ones. There are, fortunately, a few happy exceptions.

Perhaps the most deservedly acclaimed review of general commercial dictionaries was that of James B. McMillan in *College English,* a journal published by the National Council of Teachers of English (NCTE).[4] McMillan, a professor of English at the University of Alabama who supervised the collection of usage data for the NCTE and who has contributed editorially to many dictionaries, set forth three basic criteria for judging dictionaries: quantity of information, quality of information, and effectiveness of presentation. Quantity included the number of entries, the number of definitions, the number of new terms (when compared with other dictionaries), the frequency of use of subject (or field) labels, synonyms, etymologies, and pronunciations. Quality embraced accuracy, completeness, clearness, simplicity, and modernity. Each of the specifically different items compared quantitatively was analyzed by each of these criteria. The inclusion of illustrative phrases, since they contribute to clearness and completeness, was considered a qualitative feature. The effectiveness of presentation included comparisons of the systems of alphabetization, the placement of etymologies within the entries, the order in which the definitions were listed, the pronunciation systems, and the typography. The front-matter essays, including the guide to the use of the dictionary, and encyclopedic or tabular sections in the back matter, were also considered. McMillan's review is thorough, balanced, and considerate and is wonderfully concise, being only eight pages long. Few people, may I say, having put as much work as McMillan did into this review, would have had the modesty and grace to confine it to so brief and essential a statement.

Other standards of comparison have been proposed. These include the year of publication, the number and quality of scholars serving as advisers, the number of pages, the number of printed characters in the volume, the average number of words per entry, and the inclusion of a specific set of new terms.[5] All of these proposals have some merit, but all have defects as well.

Copyright dates can be meaningless if an old dictionary is only superficially updated. As Edward Phillips showed in 1658, a list of prominent scholars does not necessarily guarantee lexicographic excellence or even originality. Page count may be more a function of size of type than comprehensiveness of content. More to the point, all counts of pages, characters, and words per entry imply that the bigger the work, the better it is. But if a book has more words or characters in it than others, it may be merely verbose and poorly edited. Checking to see whether a set of new terms is in a dictionary is a favorite device of reviewers to test the currency of the work; but as I have said previously, they invariably assume that whatever does not appear in the dictionary under review has been overlooked. On the contrary, it may have been considered and rejected on good grounds. Those dictionaries that too readily accept ephemeral neologisms without adequate evidence in their citation files are thus rewarded with higher ratings than those dictionaries that exercise more careful control. Even if the latter dictionaries were wrong to omit the neologisms, they are never criticized for the right reasons. Instead of questioning the editors' judgment, reviewers take such omissions as evidence of poor coverage of the contemporary vocabulary.

Furthermore, very often such lists of new words contain terms that are beyond the scope of the particular dictionary under review. For example, Kenneth Kister's *Dictionary Buying Guide* includes, on its checklist for evaluating dictionaries, the terms *laetrile, derisible,* and *nitrofurantoin.*[6] It is difficult to imagine why any of these terms should be in any but the largest of dictionaries, and maybe not even in them. *Nitrofurantoin* is the chemical name of an antibacterial drug used to treat infections of the urinary tract. There are many hundreds, if not thousands, of other antibacterial drugs that could have been included as well. *Derisible* appears neither in the Brown Corpus nor in the *American Heritage Word Frequency Book.* (It also does not appear in the Thorndike-Lorge *Teacher's Word Book of 30,000 Words.*) *Laetrile* is a chemical compound extracted from peach stones, apricot pits, and other seeds, and was much in the news for a period of time when it was alleged, without scientific basis, to be effective in treating some cancers; in ten years it will be entirely forgotten by the general public. There may be grounds for including the term in a medical dictionary, since it has been discussed and studied in the medical literature. Usages in medicine are slower to take hold than in the general vocabulary, but also slower to disappear, since scientific studies often take several years before they are published. But in the general vocabulary, many words pass swiftly in and out of circulation, and the inclusion of any word simply because it is common for a few years is a questionable practice. Unfortunately, checklists of new terms encourage lexicographers to include all such terms lest they be stigmatized for having omitted them.

Unless the reviewer has access to a large citation file, he lacks the basis for being able to decide whether the omission of any new term or sense was wise or not. On the other hand, if he confines his list to terms that are all fairly well accepted, he may be able to distinguish a dictionary that is badly out of date from others, but he will not be able to make finer distinctions of the comparative currency of two works. Certainly any checklist of terms should contain a few reasonably new terms and senses, but far too much emphasis has has been placed on novelty by dictionary reviewers and not enough on solid coverage of the basic vocabulary.

How should dictionaries be reviewed? Robert L. Chapman proposes that reviewers "use a random sampling device that covers the book from A to Z, so that the total average performance may be assessed. This might be something as simple as 'the tenth main entry on every twentieth page'" or the fifteenth or tenth page, depending on the reviewer's stamina. He recommends that each such entry be carefully scrutinized according to McMillan's criteria of accuracy, completeness, clearness, simplicity, and modernity. He would add to these substitutability of the definition and a check to see that every word used in the definition is itself defined. Finally, he urges that "referential integrity" be checked "by tracking down a number of cross-references." The reader should not be sent down blind alleys or given a runaround.[7] These are valuable suggestions from an experienced lexicographer. It makes sense to apply McMillan's standards systematically to entries throughout a dictionary.

One way to learn how to review dictionaries is by examining those few soundly based critiques that exist. It would be hard to find a more trenchant or better-documented criticism than that of the *Thorndike-Barnhart Beginning Dictionary* that appeared in a 1964 issue of *Elementary English* devoted to "The Dictionary in the Elementary School."[8] The author takes the dictionary to task for its disproportionate emphasis on Christianity in its illustrative phrases, and she documents her claim convincingly: "From *a* to *Yule,* we counted fifty-nine references to the word *Christmas* . . . [in illustrative sentences]."[9] She cites these illustrative sentences (with the word being exemplified in italic type) as typical:

> The Star in the East was the *sign* of Christ's coming.
> Christ came to *save* the world.
> Christ is called the *Rock* of Ages.
> Christ gave His disciples power to *remit* sins.
> Jesus touched the sick man. *Thereon* he was healed and arose from his bed.
> Jesus died on the *cross.*
> The sufferings and death of Christ are called the *Atonement.*

The author also shows that the dictionary's illustrative phrases consistently represented girls as good, honest, pure, truth telling, and generally wonderful; whereas boys were represented as violent, cruel, and irremediably wicked. She cites examples:

> That cruel boy *tortures* animals.
> The cruel boy *stoned* the dog.

And so forth. One can be sure that the current Thorndike-Barnhart dictionaries do not show such a pattern in the choice of illustrative sentences. I cite this example of bias in dictionaries not to denigrate the Thorndike-Barnhart dictionaries, which were without doubt the best books of their kind. Moreover, nobody could ever impute to Clarence Barnhart or to anyone associated with him any sort of conscious bias. The criticism simply illustrates that even an outstanding dictionary conscientiously edited is apt to reflect the cultural backgrounds and habits of the editors. It also illustrates the value of hindsight: society's predominant values change from decade to decade. In the 1940s, when the Thorndike-Barnhart dictionary was prepared, few questioned that America was a Christian country and prayer was common in the public schools. The didactic tone of the illustrative sentences that the reviewer also criticizes was simply a carryover of tradition from early schoolbooks. The real point of the criticism is not that the dictionary was biased, but that it had not kept up with the times. That is a fair criticism.

We have had occasion elsewhere to allude to the role of dictionaries in reflecting the values of the predominant social class. We see now that as these values change in the course of time, what was formerly as innocuous as bland background music can become intrusive and objectionable. The bright paint used to color parts of ancient Greek statuary would strike us today as tawdry. Every established dictionary reflects, however it may strive to be impartial, the prevailing biases of its times, because the biases often inhere in the very manner of expression used in its definitions. They inhere in the choice of terms to be included and in the fullness with which they are treated. Instances of bias may fairly be criticized as signs of prejudices that have since become outdated and conspicuous. Yet the indignation shown by critics, which implies that the lexicographers have naïvely betrayed their own biases, is almost always wrong-headed and unjustified.

Dictionaries should not be immune from criticism, but the critics should take into consideration practical limitations on the size and cost of the work. Theoretical recommendations for improving dictionary practice are always valuable, whether they are practicable or not. When such proposals are made in the form of serious criticism of commercial dictionaries for not having adopted them, however, we are justified in asking the critics whether they have considered the practical consequences of their recommendations. Many a dictionary has been taken to task for not having adopted policies that would have made the work treble in size if actually undertaken. In the case of academic projects, such criticisms may still be justified; but commercial enterprises have no such flexibility. Frequently, such proposals would necessitate vastly longer periods of editorial preparation and much larger staffs—in short, huge outlays of money.

309

Johnson remarks in his *Preface,* "Every other authour may aspire to praise; the lexicographer can only hope to escape reproach, and even this negative recompense has been granted to very few." There is so much substance to a dictionary that opportunities for error and omission are legion, and the challenge of criticism is not the discovery of faults but the distillation of a basis for discriminating large faults from small ones. One disposed to find fault with a dictionary can always find ample grounds to justify his sentiment, while particular merit may pass unnoticed unless one has taken the time and trouble to compare and analyze similar works.

Dictionary work is not heroic. Its reward is the patient fulfillment of distant expectation, and often that is submerged in present distress in the struggle to meet intermediate deadlines. Upon the publication of his work, the lexicographer's principal emotion may be simply one of relief, like that of a long-distance runner who has finished his race at last and can stop running. But his is an achievement of the intellect, and few works of the intellect are more useful to so many people over such a protracted period of time. The dictionary maker must look to that for his satisfaction.

Notes

Full bibliographic data for works other than dictionaries are given in the note that first refers to each source. In addition, the more important nondictionary sources are listed alphabetically by author in the *Selective Bibliography* beginning on page 333. For dictionaries, full bibliographic data are given either under the first reference in the *Notes* or in the *Critical Bibliography of Selected Monolingual Dictionaries,* arranged alphabetically by title, following the *Notes.*

INTRODUCTION

1. John P. Dessauer, *Book Publishing: What It Is, What It Does* (New York: R. R. Bowker, 1974), p. 136.

2. For an interesting history and survey of the subject, see Dennis E. Baron, "The Epicene Pronoun: The Word That Failed," *American Speech* 56:2 (Summer 1981), pp. 93–97.

CHAPTER ONE   What Is a Dictionary?

1. "A Typological Classification of Dictionaries on the Basis of Distinctive Features," in *Problems in Lexicography,* second ed., ed. Fred W. Householder and Sol Saporta (Bloomington, Ind.: Indiana University; The Hague: Mouton, 1967; hereafter referred to as *Problems*), pp. 3–24. Malkiel's article is condensed and modified from his earlier two-part essay, "Distinctive Features in Lexicography: A Typological Approach to Dictionaries Exemplified with Spanish," *Romance Phil-*

ology 12:4 (May 1959), pp. 366–399, and 13:2 (November 1959), pp. 111–155. The Householder and Saporta book is a valuable collection of lexicographic papers presented at a conference held at Indiana University in November 1960 and originally published as a supplement to the *International Journal of American Linguistics* 28 (1962).

2. However, to my mind the perspective category is weakly defined; the method of organization could just as well be considered part of the presentation. On the other hand, Malkiel is unjustly criticized by Ali M. Al-Kasimi in *Linguistics and Bilingual Dictionaries* (Leiden: E. J. Brill, 1977) for not providing categories of "discrete, mutually opposed dictionary types" (p. 16). That was not Malkiel's intention. Moreover, the typology advanced by Al-Kasimi for bilingual dictionaries does not provide for discrete, mutually opposed dictionary types any more than does Malkiel's.

3. Mary R. Haas, "What Belongs in a Bilingual Dictionary?", in *Problems*, p. 47.

4. Ladislav Zgusta, *Manual of Lexicography* (The Hague: Mouton; Prague: Academia, 1971; hereafter referred to as *Manual*), p. 320.

5. Cited by Richard S. Harrell, "Some Notes on Bilingual Lexicography," in *Problems*, p. 51.

6. A number of culture-specific culinary terms are cited by Dinh-Hoa Nguyen, "Bicultural Information in a Bilingual Dictionary," in *Theory and Method in Lexicography*, ed. Ladislav Zgusta (Columbia, S.C.: Hornbeam Press, 1980), p. 166.

7. Cited by Harrell in *Problems*, p. 51.

8. Haas, *Problems*, p. 45.

9. Zgusta, *Manual*, p. 310. For a fuller treatment of this subject, see *ibid.*, pp. 298–336.

10. *Ibid.*, p. 210.

11. Sidney I. Landau, "The Making of a Dictionary: Craft versus Commerce," *Booklist* (incorporating *Reference and Subscription Books Reviews*) 77:6 (November 15, 1980), p. 481. K. M. Elisabeth Murray is the author of *Caught in the Web of Words: James A. H. Murray and the Oxford English Dictionary* (New Haven: Yale University Press, 1977).

12. James Sledd, "Dollars and Dictionaries: The Limits of Commercial Lexicography," in *New Aspects of Lexicography*, ed. Howard D. Weinbrot (Carbondale, Ill.: Southern Illinois University Press, 1972), p. 128.

13. *Ibid.*, p. 136.

14. "The Making of a Dictionary," p. 481.

15. Allen Walker Read, "Approaches to Lexicography and Semantics," in *Current Trends in Linguistics*, vol. 10, ed. Thomas Sebeok (The Hague: Mouton, 1972), p. 161.

16. "American Lexicography, 1947–1973," *American Speech* 53:2 (Summer 1978), p. 115.

17. Edited by John B. Carroll, Peter Davies, and Barry Richman (Boston: Houghton Mifflin, 1971).

18. *Manual,* p. 217.

19. "Approaches," p. 149.

20. Springfield, Mass.: G. & C. Merriam, 1961. The *Random House Dictionary* (New York: Random House, 1966), though called unabridged, is not comparable in coverage to *NID3*. In fact, the *World Book Dictionary* (Chicago: World Book-Childcraft International, 1981; original ed. 1963; 2 vols.) comes closer to being unabridged. Funk & Wagnalls had a fully competitive unabridged dictionary in the late nineteenth century and the early decades of the twentieth, but sadly let it lapse into obsolescence by failing to revise it thoroughly. In England there is no work comparable to *NID3*. The *Oxford English Dictionary,* which will be discussed below, is a historical dictionary which, though complete in its general coverage, necessarily omits many recent words and senses because of the long period of its preparation, and by and large ignores the scientific and technical vocabulary. It cannot and does not provide complete coverage of the language as it is used today, although the *Supplements,* of which the first three volumes have been published, will improve its coverage considerably.

21. "American Lexicography," p. 114.

22. The Collins dictionary, edited by Patrick Hanks (London: Collins, 1979), is widely known as the *Collins English Dictionary.* The Longman dictionary (Burnt Mill, Harlow: Longman, 1982) is edited by Paul Procter.

23. *Thorndike-Barnhart Comprehensive Desk Dictionary,* ed. Clarence L. Barnhart (New York: Doubleday, 1951, now out of print). *The Doubleday Dictionary,* ed. Sidney I. Landau and Ronald J. Bogus (New York: Doubleday, 1975).

24. Sidney I. Landau, "Of Matters Lexicographical: Scientific and Technical Entries in American Dictionaries," *American Speech* 49:3–4 (Fall–Winter 1974), p. 242.

25. *IEEE Standard Dictionary of Electrical and Electronics Terms,* ed. Frank Jay (New York: Institute of Electrical and Electronics Engineers, distributed by John Wiley, 1977).

26. "Of Matters Lexicographical," p. 241.

27. "American Lexicography," p. 124.

28. *Progress in Medical Terminology,* ed. A. Manuila (Basel: S. Karger, 1981), p. 58.

29. But they do not include "dictionaries" of biography and geography, which deal not with words but with encyclopedic facts. Although dictionaries often include such encylopedic material, collections devoted exclusively to biography or geography are specialized encyclopedias.

30. Jones's work was revised by A. C. Gimson in 1967 (thirteenth ed.) under the title *Everyman's English Pronouncing Dictionary* (London: J. M. Dent, 1967). The Kenyon and Knott work, first published in 1944 (Springfield, Mass.: G. & C. Merriam), has been updated but never thoroughly revised and is now out of date.

31. *Dictionary of American Slang,* second supplemented edition, ed. Harold Wentworth and Stuart Berg Flexner (New York: Thomas Y. Crowell, 1975; first ed. 1960), p. xiii n.

32. For a discussion of the principles and methods of collection and a copy of the entire questionnaire (covering about 1,600 questions), see Frederic G. Cassidy, *A Method for Collecting Dialect*, Publication of the American Dialect Society, No. 20 (Gainesville, Fla.: American Dialect Society, 1953). Audrey R. Duckert contributed substantially to the formulation of the questionnaire—Cassidy writes that it is "at least half hers"—and to the subsequent development of the dictionary.

33. See *Manual*, pp. 207–208.

34. See *Progress in Medical Terminology*, pp. 13–14. For example:

> Myelofibrosis . . . has been described in the literature in English under at least 12 names, in German under at least 13, and in French under at least 31. . . . [An author] dealing with a French paper on *panmyélose hyperpasique chronique* may translate this into English as chronic hyperpasic panmyelosis. Many such neologisms, though not generally in use, persist in the literature, simply because once or twice they have found their way into reputable journals.

What Dr. Manuila calls a neologism is also a ghost term.

35. *A Dictionary of American Idioms* (first ed. 1966), edited by Maxine Tull Boatner and John Edward Gates, revised ed. by Adam Makkai, was produced originally for the deaf and then reissued under its present general title. It is a useful work, but much less sophisticated and uneven in concept than the British dictionaries cited.

36. Hereafter referred to as *Longman*. The Survey of English Usage of University College London, founded in 1960 under the supervision of Randolph Quirk, has been the source of many grammatical studies, notably the *Grammar of Contemporary English* (London: Longman, 1972), by Quirk, Sidney Greenbaum, Geoffrey Leech, and Jan Svartvik. The Survey consists of a corpus of one hundred written and one hundred spoken passages, categorized by subject and by degree of formality or intimacy. The spoken texts have been carefully analyzed and transcribed, and since 1979 substantial parts of them have been made available on computer tape by the Norwegian Computing Centre for the Humanities, University of Bergen. The corpus is composed of many different varieties of language, ranging from scholarly and scientific articles to intimate telephone talks. It is now directed by Sidney Greenbaum.

37. See *Manual*, p. 203.

38. *Manual*, p. 349. Not cited by Zgusta but also illustrative of the problem of scheduling dictionaries is the *Dictionary of the Older Scottish Tongue*, first proposed by Sir William Craigie in 1915 and begun before 1921. By 1983, now under the editorship of A. J. Aitken, some thirty fascicles had been published, reaching midway through the letter **P**, but by the editor's own reckoning the work will take at least forty-five more editor-years to complete. Thus, if three editors work full time on the project, it may be completed by the year 1998, seventy-seven years after it was begun. See A. J. Aitken, "DOST: How We Make It," *Dictionaries* 4 (1982), pp. 42–64, for a painfully honest assessment of the difficulties of producing a great historical dictionary under adverse circumstances.

39. A revised edition (hereafter *AHD2*) appeared in 1982 under the title of *American Heritage Dictionary: Second College Edition.*

40. David L. Gold, "The Ordering of Lexemes in a Dictionary," in *Papers of the Dictionary Society of North America 1979,* ed. Gillian Mitchell (London, Ont.: School of Library and Information Science, University of Western Ontario, 1981), pp. 51–80.

41. *The English Duden,* 2nd rev. ed. Edited by the Fachredaktionen of the Bibliographisches Institut, Mannheim, and the Modern Languages Department of George G. Harrap & Company Ltd., London. The original pictorial Duden dictionary was monolingual (German); from it a whole series of bilingual works has been created, with German the source language of each.

CHAPTER TWO   A Brief History of English Lexicography

1. The chief source of information for early English lexicography is DeWitt T. Starnes and Gertrude E. Noyes, *The English Dictionary from Cawdrey to Johnson, 1604–1755* (Chapel Hill, N.C.: University of North Carolina Press, 1946; hereafter *SN*), to which I am much indebted, particularly for its analysis of fifteenth- to seventeenth-century dictionaries. However, any opinions expressed of these or later dictionaries are my own.

2. Presidential Address, *Philological Society Transactions* (1882–84), pp. 509–510, quoted in K. M. E. Murray's *Caught in the Web of Words,* pp. 203–204.

3. *SN,* p. 2.

4. Harold Whitehall, "The Development of the English Dictionary," in *Essays on Language and Usage,* second ed., ed. Leonard F. Dean and Kenneth G. Wilson (New York: Oxford University Press, 1963), p. 3. Reprinted from the Introduction to *Webster's New World Dictionary of the American Language* (1958 ed.). Whitehall estimates the word stock in the fifteenth century as 100,000–125,000 words.

5. Quoted in "Dictionary," *The New Encyclopaedia Britannica* (Chicago: Encyclopaedia Britannica, 1977; hereafter *EB*), V, p. 714.

6. Frank Vizetelly, *The Development of the Dictionary of the English Language* (New York: Funk & Wagnalls, 1923), p. 9.

7. *SN,* pp. 10–11.

8. David O. Frantz, "Florio's Use of Contemporary Italian Literature in *A Worlde of Wordes,*" *Dictionaries* 1 (1979), pp. 49 and 53.

9. In "Dictionary," *EB,* Read mentions a third source, a translation of *The Book of Physicke* (1599) from which Cawdrey took a list of poorly translated English–Latin words with English endings—terms together with their English glosses. Read says that Cawdrey's dictionary "can rightly be called a plagiarism" (p. 715).

10. Quoted in *SN,* p. 27.

11. Cited in *SN,* p. 28.

12. *Ibid.,* p. 42.

13. *Ibid.,* p. 46.

14. *Ibid.,* p. 54.

15. The editor of *A New English Dictionary* is identified only by the initials J. K., and though most scholars attribute the work to Kersey, the evidence is not conclusive. Fredric Dolezal claims (in an unpublished paper given on June 11, 1983, at the Dictionary Society of North America conference in Newark, Del.) that John Wilkins's and William Lloyd's *Alphabetical Dictionary* of 1668 was the first dictionary to focus its attention on common words. The difficulty with this claim is that the *Alphabetical Dictionary,* anticipating Roget's system of classification by nearly two hundred years, depends on tables by which terms are classified, and appears to be closer in form to what we now call a thesaurus than to a dictionary. The *Alphabetical Dictionary,* however, certainly is a remarkable work deserving of further study. For example, Dolezal says that it is the first dictionary in which the words used in its definitions are themselves defined.

16. *SN,* pp. 71, 72.

17. *Ibid.,* p. 102.

18. The entry, alphabetized under *rolling,* is quoted from the 1766 edition.

19. See Esther K. Sheldon, "Pronouncing Systems in Eighteenth-Century Dictionaries," *Language* 22 (1946), pp. 27–41. Sheldon divides early pronunciation guides into three stages: the first, mere indication of stress; the second, stress placed so as to indicate "long" or "short" vowels; and the third, a diacritical system representing the pronunciation of different vowels and consonants. Bailey progressed to stage 2.

20. Some sources cite Bailey's expanded 1731 edition of *An Universal Etymological English Dictionary* as Johnson's source, but James Sledd and Gwin J. Kolb, *Dr. Johnson's Dictionary: Essays in the Biography of a Book* (Chicago: University of Chicago Press, 1955), p. 4, cite this work, as does Mitford M. Mathews, *A Survey of English Dictionaries* (London: Oxford University Press, 1933; rpt. New York: Russell & Russell, 1966), p. 28. Bailey's two dictionaries were closely related and published only a year apart.

21. *SN,* p. 119.

22. *Ibid.,* pp. 146–147.

23. See Sledd and Kolb, pp. 85–104 (especially p. 94), a chapter devoted to a detailed discussion of the *Plan* in its several versions and to Johnson's relationship with Chesterfield.

24. *SN,* pp. 156–157.

25. The number of entries in Johnson's *Dictionary* is variously reported as 41,443 by Harold B. Allen, cited by J. E. Congleton, "Pronunciation in Johnson's *Dictionary,*" in *Papers on Lexicography in Honor of Warren N. Cordell,* ed. J. E. Congleton, J. Edward Gates, and Donald Hobar (Terre Haute, Ind.: DSNA and Indiana State University, 1979), p. 60; as 43,500 entries by Read, "Dictionary," *EB,* p. 715; and as 50,000 entries by Vizetelly, *Development of the Dictionary,* p. 11. Since Allen's count appears to be actual rather than an estimate, I am inclined to take his figure as the most accurate.

26. Robert Ainsworth's *Thesaurus Linguae Latinae Compendiarius* (1736), a Latin–English dictionary often used by Johnson to cite the existence of terms.

27. Sledd and Kolb, pp. 42–43.

28. See Congleton, "Pronunciation in Johnson's *Dictionary*," pp. 59–82, especially p. 73. Congleton credits Johnson with significant innovations in the representation of pronunciation. Sheldon, in her "Pronouncing Systems in Eighteenth-Century Dictionaries," *Language* 22 (1946), takes a contrary view. Sledd and Kolb (p. 34) agree with Sheldon: "Certainly he did not influence the sounds of English, for he did not mark pronunciation."

29. R. W. Chapman, *Lexicography* (London: Oxford University Press, 1948), p. 13.

30. Sledd and Kolb, pp. 134–141.

31. *A Universal and Critical Dictionary of the English Language* (1847), p. lxiv. The allusion is to John Walker. See below, p. 57.

32. Richard Chenevix Trench, *On Some Deficiencies in Our English Dictionaries* (London, 1857). Dean Trench's two talks before the Philological Society, published under this title, are usually credited with providing the key stimulus for formulating plans that led to the development of the *OED*. Trench's specific criticisms and recommendations are discussed below in connection with the *OED*.

33. My chief sources of information on eighteenth-century pronouncing dictionaries are two articles by Esther K. Sheldon: "Pronouncing Systems in Eighteenth-Century Dictionaries," *Language* 22 (1946), pp. 27–41, and "Walker's Influence on the Pronunciation of English," *Publications of the Modern Language Association* (cited hereafter as *PMLA*) 62 (1947), pp. 130–146. I am much indebted to them. However, the opinions expressed unless specifically attributed to others are my own.

34. Sheldon, *PMLA*, p. 146; quoted from a 1928 textbook based on Walker.

35. In the International Phonetic Alphabet (IPA), /ˈdʒuˈrɔr/ for /ˈdʒʊrɚ/.

36. See Richard L. Venezky, "From Webster to Rice to Roosevelt: The Formative Years for Spelling Instruction and Spelling Reform in the U.S.A.," in *Cognitive Processes in Spelling*, ed. Uta Frith (London: Academic Press, 1979), pp. 9–30.

37. "Noah Webster," *The New Columbia Encyclopedia*, ed. William H. Harris and Judith S. Levey (New York: Columbia University Press, 1975), p. 2,948.

38. Joseph H. Friend, *The Development of American Lexicography 1798–1864* (The Hague: Mouton, 1967), p. 15. I am much indebted to this monograph for its detailed analysis of Webster's work and especially for its sensitive description of the conflict between Webster and Worcester, and their publishers.

39. Albert C. Baugh, *A History of the English Language*, second ed. (New York: Appleton-Century-Crofts, 1957), pp. 430–431.

40. Friend, p. 23.

41. Sledd and Kolb, p. 198.

42. Friend, p. 55. The examples cited above are also taken from Friend.

43. *The English Language in America* (New York, 1925), Vol. I, p. 363. Cited in part by Friend, p. 35. After comparing the faults of Webster's dictionary of 1828 with those of Joseph Worcester's *Comprehensive and Explanatory Dictionary* of 1830, Krapp concludes (p. 372) that "the totals are greatly in favor of Worcester.

One must conclude that the success of Webster has been due largely to judicious editing, manufacturing and selling."

44. Friend, p. 85.

45. James R. Hulbert, *Dictionaries: British and Amercian,* rev. ed. (London: Andre Deutsch, 1968), pp. 31–32.

46. Friend, pp. 102–103.

47. The G. & C. Merriam Co. of Springfield, Mass., had bought the Webster interests along with the 1841 edition from an Amherst firm that acquired them from Webster's heirs. Friend, p. 82 n.

48. Springfield, Mass.: G. & C. Merriam, 1934.

49. *Funk & Wagnalls New Standard Dictionary of the English Language* (New York: Funk & Wagnalls, 1913). Adam Willis Wagnalls, Funk's partner, had no role other than a financial one in the company.

50. Sledd and Kolb, p. 183.

51. The characterization of Furnivall is based on K. M. Elisabeth Murray's in *Caught in the Web of Words.* He was apparently both infuriating and charming. Too impatient to be an editor, he was nonetheless a driving force in the early years of the dictionary.

52. *A Supplement to the Oxford English Dictionary,* 4 vols. (Oxford: Clarendon Press, 1972–). Vol. I, A–G, appeared in 1972; Vol. II, H–N, in 1976; and Vol. III, O–Scz, in 1982. Vol. IV is in preparation.

53. *A Dictionary of American English on Historical Principles,* 4 vols. (Chicago: University of Chicago Press, 1936–44).

54. *A Dictionary of Americanisms on Historical Principles,* 2 vols. (Chicago: University of Chicago Press, 1951).

55. "Approaches," p. 153.

56. *The Century Dictionary and Cyclopedia,* 12 vols. (New York: Century Co., 1899–1910).

57. New York: Random House, 1947.

58. The *Thorndike-Century Senior Dictionary* (1941) was the first to use the schwa.

59. Edited by David B. Guralnik and Joseph H. Friend (Cleveland: World, 1953; hereafter *World*). The dictionary has passed through the hands of several publishers. Revised in 1970 and updated regularly, the *Second College Edition,* edited by Guralnik, is published by Simon & Schuster in New York. "Webster's" is not the exclusive trademark of the G. & C. Merriam Co.; any dictionary may be called "Webster's."

60. *The Random House College Dictionary,* ed. Laurence Urdang (New York: Random House, 1968; hereafter *RHCD*). The revised edition of 1975 was edited by Jess Stein.

61. The ninth edition, hereafter *MW9,* was edited by Frederick C. Mish (Springfield, Mass.: Merriam, 1983). The eighth edition, hereafter *MW8,* was edited by Henry Bosley Woolf (Springfield, Mass.: Merriam, 1973). Its predecessor, *Webster's Seventh New Collegiate Dictionary,* edited by Philip Babcock Gove (Springfield, Mass: Merriam, 1963), will be abbreviated *MW7.*

318

62. Personal communication from Robert Barnhart, July 1981.

63. New York: Funk & Wagnalls, 1962.

64. Allen Walker Read reminds us (in his unpublished paper, "An Obscenity Symbol after Four Decades," given at the University of Louisville, Louisville, Ky., May 7, 1976) that *The Penguin English Dictionary*, a British paperback dictionary published in 1965, included an entry for *fuck*. However, this work did not have nearly the popularity of *AHD*. In the United States it was virtually unavailable, and its inclusion of taboo words went unnoticed by the press. It is not likely to have had any appreciable influence on college dictionaries.

65. Boston: Houghton Mifflin, 1982. For comment on the many ways in which this edition differs from the first, see the bibliographic listing on page 334.

CHAPTER THREE　Key Elements of Dictionaries and Other
Language References

1. The term *lemma* (plural *lemmata*) is sometimes used to signify any word or phrase glossed or defined. Zgusta uses *lemma* to refer to both the canonical form and its pronunciation—see *Manual*, pp. 249–251. For my purposes it is better to distinguish between the headword and its pronunciation, and I shall therefore avoid using *lemma*.

2. For a scholarly and entertaining summary of the reform spelling movement in America, see Venezky, "From Webster to Rice to Roosevelt," in *Cognitive Processes in Spelling*, ed. Uta Frith.

3. *Dictionaries: British and American*, p. 49.

4. Samuel E. Martin, "Selection and Presentation of Ready Equivalents in a Translation Dictionary," in *Problems*, p. 157.

5. See Yakov Malkiel, "A Typological Classification of Dictionaries," in *Problems*, p. 9.

6. See Landau, "Of Matters Lexicographical," pp. 241–244.

7. Henry Kučera and W. Nelson Francis, *Computational Analysis of Present-Day American English* (Providence, R.I.: Brown University Press, 1967). See page 280 for a fuller discussion of the Brown Corpus in the context of computer uses in lexicography.

8. Manuila, *Progress in Medical Terminology*, p. 10. As a result of this situation, the *International Nomenclature of Diseases* was initiated in 1968 under the direction of Dr. Manuila to establish a uniform nomenclature of diseases. The effort is sponsored by the Council for International Organizations of Medical Sciences (CIOMS) and funded in part by the World Health Organization, in part by grants from participating governments.

9. These criteria follow Manuila, *Progress*, pp. 19–22.

10. *Dorland's Illustrated Medical Dictionary*, twenty-sixth ed. (Philadelphia: W. B. Saunders, 1981).

11. *Stedman's Medical Dictionary*, twenty-fourth ed. (Baltimore: Williams & Wilkins, 1982).

319

12. See Sidney Landau, "Dictionary Entry Count," *RQ* 4:1 (September 1964), pp. 6, 13–15. So far as I know, this remains the only published account describing in any detail how dictionaries count entries. The U.S. government's General Services Administration's guidelines for government purchases of dictionaries includes some description of entry counting, but it is sketchy and incomplete. (It is Federal Specification G-D-331D, last revised June 28, 1974, and may be obtained by writing the General Services Administration, Inventory Management Branch [WFSI], Specification Section, Room 6039, 7th and D Sts., SW, Washington, DC 20407.) The information was based on the recommendations of commercial lexicographers (including myself) following several hearings in the 1960s, but much of the material was written in 1942.

13. *The Concise Oxford Dictionary,* seventh ed., ed. John Sykes (Oxford: Oxford University Press, 1981).

14. See, for example, the *Thorndike-Barnhart Intermediate Dictionary,* ed. E. L. Thorndike and Clarence L. Barnhart (Glenview, Ill.: Scott, Foresman, 1974). Earlier editions did not identify the definitions to which each part of speech belonged, but merely list the parts of speech.

15. The *Harcourt Brace School Dictionary,* ed. Harrison Gray Platt (New York: Harcourt Brace Jovanovich, 1968). I was the managing editor of this dictionary, which was prepared by the Funk & Wagnalls dictionary staff.

16. Martin, "Selection and Presentation," in *Problems,* p. 157.

17. The phonemic systems used by American dictionaries are based on the pioneering work of George L. Trager and Henry Lee Smith, *An Outline of English Structure,* Studies in Linguistics: Occasional Papers 3 (Washington, D.C.: American Council of Learned Societies, 1957; first ptg. 1951). For a discussion of the phonemic systems based on Trager-Smith, see Arthur Bronstein, *The Pronunciation of American English* (New York: Appleton-Century-Crofts, 1960), pp. 311–316. Bronstein gives an admirably clear description of the articulations of speech sounds in American English.

18. Henry Cecil Wyld, *The Universal Dictionary of the English Language* (London: Routledge & Kegan Paul, 1961; first ptg., 1932). This valuable but somewhat eccentric work is chiefly distinguished by its very full etymologies.

19. *Dictionaries: British and American,* p. 54.

20. A. C. Gimson, "Phonology and the Lexicographer," in *Lexicography in English,* Annals of the New York Academy of Sciences, vol. 211, ed. Raven I. McDavid, Jr., and Audrey R. Duckert (New York: New York Academy of Sciences, 1973), p. 119. The McDavid and Duckert book is a most valuable collection of papers presented at a conference held in New York on June 8, 1973. It will be referred to hereafter as *Lexicography.*

21. "American Lexicography," p. 110, quoting Robert L. Chapman and R. W. Burchfield.

22. These criticisms are made, for example, by Robert L. Chapman, "A Working Lexicographer Appraises *Webster's Third New International Dictionary,*" *American Speech* 42 (1967), pp. 202–210.

23. "A Working Lexicographer," p. 207.

24. "Respelling: Necessity or Boondoggle?" *Papers of the DSNA 1979*, pp. 23–30.

25. The Merriam-Webster pronunciation system must be exempted from this criticism, for it employs the schwa more rigorously as a phonetic symbol in both stressed and unstressed contexts.

26. T. Magay, "Problems of Indicating Pronunciation in Bilingual Dictionaries with English as the Source Language," in *Dictionaries and Their Uses,* Exeter Linguistic Series, vol. 4, ed. R. R. K. Hartmann (Exeter: University of Exeter, 1979), p. 99.

27. *Dictionaries: British and American,* p. 55.

28. *The Origins and Development of the English Language* (New York: Harcourt Brace Jovanovich, 1964), p. 305.

29. *Progress in Medical Terminology,* p. 107.

30. Aug. 30, 1981, p. 12.

31. *SN,* p. 102.

32. Patrick Drysdale, "Dictionary Etymologies: What? Why? and for Whom?", *Papers of the DSNA 1979*, p. 45. See also Louis G. Heller, "Lexicographic Etymology: Practice versus Theory," *American Speech* 40 (1965), pp. 113–119, for examples of the deficiencies of etymologies in current dictionaries.

33. *The Universal Dictionary of the English Language,* p. ix. The passage is quoted verbatim except that where the author has abbreviated language designations I have written them in full. The symbol Þ is an Old English character called the *thorn,* representing the sound of *th,* either voiced or voiceless. The digraph *th* was used in the earliest English texts but was replaced by the thorn from about 900 to 1400. The Old English character *eth* (ð), also used to represent the *th* sound, is used in the IPA to represent the voiced *th,* as in *this.*

34. Walter W. Skeat, *An Etymological Dictionary of the English Language* (Oxford: Clarendon Press, 1961; first ed. 1879–82), p. xxviii. Skeat's dictionary is still of considerable value. The *Oxford Dictionary of English Etymology,* ed. C. T. Onions, *et al.* (New York: Oxford University Press, 1966), is a fine work and naturally more up to date (Onions was one of the *OED*'s editors). Ernest Weekley's *An Etymological Dictionary of Modern English* (1921; rpt. New York: Dover, 1967) and Eric Partridge's *Origins: A Short Etymological Dictionary of Modern English* (New York: Macmillan, 1958) are also of interest. Ernest Klein's *A Comprehensive Etymological Dictionary of the English Language* (Amsterdam: Elsevier, 1971) is another valuable work, especially in its coverage of words of Semitic origin.

35. "American Lexicography," p. 113.

36. From the *Harcourt Brace School Dictionary.*

37. "Dictionary Etymologies," p. 47.

38. *Manual,* pp. 89 ff. These concepts will be discussed at greater length in Chapter Four.

39. *Roget's International Thesaurus,* fourth ed. revised by Robert L. Chapman (New York: Thomas Y. Crowell, 1977), p. ix. It should be noted that several other thesauruses claim to be descended from the original Roget work, and given the

anfractuous publishing history of the work, their claims may have some merit.

40. *Thesauri,* also used as the plural, seems to me both pedantic and un-English. Among the alphabetical thesauruses are *The New Roget's Thesaurus of the English Language in Dictionary Form,* ed. Norman Lewis (New York: Putnam, 1964); *The Doubleday Roget's Thesaurus in Dictionary Form,* ed. Sidney I. Landau and Ronald J. Bogus (New York: Doubleday, 1977); and *Webster's Collegiate Thesaurus,* ed. Mairé Weir Kay (Springfield, Mass.: G. & C. Merriam, 1976).

41. See, for example, Chapman's Foreword to *Roget's International Thesaurus,* fourth ed., p. xv.

42. Kenneth Kister, *Dictionary Buying Guide* (New York: R. R. Bowker, 1977), p. 252.

43. There are, however, exceptions. *The Synonym Finder* (Emmaus, Pa.: Rodale Press, 1961), edited by J. I. Rodale, revised in 1978 by Laurence Urdang and Nancy LaRoche, is alphabetically arranged but extremely inclusive, and in my judgment not very successful for that reason. Inclusivity seems to work better with conceptually arranged works.

44. *Funk & Wagnalls Modern Guide to Synonyms and Related Words* (New York: T. Y. Crowell, 1968). I directed the preparation of this work by the Funk & Wagnalls dictionary staff in cooperation with Hayakawa. *Webster's New Dictionary of Synonyms* (Springfield, Mass.: G. & C. Merriam, 1973).

45. See *Manual,* pp. 294–344, especially pp. 294–297 and 312–325.

46. Robert A. Fowkes, "Preface," *Verbatim* 8:2 (Autumn 1981), pp. 9 and 15. The Preface is that of the reprint edition of *The Century Dictionary* (Detroit: Gale Research, 1982).

47. See, for instance, James R. Hulbert, *Dictionaries: British and American,* and R. W. Chapman, *Lexicography,* pp. 21–24. Hulbert writes, "As to pictures, it is so inane to point out that at a glance a picture makes many subjects . . . clearer than many words can do, that I blush to do so."

48. *Manual,* p. 256.

49. The definition is from *Harcourt.*

50. See *Larousse Illustrated International Encyclopedia and Dictionary* (Cleveland: World, 1972).

CHAPTER FOUR Definition

1. The best modern work on the subject is Richard Robinson's *Definition* (Oxford: Clarendon Press, 1965; first ed. 1954).

2. A. J. Aitken, "Definitions and Citations in a Period Dictionary," in *Lexicography,* p. 259.

3. C. K. Ogden and I. A. Richards, *The Meaning of Meaning* (New York: Harcourt Brace Jovanovich, 1923), p. 11.

4. *Manual,* p. 34.

5. *Ibid.,* pp. 38–39.

6. See David B. Guralnik, "Connotation in Dictionary Definition," *College Composition and Communication* 9:2 (May 1958), pp. 90–93. Dictionaries do attempt to recognize connotation if it is widely understood by users of the language, as Guralnik shows, by incorporating it in the definition or by adding a usage note or label.

7. *Manual,* pp. 257–258.

8. "Repetition in Defining," in *The Role of the Dictionary,* ed. Philip B. Gove (Indianapolis: Bobbs-Merrill, 1957), pp. 9–14.

9. *Ibid.,* p. 10.

10. *Ibid.*

11. The *OED*'s most recent citation for this sense of *occupancy* is from 1843.

12. "Repetition," p. 12. The original reference to truncated definition appears on p. 11.

13. Patrick Hanks, "To What Extent Does a Dictionary Definition Define?" in *Dictionaries and Their Uses,* ed. R. R. K. Hartmann, p. 36.

14. See Landau, "Of Matters Lexicographical," pp. 241–244, especially p. 243. See also Sidney I. Landau, "Popular Meanings of Scientific and Technical Terms," *American Speech* 55:3 (Fall 1980), pp. 204–209. The point is also addressed in Kemp Malone's "On Defining mahogany," discussed below on page 163.

15. Landau, "Of Matters Lexicographical," p. 242. Robinson uses the terms *lexical* and *stipulative definitions* for my *extracted* and *imposed definitions,* respectively. His discussion of stipulative definitions is full of keen insights into the nature of scientific definition. See his *Definition,* pp. 59–92, especially pp. 66–80 on the advantages and disadvantages of this kind of definition.

16. *Ibid.,* p. 241.

17. "American Lexicography," p. 124.

18. *Confessions,* trans, R. S. Pine-Coffin (Harmondsworth, Middx.: Penguin Books, 1961), p. 264.

19. *Definition,* p. 124.

20. The *OED Supplements,* it should be noted, devote considerably more attention to scientific terminology than does the *OED.*

21. *Definition,* p. 56.

22. Manuila, *Progress,* pp. 110–112.

23. *Butterworths Medical Dictionary,* second ed., ed. Macdonald Critchley (London: Butterworths, 1978).

24. *Blakiston's Gould Medical Dictionary,* fourth ed. (New York: McGraw-Hill, 1979).

25. "Definition: Practice and Illustration," in *Lexicography,* p. 256.

26. After *Manual,* p. 48.

27. Laurence Urdang writes, "Citations for names of ostensive objects, e.g., *apple, dog, microbe,* are worthless for defining purposes, though they may provide vital evidence for the existence of a term"—"The Art and Technique of Citation Reading," *Verbatim* 2:1 (May 1975), p. 5. Certainly such citations are rarely used for defining, but whether they *should* be used to provide definitions in addition to their imposed technical definitions is another matter.

28. "Problems in Editing Commercial and Monolingual Dictionaries," in *Problems*, p. 167.

29. "Approaches," p. 171.

30. It also has consequences for the way we perceive reality, for in slicing up meaning one is implicitly expressing a view of reality. The unanswered question is, Which comes first? To what extent does the way we slice up meaning influence the way we perceive the world? The interaction between language and reality has been most notably analyzed by Benjamin Lee Whorf in a series of essays, written in the late 1930s and early 1940s, based on his studies of Indian languages of the Americas. See especially *Language, Thought, and Reality* (Cambridge, Mass.: M.I.T. Press, 1956).

31. "Definition," *Lexicography*, p. 257.

32. "American Lexicography," p. 99.

33. "The Art and Technique of Citation Reading," p. 5.

34. *Manual*, p. 46.

35. "On Defining mahogany," *Language* 16:4 (1940), pp. 308–318. The quotation is from p. 312.

36. *Ibid.*, p. 313.

37. *Manual*, p. 265.

38. See Gwin J. Kolb and Ruth A. Kolb, "The Selection and Use of the Illustrative Quotations in Dr. Johnson's *Dictionary*," in *New Aspects of Lexicography* (Carbondale, Ill.: Southern Illinois University Press, 1972), ed. Howard D. Weinbrot, pp. 61–72.

39. R. W. Chapman, *Lexicography*, p. 28.

40. *Times Literary Supplement*, October 22, 1976, p. 1,336.

41. *Ibid.*, December 3, 1976, p. 1,516.

42. *Ibid.*, January 7, 1977, p. 13.

43. Allusive meaning is particularly susceptible to the kind of analysis employed by B. F. Skinner in *Verbal Behavior* (Englewood Cliffs, N.J.: Prentice-Hall, 1957). Words like *Watergate* are used to elicit a certain response, and if speaker and listener are both of a certain age and social class, the probability of a given response, which is as calculable as that of pigeons, will be high. In the United States, the name of whoever happens to be president has always had strong allusive meanings of this kind.

44. *Teapot Dome* has been cut from the A–Z section of *AHD2* and inserted as a straight geographical entry in the back matter without any clue to its former lexical importance. The unsuspecting reader might well wonder why a "Former naval oil reserve site in E central Wyo., N of Casper" merits inclusion.

CHAPTER FIVE   Usage

1. N. E. Osselton, "Some Problems of Obsolescence in Bilingual Dictionaries," *Dictionaries and Their Uses*, ed. R. R. K. Hartmann, pp. 120–126.

2. *Ibid.*, p. 123.

3. Harold B. Allen, "Introductory Remarks," *Lexicography,* p. 50.

4. Randolph Quirk, Sidney Greenbaum, Geoffrey Leech, and Jan Svartvik, *A Grammar of Contemporary English* (London: Longman, 1972), p. 15.

5. Audrey Duckert, "Regional and Social Dialects," in *Lexicography,* p. 51.

6. Hans Kurath was the editor of *Word Geography;* Kurath, succeeded by Raven I. McDavid, Jr., of *Atlantic States;* and Harold B. Allen of the *Upper Midwest.* Several other regional atlases, such as those of the southeast and middle Atlantic states, are also under way. For two recent surveys of work in regional dialectology, see Harold B. Allen, "Regional Dialects, 1945–1974," *American Speech* 52:3–4 (Fall–Winter 1977), pp. 163–261, and Lawrence M. Davis, *English Dialectology: An Introduction* (University, Ala.: University of Alabama Press, 1983), pp. 16–68.

7. Allen Walker Read, "An Obscenity Symbol," *American Speech* 9:4 (December 1934), pp. 264–278.

8. Sidney I. Landau, *"sexual intercourse* in American College Dictionaries," *Verbatim* 1:1 (n.d., issued July 1974), p. 4.

9. *Ibid.,* pp. 4–5.

10. Edited by Edwin B. Williams (New York: Charles Scribner's Sons, 1977).

11. Edited by Eugene Ehrlich, Stuart Berg Flexner, Gorton Carruth, and Joyce Hawkins (New York: Oxford University Press, 1980).

12. This caveat does not diminish the great importance of Read's paper, which was one of the first serious, scholarly efforts in modern times to address the issue of linguistic taboo in English. Moreover, the paper was written half a century ago and his views may well have changed. On May 7, 1976, Read presented a paper entitled "An Obscenity Symbol After Four Decades," at the University of Louisville, Kentucky, but did not touch upon the issues I have discussed.

13. Edward B. Jenkinson, "How to Keep Dictionaries out of the Public Schools," *Verbatim* 5:4 (Spring 1979), p. 12.

14. For example: "The American Heritage Dictionary was removed from school libraries and classrooms in Eldon, Mo., because of objectionable definitions it offered for such words as 'bed,' 'tail,' and 'nut'" (*New York Times,* April 5, 1982, p. C-11).

15. For example, Julia Stanley reported in "Homosexual Slang," *American Speech* 45:1–2 (Spring/Summer 1970), pp. 45–59, that "Of these four terms [*queer, fairy, faggot,* and *swish*], *queer* was cited by homosexuals as the one that has the strongest connotations of distaste or disgust," and that the word was considered "the worst that could be used." Yet until 1978 no dictionary other than *Doubleday* labeled it as contemptuous or offensive in this sense. Apart from the Longman dictionaries, it is still unlabeled.

16. *Booklist* 73:8 (May 15, 1977), p. 1,455.

17. See Sidney I. Landau, "The Egalitarian Spirit and Attitudes Toward Usage," *American Speech* 54:1 (Spring 1979), pp. 3–11.

18. A personal interview in Oxford on April 19, 1982, with Robert Burchfield, editor of the *OED Supplements,* confirmed that this was the method used by the *Supplement* editors.

19. Jonathan Lighter, "Some Problems of Documentation in Slang Dictionaries," unpublished paper presented at the American Dialect Society meeting in New York City in December 1981, p. 4. It was slightly altered by the author in a personal communication, January 1983. Used with permission.

20. James B. McMillan, "Five College Dictionaries," *College English* 10:4 (January 1949), pp. 214–221.

21. Thomas J. Creswell, *Usage in Dictionaries and Dictionaries of Usage,* Publication of the American Dialect Society, nos. 63–64 (University, Ala.: University of Alabama Press, 1975), p. 85.

22. "Some Problems . . ." Lighter cites entries such as *ABC's, AWOL,* spelling pronunciations like *az iz* (for *as is*), and journalistic inventions such as *circuit clout* (for *home run*), as examples of types of nonslang terms found in slang dictionaries. Terms of insult and taboo also appear in slang dictionaries, as already noted.

23. John S. Kenyon, "Cultural Levels and Functional Varieties of English," *College English* 10:1 (October 1948), pp. 31–36.

24. Martin Joos, *The Five Clocks* (New York: Harcourt Brace Jovanovich, 1967; first ed. 1961). The quotation is from p. 7.

25. *A Dictionary of Contemporary American Usage* (New York: Random House, 1957), p. vii.

26. Joos, p. 32.

27. "Lexicography and the Teacher of English," *College English* 25:5 (February 1964), p. 350.

28. Karl Dykema, "Historical Development of the Concept of Grammatical Proprieties," in *Readings in Applied English Linguistics,* ed. Harold B. Allen (New York: Appleton-Century-Crofts, 1958), pp. 2–9.

29. Robert C. Pooley, *The Teaching of English Usage,* second ed. (Urbana, Ill.: National Council of Teachers of English, 1974), p. 8.

30. Quoted in *SN,* p. 55. An obelisk is a symbol more commonly known today as a dagger (†). See also Virginia McDavid, "Dictionary Labels for Usage Levels and Dialects," in *Papers on Lexicography in Honor of Warren N. Cordell,* ed. J. E. Congleton, J. Edward Gates, and Donald Hobar (Terre Haute, Ind.: DSNA and Indiana State University, 1979), pp. 29–30.

31. I am indebted to Edward Finegan's *Attitudes Toward English Usage* (New York: Teachers College, Columbia University, 1980), pp. 18–61, for this discussion of early English and American grammars. See also Dennis E. Baron, *Grammar and Good Taste* (New Haven: Yale University Press, 1982), pp. 119–168, for a survey of English grammars of the seventeenth to nineteenth centuries. Baron discusses usage guides from the seventeenth century to the present as well (pp. 169–241).

32. Quoted by Finegan, pp. 47 and 51, the first example from Murray and the second from Samuel Kirkham.

33. Goold Brown, *The Grammar of English Grammars,* p. 271 (1875 ed.).

34. *AHD,* first ed., p. xxiii.

35. Thomas Pyles, "Dictionaries and Usage," in *Thomas Pyles: Selected Essays on English Usage*, ed. John Algeo (Gainesville, Fla.: University Presses of Florida, 1979), p. 200.

36. *AHD*, Morris Bishop, first ed., p. xxiv.

37. *AHD2*, p. 33. For an exhaustive survey of this tendency in America, see Allen Walker Read, "American Projects for an Academy to Regulate Speech," *PMLA* 51:4 (December 1936), pp. 1,141–1,179. See also Baron, pp. 99–118.

38. *Facts About Current English Usage* (New York: Appleton-Century-Crofts, 1938), p. 59.

39. Charles C. Fries, *American English Grammar* (New York: Appleton-Century-Crofts, 1940).

40. Randolph Quirk, *The Use of English*, second ed. (London: Longman, 1968), p. 87. Quirk makes the astute observation that although most of us remain unfamiliar with the sounds of our own voices and are often surprised when we hear ourselves on recordings, we know our handwriting very well (p. 90). Our consciousness of writing makes it much easier to use spelling as a standard than speech.

41. William Labov, *The Social Stratification of English in New York City* (Washington, D.C.: Center for Applied Linguistics, 1966). For a detailed description of *Social Stratification* and a critique of Labov's work, see Davis, *English Dialectology*, pp. 87–100, part of a survey of social dialectology, pp. 69–132.

42. *Ibid.*, p. 476.

43. *Ibid.*, p. 478.

44. *The Teaching of English Usage*, p. 12. The definition first appeared in Pooley's *Grammar and Usage in Textbooks on English* (1933).

45. See, for example, *Dictionaries and THAT Dictionary*, ed. James Sledd and Wilma R. Ebbitt (Chicago: Scott, Foresman, 1962).

46. "Lexicography and the Teacher of English," p. 350.

47. A typical use of *nauseous* to mean "affected by nausea" from the *New York Times* (April 4, 1982, p. 15): "In addition to oral presentations, the group was shown a film, 'Hiroshima-Nagasaki 1945,' whose explicit depiction of the effect of the first atomic bombs left many in the audience feeling stunned and nauseous." Note that the level of writing and subject matter are anything but casual.

48. Dwight Bollinger, *Language—The Loaded Weapon* (London: Longman, 1980), p. 168.

49. *The Teaching of English Usage*, p. 16.

50. Usage guidance in the eighteenth century was "for the edification and use of gentlemen, to warn them against inadvertent contamination with the language of the vulgar"—Sterling Leonard, *The Doctrine of Correctness in English Usage 1700–1800*, p. 169.

51. On the other hand, I agree with those who criticized *NID3* for not applying the "slang" label more liberally.

52. William Labov, *The Study of Nonstandard English* (Champaign, Ill.: NCTE, 1970), p. 22. Originally published in 1969 by the Center for Applied Linguistics.

53. *The Five Clocks,* p. 8.

54. Richard Allsopp addresses these issues with insight in "The Need for Socio-linguistic Determinants for Status-Labelling in a Regional Lexicography," in *Papers of the DSNA 1977,* ed. Donald Hobar (Terre Haute, Ind.: Indiana State University, 1982), pp. 64–77. Although his particular concern is Caribbean English, his analysis of status labeling is pertinent. Status labeling, he says, is "inevitably elitist" and "assignment to levels within it will be class-intuitive. . . ." Moreover, the homogeneity and stability in language implied by such labeling was probably never justified and certainly is not justified today. The effect on language of sociopolitical changes since the Victorian period has been to emphasize *"social appropriateness of discourse style as the basis of acceptability"* (p. 71, author's italics).

55. J. L. Burton, "The Logic of Dermatological Diagnosis," *Clinical and Experimental Dermatology* 6 (1981), p. 3.

56. The methodology used by *DARE,* described on pages 178 and 221–225, has identified distinctively black usages and could be applied to a wider survey of black speakers. See Jeffrey Hirshberg, "Towards a Dictionary of Black American English on Historical Principles," *American Speech* 57:3 (Fall 1982), pp. 163–182, which describes *DARE*'s method and cites fifty *DARE* vocabulary entries used especially by blacks. J. L. Dillard's *Lexicon of Black English* (New York: Continuum Books, 1977), in spite of its title is not a lexicon but a discussion of a number of terms presumed to be distinctive of Black English. See Hirshberg's review in *American Speech* 57:1 (Spring 1982), pp. 52–73, which includes an index to the terms discussed in Dillard's book.

57. Margaret Nicholson's *A Dictionary of American English Usage* (1957) was based on Fowler's work, of which a second edition revised by Sir Ernest Gowers appeared in 1965.

58. See, for example, Creswell's analysis of *AHD*'s usage notes in *Usage in Dictionaries and Dictionaries of Usage,* especially appendix 5, pp. 193–195.

59. "Grammatical Usage: Modern Shibboleths," in *James B. McMillan: Essays in Linguistics by His Friends and Colleagues,* ed. James C. Raymond and I. Willis Russell (University, Ala.: University of Alabama Press, 1977), p. 70.

60. Wilson Follett, *Modern American Usage,* edited and completed by Jacques Barzun (New York: Hill & Wang, 1966), p. 6.

61. William Morris and Mary Morris, *Harper Dictionary of Contemporary Usage* (New York: Harper & Row, 1975), pp. xiii–xiv.

62. Richard A. Lanham, "The Abusage of Usage," *Virginia Quarterly Review* 53:1 (Winter 1977), pp. 47–48.

63. Sutherland's review appeared in the *Times Literary Supplement* of October 23, 1981; the subsequent comment in that of November 13, 1981.

64. Bergen Evans and Cornelia Evans, *A Dictionary of Contemporary American Usage,* p. v.

65. Margaret Bryant, *Current American Usage* (New York: Funk & Wagnalls, 1962), p. xxii.

66. In *American English Grammar,* one of Fries's criteria for placing an informant in Group III (uneducated usage) was lack of end punctuation, the error that used to be called in freshman English papers a "run-on" sentence. If we judge a sentence to be a written statement ending with a period, uneducated writing will have, on the average, longer sentences than educated writing. Whether the same situation obtains regarding formal and informal writing is not known.

67. John Algeo, "Grammatical Usage: Modern Shibboleths," p. 70. *The Careful Writer* (New York: Atheneum, 1965); *A Dictionary of Usage and Style* (New York: Hawthorn Books, 1964); *Success With Words: A Guide to the American Language,* prepared in association with Peter Davies; David Rattray, project editor (Pleasantville, N.Y.: The Reader's Digest Association, 1983). Not just a usage book, *Success With Words* attempts to be a jack of all trades, with articles on dialect, literary subjects, special lexicons, and etymology as well as on usage questions. Its approach to dialectal variation is objective and tolerant, demonstrating an awareness of recent research and a willingness to go into detail that is surprising and even courageous in a popularization for the mass market. Best of all, it includes numerous citations illustrating different usages, but the usage recommendations themselves are generally timid reaffirmations of traditional prescriptive doctrine. We should nonetheless be grateful for the citations and the down-to-earth tone in which the usage advice is given. It lacks completely the sense of moral superiority characteristic of many traditional guides.

68. *American Usage and Style: The Consensus* (New York: Van Nostrand Reinhold, 1980).

69. Randolph Quirk, *The Use of English,* p. 39.

70. Quoted in Pooley, *The Teaching of English Usage,* p. 22.

71. See Sidney I. Landau, "*Little Boy* and *Little Girl,*" *American Speech* 45:3–4 (Fall–Winter 1970), p. 202, for a discussion of these usages, with illustrative citations.

72. See Jeffrey Hirshberg, "Computers in Lexicography: A Preview of the *Dictionary of American Regional English,*" in *Papers of the DSNA 1977,* p. 43. See also Frederic G. Cassidy, "Computer Mapping of Lexical Variants for *DARE,*" in *Theory and Method in Lexicography,* ed. Ladislav Zgusta (Columbia, S.C.: Hornbeam Press, 1980), pp. 147–160.

73. These examples are cited in Hirshberg, "Computers in Lexicography," p. 43.

74. Private communication from Frederic G. Cassidy, November 11, 1982.

75. See Jeffrey Hirshberg, "Spoken Usage, Status Labels, and *DARE,*" in *Papers of the DSNA 1979,* ed. B. Gillian Mitchell (London, Ont.: School of Library and Information Science, University of Western Ontario, 1981), pp. 109–131, especially pp. 118 and 122. The use of figures 11–12 was suggested by Hirshberg's discussion of them in this paper.

76. See *Lexicography,* pp. 302–317, especially Clarence L. Barnhart, "Plan for a Central Archive for Lexicography in English," pp. 302–306; and Robert L. Chapman, "On Collecting for the Central Archive," pp. 307–311.

CHAPTER SIX   Dictionary Making

1. *Dictionaries: British and American*, pp. 47–48.

2. *Manual*, p. 348.

3. *Ibid.*

4. Sidney I. Landau, "The Making of a Dictionary: Craft versus Commerce," *Booklist* 77:6 (November 15, 1980), pp. 481–482.

5. David B. Guralnik, *The Making of a New Dictionary* (Cleveland: World Publishing Co., 1953), p. 11.

6. Landau, "The Making of a Dictionary," p. 482.

7. "Definition: Practice and Illustration," *Lexicography*, p. 253.

8. "To What Extent Does a Dictionary Definition Define?" in *Dictionaries and Their Uses*, ed. R. R. K. Hartmann, p. 37.

9. "Definition: Practice and Illustration," p. 253.

10. "Problems in Editing Commercial Monolingual Dictionaries," in *Problems*, pp. 162ff.

11. *Ibid.*, p. 165.

12. My analysis is based in part on *Manual*, pp. 144–151. Zgusta lists a number of criteria but fails to mention stress pattern.

13. The best description of the sound pattern of compounds can be found in the celebrated work of Leonard Bloomfield, *Language* (New York: Holt, 1933), Ch. 14, pp. 227ff. Exactly what constitutes a compound is a vexed question in linguistics but one not germane to the present purpose.

14. I am most grateful to Robert K. Barnhart for permission to print Thorndike's system. It has been known informally and used by me and probably by other dictionary editors (apart from the Barnharts) for many years, but it has not been published.

15. *Chambers Twentieth Century Dictionary*, ed. A. M. Macdonald (Edinburgh: Chambers, 1972; Supplement, 1977). All dictionaries, American and British, necessarily run in idioms. The distinction being made here is chiefly in the handling of compounds and derivatives.

16. *New York Times Everyday Dictionary*, ed. Thomas M. Paikeday (New York: Times Books, 1982).

17. "Problems in Editing Commercial Monolingual Dictionaries," in *Problems*, p. 162.

18. Alexandre Manuila, ed. *Progress in Medical Terminology* (Basel: S. Karger, 1981), pp. 55–57. Reprinted by permission.

19. Personal interview with Robert Burchfield, April 19, 1982.

20. *The Development of the Dictionary of the English Language*, p. 38.

21. See, for instance, the *Macmillan Dictionary for Children*, ed. Christopher G. Morris (New York: Macmillan, 1977).

22. Unfortunately, there is no consensus of usage regarding the terms *revision* and *updating; revision* is often used to mean what I call an updating. To complicate matters further, some dictionaries list new *printings*, which may be the verbatim

reissue of the previous printing or include a few minor emendations. A new printing, of course, does not imply a new copyright.

CHAPTER SEVEN   Computer Use and the Future of Dictionary Making

1. *Longman Dictionary of Scientific Usage* (Burnt Mill, Harlow, Essex: Longman, 1979).

2. *Longman Lexicon of Contemporary English,* ed. Tom McArthur (Burnt Mill, Harlow, Essex: Longman, 1981).

3. The Stanford *Computer Archive of Language Materials* (CALM) was a step in this direction but seems to have run out of funding. See Donald Sherman, "A Computer Archive of Machine-Readable Dictionaries," in *Papers of the DSNA 1979,* ed. Gillian B. Mitchell, pp. 133-147. See also Sherman's "Retrieving Lexicographic Citations from a Computer Archive of Language Materials," in *Dictionaries and Their Uses,* ed. R. R. K. Hartmann, pp. 136-142. The Writer's Workbench Project under way at Bell Laboratories is a promising development in this area.

4. See Donna I. Arnold, "College-Level Dictionaries and Freshman Composition," *Dictionaries* 2-3 (1980-81), pp. 69-79. The quotation is from p. 71.

5. "Computer Application in Lexicography," *Lexicography,* p. 290.

6. Letter to Ronald A. Wells, quoted in Ronald A. Wells, *Dictionaries and the Authoritarian Tradition* (The Hague: Mouton, 1973), p. 119 n. For one approach to this issue in connection with tabulating word frequencies, see Laurence Urdang, "An 'Unabridged' Word-Frequency-Count of American English," *Word* 22 (1966), pp. 294-302.

7. See "France's Word Hoard," a review of Vol. I of the *Trésor,* edited by Paul Imbs, the original editor, in the *Times Literary Supplement,* October 13, 1972, pp. 1,229-1,230.

8. Thomas Paikeday, Baltimore *Morning Sun,* August 8, 1982, p. 2.

9. Personal interview, April 19, 1982.

10. Sidney I. Landau, "Computer Use in Medical Lexicography: IDMB," in *Papers of the DSNA 1981,* ed. Yeatman Anderson III (Terre Haute, Ind.: DSNA and Indiana State University, 1983), p. 64.

11. See Angus Cameron and Antonette diPaolo Healey, "The Dictionary of Old English," *Dictionaries* 1 (1979), pp. 87-96. For a description of the computer program, see Richard L. Venezky, "Computational Aids to Dictionary Compilation," *A Plan for the Dictionary of Old English* (Toronto, University of Toronto Press, 1973), pp. 307-327. For a recent bibliography on the general subject of dictionaries and computer use, see "Computer Applications in Lexicography," ed. Barbara Ann Kipfer, in *Dictionaries* 4 (1982), pp. 202-237.

12. See, for example, Robert A. Amsler and John S. White, *Development of a Computational Methodology for Deriving Natural Language Semantic Structures via Analysis of Machine-Readable Dictionaries* (Austin, Tex.: Linguistic Research Center, University of Texas, 1979).

13. For a summary of computer-generated dictionaries, now somewhat dated, and a description of how computers can help bilingual lexicography, see Harry H. Josselson, "Automation of Lexicography," *Cahiers de Lexicologie* Vol. 9 (1966), pp. 73–87.

14. This would have the great advantage of amalgamating the *OED Supplements* with the *OED* proper. Theoretically it would also enable the user to see those citations for each term that had to be suppressed from the printed volumes for lack of space. In other developments, Wang Laboratories, Inc. has acquired the electronic publishing rights to *RHD, COD,* and several thesauruses, foreign-language dictionaries, and technical dictionaries. Dictronics Publishing, a subsidiary of Wang, produces software to translate reference works into machine-readable form. Houghton Mifflin, publisher of *AHD,* markets its own dictionary database in various forms. It remains to be seen whether such services will be widely used or profitable, either to database distributors or to publishers, but they obviously do have certain advantages, such as frequent updatings and the addition of new citations, that make them very attractive, especially in the case of very large, historical, citational dictionaries such as the *OED.*

CHAPTER EIGHT   A Miscellany

1. Neville March Hunnings, *Times Literary Supplement,* April 15, 1983, p. 379. See also the issue of April 29, 1983, p. 433, for further comment, including that of Burchfield.

2. But not always. I know of one prominent lexicographer who has consistently disdained sports and deliberately omitted or given short shrift to sports terms in his dictionaries. He justifies his policy on the grounds that sports are unimportant and that the space is better used for other kinds of information.

3. Robert L. Chapman, "Dictionary Reviews and Reviewing: 1900–1975," in *James B. McMillan: Essays in Linguistics by his Friends and Colleagues,* ed. James C. Raymond and I. Willis Russell, pp. 143–162. The quotation is from p. 144.

4. "Five College Dictionaries," *College English* 10:4 (January 1949), pp. 214–221. James B. McMillan reviewed the *American College Dictionary,* the *Funk & Wagnalls New College Standard Dictionary, Macmillan's Modern Dictionary,* Merriam's *Webster's Collegiate Dictionary (MW5),* and the *Winston Dictionary, College Edition.*

5. See especially Barnhart, "American Lexicography," pp. 122–124.

6. Kenneth Kister, *Dictionary Buying Guide* (New York: R. R. Bowker, 1977), p. xix. Nonetheless, Kister's book is on the whole well informed and fair.

7. R. L. Chapman, "Dictionary Reviews and Reviewing," p. 158.

8. Ann Ediger Baehr, "An Evaluation of the 1952 and 1962 Editions of the *Thorndike-Barnhart Beginning Dictionary,*" *Elementary English* 41:4 (April 1964), pp. 413–419.

9. *Ibid.,* p. 416.

A Critical Bibliography of Selected Monolingual Dictionaries

It is not my purpose here to provide a comprehensive listing but merely to list those works that in my view are the major monolingual dictionaries in some of the fields discussed in this book. Dictionary publishers often find it expedient to publish the same work in different formats under different titles, and I have not attempted to list all such titles. This list is arranged by the title under which each book is generally known in the trade market. I have excluded children's dictionaries, since these are discussed in various parts of the text. For a discussion of usage books, see page 211. For a discussion of synonym books and thesauruses, see page 104. There are a number of excellent linguistic bibliographies that include listings of dictionaries, notably Harold B. Allen's *Linguistics and English Linguistics,* second edition (Arlington Heights, Ill.: AHM Publishing Corp., 1977). For the American dictionary market in particular, Kenneth Kister's *Dictionary Buying Guide* is most useful.

The American College Dictionary

Clarence L. Barnhart, ed. New York: Random House, 1947.
A landmark in American lexicography (see pages 72–73), the *ACD* was the first modern desk dictionary to challenge the Merriam-Webster line of dictionaries for the college market and, if imitation is the sincerest form of flattery, it has been much praised. It is now superseded by the *Random House College Dictionary.*

333

The American Heritage Dictionary of the English Language

William Morris, ed. Boston: Houghton Mifflin, 1979; original ed., 1969. (The comments applying to the first edition were written before the second edition was published. See below for comment on the second edition of 1982.)

One of the most successful recent entries in the competition for the college dictionary market. It is a good dictionary, but its definitions are not quite on a par with those of *MW8*, *RHCD*, and *World*. Its original, large-sized edition was far more attractive than any of the others, but in reduced format it is no easier to read and the pictures that so successfully adorned the large-sized edition seem rather less imposing in the smaller one. For those who like pictures, however, *AHD* will remain superior, since it has far more than any other college dictionary. Its etymologies are distinguished, and its back-matter section on Indo-European roots appeals to scholars and is an awesome document to the lay reader—like a microscopically inscribed "24k" on the inside of a yellow ring—but of questionable use for most readers. Conceived as a response to the supposed permissiveness of *NID3*, *AHD* (originally planned as an unabridged dictionary, but whittled down to size by reality) sought to restore authority as the guide to correct usage and installed a panel of experts to which it addressed questions about divided usage. Their answers were recorded by percentages for and against, as if voting for candidates for public office, and some of their comments were quoted. The composition of the panel of experts, the methods by which their opinions were solicited, and the choice of questions themselves have all been criticized. See especially Thomas J. Creswell, *Usage in Dictionaries and Dictionaries of Usage*. The commonest complaint was that the usage panel was composed mainly of older, conservative people, many of whom were known to have been critical of *NID3*. *AHD*'s usage panel received a great deal of publicity, which promoted the dictionary's sales, but it is really of marginal importance to the dictionary's chief functions. It does a dictionary publisher no harm to flatter eminent people in the worlds of letters and public communication—exactly those who might be called upon to review it—by inviting them to consider themselves authorities on good usage. As Anthony Wolk asked: "I wonder if the editors and columnists for *Harper's, Saturday Review, The New York Times, Atlantic Monthly, The New Yorker*, were likely to be a little less critical of the AHD after being invited to join its Usage Panel?" ["Linguistic and Social Bias in *The American Heritage Dictionary*," *College English* 33:8 (May 1972), p. 932.]

The American Heritage Dictionary: Second College Edition

Boston: Houghton Mifflin, 1982. No editor-in-chief is listed. Margery S. Berube is listed as Director of Editorial Operations, Pamela B. DeVinne as Project Editor. The staff of the first edition, with the single exception of William Morris, who is acknowledged in the Introduction, is not even mentioned. One would think that at least the editor-in-chief succeeding Morris, Peter Davies, and the managing editor, Norman Hoss, deserved mention.

The major changes in the second edition have been to add *College* to the title and to drop the much-praised back-matter section on Indo-European roots along with all the references to it in the A–Z section etymologies. Whereas the first edition had no abbreviations in its etymologies, the second has the usual complement (not "a few" as the Introduction states on page 7, but 125 different abbreviations by actual count).

AHD2 adopts several questionable marketing practices. It abandons the entry count war, which is all to the good, but substitutes the claim of having 200,000 "definitions," which is worse than the entry sweepstakes. The number 200,000, which most people will take to mean entries or even headwords, places *AHD2* well above its college dictionary competitors who base their numbers on entries. Further, the Introduction and jacket copy allude to *AHD2*'s ordering of definitions by currency rather than chronology as a "departure from traditional lexicography" and claim that the practice "is unique to *The American Heritage Dictionary. . . .*" (p. 6) This is false. The Funk & Wagnalls *Standard Dictionary* of 1893 initiated the practice, which was adopted by all the Funk & Wagnalls dictionaries. It was an innovation that Frank Vizetelly attributed to Isaac Funk, the *Standard*'s editor: "[The *Standard*'s] definitions were to be definitions of the day, and radical change was to be made in the order of these. Order of usage was to supersede the old-time chronological order. . . ." (*The Development of the Dictionary of the English Language*, p. 22). Moreover, the practice has been adopted by a number of other dictionaries since, notably by the *ACD* (1947), which used the Thorndike-Lorge word list "to determine with some certainty which are the common meanings and to put them first" (page xix). Its successor, *RHCD*, still employs this practice, as the anonymous Introduction writer of *AHD2* must surely have been aware. *AHD2*, being of slightly smaller trim size even than the reduced version of the first edition, has less text on each page, hence the need to shorten etymologies and probably definitions as well, especially since fifteen thousand new words and senses are said to have been added. (Fully a third of them are scientific and technical.) Compare, for example, the etymologies for *guild* and *guile:*

	AHD (1969)	*AHD2* (1982)
guild	Middle English *gilde,* from Old Norse *gildi,* payment, fraternity, contribution. See *ghelt-* in Appendix.	ME < ON *gildi.*
guile	Middle English *gile,* from Old French *guile,* from Germanic, akin to Old English *wigle,* divination, sorcery. See *weik-* in Appendix.	ME < OFr., of Germanic orig.

Apart from the omission of the appendix references and the introduction of abbreviations and symbols—which are certainly defensible—the etymologies are shortened in substance. All biographical and geographical entries have been lifted from the A–Z section, greatly expanded in number, and placed in four-column, illustrated sections in the back matter along with other encyclopedic material. This is a sensible way to save space and make updating easier. We must presume that the addition of *College* to this edition's title is an admission that Houghton Mifflin's marketing experts believe that "college" still sells dictionaries. The emphasis on pictorial illustration has not been changed.

The Barnhart Dictionary of New English Since 1963

Clarence L. Barnhart, Sol Steinmetz, and Robert K. Barnhart, eds. Bronxville, New York: Barnhart/Harper & Row, 1973.

In keeping with a very old tradition in English lexicography, this work and *The Second Barnhart Dictionary of New English* (1980) are "new word" dictionaries, consisting ostensibly of words that first became current in English in the periods 1963–1972 and 1973–1980, respectively. It took considerable courage to publish these works, which are well produced and with very full illustrative quotations. (In fact, I question whether they need be as extensive as they often are.) Everyone in dictionary work is in the authors' debt for making so much original material based on the Barnhart citation file widely available. However, it has been pointed out that a number of terms included, especially in the first volume, originated much earlier than 1963. The problem is particularly apparent in connection with scientific and technical terms, which both volumes include in abundance. The editors would maintain that they have only recently become current in nontechnical sources, but the distinction between a technical and nontechnical source is not easily made. The criterion seems to be that whenever a report of scientific research is picked up by the organs by popular abridgment, chiefly *Science News* in the United States and *New Scientist* in Britain, it is current in the general lexicon. But surely this accords such journals far too much influence. Many of their subscribers *are* scientists, and the extent of their circulations does not justify the conclusion that they reach a broad spectrum of the public.

Apart from the disproportionate emphasis on scientific and technical terminology, both volumes are commendably rich in genuine neologisms unreported by existing dictionaries. The definitions are excellent, and much peripheral linguistic information for the general reader has been added, all of it soundly based on the Barnhart citation files.

The Century Dictionary and Cyclopedia

Twelve vols. William Dwight Whitney, ed. New York: Century, 1899–1910.

The finest American historical dictionary, distinguished by its handsome design and the quality of its paper and printing. Unlike the *OED*, with which it was contemporary, it devoted considerable space to encyclopedic entries. The quality of the editing and selection of quotations is very high, and though the *Century* is now seldom used, it remains one of the most impressive achievements in American lexicography (see page 72).

Chambers Twentieth Century Dictionary

A. M. Macdonald, ed. Edinburgh: W. & R. Chambers, 1972; with Supplement, 1977.

Chambers is a venerable and conservative publisher of dictionaries, now ably edited by Elizabeth Kirkpatrick. This book employs a simplified, phonemic pronunciation system (unusual among British dictionaries) and retains the style in which different meanings and derivatives are clustered in a single paragraph without the use of numeric division of senses. This packs a great deal of information on every page. Chambers dictionaries maintain a high quality but are best appreciated by those who resist brushing away the cobwebs of past practice. That is, one feels that redactors have focused their attention on including new material and have been reluctant to disturb older definitions. This gives the work a certain charm that few other dictionaries have. In a sense it is to be admired for resisting the trend to rewrite too much for the sake of appearing modern—but it may not have been rewritten enough. Though the work is said to include 180,000 entries, a high percentage are run on without definitions, and compounds are defined very briefly. As one would expect in a work published in Edinburgh, it is rich in Scots expressions.

Chambers Universal Learners' Dictionary

Elizabeth Kirkpatrick, ed. Edinburgh: W. & R. Chambers, 1980.

In contrast to Oxford's *Hornby* and *Longman*—also dictionaries for foreign learners—the *Chambers* work has opted for simplicity. There are no elaborate codes for verb patterns, for count and mass nouns, or for the position of adjectives; instead, the entries themselves often contain information on grammar and diction. It is thus easier to use but perhaps not as powerful a pedagogical tool as the other ESL dictionaries. It rejects, as does *Hornby,* the *Longman* device of a controlled vocabulary for definition. As with all ESL dictionaries, the International Phonetic Alphabet is used in the pronunciation system, and invented illustrative sentences are copiously provided. There are no pictorial illustrations.

A Chronological English Dictionary

Thomas Finkenstaedt, Ernst Leisi, and Dieter Wolff, eds. Heidelberg: Carl Winter Universitätsverlag, 1970.

A computer study based principally on the *Shorter Oxford English Dictionary,* in which every definition of every term in that work is arranged chronologically according to its first recorded appearance in English, beginning with the Old English period and running through 1957. The antecedent language from which the form was derived is also indicated, as well as its appearance in one of several contemporary lexicons. This work is an example of an early and imaginative use of computer science applied to lexicography, though it may not have been of much practical help to scholars or dictionary makers.

Collins Dictionary of the English Language

Patrick Hanks, ed. Thomas Hill Long, managing ed. London: Collins, 1979. Informally known as the *Collins English Dictionary (CED)*. Laurence Urdang was the editorial director.

The first major British dictionary to adopt the American lexicographic style of presentation of numbered senses, coverage of the scientific and technical lexicon, and inclusion of encyclopedic material. It has also caught the American disease of entryitis, boasting of 162,000 entries. Apparently, the British public likes it, since it has been quite successful. It does, however, stick with a phonetic pronunciation system, unlike the American practice, and does not include a pronunciation key on every two-page spread.

A Concise Dictionary of Canadianisms

Walter S. Avis, ed. Toronto: W. J. Gage, 1973.

An abridgment of Avis's *A Dictionary of Canadianisms, q.v.*

The Concise Oxford Dictionary of Current English

Seventh ed.; J. B. Sykes, ed. Oxford: Clarendon Press, 1982; first ed., 1911.

The sixth edition (1976) was a complete revision of the fifth (1964); at that time, many new scientific and technical terms were included. The seventh edition, coming so shortly after the sixth, is a more modest revision. Based on the incomparable files of the *OED* and the *Supplements,* the *COD* is one of the most successful dictionaries ever published and is used wherever English is spoken. It employs a style that is a modification of the traditional run-in style used by Chambers. *COD* does run in compounds and derivative forms in a single paragraph, but it distinguishes larger groups of senses with boldface numbers. Pronunciations are indicated usually by diacritics marked on the entry word, without respelling, although part or all of the word is respelled if necessary. Definitions are written in a compressed but flowing style that is very different from American styles of defining. *COD* covers many more senses than one would expect in a dictionary of this size, but its definitions are therefore often very brief, amounting sometimes to a kind of shorthand reminder rather than a definition. When it works, it works very well indeed; one feels in private converse with a friend. When it fails, one is utterly lost and feels by turns stupid and abandoned. Long in a class by itself, *COD* now has competition from Collins *(The New Collins Concise Dictionary)* and from Longman *(Longman New Universal Dictionary),* both published in 1982. These events undoubtedly provoked *COD* to break tradition by issuing a seventh edition so shortly after the last.

Davies' Dictionary of Golfing Terms

Peter Davies, ed. New York: Simon & Schuster, 1980.

This specialized dictionary is extraordinary in several ways. It is one of the very few such works that have been written by an experienced lexicographer. Peter Davies was the chief editor of *AHD* at the time of its first publication and supervised several of the works derived from it. He has combined his fascination with golf and with etymology to produce extensive comments on the origin of golfing terms in addition to the definitions, and his wide reading in historical writing on golf has resulted in a dictionary with dated and documented citations going back to the earliest known use of each word. The book is also well illustrated (by Fran Carson), an important feature, since it would be hard if not impossible to describe how golf clubs differ from one another. Obviously a labor of love, *Davies' Dictionary* contains a wealth of information not otherwise available, and as an expression of the art of specialized lexicography it is exemplary.

A Dictionary of American English on Historical Principles

Four vols. William A. Craigie and James R. Hulbert, eds. Chicago: University of Chicago Press, 1938–44.

Craigie was one of the *OED* editors, and the *DAE* was an offshoot of the *OED*. The *DAE* was and remains the single most important source of information about words (marked with a special symbol) that originated in the United States. It also includes words distinctively representative of American culture. Although many particular entries in the *DAE* have been challenged in the light of more recent scholarship, the work remains a massive compilation of original research and is indispensable to any study of American English.

A Dictionary of American Idioms

Maxine Tull Boatner and John Edward Gates, eds. Rev. ed. by Adam Makkai. Woodbury, New York: Barron's Educational Series, 1975.

Originally published in 1966 as a dictionary for the deaf, this is one of very few works that attempt to deal with American idioms. Its coverage of idioms is spotty, and it includes many terms (e.g., *center field,* a baseball term) that one would be hard pressed to defend as idioms. It is a modest work, but full of examples—all invented—that make it useful to the foreign learner.

A Dictionary of Americanisms on Historical Principles

Two vols. Mitford M. Mathews, ed. Chicago: University of Chicago Press, 1951. Allen Walker Read, who worked on the *Dictionary of American English,* has written (in "Approaches to Lexicography and Semantics," in *Current Trends in Linguistics,* vol. 10, ed. Thomas Sebeok (The Hague: Mouton, 1972), p. 153):

> At the completion of the DAE, M. M. Mathews, who had been an assistant editor, stayed on to edit another work to be shaped out of the collections. He limited himself to "Americanisms" only, but . . . re-assessed the evidence, dropping some and adding others. . . . As his criterion for an "Americanism," he unfortunately adopted the same one of the DAE, "a word or expression that originated in the United States": This cuts out the "Americanism by survival"—a word that lasted on in America after it dropped from use in England. The criterion should be the more general

one of currency in usage, and not the cut-and-dried one of country of origin. But the richness of the work is remarkable, in being, as Mathews said (Preface, p. v), "an index to the history and culture of the American people." A weak point is the treatment of pronunciation, which was not historical but a mere shell applied without organic relation to the collected data.

A Dictionary of Canadianisms on Historical Principles

Walter S. Avis, ed. Toronto: W. J. Gage, 1967. The editor until 1960 was Charles J. Lovell. M. H. Scargill is Director of the Lexicographical Centre for Canadian English, which organized the project.

A handsomely produced volume, capably edited and modeled on the *OED*. "A Canadianism," says Avis, " . . . is a word, expression, or meaning which is native to Canada or which is distinctively characteristic of Canadian usage though not necessarily exclusive to Canada. . . ." (page xiii). This is an impressive collection of dated quotations illustrating the rich and diverse history of the indigenous peoples and pioneer settlers of Canada. It is an indispensable source from a linguistic point of view and a fascinating treasure of cultural information about Canada's past.

A Dictionary of South African English

Jean Branford, ed. Cape Town: Oxford University Press, 1978.

I cannot comment on the accuracy or completeness of the coverage, but the work appears to be a capable and careful one, modeled on the *OED*. It includes pronunciations and etymologies as well as frequent and ample illustrative quotations for its three thousand entries. Compound forms are indicated, and the editor often links the South African form with a British, Australian, or U.S. one.

A Dictionary of the English Language

Samuel Johnson, ed. London, 1755. See page 151.

Dictionary of the Older Scottish Tongue

A. J. Aitken, ed. Chicago: University of Chicago Press, 1933–

A large historical dictionary comparable in size to the *Middle English Dictionary,* chronicling the Scottish tongue from the twelfth century to the end of the seventeenth. Published in fascicles, the dictionary had reached midway through the letter **P** by 1983. See Chapter 1, note 37.

The Doubleday Dictionary

Sidney I. Landau, ed. Ronald J. Bogus, managing ed. New York: Doubleday, 1975.

Based on the much larger Funk & Wagnalls *Standard Dictionary, International Edition* (first ed., 1958, but updated many times), this work of 85,000 entries falls into the curious class of dictionaries known in America as "desk" dictionaries, smaller than college dictionaries and bigger than the usual paperback dictionaries. (Although some paperback dictionaries now boast of as many or more entries, they are not in the same class, since their coverage of sense breakdown and fullness of definition are far less adequate and they do not include etymologies.) The editors had at their disposal an ongoing citation file of about 350,000 items, of which 100,000 or so were derived from the Brown Corpus. The others were original and largely of the last twenty years, though the file did include the complete index of *American Speech,* which goes back to 1926. I personally went through the 250,000 original citations, which yielded many new terms and senses. The book has often been criticized for its small type, a condition imposed by fitting 85,000 entries into a relatively small book.

Funk & Wagnalls Cook's and Diner's Dictionary: A Lexicon of Food, Wine, and Culinary Terms

Samuel Davis, ed. New York: Funk & Wagnalls, 1968.

Not a cookbook, and perhaps not as encyclopedic, discursive, or chatty as some users might like, this book covers the basic culinary lexicon with clear, ample definitions, accompanied by illustrations that are useful as well as decorative. It is one of those rare, specialized dictionaries done by a professional dictionary house and is thus of much higher quality than most specialized works.

Funk & Wagnalls New Standard Dictionary of the English Language

Isaac Funk, ed. New York: Funk & Wagnalls, 1963; original ed., 1913.

The *New Standard,* a revision of the *Standard* of 1893, is the only truly unabridged work other than *NID3.* Unfortunately, it is now hopelessly out of date. It has never been entirely reset, and in spite of numerous slight emendations the dictionary reflects the language as it was used in 1913. In its day it was a fine dictionary and still has virtues unmatched by any existing work, but it is now of historic interest only.

Funk & Wagnalls Standard College Dictionary

New York: Funk & Wagnalls, 1968; first ed., 1963.

In its early period of preparation, the *SCD* was supervised by Ramona Michaelis (then Ramona Grayson), who remained as the pronunciation editor. Robert L. Chapman succeeded Michaelis and was the supervising editor for several years and at the time of its first publication in 1963. Following the first edition, Sidney I. Landau, who had been a staff definer since 1961 and had written most of the usage notes, became editor-in-chief, supervising a substantial revision in 1966 and a less extensive one in 1968. The *SCD* was accomplished in spite of so many misadventures that it is a marvel the book ever appeared, and Chapman in particular deserves enormous credit for bringing it off. There were numerous changes in management, false starts, low pay, and a meager citation file. Working in a former stable on East 24th Street in Manhattan (actually a more pleasant ambiance than most modern offices), the first definer to arrive every Monday morning in winter emptied a large wastebasket filled to the brim with water from a relentlessly leaky radiator by dumping the water out a window. Yet in spite of such distractions the dictionary staff had a sound nucleus of experienced definers, steps were taken to add citations, and the dictionary was done. It is imperfect in many ways. Its etymologies are undistinguished and sometimes worse. Nonetheless, in the 1960s its definitions held up well in comparison with those of other dictionaries. Unfortunately, since it has never been thoroughly revised and reset, it does not bear comparison with college dictionaries published ten years later and consistently updated.

Funk & Wagnalls Standard Desk Dictionary

Sidney I. Landau, ed. New York: Funk & Wagnalls, 1966. An abridgment of the *Funk & Wagnalls Standard College Dictionary, q.v.*

Gage Canadian Dictionary

Walter S. Avis, Patrick D. Drysdale, Robert J. Gregg, Victoria E. Neufeldt, and Matthew H. Scargill, eds. Toronto: Gage, 1983.

This handsomely produced book, a revision of the *Canadian Senior Dictionary* (1979), is the flagship of the line of graded Gage dictionaries and is intended for the adult (high school, university, and general) audience. Since a number of entries are "based on materials collected for a *Dictionary of Canadianisms on Historical Principles,*" the claim that this dictionary gives greater attention than others to Canadian usage appears to have merit.

Jazz Talk

Robert S. Gold, ed. Indianapolis: Bobbs-Merrill, 1975.

A well-researched example of specialized dictionary making, and a rare example of a thoroughly professional effort brought off by one diligent and knowledgeable person. A historical dictionary with numerous illustrative quotations.

The Kenkyusha Dictionary of Current English Idioms

Sanki Ichikawa, *et al.,* eds. Tokyo: Kenkyusha, 1964.

An impeccably researched and produced work by Japanese scholars, but one that falls short of being either up to date or comprehensive. It is nonetheless a valuable work with copious citations. See page 28.

Longman Dictionary of Contemporary English

Paul Procter, ed. London: Longman, 1978.

An innovative and impressive dictionary for the foreign learner. All entries are defined by a controlled vocabulary of two thousand words, which are listed in an appendix. In theory, if the reader masters the core vocabulary he will be able to understand the definition of any entry in the dictionary. Some lexicographers are dubious that language acquisition works this way and argue that the restricted vocabulary makes the phrasing of definitions unnatural or ambiguous. I am of mixed minds on the question. When controlled vocabularies are applied to children's dictionaries and textbooks, as they have been, they simplify too much, discourage experimentation, and squelch the sense of play and mystery that can make learning fun. (They may, however, be most helpful for children having special difficulty with learning.) For adult learners, the qualities of experimentation and play may be of less importance. There is no doubt that a controlled vocabulary makes for a duller text, and there is probably some merit to the charge of awkwardness, but the foreign learner may be better served by sacrificing all else to basic understandability of sense.

Longman Dictionary of English Idioms
Thomas Hill Long, ed. Burnt Mill, Harlow: Longman, 1979. See page 29.

Longman Dictionary of Scientific Usage
Burnt Mill, Harlow: Longman, 1979. See page 273.

Longman Lexicon of Contemporary English
Tom McArthur, ed. Burnt Mill, Harlow: Longman, 1981. See page 273.

Longman New Universal Dictionary
Paul Procter, ed. Burnt Mill, Harlow: Longman, 1982.

The *New Universal*, a revision and abridgment of the database of *MW8*, continues the Longman tradition of innovation in lexicography. It is an admirable work in many ways and as a dictionary is excellent, drawing upon original citations from many different sources. It aspires, however, to be more than a dictionary by including over one hundred pages of full-page illustrations and tables, thus incorporating some features of an encyclopedia (as do the Larousse encyclopedias), and the combination does not entirely succeed. Let me first consider the work strictly as a dictionary.

Unlike the other Longman dictionaries, the *New Universal* is intended particularly for the British market. It gives comparatively little attention to American spellings and pronunciations, and its word list (including terms like "Common Entrance examination") reflects the native emphasis. The definitions are of high quality, and the entry list is up to date. It was obviously of immense advantage to begin building a dictionary with such solid material as that of *MW8*, but it is to the credit of the editors of the *New Universal* that they succeeded beautifully in integrating it with their own material to produce a work that does not appear to be derived from any other. Every definition from the Merriam database has clearly been reexamined and altered when necessary, with new or revised illustrative phrases substituted, and a number of distinctively British entries have been added, although the overall length of the *New Universal* is much shorter than that of

MW8. The usage information in the *New Universal* shows the same freshness of approach that characterizes the other Longman dictionaries; for example, *queer* (homosexual) is noted as derogatory, and *cunt,* apart from its notation as vulgar, is noted as being "used by men" in the sense of sexual intercourse. Linking usage with typical users is a welcome step forward in lexicography. The pronunciation system departs from British tradition by employing a non-International Phonetic Alphabet system; this makes sense in a work for native speakers, but from an international point of view it is unfortunate, since it may lead other British publishers to rely on various parochial phonemic systems such as those used in American dictionaries. The *New Universal* follows Merriam-Webster in using the ISV (International Scientific Vocabulary) designation in its etymologies of scientific terms and in using the stress symbols for compound entries and omitted syllables popularized by *NID3.* The *New Universal* defines 50,000 words and contains either 70,000 or 100,000 entries overall, depending on whether one believes the Preface (70,000) or the dust jacket (100,000). I believe the Preface. It is amusing to witness how avidly publishers compete to claim a dictionary as their own once it has proved itself to be an enduring classic, when one reflects how meager and grudging is their support for dictionaries now in preparation. Longman may be an exception in the latter case, but not in the former, since both the Foreword (by Randolph Quirk) and the Preface (by John Ayto) lay claim for Longman as the publisher of Johnson's dictionary. This is like saying that Henry Bradley was the editor of the *OED.* The Longman firm was one of five sponsors of Johnson's dictionary, the others being Robert Dodsley, Andrew Millar, Charles Hitch, and the firm of John and Paul Knapton.

The illustrations and tables in the *New Universal* comprise a major portion of the work—almost 10 percent of the space—far more than in any other English dictionary except perhaps the *AHD.* The pictorial illustrations fall into two categories: those that are essentially linguistic, like the anatomical drawings identifying parts of the body, and those that are essentially encyclopedic, describing, for example, how evolution works or how animals defend themselves against predators. Falling between these two types are the technologically *au courant* displays for "computer," "television," and "telecommunications," in which, incidentally, Viewdata is illustrated twice. Longman evidently wants to establish itself as being first in technological know-how and use, and it therefore devotes lavish space to some very boring and static displays of gray boxes, familiar telephones, and spools of tape, in the hope that the idea of modernity will be sufficient in itself to charge such dead wood with vitality. Unfortunately, computers are better described than depicted. I don't see what is to be gained by showing us large gray file cabinets labeled "processor." Some of the illustrations are just silly. To devote an entire page (under *unit*) to an enormous thermometer, two bottles, and two elephantine tablets is an unconscionable waste of space, and the list of words for Scrabble players (at *word*) has no place in a general dictionary. More serious was the unwise decision to limit the running heads at the top of each page to the first three letters of the initial entry. Thus, there are six consecutive pages headed COM within which the reader has no guidance whatever in finding the word sought.

The illustrations, which sometimes run to six or more consecutive pages, break up the dictionary text and make words even harder to find, and they sometimes necessarily fall out of strict alphabetic sequence. Thus, *first aid,* to which six pages are devoted, follows FIS. One can imagine someone bleeding to death while trying to find first aid in this dictionary. On the other hand, the linguistic illustrations, those for *nerve, anatomy,* and especially for *reproduction,* are of high quality and evident usefulness, and the four-page table and map at *language* is superbly thought out and richly informative. This is Longman at its best, and at its best the *New Universal* is a very impressive dictionary.

The difficulty in attempting to combine pictorial encyclopedic material with dictionary text is that it detracts from the essentially referential nature of a dictionary. Lexical units are harder to locate and one can never be sure, since this is not, after all, an encyclopedia, whether any particular encyclopedic fact will be included. Suppose one wants to know who the chief adversaries in World War I were—surely not an obscure fact and one that every encyclopedia would contain. One will not find the answer in the *New Universal,* in spite of a six-page summary of British history which in its own way is quite well done. In short, the nonlinguistic illustrations function as a teaching tool, not as a reference guide, and their relevance in a dictionary may be questioned. They do, however, help to distinguish the *New Universal* from other dictionaries and enhance its sales appeal.

The Macquarie Dictionary

Arthur Delbridge, ed. St. Leonards, NSW, Australia: Macquarie Library, 1981.

This large, handsomely produced work is the first general dictionary devoted to the informed representation of the English of Australia, with some attention given as well to that of New Zealand. It is, Delbridge says in the Introduction, "not merely a dictionary of Australianisms; that is, of the words and phrases that are peculiar to Australia. . . ." It attempts to take stock of the entire range of the lexicon from an Australian view and thus record senses of words like *station, yard, track, house, terrace,* and *flat* with "uses in Australia that are not adequately covered in any of the great dictionaries of the world . . ." (page 12). The lexicon was based on that of the *Encyclopedic World Dictionary* (Hamlyn, 1969), an updating and Anglicization of the *ACD* (first published in 1947, not 1969, as stated in the Introduction). The *Macquarie Dictionary* represents, then, a revision based on older materials, considerably reworked and updated by including new terms and senses, by the inclusion of terms that are Australianisms, and by the revision of definitions to include or amplify Australian usage. This is not a historical dictionary, and it is not the last word on Australian usage, but it is a major and honest effort to represent Australian usage in the context of a general dictionary. Its approach to stylistic varieties is unusual: "colloquial" is the only label used. It is up to the reader to decide what, for example, is vulgar or nonstandard. The *Macquarie*'s definition of *colloquial,* consistent with this policy, is worth quoting:

> appropriate to or characteristic of conversational speech or writing in
> which the speaker or writer is under no particular constraint to choose

standard, formal, conservative, deferential, polite, or grammatically unchallengeable words, but feels free to choose words as appropriate from the informal, slang, vulgar, or taboo elements of the lexicon.

Obviously an imposed definition! It appears to me that what is represented as a definition is actually a description (better placed in the front-matter guide) of how the "colloquial" label is used in the dictionary. The pronunciation system used is that of the International Phonetic Alphabet, with a guide printed at the foot of every page. Etymologies are included, but syllabication is not indicated.

Middle English Dictionary
Hans Kurath and Sherman M. Kuhn, eds. Ann Arbor Mich.: University of Michigan, 1956–.
A massive, ongoing effort to chronicle the use of English during the twelfth to fifteenth centuries. Published in fascicles, the dictionary had reached the letter **P** by 1983.

The New Collins Concise Dictionary of the English Language
William T. McLeod and Patrick Hanks, eds. London: Collins, 1982.
An abridgment of the *CED* (formally the *Collins Dictionary of the English Language*), this work is said to include 96,000 entries, of which 53,000 are headwords, a percentage the jacket blurb correctly asserts is higher than that of most other dictionaries. A capably edited and thoroughly up-to-date work, the *Collins Concise* follows *CED* in almost all particulars, employing the International Phonetic Alphabet in its pronunciation and adopting the helpful etymological practice of identifying the century when each word made its first appearance in English. Like the *CED,* the *Concise* has no illustrations and little in the way of tabular matter. It follows the *CED* practice of numbering definitions and to the publisher's credit has not reduced the size of type, which is quite readable. The *Collins Concise* is a good, sound, conventional dictionary, and it should give the *COD* a run for its money.

The New York Times Everyday Dictionary
Thomas M. Paikeday, ed. New York: Times Books, 1982.
An innovative desk dictionary employing a variety of the clustered treatment of entries used in the *COD* and in the Chambers dictionaries (see page 337), but depending heavily on illustrative phrases and sentences to convey meaning. Its pronunciations are given selectively for words presumed to need them, and the system eschews all nonalphabetic characters, relying entirely on respelling to provide a rough-and-ready guide. The pronunciations will not tell one how to pronounce a word that he is thoroughly unacquainted with, but if one is wondering whether to use pronunciation A, B, or C, they will usually provide a contrastive basis for mak-

ing a decision. Etymologies are not included. The type is readable, the word list up to date, and the definitions and illustrative sentences provide quite serviceable treatment of sense. All things considered, Paikeday's dictionary is a most encouraging development in North American lexicography, since it has abandoned the attempt simply to reduce all the features of a college dictionary to smaller size, but has instead staked out a new and more concise method for rendering those elements of the dictionary entry that can be conveyed in a shorter dictionary: namely, meaning, spelling, syllabication, and contrastive pronunciation.

Oxford Advanced Learner's Dictionary of Current English

Third ed. A. S. Hornby, with A. P. Cowie, eds. Oxford: Oxford University Press, 1974; first ed., 1948.

The standard ESL dictionary for the foreign learner who has mastered more elementary works. The name *Hornby* is synonymous all over the world with quality dictionaries for the foreign learner of English. It is, of course, British English that is chiefly represented. See page 30.

Oxford American Dictionary

Eugene Ehrlich, Stuart Berg Flexner, Gorton Carruth, and Joyce M. Hawkins, eds. New York: Oxford University Press, 1980.

The publishers of the *OED* do themselves no credit by preposterously writing about this modest and flawed work as though it were the culminating triumph of the editors of the *OED*. (I refer to the "Publisher's Note: From OED to OAD," pages xi–xvi.) The *OAD* is apparently an Americanization of the *Pocket Oxford Dictionary*, with some new terms and senses added. It is compiled by four editors, only two of whom (Flexner and Hawkins) have had previous experience in lexicography.

The jacket blurb identifies Gorton Carruth as the "former Editor-in-Chief of Funk and Wagnalls" and may give the impression that he was a lexicographer with that company. I was the editor-in-chief of Funk & Wagnalls dictionaries from 1963 to 1970. After the *Reader's Digest* acquired Funk & Wagnalls in 1966, Carruth was hired to direct the reference department of Reader's Digest Books for the parent company, and in this capacity he was briefly my administrative superior, though concerned mainly with books other than dictionaries. At no time did he contribute lexicographically to any Funk & Wagnalls dictionary.

The *OAD* attempts to capitalize on the success of the *AHD* by providing usage guidance to the insecure reader, but its notes are based on nothing other than the opinions of the editors. Even the *AHD* attempted to maintain a degree of objectivity with its usage panel, however imperfect the attempt was in execution. But the *OAD* has taken a step backward in lexicography by reaffirming the *ipse dixit* assertions of nineteenth-century grammarians. It claims to have an authority that no dictionary can have and serves to perpetuate the mischievous belief that the makers of a dictionary have the power to determine what good usage is.

Oxford Dictionary of Current Idiomatic English

Two volumes. For Vol. 1, A. P. Cowie and R. Mackin, eds. For Vol. 2, Cowie, Mackin, and I. R. McCaig, eds. London: Oxford University Press, 1975 and 1983. See page 28.

The Oxford English Dictionary

Twelve vols. James A. H. Murray (chief ed.), Henry Bradley, W. A. Craigie, and C. T. Onions, eds. Oxford: Clarendon Press, 1882–1928. A Supplement was published in 1933. Published originally under the title of *A New English Dictionary on Historical Principles*. Now also available in two volumes in which the original pages are greatly reduced, and sold with a magnifying glass. The keen-eyed might be able to read the definitions with unaided eye even in this set, but the illustrative quotations, printed in yet smaller type, are microscopic.

The *OED* is truly the basis of all modern monolingual lexicography in English. There would be dictionaries without it, but they would not be nearly as good as they are. The influence of the *OED* is especially strong in the basic word stock of the language but much less so in twentieth-century coinages, new senses, Americanisms, and scientific terminology, although Burchfield's *Supplement* will extend the reach of the *OED* in all of these areas. The *OED* is discussed in many parts of this book, but see especially Chapter 2. See also *A Supplement to the Oxford English Dictionary* (page 349).

The Random House College Dictionary

Laurence Urdang, ed. Stuart Berg Flexner, managing ed. New York: Random House, 1975; first ed., 1968. The revised editions have been edited by Jess Stein, Laurence Urdang having left Random House to form his own company.

Based, we are told, on the "unabridged" edition, pound for pound this is a better dictionary and a better buy, since the superfluous heft has been stripped away, revealing a good sound college dictionary. Random House dictionaries are very sensitive to scientific and technical terminology and to current slang, perhaps too much so. But *RHCD* is without a doubt among the best of the college dictionaries. Its in-house staff fluctuates drastically and at times has been almost nonexistent; yet the enduring commitment of Jess Stein has succeeded, often against great odds, in maintaining the quality of Random House dictionaries. Upon his retirement, Stuart Flexner assumed the editorship of dictionaries.

The Random House Dictionary of the English Language

Jess Stein, ed. New York: Random House, 1973; first ed., 1966.

The so-called unabridged edition, about the size of one and a half college dictionaries. It is much less than an unabridged dictionary and is replete with encyclopedic terms that inflate its entry count. Nonetheless, having the rich store of the *ACD* (of which Jess Stein was the managing editor) and its subsequently collected citation files to draw upon, *RHD* is a major contribution to American lexicography. Random House dictionaries are especially notable for their excellent coverage of scientific and technical terms and of current slang. Indeed, the quality of its definitions in general is very high.

348

The Scribner-Bantam English Dictionary

Edwin B. Williams, ed. New York: Charles Scribner's Sons, 1977.

A monolingual dictionary put together chiefly by bilingual lexicographers, originally under the auspices of Bantam Books with the help of the American lexicographer Walter Glanze. Professor Williams, who died in 1975, was a distinguished scholar of Spanish lexicography. Unfortunately, the initial advertising claimed 80,000 entries for this dictionary, whereas it probably has no more than 60,000 by the traditional methods of entry counting described in this book. It is a serviceable if not outstanding work, with very large type and, for a dictionary of such modest scope, a large number of synonym discriminations and synonym lists that take up a disproportionate amount of space. Nothing is said about how the entries were selected, and since there is no designated parent dictionary and no clue as to whether a citation file existed, the basis of selection is a mystery. Certainly some of the included entries are questionable. The guide to the dictionary by Walter Glanze is unusually thorough and valuable in its own right.

The Second Barnhart Dictionary of New English

Clarence L. Barnhart, Sol Steinmetz, and Robert K. Barnhart, eds. Bronxville, New York: Barnhart Books, 1980. See *Barnhart Dictionary of New English*.

6,000 Words: A Supplement to Webster's Third New International Dictionary

Mairé Weir Kay, Frederick C. Mish, and H. Bosley Woolf, eds. Springfield, Mass.: G. & C. Merriam, 1976.

Webster's answer to the Barnhart dictionaries of new words, but with far fewer citations, a less attractive format, and a more perfunctory treatment of meaning. However, its price is also less. It suffers from all the defects noted in connection with the Barnhart works, particularly the profligate inclusion of chemicals, such as *phosphoenolpyruvate,* defined as "a salt or ester of phosphoenolpyruvic acid," or enzymes like *phosphofructokinase.* Since many new enzymes are identified each year, one wonders on what basis the included enzymes were selected. Nonetheless, the work does contain many genuinely novel terms that merit inclusion. The elaborate pronunciations, defensible in an unabridged work, seem altogether out of place in this slim volume.

A Supplement to the Oxford English Dictionary (in progress)

Four vols. R. W. Burchfield, ed. Oxford: Clarendon Press, 1972– . Vol. I (A–G) was published in 1972, Vol. II (H–N) in 1976, Vol. III (O–Scz) in 1982. See page 71.

The issuance of the *Supplements* makes it necessary for one to skip back and forth between the original volumes of the *OED* and the *Supplements,* both for the addition of new terms and senses and for the correction or insertion of information inadvertently omitted. But the trouble is well worth it. The *Supplements* are superbly researched and edited. When one considers that the original work had reached only the letter G by 1900, the *Supplements* quite literally bring the *OED* into the twentieth century, though they cannot, of course, bring it as up to the minute as American dictionary users have come to expect of their college dictionaries.

The Universal Dictionary of the English Language

Henry Cecil Wyld, ed. London: Routledge & Kegan Paul, 1961; original ed., 1932.

An unusual and impressive work by an eminent scholar who was chiefly interested in etymology but who could define expertly as well. Its full etymologies, however, are the most valuable feature of his dictionary today. It is an elegant work, but with some of the eccentricities one might expect of an individual effort. The lexicon itself is now of historical interest only.

Webster's New Collegiate Dictionary

Eighth ed. Henry Bosley Woolf, ed. Springfield, Mass.: G. & C. Merriam: 1977; 1st printing of this ed., 1973. See *Webster's Ninth New Collegiate Dictionary.*

Webster's New World Dictionary of the American Language

Second College Edition. David B. Guralnik, ed. New York: Simon & Schuster, 1976; first printing of this ed., 1970.

First published in 1953, *World* has taken its place as one of the finest desk dictionaries in America. It is one of the very few to boast of a permanent dictionary staff and an active, ongoing citation file. It has been unjustly denigrated because it dared to call itself "Webster's" and because it has never dressed up its advisory boards with long lists of prominent linguists. Through aggressive merchandising it has been hugely successful, though in second place to G. & C. Merriam. Its success is deserved. The book is kept up to date, and in its way it is as good as any dictionary of its size and better than most.

Webster's Ninth New Collegiate Dictionary

Frederick C. Mish, ed. Springfield, Mass.: G. & C. Merriam, 1983.

The ninth edition owes much of its excellence to the sweeping changes made by the eighth, which discontinued the heavy reliance on the peculiar cross-reference definitions of the seventh edition, edited by Philip Babcock Gove. Many definitions of *MW8* have been left unaltered, although many new senses and new terms have been added. Both *MW8* and *MW9* are distinguished for their fine but concisely stated definitions and for their outstanding pronunciations, which are more accurate than those of any other American dictionary. Their illustrative phrases supplementing definitions are well chosen and ample, employing both invented and actual quotations.

Based on the *NID3* and Merriam's huge citation files (the importance of which Merriam naturally exaggerates), and the heritage of past excellence (the importance of which cannot be exaggerated), *MW8* and now *MW9*, the latest in a line of college dictionaries going back to 1898, deserve their eminence, although they have not been in a class of their own. *RHCD, World,* and *AHD* remain worthy competitors in the United States, as does the *CED* in Britain. (The *COD* and the

Shorter Oxford English Dictionary are not comparable, the first because it is smaller and the second because it is historical.)

In order to make room for thousands of new entries and other additions in *MW9*, the dimensions of the type page have been enlarged (each column of *MW9* being a pica wider than that of *MW8*) and the very bold, expanded, sans serif type used in *MW8* for headwords (and wherever the style called for boldface) has been replaced in *MW9* by a much more condensed serif type that is not as easy to read. This change alone must have saved an enormous amount of space, but it comes at a price. The boldface in *MW9* simply does not stand out as instantly legible. Readers with imperfect sight will have to use their fingers more often than in the past to find the entry they want. In another and much less arguable space-saving maneuver, abbreviations have been moved to the rear of the book.

MW9 makes much of two novel features, and in fact both will be of genuine appeal to many readers. First, immediately following its etymologies, a date is given that is said to indicate "when the earliest example known . . . of the use" of the first sense was written or printed. Thus one can see that *whippet* first appeared in 1610 and *Ms.* in 1950. The practice is a familiar feature of historical dictionaries, in which the earliest occurrence is always cited, and *CED* introduced the policy of giving the century in which entry words appeared; but *MW9* has taken the idea one step further in synchronic dictionaries than anyone had before. Second, an unspecified number of usage notes are included to provide guidance to readers about questionable usages. The advice given is "never based merely on received opinion, though opinions are often noted, but typically on both a review of the historical background and a careful evaluation of what citations reveal about actual contemporary practice" (Preface, page 6). Based on my reading of a number of notes, the claim seems justified; the quality of information, both historical and citational, exceeds anything else available and merits high commendation. The number of such notes appears to be comparatively small, but they represent a major step forward in the presentation of informed usage advice. (See, for example, *ain't,* expanded and improved from the brief note in *NID3,* or *disinterested,* or *fulsome.*)

One of the few unsuccessful features of *MW8* was the fiction that a "shared meaning element" sufficed to satisfy the reader's curiosity about the synonymy of semantically related words. It was a space-saving method by which one could claim to have synonym discussions without really having them. Happily, *MW9* has abandoned this exercise in specious precisionism and returned to the practice of giving full synonym discriminations.

With *MW9*, G. & C. Merriam continues its craven deference to the mercantile interests of trademark owners. As in *MW8*, the Preface states: "Those entries known to be trademarks or service marks are so labeled and are treated in accordance with a formula approved by the United States Trademark Association." Many of us have had to make occasional compromises with integrity to preserve the security of our livelihoods, but we do not usually go about announcing them in public. *MW9*'s treatment of trademarks is disgraceful. Will other pressure groups next insist on specifying the formulas by which the words they care about be defined in *MW10*? We can then expect to find additional statements, such as: "Those entries known to have religious import are treated in accordance with a formula approved by the United Council of Churches." Or is *MW9* perhaps already employing other such formulas without telling us about them? *MW8*, though representing *Xerox* in the manner specified by the United States Trademark Association ("*trademark*—used for a xerographic copier"), at least entered the universally known verb, *xerox*, and defined it as "to copy on a Xerox machine." *MW9*, on the other hand, pretends no one has ever said, "Would you xerox this for me?" and omits the verb entirely. (See page 298 for further comment about trademarks in dictionaries.)

Apart from trademarks, *MW9*'s coverage of the vocabulary of English is reliably up to date, though I was surprised not to find either *friendly* or *user-friendly* in the now-familiar sense meaning "helpful in explaining how to use a computer," commonly used of software. It has, however, expanded its coverage of taboo words from that of *MW8*, and one notes with some satisfaction its most elegant expression, as it were, from **A** to **Z**, in the placement of *motherfucker* directly above *Mother Goose*.

Webster's Sports Dictionary

Robert Copeland, ed. Springfield, Mass.: G. & C. Merriam, 1976.

Definitions, based on citations that are occasionally cited in the text, are full and clearly written for the nonexpert. Each definition is labeled according to the sport in which it is used. This is a successful amalgam of encyclopedia (rules governing each sport are included) and dictionary.

Webster's Third New International Dictionary of the English Language

Philip Babcock Gove, ed. Springfield, Mass.: G. & C. Merriam, 1961.

The only truly unabridged synchronic dictionary in English. All things considered, a masterpiece of the art of lexicography, but irritatingly wrong-headed in many small yet troublesome ways. See, for example, page 125ff. for a critical discussion of Gove's concept of definition. *NID3* is discussed in many parts of this book.

The World Book Dictionary

Two volumes. Clarence L. Barnhart and Robert K. Barnhart, eds. Chicago: World Book–Childcraft International, 1981; original ed., 1963. See page 74.

This dictionary is intended to complement the *World Book Encyclopedia* and therefore includes no proper names. The 1981 edition reportedly contains about 264,000 entries, though it advertises only 225,000. In keeping with the *World Book Encyclopedia*, which is written for various age levels, the definitions of *WBD* are marked by extraordinary clarity and simplicity and consume much more space than most dictionaries can afford to use. (Hence the comparatively high price of *WBD*.) The size of the work and the large number of illustrative quotations used— and they are quoted more fully than in *NID3*—make this the only dictionary comparable in some measure to *NID3*. In the United States, Barnhart's citation files, which include *The Century Dictionary* citations on which the *ACD* was based, are second only to Merriam-Webster's in size and are kept up to date. *WBD*'s definitions are simpler and fuller than *NID3*'s, but the word list is not as extensive and sense breakdown is not as fine. What the *World Book Encyclopedia* is to *Encyclopaedia Britannica*, *WBD* is to *NID3*. *WBD* is in effect an unabridged dictionary at the senior high school level.

A Selective
Bibliography of
Nondictionary Sources

What follows is a selective bibliography of the more important nondictionary sources referred to in this work. Items are arranged alphabetically by author or editor. See also the preceding *Critical Bibliography of Selected Monolingual Dictionaries*.

Algeo, John, ed. *Thomas Pyles: Selected Essays on English Usage.* Gainesville, Fla.: University Presses of Florida, 1979.

Baehr, Ann Ediger. "An Evaluation of the 1952 and 1962 Editions of the *Thorndike-Barnhart Beginning Dictionary,*" *Elementary English* 41:4 (April 1964), pp. 413–419.

Barnhart, Clarence L. "American Lexicography, 1947–1973," *American Speech* 53:2 (Summer 1978).

———. "Problems in Editing Commercial Monolingual Dictionaries," in *Problems in Lexicography,* second ed., Fred W. Householder and Sol Saporta (Bloomington, Ind.: Indiana University; The Hague: Mouton, 1967), pp. 161–181.

Baugh, Albert C. *A History of the English Language.* Second ed. New York: Appleton-Century-Crofts, 1957.

Carroll, John B., Peter Davies, and Barry Richman. *The American Heritage Word Frequency Book*. Boston: Houghton Mifflin, 1971.

Chapman, Robert L. "A Working Lexicographer Appraises *Webster's Third New International Dictionary*," *American Speech* 42 (1967), pp. 202–210.

Chapman, R. W. *Lexicography*. London: Oxford University Press, 1948.

Congleton, J. E., J. Edward Gates, and Donald Hobar, eds. *Papers on Lexicography in Honor of Warren N. Cordell*. Terre Haute, Ind.: Dictionary Society of North America and Indiana State University, 1979.

Creswell, Thomas J. *Usage in Dictionaries and Dictionaries of Usage*. Publication of the American Dialect Society, nos. 63–64. University, Ala.: University of Alabama Press, 1975.

Finegan, Edward. *Attitudes Toward English Usage*. New York: Teachers College, Columbia University, 1980.

Friend, Joseph H. *The Development of American Lexicography 1798–1864*. The Hague: Mouton, 1967.

Fries, Charles C. *American English Grammar*. New York: Appleton-Century-Crofts, 1940.

Gove, Philip B. "Repetition in Defining," in *The Role of the Dictionary*, ed. Philip B. Gove (Indianapolis: Bobbs-Merrill, 1957), pp. 9–14.

———, ed. *The Role of the Dictionary*. Indianapolis: Bobbs-Merrill, 1957.

Hartmann, R. R. K., ed. *Dictionaries and Their Uses*. Exeter Linguistic Series, vol. 4. Exeter: University of Exeter, 1979.

Hobar, Donald, ed. *Papers of the Dictionary Society of North America 1977*. Terre Haute, Ind.: Indiana State University, 1982.

Householder, Fred W., and Sol Saporta, eds. *Problems in Lexicography*. Second ed. Bloomington, Ind.: Indiana University; The Hague: Mouton, 1967.

Hulbert, James R. *Dictionaries: British and American*. Rev. ed. London: Andre Deutsch, 1968.

Joos, Martin. *The Five Clocks*. New York: Harcourt Brace Jovanovich, 1961.

Kenyon, John S. "Cultural Levels and Functional Varieties of English," *College English* 10:1 (October 1948), pp. 31–36.

Kister, Kenneth. *Dictionary Buying Guide*. New York: R. R. Bowker, 1977.

Kučera, Henry, and W. Nelson Francis. *Computational Analysis of Present-Day American English*. Providence: Brown University Press, 1967.

Labov, William. *The Social Stratification of English in New York City*. Washington, D.C.: Center for Applied Linguistics, 1966.

———. *The Study of Nonstandard English*. Washington, D.C.: Center for Applied Linguistics, 1969.

Landau, Sidney I. "Computer Use in Medical Lexicography: IDMB," in *Papers of the Dictionary Society of North America 1981*, Yeatman Anderson III, ed. (Terre Haute, Ind.: DSNA and Indiana State University, 1983), pp. 61–67.

———. "Dictionary Entry Count," *RQ* 4:1 (September 1964), pp. 6, 13–15.

———. "The Egalitarian Spirit and Attitudes Toward Usage," *American Speech* 54:1 (Spring 1979), pp. 3–11.

355

————. "*Little Boy* and *Little Girl*," *American Speech* 45:3–4 (Fall–Winter 1970), pp. 195–204.

————. "The Making of a Dictionary: Craft versus Commerce," *Booklist* (incorporating *Reference and Subscription Books Reviews*) 77:6 (November 15, 1980), pp. 481–483.

————. "Of Matters Lexicographical: Scientific and Technical Entries in American Dictionaries," *American Speech* 49:3–4 (Fall–Winter 1974), pp. 241–244.

————. "Popular Meanings of Scientific and Technical Terms," *American Speech* 55:3 (Fall 1980), pp. 204–209.

————. "*sexual intercourse* in American College Dictionaries," *Verbatim* 1:1 (n.d., issued July 1974), pp. 4–5.

Lanham, Richard A. "The Abusage of Usage," *Virginia Quarterly Review* 53:1 (Winter 1977), pp. 32–53.

Leonard, Sterling A. *Current English Usage.* English monograph, no. 1. Chicago: National Council of Teachers of English, 1932.

————. *The Doctrine of Correctness in English Usage 1700–1800.* Studies in Language and Literature, no. 25. Madison: University of Wisconsin, 1929.

Malone, Kemp. "On Defining mahogany," *Language* 16:4 (1940), pp. 308–318.

Manuila, Alexandre, ed. *Progress in Medical Terminology.* Basel: S. Karger, 1981.

Marckwardt, Albert H. and Fred G. Walcott. *Facts About Current American Usage.* New York: Appleton-Century-Crofts, 1938.

McDavid, Raven, I., Jr., and Audrey R. Duckert, eds. *Lexicography in English.* Annals of the New York Academy of Sciences, vol. 211. New York: New York Academy of Sciences, 1973.

McMillan, James B. "Five College Dictionaries," *College English* 10:4 (January 1949), pp. 214–221.

Mitchell, Gillian, ed. *Papers of the Dictionary Society of North America 1979.* London, Ont.: School of Library and Information Science, University of Western Ontario, 1981.

Murray, K. M. Elisabeth. *Caught in the Web of Words: James A. H. Murray and the Oxford English Dictionary.* New Haven: Yale University Press, 1977.

Pooley, Robert C. *The Teaching of English Usage.* Second ed. Urbana, Ill.: National Council of Teachers of English, 1974.

Pyles, Thomas. *The Origins and Development of the English Language.* New York: Harcourt Brace Jovanovich, 1964.

Quirk, Randolph. *The Use of English.* Second ed. London: Longman, 1968.

————, Sidney Greenbaum, Geoffrey Leech, and Jan Svartvik. *A Grammar of Contemporary English.* London: Longman, 1972.

Raymond, James C., and I. Willis Russell, eds. *James B. McMillan: Essays in Linguistics by His Friends and Colleagues.* University, Ala.: University of Alabama Press, 1977.

Read, Allen Walker. "Approaches to Lexicography and Semantics," in *Current Trends in Linguistics,* vol. 10, ed. Thomas Sebeok (The Hague: Mouton, 1972).

————. "Dictionary." *The New Encyclopaedia Britannica* (Chicago: Encyclopaedia Britannica, 1977), V, pp. 713–722.

————. "An Obscenity Symbol," *American Speech* 9:4 (December 1934), pp. 264–278.

Robinson, Richard. *Definition.* Oxford: Clarendon Press, 1954.

Sebeok, Thomas, ed. *Current Trends in Linguistics.* Vol. 10. The Hague: Mouton, 1972.

Sheldon, Esther K. "Pronouncing Systems in Eighteenth-Century Dictionaries," *Language* 22 (1946), pp. 27–41.

————. "Walker's Influence on the Pronunciation of English," *PMLA* 62 (1947), pp. 130–146.

Sledd, James, and Gwin J. Kolb. *Dr. Johnson's Dictionary: Essays in the Biography of a Book.* Chicago: University of Chicago Press, 1955.

Starnes, DeWitt T., and Gertrude E. Noyes. *The English Dictionary from Cawdrey to Johnson, 1604–1755.* Chapel Hill, N.C.: University of North Carolina Press, 1946.

Trench, Richard Chenevix. *On Some Deficiencies in Our English Dictionaries.* London, 1857.

Venezky, Richard L. "From Webster to Rice to Roosevelt: The Formative Years for Spelling Instruction and Spelling Reform in the U.S.A.," in *Cognitive Processes in Spelling,* ed. Uta Frith (London: Academic Press, 1979).

Vizetelly, Frank H. *The Development of the Dictionary of the English Language.* New York: Funk & Wagnalls, 1923.

Weinbrot, Howard D., ed. *New Aspects of Lexicography.* Carbondale, Ill.: Southern Illinois University Press, 1972.

Zgusta, Ladislav. *Manual of Lexicography.* The Hague: Mouton; Prague, Academia, 1971.

————, ed. *Theory and Method in Lexicography.* Columbia, S.C.: Hornbeam Press, 1980.

Index

Facts About Current English Usage
(Marckwardt and Walcott),
199
fad words, 161–62
fair use concept, 298
Fernald, James C., 109
field labels, 181–82
Finegan, Edward, 196
Flexner, Stuart Berg, 25, 101, 220
Florio, John, 39, 55, 183
Follett, Wilson, 204, 213
foreign terms, 156
formal style of usage, 192–93, 206–
7, 209, 215, 219–20
Fowler, F. G., 211
Fowler, H. W., 211
Francis, W. Nelson, 280
Fraser, W. Lewis, 111
free-lance staff, 234
French Academy, 50, 54, 67
French glossaries, 37–38
frequency of use, labeling of, 176
Friend, Joseph H., 62, 64, 73
Fries, Charles C., 73, 192, 200–202,
204
frozen style of usage, 193
front matter, 115–16, 117
functional varieties of usage, 191–92,
208
Funk, Charles Earle, 73
Funk, Isaac Kauffman, 65
Funk & Wagnalls' dictionaries, 65–
66, 73, 96, 103–4, 238
Furnivall, F. J., 68, 69

gender discrimination, masculine
pronoun usage and, 3
*General Dictionary of the English
Language, A* (Sheridan), 57
generic meanings, 299
of trademark terms, 299–302
genus and *differentia,* definition by,
120
geographical entries, 239, 253
ghost word, 27–28
Glossographia (Blount), 42–43
Gold, Robert S., 22
"good English," 204
Goodrich, Chauncey, 62, 63
"good usage," 197

Gove, Philip Babcock, 18, 64, 73,
109, 126–29, 194, 204
graded vocabularies, 15–16
grammar
as instrument for teaching usage,
194–98
information on, in dictionary
entry, 88–92
Grammar of English Grammars, The
(Brown), 196
grammatical function, definition in
accord with, 134, 138–44
*Grammatical Institute of the English
Language, A,* 59
Greet, W. Cabell, 73, 183, 204
Grimm, Jacob and Wilhelm, 31, 61,
65, 68, 100
Grimm's Law, 65
Grose, Francis, 185
Guralnik, David B., 73, 231

Haas, Mary R., 9–10
halftones, 112–13
Hall, J. Lesslie, 198
Harcourt Brace School Dictionary,
90, 260
hard words, 37, 41, 43, 44, 195
*Harper Dictionary of Contemporary
Usage* (Morris), 213
Harris, John, 44
Hartmann, R. R. K., 1
Hayakawa, S. I., 109
headword
in entry count, 84, 87, 88
form, 76–81, 87
participle as, 91
placement of, 82–84
high school dictionaries, 16
historical dictionaries, 31, 66–72,
101
Hornby, A. S., 30–31, 88, 89, 114,
117
Hortus Vocabularum, 38
Hulbert, James R., 72, 77, 95, 97,
111, 228
Huloet, Richard, 38

idioms, 82, 85–86
dictionaries of, 26, 28–29
"illiterate" usage, 199

Ogilvie, John, 72, 111
Onions, Charles Talbut, 22, 24, 69
On Some Deficiencies in Our English Dictionaries (Trench), 67, 104
orthography. *See* spelling
ostensive definition, 135
Oxford Advanced Learner's Dictionary of Current English, 30–31, 88, 89
Oxford-American Dictionary, 184
Oxford Dictionary of Current Idiomatic English, 28–29
Oxford Dictionary of English Etymology (Onions), 22, 24
Oxford English Dictionary (OED), 11–12, 24, 31, 36, 56, 137, 152, 157, 172, 229, 238, 290, 297
  achievement of, 69, 71
  editors and editorial process in, 69
  generalist approach in, 71, 253
  origins of, 68–69
  revisions and supplements to, 71–72, 187, 253, 284, 301

Paikeday, Thomas, 283–84
paper, choice of, 265–66
paperback dictionary, 19
parenthesis, use of, in defining, 143
participle, as main entry, 91
Partridge, Eric, 25
parts of speech, defining by, 134, 138–44
Phillips, Edward, 43, 44, 53, 171, 195
Philological Soceity, 67, 68, 69, 229
phonemic system, 92–93, 94
photographs, 112–13
phrasal entries, 139, 144, 239
picture dictionaries, 14
picture editor, 258–59, 260
picture research, 258
Piozzi, Hester Lynch (Thrale), 104
plagiarism *vs.* fair use, 296–98
Plan of a Dictionary of the English Language (Johnson), 48–51
pocket dictionary, 19
"poetic-," style label, 176
polysemy, 44, 52, 249, 278
Pooley, Robert C., 204, 206, 209

Porter, Noah, 64
prepositions, defining of, 144
prescriptiveness, 32
prestige dialect, 177
Priestly, Joseph, 197
printer's errors (PEs), 264
Procter, Paul, 30
Promptorium Parvulorum sive Clericorum, 37
pronouns
  defining of, 144
  masculine, 3
pronunciation, 50, 55, 57, 65, 71, 73, 75, 253
  dictionaries of, 24, 56–59
  keys, 263
  phonemic-phonetic systems of, 92–94
  preferred dialect in, 94–95
  representation of variations in, 95–96, 97
  respelling of, 96–97
  for scientific and technical vocabulary, 97
  usage guides to, 211–12
Pronouncing and Spelling Dictionary (Johnston), 57
Pronouncing Dictionary of American English, A (Kenyon and Knott), 24, 98
proofreading, 256–57, 263–65
proverbs, 26, 46
Pyles, Thomas, 98–99, 197

Quemada, Bernard, 283
Quirk, Randolph, 30, 167–69, 177, 281
quotation marks, significance of, 218
quotations. *See* illustrative quotations

Random House College Dictionary (RHCD), 73, 74, 143, 184, 300, 303
Random House Dictionary, College Edition, 73
Random House Dictionary of the English Language, The, 19, 73, 289
Rask, Rasmus, 65, 100
Read, Allen Walker, 17, 38, 44, 72, 158, 183–85